Orientalists, Islamists and the Global Public Sphere

Comparative Islamic Studies
Series Editor: Brannon Wheeler, US Naval Academy

This series, like its companion journal of the same title, publishes work that integrates Islamic studies into the contemporary study of religion, thus providing an opportunity for expert scholars of Islam to demonstrate the more general significance of their research both to comparatavists and to specialists working in other areas. Attention to Islamic materials from outside the central Arabic lands is of special interest, as are comparisons which stress the diversity of Islam as it interacts with changing human conditions.

Published

Notes from the Fortune-Telling Parrot:
Islam and the Struggle for Religious Pluralism in Pakistan
  David Pinault

Earth, Empire and Sacred Text:
Muslims and Christians as Trustees of Creation
  David L. Johnston

Forthcoming

Ibn Arabi and the Contemporary West:
Beshara and the Ibn Arabi Society
  Isobel Jeffery-Street

Prolegomena to a History of Islamicate Manichaeism
  John C. Reeves

Prophecy and Power:
Muhammad and the Qur'an in the Light of Comparison
  Marilyn Robinson Waldman
  Edited by Bruce B. Lawrence

The Qur'ān:
A New Annotated Translation
  Edited by A. J. Droge and Umair Khan

East by Mid-East
Studies in Cultural, Historical and Strategic Connectivities
  Edited by Brannon Wheeler and Anchi Hoh

Orientalists, Islamists and the Global Public Sphere

A Genealogy of the Modern Essentialist Image of Islam

Dietrich Jung

SHEFFIELD OAKVILLE

Published by Equinox Publishing Ltd.

UK: Unit S3, Kelham House, 3 Lancaster Street, Sheffield S3 8AF
USA: DBBC, 28 Main Street, Oakville, CT 06779
www.equinoxpub.com

First published 2011

British Library Cataloguing-in-Publication Data

A catalogue record for this book is available from the British Library.

ISBN: 978-1-84553-899-6 (hardback)
          978-1-84553-900-9 (paperback)

          Library of Congress Cataloging-in-Publication Data

Jung, Dietrich, 1959–
Orientalists, Islamists and the global public sphere : a genealogy of
the modern essentialist image of Islam / Dietrich Jung.
p. cm. — (Comparative Islamic studies)
Includes bibliographical references and index.
ISBN 978-1-84553-899-6 (hb) — ISBN 978-1-84553-900-9 (pb) 1.
Orientalism—History. 2. Islam—Public opinion. 3. Middle
East—Foreign public opinion, Western. 4. Islam—Relations. 5. East
and West. I. Title. DS61.85.J86 2011
305.6'97—dc22
          2010008981

Typeset and edited by Queenston Publishing, Hamilton, Canada
Index by Richard Bartholomew
Printed and bound in the UK by the MPG Books Group

To Marianne, Oskar,
and my parents,
Margarete and Herbert Jung

Contents

Preface

Reading Edward Said's *Orientalism* as an undergraduate gave me a shock. I had just taken up my studies in the social sciences and Islamic studies when Edward Said's book told me that I had been driven into the field of Islamic and Middle Eastern studies by my romanticist orientalist attitudes toward the East. Indeed, when I actually set my feet on North African soil for the first time in 1978, I was full of both adventurist and romanticist expectations. In the jargon of post-colonial critique, I was longing for difference and otherness. However, the intense study of social theory together with working and living in the Muslim world fundamentally changed my attitude toward the Middle East. Borrowing from Max Weber's terminology I would call this change a quick and lasting process of disenchantment. Under the impact of my studies, I was no longer looking for differences, but increasingly discovering similarities. The Middle Eastern "other" became gradually familiar and therewith akin. Having once been the stage for my romanticist dreams, the Middle East became a scholarly problem. I no longer perceived the region as being full of mysterious and unfamiliar forces, but as a specific field for rational academic enquiry. The projection of otherness was replaced by scholarly analysis based on general concepts and models from the social sciences. The region became a reservoir of unsolved puzzles, a field of scholarly problems which had to be understood by scholarly means.

This book is a direct result of this personal disenchantment process. The longer my engagement with the Middle East has lasted, the more I have asked myself why Islam is so frequently represented in the holistic terms of an all-encompassing socio-religious system. How is the persistence of this specific image of Islam to be explained against all empirical evidence? Having worked and lived in various Muslim countries in the Middle East and beyond, I have been confronted with so many different Islams. No scholarly erudition is required to see the enormous variety in both the political institutions and the walks of life in the Muslim world. Why, so the mind-boggling question, do then so many Muslims and non-Muslims nevertheless retain this essentialist image of "true Islam" in their minds? Where do our convictions come from regardless of all instances of reality that could prove this knowledge wrong?

With these questions in mind, I set out to design a research project in 2004. The project was triggered by the reading of Andreas Reckwitz' book *Die Transformation der Kulturtheorien*. Reckwitz, a fellow student at Hamburg University, where we both received our academic education, analyzes the "cultural turn" in the social sciences and argues for a convergence of structural and hermeneutic approaches in social theory. To be sure, his book has nothing to do with Islam, not even with religion as such. Reckwitz' elaborations do not have an empirical object. Yet putting my questions, empirical knowledge and field experience into the framework of his theoretical discussion, I envisaged a way in which I could tackle the above-mentioned problem complex. Bringing these two different theoretical perspectives of the social sciences together could resolve the issue of unity and difference which is at the heart of the emergence and global spread of the modern essentialist image of Islam, the core theme of this book. It must be emphasized here that the whole starting point for my project was a fresh reading of sociological theory; and it is this theoretical impact that runs throughout the book.

From the beginning, I was lucky to receive the full support of my then head of department, Neil Webster, and from Nanna Hvidt, the director of the Danish Institute for International Studies, where I was employed at that time. Working for an institution whose rationale is partly based on the idea of applied social research, such support is by no means a matter of course. In financial terms, I am grateful to the Danish Social Science Research Council which awarded me with a research grant paying half of my salary for two years and therewith liberating me from a number of time-consuming tasks at the institute. Moreover, I had the opportunity to discuss my project on the invitation of such different research environments as various academic associations, the universities of Heidelberg, Marburg, Pretoria, Tsukuba and Washington, and the Jawahrlal Nehru University in New Delhi, as well as the Islamic universities of Aligarh, the Jamia Millia Islamia in Delhi, and the International Islamic University of Malaysia in Kuala Lumpur. I thank all these institutions for their indispensible help developing my research for this book.

Equally important was the support of colleagues and friends. I would like to express my gratitude to those who willingly took on the effort of reading parts of the manuscript and developed my work further with their insightful comments. This applies in particular to Thomas Brudholm, Burkhard Conrad, Martin H. Jung, Goetz Nordbruch, Frederik Rosén, Thomas Scheffler and Klaus Schlichte, with all of whom I was able to discuss substantial parts of the text. Klaus Schlichte, an old friend and colleague from the times in Hamburg, went through the whole manuscript and has always been a source of inspiration in my research efforts. With regard to the specific subject of this book, my brother, Martin H. Jung, helped me a lot in understanding nineteenth-century Protestant reform movements, a field of study with which I was previously not familiar. Moreover, I would like to thank the three anonymous reviewers for their valuable suggestions, which helped a lot to enhance the quality of my text. Last but not least, Catherine Schwerin again did a great job in carefully correcting the errors and mistakes that mar the English of the non-native writer. The support of these people and institutions shows that scholarship indeed is a collective enterprise. However, remaining errors and mistakes are the responsibility of the author alone.

In January 2009, I took up the position of Professor for Contemporary Middle East Studies at the University of Southern Denmark, where this book was finalized. In the editor of the "Comparative Islamic Studies Series" of Equinox, Brannon Wheeler, and Equinox founder Janet Joyce, I met with dedicated and strongly supportive publishers. I am indebted to them both in helping me turning my research project into a book.

Dietrich Jung
Copenhagen

1

The Problem: The Essentialist Image of Islam

> The sacred Law of Islam is an all-embracing body of religious duties, the totality
> of Allah's commands that regulate the life of every Muslim in all its aspects.
>
> (Joseph Schacht)

With these words, the Columbia Professor Joseph Schacht (1902–1969) began his famous introduction to Islamic law (1964, 1), and hardly any contemporary Islamist activist would contradict him in this matter.[1] Precisely this is the problem: the overwhelming majority of both Western scholars in oriental studies and followers of Islamist movements have defined Islamic culture first and foremost by its sacred moral and legal codes. Based on the almost axiomatic assumption that in Islam religion and politics are inseparably knitted together, they both view Islamic culture as intrinsically different from the modern democratic culture of the West. In their ideal conceptualizations, the Muslim religion is represented as a holistic unity of social, political, cultural and economic institutions. Islam, according to their reading, is more than just a religion; Islam is a comprehensive, unique and unifying way of life encapsulated in the scripture of revealed texts and the example of the Prophet. From a scholarly perspective, Schacht's definition of Islamic law as a sacred, all-embracing, total, and comprehensive regulative system epitomizes this "essentialist" modern image of Islam, by conceptualizing the Muslim religion in sharp distinction from the pluralist culture of the West. It is this essentialist image that to a large extent informs the global public discourse on Islam, and it is without any doubt the predominant idea voiced on both Western and Muslim sides in the contemporary debate about Islam and the West.[2]

---

1. Joseph Schacht (1902–1969) was a leading scholar in Islamic studies. He was born in Silesia and educated in Germany where he studied theology and Semitic languages. In 1934, then a professor at Königsberg (today Kaliningrad), Schacht left Germany protesting against the Nazi government. He later held university positions in Cairo, Oxford and Leiden before he finally took over a chair in Arabic and Islamic studies at Columbia University in 1954.

2. If not specified in another way, I will use the terms Islamism or Islamists as a residual

To be sure, this essentialist image of Islam has not remained undisputed.[3] From a scholarly point of view, many of its critics take a so-called constructivist position. They reject the essentialist assumptions by stressing the generally constructed nature of social and cultural phenomena. In this way, they direct their critique against the questionable assertion of cultural determinism on which the idea of a closed Islamic system rests. From this constructivist angle, juxtaposing Islam and the West as distinctive cultural wholes is equally false.[4] There is also no doubt that the field of Islamic studies has experienced important changes with regard to objects and methods in the course of recent decades. Contemporary scholarship on Islam has developed into an academic enterprise employing the critical theories and varied methods of modern cultural studies and the social sciences. In the more narrowly defined field of Islamic studies, the essentialist tradition is meanwhile only represented by a minority of scholars. Yet beyond the disciplinary confines of Islamic studies proper, many Western scholars and media pundits have retained the image of Islam as a holistic system. In light of Edward Said's critique (1978), this continuing strand of essentialist interpretations has been branded as "new orientalism" (Sadowski 1993). In taking up issues about democratization and modernization in the Muslim world, these new orientalists have perpetuated the approach of their predecessors and still perceive Islam as the determining explicative variable for the understanding of Muslim societies. Prime amongst them within the field of Islamic studies is Bernard Lewis, who asserted, for example, that with the establishment of the Islamic Republic in Iran an "unnatural aberration" of the separation of religion and politics in this country had come to an end (Lewis 1988, 2). From this perspective, the general absence of democratic rule in Muslim countries is almost naturally associated with a specific role of the Islamic religion.[5]

---

category throughout this book. In this application of the terms they only signify the very general idea of relating religious norms and values to policies of establishing an "Islamic social order" in predominantly Muslim societies. Therefore, the term Islamism lumps together a broad range of very different political actors and ideologies such as the moderate Turkish "Justice and Development Party" (AKP) or the Egyptian "Wasat," on the one hand, and militant Islamist movements on the other.

3. In contrast to orientalist studies, for instance, anthropologists emphasized the study of "local Islams." In observing the multiplicity of Muslim social practices, they strongly criticized the orientalist notion of one single and all-encompassing Islam base on textual sources alone (cf. Anjum 2007 and Abu-Lughod 1989).

4. Having said this, the readers will nevertheless be surprised to find the "essentializing" terms *Islam* and *the West* throughout the book. This is due to the fact that these terms are difficult to circumvent since they have a long tradition of meaning for people and have no suitable alternatives. Although I indicate their critical character and analytical limitations right from the beginning, I retain these terms for mere convenience rather than trying to conjure up new ones.

5. For an example of this debate about the relationship between Arab or Muslim culture and democratic rule in the post-September 11 era, see the *Debate* in *Journal of Democ-*

The necessary and justified critique of the essentialist image of Islam, however, increasingly loses its relevance in the face of a global reality in which essentialist protagonists of a confrontation between the Muslim and the Western worlds, such as Osama bin-Ladin or Samuel Huntington, have taken the discursive lead. Consequently, the public political debate after September 11, 2001, has reinvigorated the very same theme of difference between Islam and the West. The terror attacks in New York and Washington set off an avalanche of more or less academic publications, aiming at an explanation of the recent waves of Islamist militancy. In this global debate, the different camps draw on a variety of essentialist or constructivist arguments in order to confirm or to reject the assumption that we might experience a clash between Western and Islamic cultures. Focusing on the paradigm of conflict between Islam and the West, these often hastily written analyses have contributed to extending further the already extensive literature on the politicization of Islam rather than to broadening our understanding of the gradual rise of Islamist world views.[6]

This predominance of quantity over quality is largely due to the fact that neither the underlying concepts nor the questions posed have changed. By using two contradictory general concepts about "true Islam," either that it is intrinsically hostile to or principally compatible with modern democratic culture, the post-September 11 debate has gone full circle.[7] Against this background, this book aims at a change of perspective. Instead of explaining differences, it aims at understanding similarities. It will depart from the observation that both Western orientalists and contemporary Islamists have conceptualized Islam as an all-encompassing, determinant, and unchanging cultural entity. Leaving behind the increasingly circular debate between essentialist and constructivist conceptualization of true Islam, this book investigates the origin, spread, and conflictive potential of a historically particular but extremely influential modern image of Islam. In doing so, my study is organized around the following core question: Why do orientalists and Islamists similarly define Islam as an all-encompassing religious, political and social system? Related to this question, I look at the ways in which this image attained the status of popularly accepted knowledge on Islam in a global dimension and how it is associated with the assumption of a

---

racy, 15 (4), October 2004.

6. For a good and critical overview of a part of this literature that appeared immediately after September 11, see Geertz (2003a and b).

7. However, outspoken representatives of the relativist position do not entirely escape certain tendencies to essentialize Islam either. In their book *Islam and Democracy* the two Georgetown Professors John Esposito and John Voll state from the outset that Islam is in principle compatible with both authoritarian and democratic forms of rule. Nevertheless, they start their investigation, which is predominantly based on six case studies, with a general chapter on the "conceptual resources within Islam for democratization" (Esposito and Voll 1996, 7). In this way, Islam as a whole again appears to have the quality of being the essentially independent variable with regard to democratization processes in the Muslim world.

confrontation between Islam and the West.

Although principally sympathetic to the constructivist position, viewing Islam as open to historical, social and cultural contingencies, I would not easily dismiss the confrontational scenario. It is not the interpretations of scholars, but the perceptions of actors that turn contingencies into historical realities and shape the contours of political conflicts. The modern essentialist image of Islam is such a historical reality. It is firmly anchored in the minds of both Muslims and non-Muslims and plays a crucial role in shaping the global discourse on religion in general and on Islam in particular. We have to face this historical reality of the current hegemony of essentialist conceptualizations of Islam in public discourses, on which not only militant Islamists and Islamophobic Western analysts have based their political world views.[8] Given the fact that these discourses take place in the midst of asymmetric international power relations, the likelihood of conflict is unfortunately given. My investigation of the rise of this modern concept of Islam will be guided by the hypothesis outlined in the following.

The notion of Islam as an all-encompassing social system has to be understood against the theoretical framework of an emerging global modernity. As an instance of globalization, it can be traced back to both the emergence of the academic discipline of Islamic studies in the late nineteenth century and the parallel rise of an Islamic modernism whose ideas represented an amalgam of various teachings of Islamic reform, the encounter with indigenous and colonial faces of modernization, and intellectual debates about scholarly and literary interpretations of Muslim culture by the West. This amalgam of ideas became a fundament of modern knowledge about Islam, based on the reinterpretation of Islamic traditions through the lenses of modern concepts such as national state, science, religion, law, secularism and authenticity. The contemporary essentialist image of Islam, then, evolved in the course of the twentieth century in a complex process of cross-cutting (self-)interpretations of Muslim *and* Western life experiences within an emerging global public sphere. Thus, the consensus among orientalists and Islamists does not rest on the alleged "ontological essentials" of Islamic culture, but rather reflects the cognitive and semantic structures of an emergent "world society" that have shaped the global discourse on Islam. The gradual transformation from ideas of Islamic reform to ideologies of Islamist revolution took place within a social field whose major coordinates were the structures of international and national power politics and the changing character of

8. Since September 11, 2001, I have been lecturing intensively on security issues, as well as the relationship between religion and politics in modern societies, to European, Middle Eastern and Asian audiences. In the course of this, I have found the factual cross-cutting prevalence of this "essentialist" image of Islam striking. Furthermore, on a number of trips to Middle Eastern destinations I talked to a variety of people from taxi drivers, restaurant employees, students, officials, and journalists to academics. Although the overwhelming majority of these people condemn terrorism, many of them nevertheless sympathized with Islamist interpretations of world politics as characterized by an ongoing Western suppression of the Muslim world.

a global public sphere whose technologically advancing infrastructure facilitated the gradual popularization, trivialization, and dissemination of a previously elitist discourse on Islam and the West.

In order to substantiate this hypothesis, the following chapters attempt to deliver a historical and sociological reconstruction of some parts of this particular trajectory of modern knowledge on Islam. This reconstruction is based on a broad spectrum of primary and secondary sources, and it is methodologically inspired by a genealogical approach. As a historically oriented, critical method of analysis, the genealogy tries to make explicit the covert history of something that appears to us as a given whole. The genealogical approach can disclose some of the intermediate steps in the formation of the essentialist image of Islam and aims at a better understanding of the hidden heterogeneity of its historical origin. In other words, I do not claim to give a comprehensive narrative of the historical evolution of this modern image of Islam. This book only traces back the complex construction of this image in a very selective way, analyzing some crucial steps of its evolution. The sequence of its chapters is therefore structured by the (genea-)logic of the argument and by a theoretically guided selection of themes and representative individuals.

We will take up the chain of argumentation with a critical glance at the controversy around Edward Said's *Orientalism* (1978). His polemic study about the discursive construction of the Orient in European scholarship and literature gave a bold answer to questions about the modern imaging of Islam. According to Said, a hegemonic European discourse created the Orient as its "exotic other" and established the essentialist dichotomy between East (read here: Islam) and West. In his interpretation, this discursive nexus of knowledge and power provided a justification for the advancement of European cultural supremacy and imperialist domination. Said's book triggered a still ongoing debate on his method, sources, and findings that also has opened new avenues of research under the labels of postcolonial and colonial discourse studies. However, this strand of literature has largely focused on the linkage between oriental studies and imperial policies, neglecting the impact which the "ontology of orientalism" might have had on the self-interpretation of Islamic culture. A rare exception was Sadik al-Azm (1981) who claimed that Islamist and Arab nationalist ideologies contain elements of "orientalism in reverse." According to al-Azm, Arab nationalists and Islamists have employed orientalist stereotypes in their own ideologies, reversing them into positive elements of Arab nationalist and Islamist self-descriptions.[9] In developing al-Azm's idea further, the second chapter ends by anchoring my argument in the existing body of literature, demonstrating the conceptual needs for my own study, and explaining the historical circumscription of its genealogical steps. Hence, this review of the controversy around Said's thesis will help us map out the set of theoretical and empirical questions essential for this book.

---

9. Later works also pointed at the intellectual heritage of European romanticism and nineteenth century authoritarianism in Islamist thoughts (see Stauth 1993, al-Azmeh 1996, Salvatore 1997, Asad 2003).

The third chapter, then, will lay out the theoretical framework and the analytical tools on which this study of knowledge rests. To be frank, for some readers this chapter might appear to be a difficult and probably exaggerated exercise in social theory. Yet this conceptual discussion is not only important for a thorough understanding of my argument, but is embedded in a theoretical perspective that has framed this study right from the beginning. The theoretical frame of reference presented in chapter three has generated my research questions and organized the whole research process from which this book results. Making sense of the world first and foremost relies on the application of theoretically well-founded analytical tools within a more general theoretical framework. It is therefore the purpose of chapter three to engage the reader with an argumentative reflection on my approach. Furthermore, this chapter is intended to make a contribution to more general debates in contemporary social theory and to the field of the sociology of knowledge, the latter in particular with my analytical device of a global public sphere. Being aware that social theory is not the most preferred reading for everybody, I decided to organize the chapter in a way that might make it more easily digestible for the reader who may have less of an interest in sociology than the author of this book. The first section of chapter three therefore gives an introduction to my mode of sociological reasoning and presents the analytical key concepts of the book in a nutshell. In the following sections, I then engage in a deeper argumentative discussion of my theoretical position and the origins of the analytical language that will be applied in the empirical investigations of this book. In light of this structure, the readers may decide themselves whether they read through the whole chapter or stay content with its introduction alone. The various sections of the chapter can also serve as a theoretical reference when questions turn up at a later stage in the book.

I begin the argumentative discussion with a brief look at globalization. The global discourse on Islam has been embedded in a larger historical context to which we often refer to as globalization. I will analyze this historical context through the macro-sociological concept of world society. This concept is a sociological construct rather than a clearly visible empirical reality. With its heuristic quality of an ideal type, the concept of world society will help us to organize the multiplicity of relevant global developments in their political, cultural, and economic dimensions. Although based on classical theories of the sociology of modernity, I consciously distance my concept of world society from the neo-classical theories of modernization with their ill-fated emphasis on homogeneity and linearity. In sharp contrast to these modernization theories of the 1950s and 1960s, the theory employed here leads to an understanding of the emergence of a global modernity as the development of "multiple modernities" (Eisenstadt 2000). From this point of view, the rise of Islamic and Western modernities has been a simultaneous but asymmetric process, and their empirically distinctive features become apparent from a general theoretical vantage point.

While the concept of world society will serve as this general macro-sociological framework for my study, chapter three also gives an outline of the more specific analytical tools for the book, combining structural and hermeneutic theories with the idea of a global public sphere. I will borrow from theoretical approaches that conceptualize culture from a semiotic perspective.[10] These theories define cultures as emergent symbolic orders of a collective nature, yet open to individual interpretation and social change. For this purpose, I will draw on a combination of theoretical elements inspired by the concepts of *episteme* (Michel Foucault), of the "social habitus" (Pierre Bourdieu), of "cultural interference" (Clifford Geertz), of "social imaginaries" (Charles Taylor), and of the "fusion of horizons" (Hans-Georg Gadamer).[11] Despite their differences in theory and method, the works of these authors tend to converge in some points crucial for my own investigation. From this perspective of convergence instead of difference, it seems to me possible to bridge general theoretical divides such as between structure and agency, universal and particular patterns of meaning, and between orders of knowledge and the self.

I shall complement this theory of knowledge with two other strands of social theory: theories of the public sphere and theories of power. I will conceptualize the global public sphere as the "social site," a mesh of discursive orders of knowledge, of social practices, and asymmetric power relations (Schatzki 2002), on which the historical configuration of the essentialist image of Islam has taken place. In so doing, I take the classical work of Jürgen Habermas as my departure point, but deviate from it in two essential aspects. First, my model of a global public sphere will play down the normative aspects of Habermas' approach, his emphasis on liberal democratic politics and the role of the public sphere to provide a means for discussing and controlling the state's exercise of power by its citizens.[12] Second, I will extend Habermas' model beyond national borders, conceptualizing the public sphere in the context of international power relations in a global dimension.

In this study, I employ the global public sphere as an analytical tool, referring to a social site whose operational fundaments are the cognitive deep structures of world society. These cognitive deep structures facilitate communication

---

10. In this study the meaning of the term "knowledge" refers to what Russell Hardin called "ordinary knowledge," bodies of putative popular knowledge that "must not be justified in a philosophical sense" (Hardin 2009, 25–27).

11. All these theories understand cultures no longer in the tradition of Herder—as historically unfolding, all-encompassing, holistic entities—but as emergent symbolic orders. Yet this deviation from the Herderian tradition and its essentialist assumptions has to be understood in a qualified way. Also these theories show, more or less, certain tendencies toward the "myth of cultural integration," that is to say the inclination to conceptualize culture as "a symbolically consistent universe" (Archer 1988, xv). This qualification applies in particular to Taylor's work. The Canadian Charles Taylor might be better known as a political thinker who has been advocating "communitarian positions" in the democracy debate in the United States.

12. The majority of literature on the public sphere focuses on these normative aspects (cf. Calhoun 1997, Alejandro 1993, McGuigan 1996, Marden 2003).

among a variety of actors with different semantics that allow both cooperative and confrontational communications and actions over the globe. I, thus, perceive the empirical emergence of Western and Islamic public spheres as interrelated processes of establishing a global platform for the evolution of modern forms of knowledge. The formation, extension, and dissemination of knowledge have historically never taken place without the moderation by and the modification through social power relations. The crucial historical developments of this study —the evolution of the modern concept of religion, the scholarly reconstruction of Islam as a modern religion, the incorporation of orientalist stereotypes into Islamist ideologies, and the transformation of the reformist ideas of Islamic modernism into radical political ideologies—cannot be explained by cognitive processes alone. The emergence and relative global hegemony of the modern essentialist image of Islam must also be viewed through the lenses of concepts of power.

The main body of my empirical investigation will then be presented in chapters four and five. As already mentioned, I am going to relate my own research closely to some of the main disputes in the controversy around Edward Said's *Orientalism*. This applies not only to the specific questions of my empirical chapters, but also to the above-presented selection of theories and analytical concepts that represent the analytical framework for the whole argumentation of this book. In taking the global public sphere as the social site—the stage—of my analysis, it is important to address both its cognitive and semantic macro-structures, as well as the micro-sociological aspect of individual exchanges that have taken place among and between Western and Muslim intellectuals. Although the modern image of Islam has largely been shaped by rather invisible discursive structures, I try to give the reader an idea of in which way collective actors and individuals have actively participated in enacting and semantically transforming these structures over the course of two centuries. In terms of time, however, my focus will be on the period between 1850 and the First World War. I consider this period to be crucial because it has seen both the evolution of modern Western Islamic studies as a distinct academic discipline and the emergence of a variety of modern Islamic reform movements. It was in this period of time in which a public sphere of intellectual deliberation between Western and Muslim thinkers emerged in the political context of European imperialism; and it was during this crucial period that fundamental concepts of Islamic traditions were bestowed with a modern meaning.

In an attempt to combine macro- and micro-sociological dimensions, my empirical investigation presents a combination of both the analysis of important public debates with their conceptual foundations and the role of specific individuals in enacting, shaping, and consolidating these discursive structures. We will set out with a more general examination of the conceptual and thematic patterns with which the emergence of modern society in Europe was publicly discussed throughout the nineteenth century. In particular the changing conceptualization of and the shifting relationship between religion, state and science will be addressed. In this discussion, I employ the concept of science in the meaning of the German term *Wissenschaft.* In contrast to "science" in English, *Wissenschaft* does not predominantly refer to the natural sciences, but comprises modern scholarship in a more comprehensive sense. My usage of science, therefore, includes fields of knowledge such as anthropology, comparative religion, history, theology, philology and sociology, which are crucial with regard to this study on the modern image of Islam.

In my analysis, I will put the focus more explicitly on the variations with which European societies reacted to the challenge that modern science posed to the revealed knowledge of Christianity. It was the discursive competition among positivists, traditionalists and a broad, very diverse range of Protestant and Catholic apologists that eventually shaped the modern European perception of religion in general. In this competitive process, the French Catholic turned positivist Ernest Renan and the Scottish liberal Protestant apologist William Robertson Smith played key roles in reflecting on the relationship between science and religion. Even more important for the topic of this book, Renan and Smith as two almost paradigmatic scholars of classical orientalist studies influenced modern knowledge on Islam and the formation of Islamic studies in Europe and beyond. From the perspective of the history of the modern sciences, this struggle to shape an acknowledged understanding of modern society culminated in the establishment of sociology as an academic discipline. Consequently, I have chosen, in addition to Renan and Robertson Smith, Emile Durkheim and Max Weber as representative individuals for the general theme of chapter four. They are not only two of the founding fathers of sociology, but eminent figures in the sociologies of religion and knowledge. Much of what we think we know about religion today can be traced back to their sociological conceptualizations whose origins partly lay in the modern revision of Christianity by liberal Protestant theology.

In chapter five we narrow our focus and will look at the representations of Islam within the emerging field of a distinct discipline of Islamic studies. We will start with a brief analysis of the emancipation of Islamic studies from the broader field of oriental studies in Germany. I have chosen the German example as it seems paradigmatic for the general development of Islamic studies as an autonomous academic discipline. Moreover, the German context was far less conditioned by colonial interests and thus might serve as a corrective to Edward Said's preoccupation with oriental studies in France and Great Britain. Once again four individuals who were closely linked with each other through personal and scholarly ties are at the center of my analysis. First I analyze the life and work of two founding fathers of Islamic studies, the Hungarian scholar Ignaz Goldziher and the Dutch orientalist and colonial advisor Christiaan Snouck Hurgronje. The methods, topics, and findings of both scholars provided the very foundation for designating the academic contours of the new discipline. In addition, both had very close ties with German scholarship, maintained intensive contact with Muslim thinkers and were widely reputed in Muslim intellectual circles. I then move back to the German scene and two scholars who lobbied intensively, and for a certain time successfully, for the institutional establishment of a modern science of Islam (*Islamwissenschaft*) in Imperial Germany: C.H. Becker and Martin Hartmann. Moreover, their view of Islam as a religion and civilization made a strong impact on politicians and on the learned public. In this sense, they are also exemplary of the spread and dissemination of scholarly acquired knowledge on Islam within the broader public sphere.

Due to the complexity of the topic and the enormous amount of data to be scrutinized, this book has its limits. It therefore predominantly deals with the construction of the modern image of Islam by European scholars and the conceptual fundaments in which this image is rooted. To a certain extent, this bias gives my study a kind of uneven nature. However, in order to balance this unevenness and to support my hypothesis of the mutual interaction among European and Muslim intellectuals, the historical developments in the Muslim world and the role of important figures of the Islamic reform movement will constantly serve as additional empirical reference points. To this end, the dominant European narrative will be accompanied from the outset by a secondary narrative about the Muslim world. This secondary narrative indicates the ways in which influential Muslim actors were engaged in the European (read: "global") discourse about religion, state, and science, thereby linking modern debates and concepts with their own traditions and to their struggle against Western colonial domination.

This group of Muslim intellectuals comprises first and foremost three well-known and enormously influential figures who became known in Western scholarship under the label of the modernist Salafiyya movement: Jamal al-Din al-Afghani, Muhammad Abduh, and Rashid Rida.[13] Their reformist ideas developed not only in close contact with each other, but also in discursive and social exchanges with the Islamic studies of the afore-mentioned orientalists and in light of general European debates about state, religion and science. In addition, I make references to a number of non-Arab Muslim intellectuals, most specifically to the Ottomans Namik Kemal and Ziya Gökalp and to the Indian poet and philosopher Muhammad Iqbal. They also belong to the broader stream of Islamic modernism, however, without being associated with such a close intellectual movement as the above-mentioned three Arab thinkers. Reflecting on imperial domination, nation-building, social reform and the role of religion in modern societies, these Muslim intellectuals intensively contributed to shaping the modern image of Islam. It is important to note that in political terms the course of Islamic reform for the decades to follow remained open to both Islamist and secularist ideological alternatives (cf. Sharabi 1970). The concrete historical paths that the emerging Muslim national states have taken were largely due to the power configurations and the concomitant ideological justifications on which their

---

13. These three Muslim intellectuals advocated the "Salafi method," that is to say a return to the primary religious sources in their efforts to re-interpreting Islam in the context of modern times. However, they themselves apparently did not refer to their intellectual movement with the term Salafiyya. This label seems to be a later invention by Western scholars of Islam.

respective nation- and state-builders relied. Thus, Muhammad Iqbal became the ideological father of the Islamic state of Pakistan, while Ziya Gökalp is remembered as the leading Turkish nationalist intellectual behind the political elite of the secularist Turkish republic.

In order to finally answer my central research question, the concluding chapter will emphasize the "Muslim narrative" more. First we will look more closely at the interaction of Islamic reformers with Western orientalists and their intellectual and scholarly milieus. This section will demonstrate the close interconnection between the Muslim reform movements in India, the Ottoman Empire and Egypt with the European scene. The emergence of an Islamic public sphere will thus be explained as an inherent part of the rising global public sphere. The second step will look more closely at some of the conceptual revisions with regard to Islamic traditions which characterized the reformist thought of Jamal al-Din al-Afghani, Muhammad Abduh and Rashid Rida. I shall analyze the ways in which these Islamic reformers reinterpreted their religious traditions in the modern social context. The third part of the chapter, then, sketches out the gradual transformation of various ideas of Islamic reform into elements of a militant ideology of Islamist revolution. Again I organize this section around the role of four influential individuals: Hasan al-Banna, Abu al-Ala Mawdudi, Sayyid Qutb and Abdallah Azzam. All four decisively contributed to the popularization, politicization and eventual militarization of Islamist thought for which an intellectual platform developed in the nineteenth and early twentieth centuries through the social and cultural exchanges of Muslim reformers among each other and with Western scholars. This chain of important personalities, however, should not be confused with the idea of a linear line of development. There is no teleology leading from Afghani to Azzam. On the contrary, this chain is the construction of a contingent historical process in retrospect. Its individual personalities have been chosen selectively from a genealogical perspective; they represent nodal points in the understanding of a present situation, whose historical evolution has been submerged.

Yet before now taking up our argumentative thread, some words of caution seem to be necessary. With this study, I do not pretend to completely rewrite the history of Islam and the West. Rather, it is the purpose of this book to integrate a variety of already known histories and to present them from a different theoretical perspective. For me, the social sciences are first and foremost an interpretative enterprise. Therefore, the primary aim of this study is to provide a theoretically informed new interpretation of at least in part widely known "facts." The original quality of this interpretation may be found in its particular composition of various elements of the sociology of knowledge with historical, biographical, and text-based sources of both Muslim and Western thinkers and their historical and intellectual environments.

Generally speaking, the book pursues a twofold aim. Firstly, it is intended to enhance our understanding of the origin and evolution of a specific modern image of Islam. More precisely, it investigates the linkages between European scholarship on religion and Islam with the ideas of Islamic modernism in shaping the modern essentialist image of Islam on which Islamist ideologies and Western perceptions of Islam largely rely. In doing so, it also adds to reflections about the historical emergence of the discipline of Islamic studies. Secondly, in introducing and applying the analytical device of a global public sphere, this book is intended to contribute to the field of the sociology of knowledge in empirical and theoretical terms. The search for similarities has not only guided my analysis of Islamist and orientalist thinking. I also knit together a variety of quite different social theories, oriented toward their shared potential to bring us closer to answers on mutually asked questions. Instead of focusing on divergence, it is the search for convergence in both historical developments and theoretical perspectives that interests me. Consequently, the readers should not expect this book to be a large compilation of previously unknown "facts" nor a rigorous "test" of social theories.

The ultimate purpose of this book is to question from a theoretically elaborated perspective a particular form of accepted knowledge about Islam that has permeated our public debates. I am challenging this knowledge by writing an interpretative history of its emergence. In the academic jargon of our times, this might be labeled a "deconstructionist" approach. Personally, however, I prefer to understand myself rather as what Max Weber once called an "interpretative specialist." In Weber's understanding, the scholarly "artistry" of these specialists lies in their "ability to produce new knowledge by interpreting already *known* facts according to known viewpoints" (Weber 1904, 112). Whether I have been successful in this undertaking or not I leave to the judgment of the reader.

2

Orientalism: Edward Said and His Critics

> The distortion of the subject matter of *Orientalism* is so fundamental that to ac-
> cept its broad framework as something to work with and then correct would be
> merely to waste one's time.
>
> (Robert Irwin)

The ongoing scholarly debate about *Orientalism* has undoubtedly uncovered a
number of errors and flaws in Edward Said's work. Yet, accepting the relent-
less verdict cited above would render any critical analysis of Edward Said's book
superfluous. Contrary to Robert Irwin, I perceive *Orientalism* not as a "work of
malignant charlatanry" (2006, 4), but as—although not in terms of age—a classic.
Less than 25 years after its first publication in 1978, the book had been translated
into 36 languages. Edward Said's book triggered ongoing debate and contributed
influentially to the accusation of the Eurocentric character both of the social sciences and the humanities. In addition, *Orientalism* stimulated the exploration of
new avenues of research in fields such as post-colonial or colonial discourse studies. Not that Edward Said's argument was entirely new. The theme of Islam and
the West had a series of predecessors in the decades before Said's publication.[1]
Rather, its outstanding success was due to the particular political, societal and
scholarly context in which *Orientalism* appeared. It was the learned polemic of a
"Western scholar with oriental roots," voiced in the new language of so-called
post-structuralist criticism and surfing on the waves of Third-Worldism.

   In the field of Middle Eastern and Islamic studies, for instance, Said's book has
since then been an obligatory reference for many; and this both for scholars who
have read him and those who only felt the obligation to quote him. Given this
almost stifling omnipresence of *Orientalism* and the suspicion that it might have
been much more talked and read about than actually read, it is in my opinion
well worth looking more closely once again at Said's argumentation. Therefore, I
have not followed Robert Irwin's advice. Instead, I decided to re-read *Orientalism*
in light of the general question of my own research project. In the end, this is

---

1. Prime amongst them are: Daniel (1960); Frye (1956); Hitti (1962); Rodinson (1974);
    Schwab (1950); Southern (1962); Tibawi (1963); Watt (1972).

precisely what defines a classic: a text maintaining its quality of being a source of inspiration for new scholarly ideas over generations.[2]

Edward Said was an American Palestinian and a Professor in the Department of English and Comparative Literature at Columbia University, New York.[3] He based the general argument in *Orientalism* on the analysis of academic and literary texts about the Orient. In this body of literature, Said discerned an ontological and epistemological difference that distinguishes an unchanging Orient from an absolutely different and dynamic West (Said 1978, 96). Based on this binary code between East and West, according to Said, the European orientalists have produced a hegemonic discourse over the orient, not only creating an exotic other, but also legitimating the colonial oppression of this inferior mirror image by the superior Western culture. In reference to Michel Foucault's theory of power, Said viewed the birth of the oriental as the result of a specific nexus of power and knowledge which has characterized the relationship of the East, in particular the Muslim world, with the leading powers of the West. In producing an "imaginative geography," orientalist scholars have invented and constructed a geographical space that provided the necessary knowledge for "the mapping, conquest, and annexation of territory" (Said 2000, 181). In this way, the scholarly and literary representation of the Orient by the texts of orientalists became an imperial institution, facilitating and justifying colonial domination.

The above paragraph contains in a nutshell Said's central argument. In this form it became accepted knowledge in academia and outside the mere scholarly realm. Exemplary for many reviewers, Bayly Winder identified a "trinity" in the argument of *Orientalism*: "Edward Said analyzed Orientalism in three ways: as an academic discipline, as a style of thought, and as a corporate institution" (1981, 615). However, this summary account largely levels out the nuances, complexities and contradictions of *Orientalism*. In its themes and theses, Edward Said's book is by far richer and more ambiguous than this trinity and the mainstream of the subsequent controversy about *Orientalism* would lead one to believe. It is the purpose of this chapter, firstly, to present some of these complexities and nuances of Said's argument that have been submerged in the general debate. In a second step I put his complex and sometimes inconsistent argumentation into the context of the major points of critique which *Orientalism* has had to face. Finally, I link these major themes of the "Said controversy" to the central ques-

---

2. As one of Said's critics, the German historian Jürgen Osterhammel said with regard to the future role of *Orientalism*: "It is the theoretical constellation of knowledge and power, the critique of science, the constructivist epistemology and power analysis that will continue to be a stimulation" (Osterhammel 1997, 604). Indeed, the mere combination of different theoretical and historical inquires will also in future guarantee new readers for Said's book.

3. Robert Irwin is also a good example of the strong partisanship of the debate, which seems to survive the author of *Orientalism*. In the section *The Man of the Book* (Irwin 2006, 277–280) Irwin even tries to deconstruct Said's identity construction of being a Palestinian Arab "out of place."

tions of my own study. In this way, the conclusion explains the ways in which my re-reading of Edward Said's work has influenced the research design of my own project and maps out the chapters to come.

The Argument and Recurrent Themes

In the new introduction to the 25th anniversary edition of his book, Said seriously criticized both the ongoing stereotypical approach of U.S. policy experts to the Middle East and the uncomprehending anti-Americanism in the Arab World. Again, Said positioned himself as a person and author who feels "out of place." This became the title of his memoirs (Said 1999), a personal history of felt exclusion and of a continuing lack of belonging which tells much about Said's motivation for writing a polemic but nevertheless scholarly book such as Orientalism. In the Afterword, written 1994, Said explicitly states: "Orientalism is a partisan book, not a theoretical machine" (1994b, 339). Already in the 1978 edition, the introduction points to the fact that his book is definitely not an exclusively academic matter. On the contrary, it originates in the awareness of the author of being an "Oriental" himself, whose early life was shaped by the political framework of British colonialism (1978, 25–27). Said reiterated this personal attachment to his subject in Culture and Imperialism, a kind of updated version of his argument in Orientalism. In Said's words, this book was written by an exile who belongs to "both sides of the imperial divide" (1994a, xxvii).[4]

This personal insight is Edward Said's general point of departure. In his project of analyzing how Europe has shaped the Orient and has been gaining strength and identity in setting itself apart from it, Said's personal attachment is deeply inscribed (1978, 3). In analyzing orientalism, he attempts to "show the field's shape and internal organization, its pioneers, patriarchal authorities, canonical texts, doxological ideas, exemplary figures, its followers, elaborators, and new authorities" (1978, 22). Orientalism is a study that approaches the micro- and the macro-levels of the problem at the same time. In attempting a deconstruction of the Orient and the so-called oriental mind as they are represented in the texts of Western orientalists, Said deals not only with the discursive macro-structures that have systematically created the Orient, but he also aims at a better understanding of his personal feeling of being out of place. Moreover, in taking his theoretical inspiration from Michel Foucault, Said wants to question the "liberal consensus" on the disengaged character of scientific knowledge, showing the highly political character of knowledge production as a process permeated by power relations (1978, 10).

Despite all the nuances and contradictions that characterize his book, it is to a certain extent possible to synthesize Said's claims into a multi-varied general thesis about orientalism as a discipline. He outlines the development of a holistic

---

4. Another book which Said wrote in continuation of Orientalism was Covering Islam (1981). The book basically builds on the same arguments, while taking its examples from American media coverage of Islam.

system of knowledge about the Orient that was made possible by the scholarly works of orientalists (1978, 94). In his eyes, an orientalist is anybody who teaches, writes and/or researches the Orient within a particular discursive structure. This discourse has been supported by academic and non-academic institutions, a specific vocabulary, forms of scholarship, and by a number of disciplinary doctrines that have produce a body of consistent, holistic knowledge about the Orient. A core feature of this oriental knowledge is the ontological and epistemological distinction made between the Orient and the Occident (1978, 2). This essential cognitive binary differentiation is fused with a particular value attitude expressing the distinction between Western superiority and oriental inferiority (1978, 42), together creating a radical code of difference (1978, 45). Initially being a scholarly discipline based on a set of inherited structures, orientalism underwent a transformation from a scholarly discourse to an imperial institution (1978, 95).

In clear distinction to the mere disciplinary content of the terms "orientalist" and "orientalism" in the nineteenth century, Said extends their notion enormously. Once the designations for an academic avant-garde, Said's book turned them into pejorative labels for stereotypical Western thinkers and concepts that claim the absolute superiority of the West over the East. In the course of the text, Said defines orientalism as variously as follows: a mode of discourse; a style of thought; a corporate institution for dealing with the orient; a sign of Euro-Atlantic power over the Orient; a created body of theory and practice; a system of knowledge; a distribution of geopolitical awareness in aesthetic, scholarly, economic, sociological, historical, and philological texts; a justification of colonial rule; a kind of intellectual power; a political vision of reality; a generic term to describe the Western approach to the Orient; a topic of learning, discovery and practice; a collection of dreams and images; a form of specialized knowledge; a school of interpretation; an academic tradition; and an area of general societal concern. In sum, orientalism becomes an all-encompassing and ideological concept for the oppression of the Orient by the West.

In historical terms, Said understands orientalism as a specific system of theory and practice that assumed its modern face in a process based on a set of inherited structures of previously religiously defined stereotypes about the Orient and Islam. Within the inseparable coordinates of power and knowledge, this stereotypical legacy was secularized, re-disposed, and re-formed by the oriental disciplines in the course of the eighteenth and nineteenth centuries. Orientalism was molded by both the secularizing elements of Western culture and the experience of colonial expansion and historical confrontation. In this way the old religious patterns and paradigms in which Europeans viewed the non-Christian world were partly replaced and partly reconstituted within a secular framework based on a new, scientific and rational platform (1978, 120–122). This new "scientific" knowledge about the Orient, then, underwent a process of trivialization and popularization. Orientalist knowledge trickled down to society at large as reflected in the striking traffic "between what scholars and specialists wrote and what poets, novelists, politicians, and journalists then said about Islam" (1994b, 343).

Given Said's partly erratic way of writing, his sometimes contradictory formulations, and the polemic style of his book, it seems reasonable to use *Orientalism* as an inspiration rather than a paradigm for one's own study. Working with *Orientalism* is not synonymous with an attempt to correct it. Besides taking the approach of writing an overall critical sociology of knowledge, Said detected five recurrent themes in the orientalist conceptualization of Islam that are significant for my own analysis:

1. the systemic holism of orientalist perceptions;
2. Islam (and therewith religion) as the core variable in understanding the Muslim world;
3. scriptualism as method and basis for the cultural theory of orientalism;
4. the intrinsically political nature of Islam in orientalist analysis;
5. and the presentation of Islamic history as a process of decline by orientalists.

First of all, there is the holistic character of the West's perception of the orient, visible in the general applicability of the adjective "oriental" such as in oriental arts, oriental life, oriental mind, oriental mode of production, oriental personality and so forth (1978, 31–32). In its absolute difference from the West, the Orient is presented as an unchanging whole, as a systematic unity of "otherness." The core variable in understanding this otherness is religion, more specifically Islam; and while other orientalist sub-disciplines such as Indology or Sinology have subsequently revised their essentialist ideas, "only the Arabist and Islamologists still function unrevised" (1978, 301). Second, from an orientalist perspective, historical, political, economic and social developments in the Muslim world are more or less accidental processes subordinated to the determining and overarching power of the cultural synthesis of Islam. In this way, religion (Islam) turns into the general oriental signifier, representing "all at once a society, a religion, a prototype, and an actuality" (1978, 299). Everything turns religious and the orientalists posit the Islamic category as the dominant one (1978, 305). Yet, how is the cultural logic of this religious oriental whole accessed? From which kind of data should we draw our knowledge about Islamic culture?

Generally speaking, and thirdly, orientalists rely on texts. The understanding of the Orient is based on the philological analysis of Islamic core texts as given in the Koran, the Sunna and the *fiqh*, the field of "Islamic jurisprudence" (1978, 52; 98).[5] Fourth, referring to Muhammad as both a religious and a political leader, Islam is by nature a unity of religion and politics (151–152), yet a religious and

---

5. With regard to these three central themes of orientalist scholarship — holism, Islam as central explicatory variable, and scriptualist approach the book by the Swiss Professor Bürgel ("Almighty of God") is a fine example that Said's definition of orientalism not only has a historical quality but is still related to a form of contemporary scholarship (Bürgel 1991).

political system that is inferior to the modern West with its attributes of being rational, liberal, logical, and without natural suspicion (1978, 49). Grounded in the scientist spirit of nineteenth century secular positivism, the West has to teach the Orient the meaning of liberty in order to free the orientals from their self-inflicted status of inferiority (1978, 172). Finally, this status of oriental inferiority vis-à-vis the West is the result of a historical process, analyzing Islamic history as a history of decline. Only the reconstruction of the Orient according to the model of the modern West will "restore a region from its present barbarism to its former classical greatness" (1978, 86).

The Said Controversy

It comes as no surprise that Said's book met with a long and broad stream of critical reviews. Less than eight years after its first edition, *Orientalism* had been reviewed in over 60 scholarly journals (Mani and Frankenberg 1985, 178). It goes without saying that these reviews were not all of a positive kind. A polemic undoubtedly causes counter-polemics, and in particular some scholars of Middle Eastern affairs spearheaded these counter attacks in the subsequent controversy *Orientalism* had stirred. Malcom Kerr, for instance, conceded that the book had its merits and contained many excellent sections and telling points. However, he saw these achievements almost completely spoiled by Said's "overzealous prosecutorial argument" (Kerr 1980). More outspoken and not less prosecutorial was Bernard Lewis in his response. The Princeton Professor of Islamic history not only had to defend his discipline, but essentially himself. During the whole controversy, Said took Lewis as one of his prime adversaries among those scholars whom he branded as contemporary orientalists. Lewis paid back in the same partisan and polemic way and accused Said of poisoning the debate by a form of "intellectual pollution" that rendered the rational application of the terms orientalism and orientalist impossible (Lewis 1993, 251). In assessing the scholarly quality of the book, Lewis saw Said's efforts oscillating between a form of "honest historical ignorance" and the conscious "transmutation of events to fit his thesis" (1993, 259). With regard to Said's almost complete exemption of German and Russian orientalists, Lewis even considered the success of the book to be a result of Said's profound hatred and hostility toward the West and its liberal democratic culture (1993, 264).

Apparently, these polemic exchanges took place on the literary battlefield between scholars who were intransigent in both their own convictions and the mutual condemnation of their respective opponents.[6] In terms of scholarly sur-

---

6. In 1996, for example, Edward Said, in an article in *The Nation,* made the accusation against Lewis that the so-called expert on Islam was turning "Muslims into objects of a therapeutic, punitive attention" (Said 1996). Even more aggressive were the attacks against Lewis by A.L. Tibawi. He blamed Lewis for having the "habit of citing obscure references" and the inclination to "decorate his pages with foreign words" in order to project linguistic knowledge which he actually lacked (Tibawi 1979, 32).

plus, the most heated replies did not contribute too much; polemical attacks were made at the expense of valuable points of critique. Yet, a large part of the controversy raised interesting points of critique that seriously challenged the theoretical and empirical validity of Said's work. In synthesizing various arguments from a number of critical reviews of *Orientalism*, I can discern five clusters of critical remarks which are of clear relevance for my own study:

1. Said's questionable application of "post-structuralist" theory, in particular the discourse theory of Michel Foucault;
2. His instrumental and self-evident connection between colonial policies and orientalist scholarship;
3. His neglect of the phenomenon of reversed orientalism;
4. His a-historic thesis of a continuation of orientalist stereotyping from ancient times to the present;
5. His selection of cases and usage of sources;

The examination of these five clusters of critique has informed my own research process. Thus, looking closer at the Said controversy will help the reader to understand better the argumentation of my book. I will point to the interconnectedness of these critical arguments against *Orientalism*, which all can be related to specific theoretical and empirical shortcomings in Said's book. However, the purpose of this literature review is not to check the critique against the backdrop of Said's work and his replies to his critics. The focus here is not on the controversy as such. Instead, I will discuss his critics in light of their relevance for the development of my own argumentation.

Theoretical Inconsistencies and the "Real Orient"

In his introduction to a reader with core texts on the *Orientalism* controversy, the editor A.L. Macfie indicated that a number of Said's critics, in particular historians of the Middle East, were "firmly wedded to a traditional (realist) approach to the writing of history." Insisting on the mere validity of so-called historical facts, these historians were, according to Macfie, due to their methodological positions, not really able to communicate with Said, who approached his subject with the help of postmodern philosophy (Macfie 2000, 5). Indeed, given the various audiences that Said's book addressed, it is not surprising that a good deal of critique was also related to misunderstandings and particularistic readings of *Orientalism*. Yet some of his theoretically better versed critics raised the question of whether Said himself really understood the theoretical approach he claimed to use in *Orientalism* (cf. Ahmad 1991; al-Azm 1981; Bhaba 1997; Irwin 2006; Osterhammel 1997; Richardson 1990).

This question specifically has been posed concerning Said's application of Michel Foucault's discourse theory.[7] Said claimed to write from a Foucaultian perspective

---

7. Said applies a broad and multiple usage of the concept. Therewith, he follows the "widespread consensus" of relating the origin of this broad usage of discourse to Fou-

and, on the surface, he basically did so in two ways: first, in framing the field of orientalism as a discursive institution with a holistic and determining character; second, in analyzing the oriental discourse through the inseparable relationship between structures of social power and structures of knowledge. Contrary to that of Foucault, however, Said's approach is characterized by a strong subjectivist component. His strong sense of "humanism" (cf. Said 2004) clearly contradicts the fundaments of Foucault's anti-subjectivist and anti-humanist philosophy. For Said, individual writers play an eminent if not determining role in shaping the discursive field of orientalism, which he analyses "as a dynamic exchange between individual authors and the large political concerns shaped by the three great empires—British, French, American" (Said 1978, 14). We will see that this deliberate deviation from Foucault's discourse theory stirred some confusion on the side of Said's reviewers, but also in the argumentation of his book itself.

Edward Said claimed to borrow his "Foucaultian perspective" from *The Archaeology of Knowledge* and from *Discipline and Punish* (Said 1978, 3). Like *The Order of Things*, *The Archaeology of Knowledge* belongs to the early works of Michel Foucault, which in my reading are of a structuralist rather than a post-structuralist character. In these works, discourses have an almost autonomous character. They are not mentally anchored but they exist in historically specific discursive practices which are not the result of but the conditions for intersubjective exchanges.[8] In *The Order of Things* Foucault developed his discourse theory with respect to changing bodies of knowledge. He was concerned with the phenomenon of three totally different systematizations of knowledge that separate the *episteme* of modern times from previous epochs. In classical times, according to Foucault's analysis, knowledge built on a universal science of measurement and order with regard to the relationship between things, a relationship that classical knowledge methodologically ordered according to the intrinsic categories of identity and difference. The classical *episteme*, therefore, did not assign a role to the ordering perspective of an observer. Modern knowledge, however, shows a completely different logic. In the patterns of meaning in modernity, the subject enters the field and becomes both observer and observed, that is to say both the subject and object of knowledge. The modern *episteme* introduced the ordering

---

cault's work. However, Keith Sawyer showed convincingly that this usage of discourse theory does actually not originate with Foucault and largely contradicts the theoretical quality of Foucault's "more limited technical usage" of discourse (Sawyer 2002, 435).

8. Although Foucault dissociated himself strongly from a structuralist approach, especially in the conclusions of *The Archaeology of Knowledge*, where he also remarked on not having used the word "structure" a single time in his previous *The Order of Things* (Foucault 1989, 221), his "archaeological method" and concepts such as discursive formations, positivities, and *episteme* are, in my opinion, of a structuralist nature. In my interpretation, Foucault is not distancing himself from a structural approach, but rather from the French schools of structuralist analysis in the tradition of Saussure and Lévi-Strauss, with their trans-historical and mentalist pretension. Foucault locates meaning not in universal mental structures, but in historically specific codes observable in texts.

subject into a world of objects (Foucault 1994).

Yet it would be absolutely wrong to consider this introduction of the subject into modern knowledge as coming a step closer to "scientific truth." For Foucault, the appearance of man at the centre of modern epistemology only indicates a radical change in the unconscious discursive structures on which human knowledge generally rests. In this sense, the move from classical to modern knowledge should not be misunderstood as a process of scientific progress. Foucault did not interpret the ontological and epistemological priority of the subject in modern knowledge in terms of a progress of reason, but simply as a historical change in forms of *episteme* in modern times. In Foucault's eyes, both subjects and objects of knowledge are only results of discursive practices. Theoretically, individual actors are nothing more than "discursive effects" (Reckwitz 2000, 282). There is no progress in human knowledge and human actors themselves are a product of the unconscious application of historically different, discursive paradigms of knowledge.[9] In *The Order of Things*, however, Foucault focused on the order of "networks of concepts," whereas *The Archaeology of Knowledge* had the discursive regularities of their formation as its topic (Foucault 1989, 72).

Against this theoretical background, Edward Said did not only deviate from Foucault. In prioritizing the individual and adding a voluntary component to his approach, he actually undermined the theoretical edifice of the French scholar. Aijaz Ahmad clearly pointed to this problem in his critique:

> In the Foucaultian definitions, representations cannot be referred back to any truth outside or beyond themselves, nor to the intentionality of the representer, because the structure of the representation is already inscribed in and always regulated by the power of discourse. Representations correspond thus not to an external object, a truth, a subjectivity, a purpose, a project, but to the discursive regularity alone. (Ahmad 1991, 292)

From a Foucaultian perspective, orientalists cannot deliberately invent an Orient in order to provide the necessary knowledge for "the mapping, conquest, and annexation" of a geographical space. When Said presents oriental scholarship in terms of the intended actions of rational actors, he definitely cannot base this thesis about the close and intended cooperation of orientalists and colonizers on Foucault. Rather, Said's approach reflects the tradition of critique of ideologies which goes back to Karl Marx and Feuerbach. While it might be possible to view Foucault's critique of the human sciences as an extension of the same line of tradition (Marti 1988, 36), the nature of this critique is fundamentally different. Foucault aims not to reveal hidden interests and institutional rationalities, but to understand the deep structures on which the whole edifice of social interests, institutions, and knowledge rests. The archaeological method tries to discover the regularities of discursive practices that give rise to a corpus of knowledge and therewith to the emergence of various but distinct "scientific disciplines"

---

9. In chapter three, I will elaborate more on Foucault's discourse theory with regard to what I have called a "cognitive deep structure" on which the semantics of the global public sphere rest.

(Foucault 1989, 210). *Orientalism* analytically remains on the level of the analysis of a concrete disciplinary discourse, whereas *The Archaeology of Knowledge* attempts to discover the intrinsic regularities of general discursive practices out of which the different sciences of man emerged (Foucault 1989, 69).

Said's introduction of voluntarist components into a structuralist body of theory caused further confusion with regard to the question of the "real orient." In accordance with his Foucaultian approach, Said insists throughout the book that neither the West nor the East have any kind of "ontological stability" (Said 1978, xvii). At several points in *Orientalism* he emphasizes that he does not want to suggest something like the existence of a "real orient."[10] This position, however, Said often contradicts only a few pages later on. In labeling orientalism as "distorted knowledge" (1978, xxii) or in accusing scholars such as Bernard Lewis of "distorting the truth" (1994b, 331), Said himself implies the existence of something "real" to be distorted. The consistent application of a Foucaultian framework would have excluded this dichotomy of distorted and true realities that, despite Said's defense, nevertheless runs throughout the whole book. Moreover, it would have eased his task of rejecting less theoretically couched critical questions such as whether Said could really so easily deny "that the Islamic religion has always exerted a pervasive influence on the culture and society of its adherents?" (Kerr 1980, 545).[11]

Colonial Policies and Oriental Scholarship

The discussion of theoretical inconsistencies in Said's argumentation brings us to a second important cluster of critique: Said not only claims there is an instrumental linkage between the work of scholars and colonial policies, but also presents this linkage as an almost self-evident core feature of his argument. Sadik al-Azm, in his reply to Said, distinguishes between forms of "institutional orientalism" and "cultural-academic orientalism," the former defining the whole set of political, economic, and ideological institutions that characterized the global expansion of modern Europe, and the latter indicating a specific academic field of knowledge about the Orient. In claiming that the epistemological framework of cultural-academic orientalism was decisive in shaping the course and forms of institutional orientalism, according to al-Azm, Said completely fell hostage to his "excessive fascination with the verbal, textual and linguistic" (al-Azm 1981, 226). In al-Azm's judgment, Said completely disregards the reality of political and eco-

---

10. Even in his last book, published *post mortem*, Edward Said reiterated: "My critique was premised on the flawed nature of all representations and how they are intimately tied up with worldliness, that is, with power, position, and interests. This required saying explicitly that my work was not intended as a defense of the real Orient or that it even made the case that a real Orient existed" (Said 2004, 48).

11. This confusion with respect to the problem of the "real Orient" has also entered secondary literature on Said. Zachary Lockman, for example, writes: "For Said, Orientalism (...) had created and perpetuated a certain image or 'representation' of 'the Orient,' a representation that had little to do with what the parts of the world so depicted were actually like" (Lockman 2004, 184). So what are they actually like?

nomic interests and "sublimates the earthly realities of the Occident's interaction with the Orient into the ethereal stuff of the spirit" (al-Azm 1981, 221).

While al-Azm criticized Said for his methodological bias toward linguistic analysis, Richard Minear, for instance, tried to prove empirically wrong Said's self-evident association of orientalist scholarship with colonial domination. In his article on Western studies about Japan, Minear comes to the conclusion that in the Western discourse on Japan we can find attitudes which closely resemble those of Said's orientalism. Like the orientalist discourse on Islam, the Western discourse on Japanese culture focuses on motives of absolute difference and Western scholars extol the Japanese past and castigate the country's present (Minear 1980, 510). Contrary to Said's claims, however, these orientalist stereotypes about Japan do not have any kind of religious appeal nor were they able to serve Western military domination over the country (Minear 1980, 515). Minear's study thus clearly refutes Said's claim of an inherent and automatic linkage between orientalist attitudes and imperialist policies.

Bernard Lewis made a valid point, although polemic in tone, in criticizing the implicit contradiction between Said's focus on scholarship on the Arab Middle East and the fact that the actual impact of colonialism in this region was much more indirect and mediated than in many other parts of the world (Lewis 1993, 261). In addition, several authors emphasize that Said's orientalist stereotypes might be better explained by the in general ethnocentric, reductive, and often hostile tendencies of cross-cultural perceptions than by the subordinating purpose of colonialist powers (cf. Kopf 1980; Mani and Frankenberg 1985; Minear 1980). From al-Azm's point of view, the Occident only did what all cultures do: "domesticating the alien" in representing them through indigenous and therewith culturally familiar concepts (al-Azm 1981, 222). The travel accounts of Western "orientalists" such as Julius Euting (1896 and 1914) or William Robertson Smith (1880–1881) support this argument further. On their journeys through the Fertile Crescent and the Arab Peninsula, they met with a whole set of stereotypes about Christian people among the local population which were not less denigrating than the orientalist images about them. In short, negative attitudes vis-à-vis alien cultures have been a widespread phenomenon and they are a far cry from characterizing colonial imaging alone.

Orientalism in Reverse

Said's tendency to neglect the reciprocity in processes of stereotyping the self and the other (cf. Richardson 1990) by describing the relationship between orientalists and Orientals merely as a one-way-street has raised another set of critical questions which are epitomized in Sadik al-Azm's postulation of an "orientalism in reverse." It was al-Azm who first argued that Orientals not only perceive Western people through similar stereotypical lenses, but that they even have also firmly incorporated some of the orientalist stereotypes in their self-image (see also Halliday 1993; Sivan 1985; Soguk 1993). In the second part of his critique, "Orientalism and Orientalism in Reverse," al-Azm applauds the "most prominent and interesting

accomplishments of Said's book," the deconstruction of the still-powerful orientalist pretensions of a principle epistemological and ontological difference
between the East and the West. This essentialist image of the Orient (Islam), as
I designated it in the introduction to this book, al-Azm labels as "ontological orientalism," as the firm belief in the enduring cultural essence, the fundamental
and unchangeable attributes of the Orient or Islam (1981, 230). In light of Said's
warning not to apply the readily available stereotypes of orientalism upon themselves, al-Azm contends that these applications "not only did take place, but are
continuing on a fairly wide scale" (1981, 231). He discerns these self-applications
of orientalist concepts in both Arab nationalist and Islamist ideologies.

In his analysis of Arab nationalist ideologies, al-Azm finds particularly striking
the way in which the "Orientalist obsession with language, texts and philology"
made its inroads into the ideological cosmos of Arab nationalism. He accuses
Arab nationalists of "obediently and uncritically" adopting the textual attitude
of orientalists to human reality. Following the fashion of Renan's Semitic studies,
Arab nationalist ideologues discover the "Arab mind" in the vocal and grammati-
cal structures of the Arabic language. Yet, contrary to Renan's verdict on Semitic
culture, they do not conclude that the Arab mind is inferior to the thought processes of Western culture. According to al-Azm, their philological and linguistic
studies prove the superiority of Arab civilization over the West (al-Azm 1981,
231–233). A similar form of ontological orientalism characterizes Islamist thinking in which not Arab culture, but the religious factor, Islam, becomes the central
variable for the factual superiority of Muslim over Western culture. Both Arab
nationalists and Islamists work with essentialist images of a monolithic, hermetically closed and unique culture, eternally different and distinct from the West. In
al-Azm's words, they "simply reproduce the whole discredited apparatus of classical Orientalist doctrine concerning the difference between the East and West,
Islam and Europe" (1981, 234).[12]

In more general terms, al-Azm accuses Edward Said of not grasping the "inter-
active process of the Orientalist discourse" (Mani and Frankenberg 1985, 177).[13]
The fact is that, despite all asymmetric power relations, discursive structures

---

12. Despite the example of Ayatollah Khomeini, al-Azm does not refer to typically Islamist
    thinkers, but to what he calls representatives of an "Islamanic trend." The most promi-
    nent figures of this trend, according to his analysis, come from the ranks of the former
    Arab left and he quotes, for example, the Lebanese writer Adonis (al-Azm 1981, 234).

13. Reading *Orientalism* carefully this accusation is not entirely just. There are a few pages
    in *Orientalism* where Said implies the self-reception of the orientalist stereotypes by the
    Orientals. He mentions that "the Orientalist notions influenced the people who were
    called Orientals as well as those called Occidental" (1978, 42) and that orientalism exert-
    ed its force "on the Orient, on the Orientalist, and on the Western 'consumer' of Orien-
    talism" (1978, 67). Moreover, Said seemed to be aware of the fact that Arab authors also
    took up stereotypical discourses about Islam and the "Arab mind" (1978, 322). However,
    this awareness remained at the margins of his argumentation and he never elaborated
    further on the aspect of the oriental adoption of orientalist stereotypes.

do not function as a one-way street, that is to say do not simply impose the stereotypes of the more powerful side on the weaker other. Therefore, according to David Kopf, Said misunderstood the nature of orientalism in South Asia, the "intercivilizational encounter between the European and Asian intelligentsia" manifested in the historical fact that "British orientalism gave birth to the Bengal Renaissance" (Kopf 1980, 501–502). In a similar way, the cultural encounter between East and West in the Middle East never has been one of "Oriental silence" and "Western writing" as, for instance, the factually "dialogic relationship" between writers from Iran and Europe shows (Tavakoli 1996). Another example is the advocacy of Chinese cultural uniqueness, by the People's Republic's Communist regime. Chinese intellectuals took part in a discursive practice in which they creatively appropriated and constructed both "Occidentalist images of the West and "Orientalist" images of China's past (Chen 1995, 5).[14] The stereotyping of the other is apparently not only a general feature of cross-cultural perceptions, but these perceptions are themselves derived from a discursive process of intercultural exchange. It is this process of intercultural exchange which is at the heart of our problem: the continuing and mutually re-enforcing dominance of a holistic and systemic modern image of Islam. Sadik al-Azm's thesis of an orientalism in reverse is perfectly suited to complement the rather one-sided analysis of Said.

The Historical Continuity Thesis

To be sure, if Edward Said had followed Foucault more closely, this reciprocity in the shaping of images would not have escaped his attention. In a purely Foucaultian sense, however, it is not the reciprocity of actors, but the creative power of the invisible structures of a discursive formation that generates a phenomenon like orientalism in reverse. Sticking to Foucault would also have helped Said in confronting another strand of recurring criticism. Several of his critics rejected his argumentation as a-historical. In complete disregard of the in principle historical limitation of Foucault's knowledge structures, Said presents the Orient as a European invention since antiquity. In an almost trans-historical way, Said even traces orientalist images back to Homer (Said 1978, 11; 56). In this way, he gives orientalism "an almost metaphysical power to pervade very different epochs" (Halliday 1993, 158). Some of Said's Arab critics compared this continuity thesis with the a-historical and essentialist pretensions of Arab nationalism (Sivan 1985, 136). In applying the historically limited and non-subjectivist method of discourse analysis correctly, the orientalist representations of the nineteenth century can only be interpreted as based on totally different cognitive deep structures than those of their predecessors. The congeniality of institutional and academic forms of orientalism is an entirely modern phenomenon. The specific interplay of power and knowledge in colonial times was decisively different from pre-modern times. Contrary to the extremely asymmetric power relations in the nineteenth century, in the Middle Ages and under Ottoman rule

---

14. For the phenomenon of "occidentalism," see: Buruma and Margalit (2004), Carrier (1995) and Chen (1995).

the Muslim East was a formidable competitor and powerful rival to the "West" (cf. Southern 1962).

Nevertheless, quite an impressive number of the orientalist images and narratives which Said presents to his reader resemble older stereotypes. Said's continuity thesis links his book up with a previous study by Norman Daniel who focused on the emergence of the medieval image of Islam. According to Norman Daniel, the medieval canon of knowledge about Islam was entirely based on Christian concepts. Although the scholastics often took Islam as the "sum of all heresy," Muhammad's "heretical teachings" were interpreted as a "corroboration of the Gospel" and a "witness to the truth of the Christian faith" (Daniel 1960, 272). In rejecting Muhammad's prophetic character, Christian apologists saw him as a "deliberate deceiver" who invented Islam by borrowing randomly from existing religions. In Christian opinion, the Prophet was not distinguished by receiving a divine revelation, but by his "sexual license" and "violent nature." Consequently, Islam was perceived as a "practical religion," i.e. preoccupied with worldly affairs, with determinist ethics and established by force (Daniel 1960, 272–275). In Daniel's eyes, this medieval concept of Islam proved to be extremely durable and still visible in post-Reformation times. Whether in presenting Muhammad and Islam as the head and body of the Antichrist, the use of the Muslim faith as a suitable mask by the Rationalists of European Enlightenment to attack Christianity itself, or in the approach of the Romantics who turned the pejorative image of Islam upside-down, from the Western perspective it was always Christianity that formed the central point of reference in dealing with Islam (Daniel 1960, 274–294).

To a certain extent, this medieval canon is indeed still visible in the modern image of Islam. The contemporary debates clearly show an inclination to associate Islam with violence, normative and moral determinism, and a tendency to promote practical activities at the expense of belief. Yet it is utterly wrong to turn these apparent analogies into a form of linear continuity. In fact, Christian-Muslim relations and Europe's encounter with Islam have been much more varied than Said's continuity thesis pretends (cf. Goddard 2000; Goody 2004). In his account of Islam and the West, the French scholar Maxime Rodinson emphasized the decisive changes and transformation in this relationship. In the eighteenth century, for example, Muhammad's afore-mentioned "practical attitude" was turned into the positive image of the Muslim Prophet as a "sovereign and law-giver who was tolerant and wise" (Rodinson 1988, 48). While in the Middle Ages the Islamic world represented an "utterly different civilization," the Orientals of the Enlightenment were despite their "alien" appearance above all human beings of principally the same kind (1988, 60). Moreover, the positive evaluation of Islam by Western philosophers in the nineteenth and twentieth century often contradicts Said's view and can only be understood in light of their function "as the basis for a critique of Christianity" (Turner 1983, 23).

In a similar way, the continuing narrative about Islam and violence only hides fundamental cognitive and normative changes in European societies. Before the monopolization of physical force and the subordination of the Christian clergy and church by the absolutist state, the application of violent means against non-believers was often perceived as a positive service in the name of God. In comparison to Europe's confessional wars in the sixteenth and seventeenth centuries, however, the Ottoman Empire or the Mogul Empire in India were characterized by a high level of personal and collective security also for religious minorities (Scheffler 2002, 217–218). The continuing references to the violent character of Islam in European sources served very different purposes and were predicated on changing cognitive and normative categories. Furthermore, this image of violence was always employed according to the historically specific societal and political situations in Europe itself.

The Critique of Said's Sources

The above examples may be enough to prove the ambivalent nature of Said's continuity thesis. It would be wrong to deny a certain continuity of stereotypes and narratives about Islam from medieval to modern times. However, it is equally flawed to read an unjustified linearity into this sequence. To draw a consecutive line from Homer to Henry Kissinger is only possible in retrospect and in applying the normative and cognitive concepts of our present times in an anachronistic way. To a certain extent, it is also related to the analyzed sources whether we put our emphasis on the idea of continuity or of change. Not surprisingly, the use and selection of sources also forms an important area of critique against Said. In particular the historians of the Middle East accuse Said of relying exclusively on sources which confirm his thesis. We already had the example of Bernard Lewis who even insinuated that Said was consciously following a deceptive strategy (see also Irwin 2006).

In criticizing Said's selection of leading orientalists, many reviewers point to the almost complete omission of orientalist scholars who were not nationals of the two colonial powers Britain and France or the following international hegemonic power, under the United States. Especially his peripheral treatment of German Oriental scholarship has been a recurrent theme of critique, although Said himself already acknowledged his rather biased selection of sources in the introduction to the first edition of *Orientalism* (Said 1978, 17). Bayly Winder added to this list of omissions Said's exclusion of "the considerable Arabic literature on Orientalism" (1981, 617). Indeed, taking into consideration the work of Muslim thinkers such as Muhammad Abduh, Rashid Rida, Kurd Ali, or Ziya Gökalp could have opened Said's eyes more for the argument of orientalism in reverse. Rashid Rida, for instance, today often presented as the founding father of so-called neo-fundamentalist ideologies, expressed some appreciation for the achievements of Western orientalists with regard to their knowledge of early Islam (Fähndrich 1988, 184). In a similar way, contemporary Arab intellectuals have acknowledged the merits of Oriental studies in some areas, especially in Islamic history and Koranic studies (Sivan 1985, 139).[15]

---

15. It goes without saying that Western studies of Islam have also been faced with a mul-

Post-Colonial Studies

This review of the controversy around Said's book would be incomplete without having a brief look at the field of post-colonial and subaltern studies. Besides stirring a controversial and ongoing debate, *Orientalism* also turned into "a paradigm for a new generation of historians and anthropologists" who are commonly lumped together under the label of post-colonial studies (Ashcroft *et al.* 1995, 141). Since the early 1980s, post-colonial studies have developed into an extremely diverse "discipline" whose discussions revolve around concepts such as resistance, identity, representation, stereotypes, ambivalence, power, and knowledge, and for which *Orientalism* became one of the major source books in teaching and research (Spivak 1985, 200; Young 2003, 8). In particular with regard to the nature, shape, production and dissemination of knowledge, Edward Said's book has stimulated the field of post-colonial studies (Mongia 1996, 4). This stimulation, however, was not taken uncritically. Homi Bhaba, one of the discipline's leading figures, criticized Said for his instrumentalist notion of the power and knowledge complex. In particular Said's inclination to place power and discourse exclusively on the side of the colonizers was for Bhaba a historically and theoretically unacceptable simplification of the subject. Rather, he suggested, we should understand the orientalist stereotypes in terms of "fetishism" (Bhaba 1997, 42–44), that is, that European concepts of modernity became a stereotypical and unconsciously applied blueprint for the indigenous post-colonial elite to shape their discursive and institutional framing of national modernization processes.

Bhaba's critique of Said's preoccupation with the West points to the common denominator behind the theoretical and methodological pluralism of post-colonial studies. The discipline aims not only to deconstruct European thought, but also to problematize the politics and national narratives of the indigenous post-colonial state elite. There is a visible shift of focus from colonizers to the colonized, which has become particularly relevant among scholars who have formed the Subaltern Studies Group. Initiated by Ranajit Guha, this group of historians of mostly Indian origin took its point of departure in a critique of India's post-colonial nationalist history writing. Against the dominance of either colonial or post-colonial nationalist narratives, Guha wanted to develop an alternative history of modern India in "recovering the voices of the subaltern," that is to say in an attempt to write history from below (Sivaramakrishnan 1995, 398).

From the beginning, this has also been an explicitly normative project. The search for human agency among the powerless was perceived as a simultaneous move "to restore dignity and purpose to the actions of the anonymous poor peasantry in colonized worlds" (Sivaramakrishnan 1995, 418). In his project of *Provincializing Europe,* for instance, Dipesh Chakrabarty extended this approach to a wholesale critique of the Eurocentric social sciences. The histories of the majority of humankind, according to Chakrabarty, have been subordinated to

---

tiplicity of criticism in the Arab world (cf. Tibawi 1979).

the master narrative of European history as the "scene of birth of the modern" (Chakrabarty 1992, 2–4). In this sense, Indian history has remained an imitation of European history privileging "the modern" Europe. In universalizing the modern national state, both European imperialism and Third World nationalism participated in constructing the European story of the modern. Without falling into the trap of cultural relativism, he calls to write a new history of modernity in which its own ambivalences, contradictions, and repressive practices are visibly inscribed (1992, 19–21).

By 2004, the Subaltern Studies Group alone had produced 11 books against the dominance of colonial and nationalist history writing in India, and its call for the restoration of the voices of the subaltern has become a visible trend within the whole field of post-colonial studies (Pouchepadass 2004, 67). Yet the discipline's diversity and normativity has also turned into its major predicament. The author of a recent "very short introduction" into the field describes post-colonialism as being a broad set of perspectives instead of a specific scientific theory (Young 2003, 7). The following pages of his book, then, read like a collage of issues, aims, and the ideas of a multiplicity of social movements whose common ground is their opposition to "the West." This West, however, remains to be nothing more than the amorphous enemy of all who might be labeled as subordinated: women, indigenous people, homosexuals, socially marginalized people and so forth. In homogenizing "the evils of modernity" as the West, post-colonialism has substituted Eurocentrism by an equally dichotomizing way of thinking. The field of Post-colonial studies confronts us with a similar system of stereotypical concepts and images as orientalism, and in delimiting its agenda the discipline has lost its critical strength (Pouchepadass 2004, 75). In a more critical vain, Aijaz Ahmad has always seen this "strength" as rather feeble, because *The Politics of Literary Postcoloniality* "gathered force through a system of mutual citations and cross-referencing among a handful influential writers" (Ahmad 1991, 281). From this perspective, the discourse about colonial discourse has developed into a closed discourse of its own.

Conclusions: Mapping the Chapters to Come

In spite of all waves of often harsh and substantial criticism, *Orientalism* undoubtedly has its lasting merits. With its huge popularity Said's book set a new agenda for studying phenomena such as representations, identity constructions, the emergence of bodies of knowledge, and the relationship between knowledge and power. His particular reading of "the Orient" engendered the emergence of a vast field of critical studies in domains such as literature, theatre, music, architecture, science, politics, journalism, and travel accounts (cf. Scheffler 1995). Said popularized the understanding of academic knowledge as developing within a context of social power and he showed the ways of its dissemination in society at large. Looking at orientalist stereotypes in the world view of poets, novelists, politicians and journalists, Said emphasized the traffic of ideas between academic and common-sense knowledge.

Said's approach is crucial to my own study in two ways. First of all, he localized the origin of popular stereotypes in academic work. In my genealogical approach I will therefore focus on this origin of modern knowledge on Islam and investigate the lives and works of scholars rather than the writings of journalists, novelists or the autobiographical accounts of politicians and diplomats. Whereas the latter have been instrumental in the broader dissemination process, the scholars constructed the intellectual foundations from which this dissemination has taken place. Secondly, I will add Said's perspective with regard to the trivialization and spread of orientalist knowledge in the West to the appropriation and simplification of concepts and ideas of Islamic modernism by Islamist ideologues. Here, we can observe a similar process of the trivialization and popularization of previously elitist intellectual ideas and their dissemination among the broader public. Even more important, the, in al-Azm's term, specific form of ontological orientalism that was discerned by Edward Said resembles more or less the conceptual foundations of the contemporary essentialist image of Islam. The current debate on Islam and the West relies heavily on a trivialized and popularized vocabulary that partly has its origin in the much more complex and versed studies of orientalist scholars and the intellectual deliberations of Islamic modernists. The five core themes of Said's ontological orientalism—holistic in form, scriptualist in its sources, Islam as its central explicative variable, the in general political nature of Islam, and Islamic history as decline—are prime features in the essentialist image of Islam that has preoccupied the perceptions of both Western and Islamist constituencies.[16]

From this perspective, *Orientalism* can tell us something about the features and origins of the modern image of Islam. However, Edward Said largely remained silent about the process of this body of knowledge becoming relevant in a global dimension. In particular, Said's book does not reflect the appropriation of orientalist thinking by Muslim intellectuals and Muslim societies at large. In developing this reciprocal aspect of my research, it was not Said, but his critics who have been extremely helpful. Prime amongst them is Sadik J. al-Azm. His thorough critique of *Orientalism*, largely based on Said's own premises and not on those of the reviewer, articulates a number of issues relevant for my own study. First of all, there is the basic idea of reciprocity that leads to the phenomenon of orientalism in reverse. This idea is crucial in my own study and I intend to show how the phenomenon can be traced back to the very same period of time in which ontological orientalism as a body of knowledge emerged. Therefore, my study is both an enquiry into the concepts of Western scholarship on Islam and into the discussion, rejection, and incorporation of these concepts by Islamic reformers.

Another important point of critique, emphasized by al-Azm and others, is that of the theoretical flaws in Said's work. In my opinion these are twofold. First of

---

16. It is especially striking to observe in which way Islamists conceptualize Islamic history according to the European narrative of the nineteenth century in which the high civilizational level of old oriental cultures served to justify the denigration of the contemporary oriental culture. In this way, the "back-to-ancient-roots" approach of Islamist thinking is a clear product of nineteenth-century romanticism.

all, many of the contradictions in Said's book are due to the absence of a clear general theoretical framework for his study. Contrary to Said's eclectic usage of social theory, my own selective application of different conceptual elements of social theory is anchored in the broad framework of the sociology of modernity. As mentioned in the introduction to this book, I will outline this—in my opinion—necessary sociological framework under the category of world society in the next chapter. There, it will also become clear in which way my inspiration by Said is clearly distinguished from the whole body of so-called post-colonial theories. From the perspective of social theory, I personally do not see in post-colonial theorizing a real shift of paradigms. Presenting oneself as an avant-garde should not be confused with having introduced complete theoretical innovation. This becomes strikingly evident in the conceptual help with which some of the leading theoreticians in post-colonial studies have tried to give the "insurgent knowledge" (Young 2003, 20) of the subaltern a voice. In an article about the "deconstruction of history," Gayatri Chakravorty Spivak, for example, deals with the attempt of subaltern studies to give back some of the agency of which the suppressed and dispossessed peasants of India have been deprived by European and Indian nationalist historiographies. Yet in referring to more than 20 "Western" philosophers, the article reads rather like a Who's Who of the philosophy of modernity from German idealism to French post-structuralism (Spivak 1985). A theoretically very sophisticated article, indeed, but fully integrated in the mainstream discourse of modernity on which also my general approach will be based.

Secondly, and equally problematic, is Said's application of so-called discourse theory. The problem is not that Said deviates from Foucault. Michel Foucault himself revised his rigid structuralist approach by introducing the role of human agency in later works. What confuses the reader rather is the inconsistent way in which Said deviates from Foucault's theory of discursive formations. Instead of introducing a conceptual arrangement that is able to combine structure and agency in the context of Foucault's theory, Said continuously shifts throughout the book from structuralist to individualist semantics thereby causing complete confusion about his approach among his readers. In chapter three, I will therefore also deal with this problem of different levels of analysis and the question of linkages between the macro-structures and the individual. Based on a number of authors in the field of cultural theory, I will develop an analytical device that attempts to combine elements of theories based on structures on the one hand, and theories based on forms of collective and individual agency on the other.

The third strand of criticism that has been relevant for my own study concerns the contextualization of the emergence of orientalist knowledge. Indeed, with its obsession with the theme of colonial interests and its focus on international politics, Said's work is myopic. Probably based on his very personal engagement with the topic, Said's straight equation of orientalist scholarship with colonial domination leaves aside all the leading political, economic and societal questions that occupied European and Muslim intellectuals in their encounter with modernity in the nineteenth and twentieth centuries. To be sure, the impact of colonialism was important for both sides. The imperial relationship provided the power configuration in which the essentialist image of Islam evolved. However, this international context of power should not blind us for the importance of domestic power relations that left its marks on the intellectual deliberations about religion in general and Islam in particular. My empirical chapters therefore will discuss to a certain extent the domestic political environments of France, Great Britain, The Netherlands, Hungary and Germany, as well as Egypt, the Ottoman Empire and India, within which the individual protagonists of my study developed their ideas.

In addition, I will criticize the almost complete confusion of imperial policies with the leading motivations behind orientalist scholarship by Said and his epigones. Rather than writing with an imperialist agenda, European orientalists shared a "colonial habitus," an attitude of European civilizational superiority with regard to the rest of the world. The world views of most of the founding fathers of Islamic studies was molded by similar ideas about modern civilization and progress; and while many of them perceived it as an honorable task to bring this modern civilization to the Muslim world, some of them wanted rather to safeguard oriental authenticity from the infringements of modernity. My analysis of the works of Ignaz Goldziher and other scholars of a "non-colonial background," as well as my bias toward the German scene, will underpin the assertion that this general colonial habitus of European intellectuals renders meaningless both Said's obsession with colonialism and the whole debate about the selective choice which Edward Said allegedly made in analyzing only the work of orientalists with a specific national background. In the sense of a shared habitus, the "colonial impact" was a cross-border phenomenon irrespective of the national origin of individual scholars.

This leads me to the fourth point of contention: Said's sources. In writing from an interpretative perspective, I view the frequent accusations that Said is only using sources that fit his case as essentially flawed. The ongoing and varied controversy around *Orientalism* is proof in itself of the principle openness to academic criticism of Said's argumentation. Said has chosen his sources in order to make strong points in interpreting the emergence of a particular form of knowledge about the Orient. He has done so in an often convincing and certainly transparent enough way, emphasizing his core argument through the selection of relevant sources. In my opinion, *Orientalism's* argumentation is not fashioned in order to make it immune to criticism. Anyone who subscribes to Karl Popper's principle of falsification should be content to see this principle anchored within the inter-subjectivity of the academic community at large. Again, the whole controversy has shown that Said's work is open enough to attempts of "falsification," if we only perceive Popper's postulate as a collective means of scholarly critique and control. Nevertheless, in order to deflate this source critique further, I decided to focus in my study on a number of orientalist scholars who play only a peripheral role in Said's book. These scholars—Becker, Goldziher, Hartmann and Snouck Hurgronje—however, held decisive positions in making Islamic studies an independent discipline. Moreover, my core group of European intellectuals assembles individuals who resided in five different European states—France, Germany, Great Britain, Hungary and the Netherlands—representing quite different positions in the international politics of nineteenth-century Europe.[17]

Finally, Said's pretension of historical continuity plays an important role in shaping my own study. Unfortunately, here again the theoretical weaknesses of *Orientalism* might have caused a lot of misunderstandings. On the one hand, Said claims there is a continuity of orientalist stereotypes from modernity through Christianity back to Greek antiquity. On the other hand, he writes that orientalist scholars replaced and reconstituted the old religious patterns and paradigms with which the Europeans viewed the non-Christian world. It is the latter form of continuity, the incorporation and transformation of traditions that also informs my study. Indeed, European scholars have continuously conceptualized religion through the lenses of Christianity. In this way, even the staunchest secular positivists of the nineteenth century viewed other religions through conceptual lenses that were derived from the history of Christianity. Yet this history was itself subject to fundamental transformations. The recurrent stereotypes and narratives to which Said refers are therefore only templates which have conveyed entirely transformed meanings. In this way, continuity is change. The fourth chapter of my book will take up this motive of continuity in a specific way and analyze the impact of biblical studies and Christian apologies on the modern image of religion in general and the modern image of Islam in particular. In the course of my own research, I have become more and more convinced that it was one of the most salient shortcomings of Said's book not to do justice to the major role that biblical criticism in general and the nineteenth-century school of liberal Protestant theology in particular have played in shaping global knowledge on religion and Islam.[18]

---

17. Only Ernest Renan and William Robertson Smith are from France and Britain respectively, representing the major colonial powers of the nineteenth century. However, the founding fathers of Islamic studies with which I deal in chapter five cannot be associated with French and British colonialism. It also should be noted that these scholars, although growing up in the orientalist tradition of Europe here represented by Renan and Smith, were quite different in method and approach from the classical orientalist scholars to whom Said's study mainly refers.

18. Said indicated this omission himself (1978, 17–18), however, seemingly without being aware of the core function which in particular the German school of Protestant biblical criticism actually had in shaping the modern contours of religion and therewith also of Islam. Especially chapters four and five will discuss this eminent role of biblical criticism and Protestant theology in the development of the social sciences and the humanities in general and orientalist scholarship in particular.

3

Observing Multiple Modernities:
Globalization, World Society, and the Global Public Sphere

> We're not just individuals, we're part of a larger whole and we must constantly
> have regard for that larger whole, we're dependent on it, beyond doubt…
>
> (Theodor Fontane)

This conclusion, arrived at by Geert von Innstetten, a central protagonist in
Theodor Fontane's (1819–1898) late novel *Effi Briest* (1895, 177), expresses a more
general feeling of nineteenth-century social awareness. At least in intellectual
circles, the modernization of Europe gave rise to a new consciousness of "society." In line with this new consciousness, Innstetten refers to society as a larger
whole, as an integrated structure that is more than the sum of its individual elements. During the nineteenth century the scope of notions of the social steadily
expanded and the concept of society turned into a designation for the "sum-
total" of social relations. Society attained the quality of being the totality of
the social that is external to individuals and wields coercive power over them
(Schatzki 2002, 124–126). The French sociologist Emile Durkheim defined this
larger whole as a *fait social*, as a social fact, making society the *sui generis* object
for the new scientific discipline of sociology. Yet where are the limits of this
social whole? Does this modern concept of society have specific territorial, cultural or political boundaries?

The discipline of sociology has not given clear answers to these questions.
Society as a concept and its theoretical value for the discipline have remained
contested, although there is a strong tendency to identify the scope of societies with the borders of national states. Contrary to this mainstream perspective
of the equivalence of society and state, I argue that there exists a possibly less
prominent but nevertheless continuing tradition among sociologists of acknowl-
edging the, in principle, unlimited scope of society. In this sociological tradition,
modern society is world society. This idea of world society can be traced back
to the founding fathers of sociology. Parallel to the historical evolution and scientific examination of national societies in the nineteenth and early twentieth
centuries, major figures of social thought conceived the emergence of modern

society as a dynamic process with principally global dimensions. A few examples may illustrate this tradition.[1]

In 1835, Alexis de Tocqueville described in his introduction to *De la démocratie en Amérique* a powerful structural development that he called the "great democratic revolution." At the center of this fundamental social process, Tocqueville located a gradual development of principal equality that, across political borders, was increasingly shaping social relationships in a similar way (Tocqueville 1986, 37–54). From a different angle, Karl Marx and Friedrich Engels observed the very same development as the global spread of economic competition which gradually replaces traditional personal relationships by abstract money relations. In the *Communist Manifesto* (Marx and Engels 1848), they identified capitalist economics as the driving force behind the emergence of a world history in whose course the "former natural exclusiveness of separate nations" will eventually be dissolved. For Marx and Engels the systemic logic of modern capitalist society had an inherently global dynamic, destroying all kinds of "pre-modern" communities based on tribal, religious or ethno-cultural allegiances.

In his very short essay *The Market: Its Impersonality and Ethic*, Max Weber makes a similar point in defining the archetype of modern rational social action as "consociation through exchange in the market" (Weber 1978a, 635–640). For Weber, modernity was first and foremost characterized by the principle of formal rationality. In its bureaucratic forms, Weber discerned formal rationality in institutional structures and practices such as the division of labor, functional specification, and expert training. The evolution of modern society, in Weberian terms, can be described in terms of the increasing social relevance and global advancement of principles of formal rationality. In his reading, modernization is an ongoing and non-limited rationalization process, creating social relationships with a tendency to transcend the boundaries of all kinds of previously established historical communities. Norbert Elias, to mention a last example, conceptualized the rise of an ever-larger social whole as a civilizing process. In his seminal 1936 study *The Civilizing Process*, Elias combined micro- and macrosociological perspectives and focused on the interrelated processes of modern state building and the formation of a more differentiated and stabilized self-control of the individual (Elias 1994). These examples should suffice to show that, from the outset, the social sciences have known a tradition conceptualizing the rise of modern society as an essentially unlimited process of social emergence. In the words of the German sociologist Ferdinand Tönnies, their different theories converged in the idea that "society is the world" (Tönnies 1887, 3).

In this chapter, I will depart from this nineteenth-century discovery of society as an, in principle, unlimited sum-total of social relations. In so doing, a number of insights from classical sociology will serve me as foundational stones for the formulation of a general theory of modernity under the encompassing framework

---

1. I have elaborated on this tradition of the classics more extensively in two essays: Jung (2001b, 2004a).

of world society. In sharp distinction to its mere descriptive and often normative notions in public and scholarly debates, I will employ world society predominantly as an abstract and analytical category. I do not share the assumption that the implicit global social unity of world society has to be simultaneously expressed in an empirical reality or that this unity ought to be brought about by deliberate political action. Thus, my usage of world society should not be confused with "cosmopolitan approaches" such as those of Ulrich Beck and Jürgen Habermas (Beck and Sznaider 2006; Habermas 2005, Chapter 11) or with its reductionist and descriptive usage in International Relations theory (cf. Buzan 2004). To be sure, the constitution of concepts and the objects of social research are inseparably interrelated. Yet, this interrelatedness does not mean that the formation of concepts and historical developments necessarily coincide. In this book, world society represents an exclusively theoretical framework into which I will place my inquiry into the emergence of the modern essentialist image of Islam.

As an overarching theoretical perspective, the concept of world society binds together an abstract arrangement of analytical concepts serving two specific purposes. On the one hand, it delineates the general theoretical presumptions on which my research questions rest. The specific problem complex and the course of inquiry of this book have developed within the coordinates of this theoretical framework. The following discussion of globalization, modernity and religion in social theory is thus intended to make the reader familiar with the essential theoretical standpoints relevant for the understanding of this study. On the other hand, I use the concept of world society for the analytical ordering of the diffuse set of phenomena which we associate with macrosocial processes such as modernization or globalization. Without such an overarching theoretical framework the puzzling images of a heterogeneous globality escape our analytical understanding. Departing from these general theoretical positions, this chapter discusses the analytical tools that have guided my interpretation of the evolution of a globally accepted body of knowledge on Islam as an inherent part of the global expansion of modern society. I will put forward my theoretical arguments in five steps, related to scholarly debates on globalization, modernity, world society, religion (Islam), and the public sphere. The final pages of this introduction to the chapter will present these steps in a nutshell without going into detailed argumentation and references. In this way, readers with a limited interest in social theory will be able to gain a presumably sufficient overview of the theoretical background of my study that might enable them to continue with the empirical part which starts with chapter four. It goes without saying that I personally invite all readers to engage in the theoretical elaborations of the various sections of this chapter, otherwise I would not have included them in this book.

In the first section I will position this study within the larger globalization debate. Given the omnipresence of globalization in both sociology and Islamic studies, I decided to start my theoretical exposition with regard to this rather elusive debate. I shall begin with the discussion of a number of controversial views on globalization. Then I take up the topic of religion and globalization, moving on to the relationship between Islam and globalization. My inevitably selective inquiry is inspired by two interrelated questions: In which sense can we understand the rise of the essentialist image of Islam as an instance of globalization? Does the globalization debate provide us with conceptual tools to understand this phenomenon? In conclusion, I define globalization as the often contradictory and puzzling historical process of the rise of a global modernity. The formation of the modern essentialist image of Islam can be perceived as part and parcel of this historical process. My review of the scholarly debate about globalization, however, comes to the result that theories of globalization have resembled the contradictory picture of the very same phenomena they are intended to explain. In my view, they do not provide the necessary analytical tools for my study. Contemporary theories of globalization are characterized by a very selective, incoherent and often also inconsistent usage of concepts related to the sociology of modernity. With regard to religion, they have a tendency to uncritically apply comparatively crude versions of secularization theories. This applies in particular to the representation of Islam in globalization literature, which tends to deal with the Muslim world under suggestive headings such as fundamentalism or religious terrorism and often represents Muslim countries and peoples within the familiar neo-orientalist narrative of a blocked modernization process.

This conclusion points directly to the second step of my theoretical exposition, a brief explication of my own understanding of globalization within the theoretical paradigm of modernity. In light of the massive challenges to the validity of sociological concepts of modernity, the second section of this chapter will primarily tackle the questions of whether and in which ways "modernization" can still serve as a useful theoretical perspective on globalization at all. In distancing my approach sharply from the linear developmental ideas and normative pretensions of the modernization theories of the 1950s and 1960s, I nevertheless try to salvage major insights of the sociology of modernity in a kind of "neo-modernist" framework.[2] I shall develop my perspective in making a distinction between globalization as a more or less residual category for sequences of empirical instances and modernization as a dynamic analytical concept. Then I introduce the idea of perceiving modernization as the emergence of "multiple modernities," refuting the confusion of modernization with Westernization (Eisenstadt 2000).

The section will conclude with a brief discussion of the more recent social theories of reflexive modernity and post-modernity. I will argue that both bodies of social theory seemingly remain within the broader paradigm of modernity. Instead of making the heritage of sociological classics obsolete, the postmodern critique represents an important revitalization of the often suppressed pluralist

---

2. I use the term neo-modernist in keeping with Jeffrey Alexander's usage of the term, designating a new stream of sociological thinking that has been challenging the predominance of postmodern reasoning and its complete rejection of the modernist pretension that we can observe a kind of convergence among empirically distinct societies. However, I do not identify with the ideological tendencies in the political realm that Alexander has associated with neo-modern reasoning (cf. Alexander 2003, 213–228).

dimension of classical sociology. I view the postmodern and classical social philosophies as complementary to our understanding of the modern condition rather than seeing these areas as being mutually exclusive. Therefore, the concepts
of classical sociology remain reasonable starting points for the conceptualization
of a general theory of modernity. However, the theoretically postulated unity
of this global modernity has not translated into a general global convergence of
social reality as assumed by many social scientists in the 1950s and 1960s. On the
contrary, empirically, this alleged unity appears to be diversity, which we can
observe as the emergence of multiple modernities.

This striking discrepancy between theoretical unity and empirical diversity
leads me to emphasize the character of world society as a sociological construct.
Given the empirical rather invisible nature of society as a global social whole, it is
the task of the sociologist to comprehend this social unity through a set of analytical concepts such as state formation, capitalist expansion, differentiation and individualization.[3] Posing the question of the social logics of modern society as world
society, the third section will therefore present the methodological prerequisites
and the analytical content of world society as a theoretical framework. In terms
of method, I rely on the Weberian approach of constructing ideal types. From
this perspective world society represents the general frame for an assemblage of
analytical concepts which have the quality of heuristic instruments. In combining society with the world, world society is the abstract cipher for an essentially
unlimited process of modern societal integration; yet a form of integration that is
not predicated on normative consensus, but on the reflexive adjustment of social
forms to a horizon of institutional patterns through both consensus and conflict.
In its conceptual quality, world society is a real abstraction from global social in-
terdependencies whose mediation takes place in an indirect way. World society is
therefore both a relational category and a process model.

In addition, section three introduces the reader to some of the core concepts—
society, social emergence, functional differentiation—on which my theoretical
perspective rests. In conceptual terms, this section justifies my approach to perceiving the intellectual deliberations of Muslim thinkers and Western scholars
as an integrated process of global knowledge production. I will make the reader
familiar with the specific conceptual lenses through which I later interpret the
societal context in which the lives and works of my individual protagonists were
embedded. In so doing, I fuse the perspective of classical sociology and elements
of modern systems theory, in particular the definition of modernization as the
global spread of patterns of functional differentiation. According to systems
theory, the macrosociological fabric of modern society is characterized by the

---

3. Given the scope of this book, the reader should not expect an exhaustive presentation
of these conceptual tools. Many of the concepts used are quite well known to social
scientists and do not need a more detailed elaboration at this stage. In the course of
the book, however, I will become more explicit about some concepts at the very point
at which I use them. This chapter only sets the stage for later conceptual reflections
which will then be embedded in the historical analysis.

predominance of functional differentiation, dividing society as a whole into relatively autonomous sub-systems such as politics, economy, law, religion, etc. In addition, I will introduce two dichotomies intimately linked to the concept of world society. The first of them is the classical differentiation between tradition and modernity, which as an ideal-typical polarization enables us to order societal developments by describing them as processes of economic, political and cultural modernization. The second dichotomy is between functional and social integration. At different levels of analysis, modern societal integration is characterized by both the abstract coordination of consequences of social actions (functional integration) and the concrete motivation and apprehension of social action through culturally specific programs (social integration). While the first refers to the macrostructures of social systems, the latter relates to the social practices that characterize the mesa- and microlevels of social organizations and social interactions. In the light of these two dichotomies, global social integration appears to be both increasing homogenization or isomorphism of formal institutions and visible cultural heterogeneity and social fragmentation.[4] Using the Ottoman historical experience as an example, the section ends with a brief discussion of the process of modern state formation that provides the power context in which multiple modernities have emerged. It is this context of power which represents the crucial linkage between forms of formal and social integration, which shape the historically concrete paths of modern developments.

Given my focus on the modern image of Islam, the analytical framework for this study also needs to discuss the concept of religion, which has raised enormously controversial debates in scholarly circles. Section four therefore zooms in on questions about the definition and status of religion in modern society. In partly grounding my theory of world society in the structural dominance of functional differentiation, I will conceptualize religion accordingly as a social subsystem with its own specific modus of operation. Modern concepts of religion have emerged within the broader context of increasing social differentiation, a complex historical process whose various features have been lumped together in a catch-all idea about secularization. In its simplistic version, this theory of secularization has been equated with modernization as such, whereby religion and modernity are viewed as being embedded in a zero-sum game. In criticizing this assumption of an essentially secular modernity, I will elaborate a concept of religion that is both universally applicable and historically conditioned. Based on a discussion of scholarly attempts to define religion, I suggest a definition of "modern religion" that is integrated in the broader theoretical context of world society.

---

4. In his reflection on globalization Georg Ritzer refers to this contradictory feature of simultaneous processes of formal homogenization and substantial fragmentation as the dichotomy between nothing and something. Accordingly, globalization is the appearance of both general social forms devoid of any distinctive substantial content and indigenously conceived forms of distinctive substantial social and cultural content (Ritzer 2003, 195).

I argue that the revision of Protestant Christianity laid the foundations for a general notion of religion in modern society. This reconstruction of the Christian faith took place under the societal imperative of functional differentiation that was observed as the gradual separation of religion from other realms of social action such as politics, education or law. Classical theories of secularization rationalized this process as a "decline of religion" in modern society. More recent approaches to the sociology of religion, however, have emphasized the paradoxical character of this process. While religion has lost its all-encompassing character, the religious field has attained at the same time a much more visible and identifiable logic through its separation from the social environment. Even more important, the institutional separation of state and religion does not necessarily imply a decline in religion at societal or individual levels. On the contrary, in historical terms processes of institutional secularization have been accompanied by strong movements of religious awakening. Secularization is not a linear process, and it can be interpreted in terms of cyclical, dialectical and even paradoxical patterns (Goldstein 2009).

From this perspective, the concept of modern religion has been defined as a specific and relatively autonomous form of communication and social interaction with the supernatural. The distinction between transcendence and immanence became the systemic borderline between the global religious system and its environment (Beyer 2006). Moreover, making the supernatural the specific difference when defining religion has become a central frame of reference for the global modern reconstruction of religious traditions. Worldwide, religious and secular intellectuals have explicitly or implicitly employed this definition regardless of whether their religious reconstructions endorse or refute the assumption of an exclusively transcendental nature of religion. For the latter position, the essentialist claim that Islam is a comprehensive social system, an all-encompassing way of life, is a prime example.

Finally, I shall present my concept of the global public sphere, which I perceive to be the major theoretical contribution of this book to a global sociology of knowledge. I define this global public sphere as the "social site" on which the modern image of Islam has been constructed in an increasingly dense net of cultural exchanges. On the one hand, this social site is an observable emerging reality; it represents a field of discursive relations and social interactions on a global scale. On the other hand, I use the global public sphere as an analytical device, serving me in the ordering of the complex historical set of data upon which the central arguments of this study are built. It is this analytical dimension of the global public sphere that guided my data collection and its analysis in the following empirical chapters.

In order to make this device operative for my study, I apply theoretical elements of both structural and hermeneutic approaches. I differentiate between four analytically distinct levels of observation with regard to both macrostructures and individual and collective actors. Firstly, this social site is defined by a cognitive deep structure that provides the conceptual basis for apprehending social change as a move to functional differentiation. On this level, we find the foundations for a communicative space with different but mutually intelligible semantics. Secondly, related to this cognitive deep structure, a field of basic themes has emerged. These themes reflect the social transformations with regard to the systemic imperatives of modern society. The central questions observable at this level revolve around ideas of identity and authenticity, referring to the demarcation of borders among social subsystems and the relationship between collectives and individuals. Thirdly, these general themes are articulated through different semantics which are based on various symbolic and moral orders, linguistic environments, and historically distinct narrative traditions. Positivism, Christian and Muslim apologetics, traditionalism, secularism or Islamist ideologies are examples of these semantics that are relevant for this book. This level is the core site for my empirical investigation; it is "the world" that we experience as historical reality. Finally, we can observe on a microsociological level that these predominantly discursive practices are also accompanied by direct forms of personal interaction. On this level, we can observe the exemplary character of the life, work and influence of important individuals who represent nodal points in the network of the global public sphere.

Employing this analytical instrument of a global public sphere, my historical investigation is guided by observations which take into consideration all four analytical levels. In the empirical part of this book, I will answer my leading questions—concerning the origin of mutually shared essentialist conceptions of Islam by orientalists and Islamists, the way in which these conceptions became broadly accepted forms of public knowledge, and their association with a confrontation between Islam and the West—by investigating the modern image of Islam as an interplay of social actors and discursive practices that we can reconstruct in applying the different perspectives of these four levels of observation. In each of the empirical chapters I will enter this social site by presenting the works and lives of a number of exemplary individuals and will analyze them in the light of their historical and structural contexts.

To sum up, the purpose of this chapter is first and foremost to acquaint the reader with the theoretical perspective and analytical tools on which my study of the modern image of Islam rests. Under the category of world society, it presents a theoretical framework in which more specific concepts such as modern statehood, religion or the public sphere are embedded. At the same time, two considerations have guided my selection of theoretical references. In the first place, there is an autobiographical dimension. In one or the other way the theoreticians on whom I draw in this chapter have accompanied my own career and academic education to a greater or lesser extent. Second and even more important, the selection of theories is also guided by a sense of convergence across time and methods. I perceive the simultaneous reading of sociological classics and of more recent representatives of social theory as equally important to bridging the methodological boundaries that have separated structuralist and hermeneutical approaches in the social sciences. In order to avoid the handy but artificial separation of the theoretical and empirical, I try in the following sections to illustrate my conceptual discussion with empirical examples of both Western and Muslim historical experiences.

Globalization: "Academic Monster" or Historical Reality?

According to Roland Robertson, the period between 1870 and 1925 marked the take-off phase of contemporary globalization. In this time period we can observe the accelerated differentiation and internationalization of modern sciences and the "nostalgic encounter" of European intellectuals with the so-called East (Robertson 1993, 2). At the same time, Muslim intellectuals intensified their direct and indirect encounters with the West, shaping the Islamic reform movement in the course of which the foundations for the construction of the essentialist modern image of Islam were laid. Both the reinvention of religious traditions from inside and the academic reconstruction of religion by Western sociologists, historians, philologists and anthropologists were intimately linked to the emerging "global field" (Robertson 1994, 121). This applies even more to the subsequent trivialization, popularization and spread of this modern knowledge of Islam through the modern means of communication in the twentieth century. If we view the "search for fundamentals" (Robertson 1992a, 166)—the modern construction of identities based on the idea of cultural authenticity—as an important element of globalization, the rise and spread of the essentialist image of Islam has to be examined with reference to the general globalization debate. In particular for Islamist movements, this search for an authentic Islam is core to their ideologies. In the following pages I will therefore discuss the relationship between the modern image of Islam and the general globalization debate and whether theories of globalization might help to better understand the evolution, dissemination and global spread of orientalist and Islamist interpretations of Islam.

Globalization has achieved the status of a leading buzz-word in both academic and media discourses. At the same time, it is a central category for the explanation of contemporary social realities and an often thoughtlessly applied in-word in public debates. It aims to represent an analytical concept, while being randomly used. Looking at the mushrooming numbers of scholarly books and journal articles referring to global issues, globalization has indeed turned into an "academic monster" (Kessler 2000, 932). Semantically, globalization represents a multifacetted, complex, and uneven process. It lumps together a bundle of very different changes affecting the economic dimensions of production, distribution, and consumption, the forms of political authority, patterns of cognitive and normative social orders, and the various traits of local life-worlds. Not only in everyday language, therefore, is the application of the term globalization characterized by vagueness, inconsistencies, confusions and conflicting value judgements. In academic research as well globalization has been discussed as a contradictory and contingent process. The academic eye simultaneously discovers patterns of homogenization and fragmentation and researchers engage in ongoing disputes about the origin, the social consequences, and the temporal and spatial dimensions of global developments. According to Mauro Guillén's review of the debate (2001), there are at least five core controversies to be discovered in the explosively growing academic literature about globalization.

First of all, scholars disagree about the very adequacy of the term globalization itself. Does the plethora of phenomena which we usually associate with globalization indeed represent social transformations on a global scale (cf. Hirst and Thompson 1995)? Strong criticism is directed against the inflated usage of the term in journalism and policy advice. The critics point to a clear lack of empirical evidence for the almost axiomatic application of the attribute "global" in political and media discourses. Even the World Bank confirmed for the beginning of the twenty-first century that despite an increase in the export of goods and services by developing countries, more than 40 percent of the world's population remained disentangled from global economic development (Huq and Tribe 2004, 919–920). This is just one example of the fact that even in the economic realm, whose changing features have been spearheading the whole globalization debate, the global dimension often seems to be more a result of habitually applied rhetoric than of empirically scrutinized evidence. The globalization debate has a tendency to become self-referential, turning every issue which enters the debate into a global event.

The second controversy addresses the cultural dimension of globalization. Does globalization lead to more cultural heterogeneity or will it result in a universal "world culture?" The "Stanford School," for instance, has strongly emphasized the thesis of growing cultural homogeneity. In their institutionalist theory, Meyer and his collaborators claim that the evolution of an isomorphic world culture is a driving force behind global developments (Meyer *et al.* 1997). They discern five global cultural principles – universalism, individualism, rational voluntaristic authority, rationalizing progress, and world citizenship as a "distinct" global culture (Boli and Thomas 1999). Other scholars define the rise of a "global culture" precisely in opposition to these universal patterns. Instead, they employ Lévi-Strauss' concept of *bricolage*, the complex fusion of different patterns of culture. Consequently, an emerging global culture does not have universal forms but is characterized by a pronounced heterogeneity of "hybrid" cultural formations (Pieterse 1995). Scholars interpret cultural globalization along different paths which together result in a simultaneous appearance of the universalization of particularisms and the particularization of universalisms (Robertson 1992a).

Closely related to these questions about social and cultural convergence are the third and fourth general disputes of the debate. These two intertwined disputes revolve around the novelty of globalization and the question of the way in which globalization differs from modernization. Does the term globalization really designate something qualitatively new or is it nothing more than a neologism for the meanwhile almost denigrated term of modernization? Indeed, modernization theories, in particular those of the 1950s and 1960s, were predicated on the assumption of a global move toward the convergence of previously distinct national societies and cultures. From their perspective, globalization is nothing new, but a logical continuation of the modernizing process toward more societal convergence. Finally, there is the ongoing discussion about the "future of the national state," which has become a central concern for political scientists. In their field, the globalization debate has been highlighted by labels such as "the end of territoriality" (Badie 1997; Ruggie 1993), the "retreat of the state" (Strange 1996), or the "de-bordering of the state" (Albert and Brock 2000). In political science, it has become increasingly fashionable to associate globalization with the progressive decline of modern statehood.

On closer analysis, Guillén's core controversies are actually deeply interconnected. Critics of the current "globalization hysteria" thus address them frequently in a more comprehensive fashion. The French scholar, Jean-François Bayart, for instance, reminds us that beyond visible tendencies in the globalization of economy, culture and politics, many observers tend to underestimate the inertia of nationally defined social, cultural and political orders. The neo-liberal euphoria of a global, open, and free market economy, according to Bayart, hardly matches the results of a historically guided analysis of the world economy. According to his data, enterprises really operating on a worldwide scale have remained comparatively rare and the spread of direct capital investments around the globe is still limited. In spite of lifting quite a number of barriers for trade, the world economy remains characterized by various protectionist regimes, serving national and regional interests in such different fields as agriculture, textiles, aerospace industries, or various aspects of the service industries. Likewise, the political sphere is a far cry from the virtual reality that the inflationary talk about "global governance" and the "decay of the state" might imply. In light of the difficulties of establishing functional international courts of justice such as the International Criminal Court (ICC), reaching mutual agreements in the UN Security Council, or safeguarding the global eco-system through international regimes like the Kyoto Protocol, the demise of national-interest politics is by no means imminent. Bayart concludes that the impact of globalization on politically and culturally demarcated social units is clearly visible. Yet, so far, the consequences of globalization still appear to be a blurred set of social convergences, cultural transformations and institutional resilience. In short, they are far removed from giving us a clear-cut picture of global developments (Bayart 2004, 16–19).

Apparently, globalization refers to a very contradictory set of social developments that makes any exclusive positioning with regard to the binary alternatives of Gullién's controversies rather difficult. Yet one does not have to be a radical constructivist in order to admit that the widespread, crosscultural debate about globalization in itself represents part and parcel of a changing global reality. Globalization is both an academic monster and a historical reality. We can interpret the globalization hysteria and its mobilizing power in domestic and international politics itself as one indicator of an ongoing global process of societal transformation whose economic, political and cultural facets must be analyzed as the complex interplay of both integrative and disintegrative forces on a global scale (Mittelman 2000, 923). Although a cliché, talk about the "global village" nevertheless reflects the growing perception of the geographical world as a common social sphere (Held *et al.* 1999, 2). In Norbert Elias' terminology, we may talk of a rising crosscultural awareness of being part of global interconnectedness, of a "social figuration" that renders the idea of limited and autonomous social entities increasingly obsolete (cf. Elias 1986).

This sense of global interconnectedness and the way in which issues of domestic and foreign policies are communicated through the globalization debate is perfectly demonstrated by the example of the Islamic Republic of Iran. The articulation of societal conflicts in post-revolutionary Iran indicates that also in a politically relatively isolated country globalization provides a communicative template for dealing with current political issues and contemporary societal change. In addressing the General Assembly of the UN in September 1998, Muhammad Khatami, the then President of Iran, made the proposal of declaring the year 2001 the "Year of Dialogue among Civilizations." President Khatami's proposal, which was taken up by the UN, basically had two political purposes. In calling for the replacement of "hostility and confrontation with discourse and understanding" in the international arena, Khatami was signalling his government's attempt to overcome the country's relative isolation in international politics. Yet this appeal to regional states and the international community was also a message being given to his own nation from the international stage. The declared foreign policy of détente by Khatami was the external twin of the domestic debate about Islamic democracy and inseparably linked to his internal policies of a gradual political and social liberalization (cf. Khatami 1998).

During Khatami's presidency (1997–2005), the struggle about changes in Iranian foreign and domestic policies was often expressed in the discursive context of the globalization debate. Raising issues of globalization offered a semantic field in which reformist and conservative political forces could publicly mediate their rather hostile political confrontations. In the language of the conservative camp around the Supreme Leader, Muhammad Ali Khamenei, the meaning of globalization was almost synonymous with Americanization. Here, globalization meant a conscious assault of the West against the cultural values and the normative order of the Islamic Republic. The supporters of President Khatami, in contrast, employed the term globalization in order to support their reformist ideas of an Islamic democracy. The reformist camp presented globalization as a massive force of structural change, confronting Iran with both challenges and opportunities to develop the Islamic system of government further.[5]

---

5. These different positions are documented in the article "Roundtable: Effects of Globalization on the Islamic Republic of Iran" that was published in the Iranian journal *Discourse* 2 (2): 1–30 (Tehran, Fall 2000). I was also able to discuss these issues around the globalization theme with scholars and bureaucrats on two shorter visits to Tehran in the years 1999 and 2001. It has to be emphasized that President Khatami's policies were not intended to abandon the Islamic system of government. Rather, his reforms aimed at adapting the *velayat-e faqih* to changing political, economic, and societal circumstances.

This example clearly shows that, despite all the justified critique about its form and content, the globalization debate itself could be taken as an expression of an ongoing complex restructuring of social and discursive spaces in a global dimension (Scholte 2000, 3). It is in this sense that globalization takes place. From a historical point of view, we might also distinguish contemporary social change from the phase of classical modernity in the visible attempts of economies and civil societies to free themselves from the territorial and juridical bonds of the national state. The fusion of nation, territorial state, and national economy, for a long time the dominant self-description of Western modernity, appears in the light of the contemporary globalization debate no longer to be the blueprint for future political orders, but rather resembles a historically particular idea of European state formation. However, a careful examination of the relationship between globalization and state formation indicates at the same time that, in this process of the reconfiguration of political authority, the national state plays a double role. State formation and globalization are not engaged in a zero-sum game and national states are both piloting globalization's course and risking being drowned in its wake (Casanova 2001, 423–425).

When analyzing globalization, we have to come to terms with the very contradictory features of these global transformations. In the political realm, the undermining of the national state's claim to power has been accompanied by a number of global developments which to a large extent have been triggered and sustained by the deliberate action of national states. The functioning of global markets, for instance, is as dependent on efficient political institutions as the flourishing of civil society organizations is on the legal frameworks that are an intrinsic element of modern legal political authority (Evans 1995). Even the International Monetary Fund (IMF) in its neo-liberally inspired adjustment programs relies on the supervisory and regulatory functions of the state (Lukauskas 1999, 284; Önish and Aysan 2000, 120–121). Moreover, the different practices of international peace-building by states, international organizations and non-governmental organizations, one of the more recent political aspects of globalization, still follow ideas about modern statehood and market structures which have their origin in the conceptual models of classical modernity (Paris 2002).

This ambiguous picture also characterizes studies about globalization and religion. There is a growing strand of literature once again making religion a topic of the social sciences in the context of globalization. However, these studies often have a tendency to take the proclaimed global resurgence of religion for granted. They often neglect to offer definitive evidence for their statements about the religious revival (Haynes 2006, 536).[6] In general, globalization theorists have ap-

---

6. James Beckford pointed to the fact that despite recurrent references to "religious resurgence," the globalization debate among social scientists, so far, has only shown passing references to religion (Beckford 2003, 103). Generally speaking, religion has been at the margins of the theoretical debate about globalization; something that is also reflected in the choice of topics that characterize one of the central reference books on the globalization debate (see Held and McGrew 2003).

proached religious phenomena from two opposing directions. On the one hand, they have been interpreting religious revival in line with classical secularization theories as an anti-modern and defensive reflex against cosmopolitan ideas and the mechanisms of liberal market economy. On the other hand, some theorists of globalization have transferred the very logic of the market model to the religious field. They view the revitalization of religion and spirituality as a consequence of the mechanisms of a globalized religious market. In short, the general globalization debate basically juxtaposes "fundamentalist" religious resurgence and the plurality of religious markets (Vásquez and Friedmann Marquardt 2003, 4).

Contrary to this rather stereotypical approach to religion provided by globalization theorists is the more diverse picture given to us by the current debates among scholars of the sociology of religion. They discuss contemporary religious phenomena under a number of competing scholarly narratives for which the general assumptions of secularization theories provide an essential common point of reference. The rational choice approach, contesting with its supply-side model of religious markets the theorists of secularization, explains the various observable forms of religious revival by an increase in religious pluralism. It postulates a constant demand on the side of religious individuals and explains historical variations in religiosity by insufficiencies on the supply-side. There is no decrease in religious demand, but a clear lack of attractive "religious commodities," in particular caused by strong alliances between churches and the state and the concomitant lack of pluralism in these religio-political arrangements. Scholars of religious fundamentalism also question the validity of secularization theories and their tendency to equate modernization with secularization. However, they are utterly at dispute about the meanings of fundamentalism and whether it indicates a reaction to or a result of the modernization process. Theories of religious reorganization and religious individualization maintain some of the assumptions of the secularization theories but emphasize them in different ways. Instead of interpreting contemporary religious developments in terms of rise or decline, they observe various forms of religious change as comprising tendencies such as individual religious eclecticism, a growing autonomy of believers from institutions, and a move from larger denominations to local congregations (cf. Spickard 2003).

While all these different approaches in the sociology of religion have some merit, most of them lack a genuinely global perspective and many of them focus almost exclusively on Christianity. Together with Roland Robertson, Peter Beyer is one of the few sociologists who has explicitly theorized about the relationship between religion and globalization. Beyer understands the ambivalent picture of religion in the age of globalization in the context of an evolving global system of religion. Within the coordinates of this global system, inherited forms of identity have been corroded and have given way to the creation and revitalization of new religious identities. In theoretically borrowing from Niklas Luhmann's modern systems theory, Beyer proposes perceiving religion as a distinct social subsystem with global dimensions. The emergence of this specific notion of religion as a societal unit is, according to Beyer, embedded in the general process of social differentiation that has characterized the evolution of a global modernity (Beyer 2003, 47). Similar to Robertson, he therefore perceives the global context as the "primary unit of analysis" for the contemporary study of religion (Beyer 1994, 2). In Beyer's approach, the development of global society not only generates universal religious macrostructures, or a global system of religion (Beyer 1998), but also simultaneously opens new spaces for the various articulations of particular religious identities. Unity and divergence go hand in hand. In addition, the, in principle, non-territorial character of religions has facilitated the "resurgence of religion across multiple confessions," making faith more significant as an identity marker for groups and individuals in the course of the globalization process (Scholte 2002, 245).

Turning to studies on Islam and globalization, the general assessment of a multifaceted ambivalence regarding the relationship between globalization and religion is also clearly visible, however, with publications interpreting the revivalist tendencies in Islam as "anti-modern" on the one hand and "fundamentalist" reactions against globalization on the other taking the absolute lead. In particular since the rise of transnational Islamist terrorism, the relation between globalization and Islam has increasingly been articulated under catchy headings, such as Markus Juergensmeyer's *Terror in the Mind of God*.[7] According to Juergensmeyer, globalization provides religiously motivated activists a fertile context for articulating radical political ideologies of change (Juergensmeyer 2003). There is no doubt that a variety of features of the globalization process such as the advancement in communication technologies, the consecutive waves of international migration, and the role of a globalized financial system have facilitated the growth of transnational religious networks of all sorts. From this angle, the global spread of the essentialist modern image of Islam is an inherent feature of the globalization process. Chapter six will take up this line of argumentation with respect to the trivialization, popularization and militarization of Islamist thinking. Yet, contrary to the violent image suggested by the heated global media debates, amongst the multiplicity of transnational religious networks, violent groups play an absolutely marginal role in these developments.

This finding applies to religions in general and to Islam in particular. Even the overwhelming majority of Islamist movements which employ essentialist understandings of Islam normally pursue their goals with peaceful means. We have to be aware of the great variety of transnational Islamic networks which range from *"Hajj to Hip Hop"* and whose historical roots sometimes go back to pre-modern times (cf. Cooke and Lawrence 2005). Moreover, while the twentieth century saw the global dissemination of the essentialist image of Islam, recent developments point to the rising challenges to this holistic interpretation. In particular on the internet, scholars observe an alteration and "creolization" of Islamic discourse in

---

7. It has to be mentioned that Juergensmeyer's book deals with case studies from different world religions and does not have its focus on Islam. However, in the public debate the title of his book has meanwhile become almost entirely associated with Islam.

which "creole pioneers," Muslim activist groups, Islamist parties, conventional missionary organizations, Sufi orders, and the governments of Muslim states compete for interpreting Islam in the twenty-first century (Anderson 1999, 54).

In sum, the globalization debate leaves us—so the rather desperate conclusion of Guillén—with the picture of "a fragmented, incomplete, discontinuous, contingent, in many ways contradictory and puzzling process" (Guillén 2001, 238). Although lacking conceptual precision, the term globalization seemingly refers to a confusing variety of developments—including various forms of religious change—which somehow really happen. Some of them indicate the convergence of societal patterns on a global scale and they postulate the emergence of nonetheless still disparate features of a global culture. Other developments rather suggest understanding globalization in terms of cultural fragmentation and in the rise of particularist identities. Yet the various bi-polar controversies described by Guillén should not be viewed in exclusive terms of either/or. Rather they represent two sides of the same coin. What remains as the common denominator is a globally spread and interculturally shared but still diffuse perception of global transformations that impact on states, economies and local life-worlds. Against this background, the problematic of this book—as in principle anything else—can also be related to the globalization process.

In theoretical terms, however, the globalization debate seems not to offer any new conceptual tools, let alone an applicable overarching theoretical framework for my own investigation. Qualifying globalization by stringing together a series of tautological adjectives, as by Guillén quoted in the paragraph above, is an expression of conceptual desperation rather than of the emergence of a new theoretical paradigm. I thus share John Urry's standpoint that an agreed-upon theory of globalization does not exist and that the debate only reflects an early stage of "recording, mapping, classifying and monitoring the 'global' and its effects" (Urry 2003, 3). In order to make sense of a particular phenomenon in the context of globalization, it is globalization itself we first have to grasp theoretically. In my understanding, and here I diverge from Urry's interpretation, the term globalization only lumps together a large bundle of problems which have been posed by the historical contingencies of global modernity. The following conceptualization of world society, therefore, tries to give a systematic theoretical framework for the ordering of these historical contingencies. Without such a systematizing concept, the description, interpretation, understanding and evaluation of contemporary global developments seem to me impossible.

From Linear Modernization to Multiple Modernities

Based on the conclusion of the previous section, I suggest approaching the puzzling facets of globalization with a critically revised theory of modernity. Globalization might be a successful and possibly necessary "successor term" to modernization (Beyer 2006, 18), but up to now I cannot see the theoretical coherence and sophistication that would allow theories of globalization to replace the paradigm of modernity. However, the terms modernity and modernization share with globalization the ambiguity which results from being both analytical concepts and buzzwords of public debates. Moreover, theories of globalization and modernization have been employed in political struggles as ideological terms with strong normative implications. They both have functioned as "metalanguages that instructed people how to live" (Alexander 2003, 199). Given this conceptual ambiguity, I shall first define in which way I use and distinguish the concepts of globalization, modernization, and world society in this study. Then I will continue circumscribing my concept of a revised theory of modernity by critically discussing it with regard to the theories of linear modernization, reflexive modernity and post-modernity. I will argue for a general theory of global modernity as an analytical instrument to understand the historical process of emerging multiple modernities.

In public debate the terms globalization and modernization are often used with overlapping meanings. In my own conceptualization, however, I relate them to two different domains of social research. I apply globalization in order to reduce the historical complexities of contemporary global social change to a common denominator. Globalization represents a residual category for the classification of empirical phenomena and historical developments. In this sense, the social construction of an essentialist image of Islam and its popularization are part of the general globalization process. Modernization, in comparison, has the quality of being a dynamic ideal type, of being a heuristic process category for the interpretation of social transformations. It provides the analytical lenses for understanding the multiplicity of empirical instances which we subsume under the category of globalization. In other words, globalization semantically refers to a non-linear and uneven historical process in whose course we can observe the global spread of various economic, political, and cultural elements of modernity. The empirical heterogeneity of this contingent process, that is to say globalization's disunity, however, can be rationalized and systematized in light of the conceptual unity of a theory of modernity based on ideal types. In conceptualizing modernity/modernization with the help of ideal types, I basically follow the methodological assumptions of Max Weber. As a means of research, ideal types are analytical instruments. They do not copy reality in a descriptive way, but refer to it in their conceptual quality. Ideal types are sociological constructs based on logically accentuated, concrete and significant historical phenomena, and their ideal status does not express any normative stance. Thus, social reality is not directly portrayed in the ideal type and the academic application of this theoretical construct does not tell us how things ought to be. Ideal types are abstract instruments of social research; however, they are constructed with reference to historically concrete social institutions (Weber 1904, 85–95).

From this methodological perspective, modernization and globalization are in my usage not at all synonymous concepts. They differ in their theoretical nature and analytical quality. While globalization is only a collective concept for the classification of historical developments, modernization is based on a logically assembled collection of abstractions for analytical purposes. This collection of ideal types I will unite under the category of world society. In this sense, globalization refers to historically specific expressions and a particular period in the evolution of modernity (Giddens 1990, 63–64), whereas world society represents an analytical framework of social theory. As my overarching theoretical framework, world society provides the rules and conceptual elements for the construction of (middle-range) theories about globalization. It is through these conceptual lenses of world society that I try to make sense of the emergence and spread of the essentialist modern image of Islam as a particular instance of globalization.

This approach is supported by the fact that despite all the contradictory and puzzling instances of globalization, the debate about them to a large extent takes the core features of modernity as its conceptual points of reference. In macrosociological terms, globalization literature regularly refers to the ordering power of modern ideal types such as the capitalist market economy, the bureaucratic organization of state authority, the monopolization of the means of physical force, or the rationally formalized orders of knowledge. In microsociological approaches to globalization, most studies employ the central patterns of action conventionally associated with modern agency: reflexivity, systematic enquiry, control of nature, societal constructivism and individual forms of participation in the constitution of social and political orders (cf. Beck *et al.* 2003; Eisenstadt 2000, 11–14; Scholte 2002, 5). In short, the analytical ordering of contemporary global phenomena is still guided by some of the essential ideal types of the classical sociology of modernity (see also Robertson 1990, 50–51). Historical developments, however, have been showing that these formal elements of modernity do not necessarily translate into a global convergence of communities and lifestyles. Modernization thought of as an encompassing process of structural differentiation apparently develops in combination with quite different cultural codes. Therefore, the idea of an abstract global modernity—world society—appears as the evolution of a historical variety of specific societal formations of the modern. The unity of global modernity shows us the face of a combination of multiple modernities. Modernization is not Westernization, but the constitution and reconstitution of a multiplicity of modern cultural programs (Eisenstadt 2000, 2).

Interpreting globalization as the rise of multiple modernities demands a critical revitalization of the conceptual apparatus of so-called modernization theories for which the classics remain a good starting point. To be sure, reverting to the classical theories of modernity raises many staunch and loud voices of criticism. A case in point is the assertion that the classics of the social sciences had a clear tendency to define society within the narrow confines of the national state.[8] Consequently, the concepts of classical sociology supposedly do not match

---

8. In Niklas Luhmann's analysis this territorial notion of society is nothing more than a remnant of the pre-modern conceptualization of society, largely based on the stratified and hierarchical social relations of a land-based aristocracy (Luhmann 1990, 177). Indeed, Luhmann's point could explain the unease of classical sociologists to com-

the contemporary situation of global transformations. Yet the mere fact that the rising national state was a central historical concern of sociological reasoning in the nineteenth and early twentieth centuries should not deceive us: the global dimension of modernity was an inherent feature of classical sociology. Although globality was not the primary level of analysis in classical sociology, the examples at the introduction to this chapter indicate the awareness of some classics about the global dynamics of modernity. Classical sociology confronts us with an interesting blend of universalist and particularist national views. The classics' emphasis on the national level is a contextual bias rather than an indispensable pillar of their theoretical edifices. Thus, the ongoing mantra about the national fixation of classical sociologies of modernity and their alleged preoccupation with questions of normative integration (see Featherstone 1995, 7) glosses over their actual potential for an adequate interpretation of global change.[9] In my opinion, this verdict about the national focus of classical sociology seems less to be the result of a precise reading of the classics, and more a reflection of the negative impact of the sociological textbooks which have been written in the spirit of the modernization theories of the 1950s and 1960s.

Under the influence of social theories like behavioralism and structural functionalism, post-Second-World-War sociology transformed the heuristic conceptual apparatus of classical sociology—their ideal types in the Weberian sense— into a catalogue of ostensibly objective and measurable benchmarks of modernity (Robertson 1992a, 11). By making classical sociology "scientific," modernization theories reconstructed the historically contradictory and contingent evolution of modernity as a linear and allegedly predictable social process. In their efforts to bestow sociology with a scientific aura equal to the natural sciences (Eisenstadt 1992, 421), many American sociologists in particular did not only reduce the complexities of classical theories to their normative and universal content (Lichtblau 1999, 7). They also added to them a linear developmental logic that closely resembled the historical evolution of the United States, thus shaping a normative blueprint for modernity as such (Lepsius 1990, 215).[10] It comes as no surprise that these academic endeavors did not originate in scientific considerations alone. In an excellent article, Thomas Bender showed how the emergence and spread of these "scientific" modernization theories were closely knitted into the economic

---

pletely strip their concepts of modern societies from all bonds of territorially based communities.

9. This awareness of the classics for the, in principle, unlimited global dynamics of the modernization process has been the theme of a large number of contemporary sociologist (see: Frisby and Sayer 1986; Lichtblau 1999; Münch 1998 and 2001; Robertson 1992b; Smelser 1992).

10. To a certain extent, it is also possible to discern the role of the United States as a model for modern society in the work of some classics. It is very obvious in Tocqueville's work and also visible and biographically explicable with regard to Weber's essays on the Protestant Ethic. However, this reference to the United States does not have the normative qualities of the modernization theories mentioned here.

and political developments of American universities after 1945 (Bender 1997).[11]

It is this orientation of the 1950s and 1960s toward their own American normative ideal, the behavioralist systematization of classical approaches and the political equation of modernization with national state formation, for which the classics unwarrantedly have been called to account (Wehler 1975, 28). In addition, the ideas of development planning and social engineering, an inherent feature of these modernization theories, led to the proclamation of the end of "grand theories" (Menzel 1991). The apparent failure of this kind of modernization theory, therefore, resulted in a general denigration of macrosociological interpretations of international developments. Yet it remains to be seen whether empiricist theories of a second order, the reductionist micro-foundation of the social sciences within the confines of instrumental rationality ("rational choice"), or the radicalization of interpretative sociology in constructivist approaches will eventually lead to more promising findings than the grand theories of classical sociology. In my understanding, these three alternative theoretical positions are themselves part and parcel of the larger paradigm of modernity.

Basing my research on the conceptual means of classical sociology, I certainly have to position my approach vis-à-vis two more recent bodies of social theory, the theories of reflexive modernity and post-modernity. The idea of a "second" or "reflexive" modernity has mainly been associated with the work of Anthony Giddens and Ulrich Beck. In 1986, the German sociologist Ulrich Beck published his study *Risk Society*, which since then has become a major reference book for the theory of second modernity. In itself a "consequence of modernity" (cf. Beck 1986; Giddens 1990), the risk society replaces the modern logic of wealth production with the logic of risk production that transcends social and national boundaries (Beck 1986, 17 ff). Modernity becomes reflexive not in the sense of being self-referential, but in the form of being a structural transformation in which the non-intended consequences of classical modernity are revolutionizing the very foundations of modern society (Beck *et al.* 2003, 1–3). The side-effects of modern developments and institutions such as the capitalist market, industrial production, technological advancement, and legal universalism create unintended results (read: risks) that undermine the modern master-narratives of formal rationality and calculability (Beck 1993, 40). "Industrial modernization is undermining industrial modernization" (Beck 1997, 5), eroding some of the major pillars of "first modernity" with its belief in linear progress, organized society and instrumental rationality.

Despite its pretension of novelty, the works of Beck and Giddens actually con-

---

11. In Bender's essay, the formation of the modernization theories of the 1950s and 1960s are a part of the more general process of higher education becoming a mass phenomenon after the Second World War. In this process, the social sciences, for example, implemented peer review processes to guarantee the scientific character of their research documentation, and Talcott Parsons was successful in trying to endow the social sciences with the status of the physical sciences in order to secure their inclusion in the National Science Foundation (Bender 1997, 13–16).

firm the classical notion of modernization as an unplanned social process with a self-reflexive and unlimited character. The theory of second modernity is hardly able to produce many insights that go beyond the classical concepts of capitalist modernity. The major theoretical axiom of reflexive modernity, that modern rationality in its systemic consequences renders obsolete the very principles on which it rests (Beck *et al.* 2003, 5), is far from new. This skeptical stance toward the promises of modernity was already a general trait of Max Weber's sociology, in particular resonating in his essay on *Science as Vocation* (Weber 1917). In his article on Weber and the cultural situation of modernity, Lawrence Scaff rightly emphasizes that the very characteristic of modern culture is "to subvert not only the traditional or pre-modern, but also those accomplishments that come to characterize 'modern culture' itself" (Scaff 2000, 103). The Frankfurt School, to name another prominent example, elaborated on this self-undermining—"irrational" —character of modern rationality in the *Dialectic of Enlightenment* (Adorno and Horkheimer 1989).

The same argument of the self-contradictory nature of modernity is related to the conceptual dichotomies between modern and postmodern theories. Contrary to the proponents of reflexive modernity, postmodern thinkers have abolished modernist ideals of political control. They reject the idea of politically managing the disruptive and disintegrative effects of globalization such as expressed in Giddens' "life politics" (1990, 154) or in Beck's "reinvention of politics" (1997, 160). Postmodern theories challenge the abstract and universalizing claims of modern social theory with the axiom of a "radical pluralism" of bodies of knowledge, discursive formations, systems of life-worlds, and patterns of humane agency (Welsch 1987, 5). Like Nietzsche in the nineteenth century, contemporary postmodern thinkers discard the abstract ethical demands and impersonal requirements of modern rationalism and question the sustainability of modern moral claims (cf. Alexander 2005, 171–176). In this sense, postmodern theories are the philosophical twins of social movements that defend cultural and religious particularities against tendencies of global cultural homogenization. At the same time, the postmodern struggle against the meta-narratives of the Enlightenment itself seems to be deeply rooted in the general discourse of modernity. The theoreticians of post-modernity can hardly avoid employing some of the universal categories they otherwise reject. The postmodern point of view only becomes meaningful in light of the conceptual framework of modern rationalism. Therefore, it is possible to interpret postmodern theories as a continuation of the philosophical critiques of modern rationality which in their different forms have always been an intrinsic feature of the modernization process. The postmodern critique does not represent a radical break with modern reasoning, rather it is an attempt to revise the grand narratives of modernity. The widespread adaptation of "poststructuralist" theorizing in the social sciences has re-articulated and newly fashioned the tradition of criticizing the pretension of modern reason since the Enlightenment (cf. Habermas 1987).

From this perspective, the theoretical dispute between modernism and postmodernism actually takes place within the modern paradigm. It expresses the continuation and globalization of the tension between rationalism and romanticism, between the instrumental and expressive forms of modern world views, which has been so central in the historical evolution of modern Europe. Given the very different combination of rationalist and romanticist conceptions with particular religious and local cultures, Erik Allardt rightly suggests interpreting nineteenth century nation-building in Europe already as the emergence of multiple modernities (Allardt 2005, 486–488). Indeed, the, in general, thoughtless usage of a concept like the West completely disregards the remarkable differences which have historically characterized the modernization of Europe and the United States. At the end of the First World War, the German novelist and later literature Nobel Prize award winner Thomas Mann (1875–1955), for example, asked the question of whether Germany was able to avoid the cultural and political invasion of the West as it was possible to escape direct Western military intervention throughout the war. In employing the then well-known German dichotomies of civilization versus culture and society versus community, Mann argued that German culture was incompatible with the democratic civilization of the West (Mann 1918, 50–59).[12] In Mann's understanding, Western culture was associated with the soulless "rationalism" of France, Great Britain and the United States. In a romanticist way, he defined German culture in sharp contradistinction to this rationalist culture of the West. This example shows the shifting connotations of a concept such as the West, the geo-political dimension of which at least has enormously increased during the twentieth century.

Later in this book, we will see that the contrast between rationalism and romanticism was also an inherent part of orientalist thinking. The romantics rediscovered the Orient as a source of their expressive critique against modern rationalism and initiated an "Oriental renaissance" in Europe (Schwab 1950). While the romantics fought against rationalist concepts of modernity, rationalists often employed orientalist stereotypes in order to emphasize the exclusively European nature of the modern world. In their eyes, Oriental culture was inhibiting processes of modernization in the East. Moreover, we will meet this contrast again in the world view of Muslim intellectuals, where the rationalism of an Islamic modernist such as Muhammad Abduh finds its romanticist counterpart in the Islamist ideology of Sayyid Qutb. Looking at this tradition of juxtapos-

---

12. Thomas Mann received the Nobel Prize for literature in 1929 for his novel *Buddenbrooks*. In 1933, he left Germany first to Switzerland and then to the USA. From 1938 to 1952, Mann lived in the United States where he held a chair at Princeton University. In *Betrachtungen eines Unpolitischen*, Thomas Mann expressed the conservative ideology typical of a large part of Germany's "cultural bourgeoisie" before World War One. The anti-democratic reflexes of this bourgeoisie were based on the idea of being a *Kulturmensch* (a cultivated person) whose intellectual liberty had to be defended against the politicization of culture. Later, Mann regretted the anti-democratic stances of his youth. He left the USA after accusations made against him under McCarthy's witch-hunting of alleged Communists. Thomas Mann died 1955 in Switzerland.

ing rationalism versus romanticism, in the social sciences postmodern theories represent a revitalization of the pluralist heritage of romanticist social theory, rather than a step beyond the modern paradigm. This factual pluralism of modern social theory was an essential part of classical sociology, although possibly less visible than its rationalizing and universalizing elements. The philosophical traces of Schopenhauer and Nietzsche in the sociological work of classics such as Max Weber and Georg Simmel are just two cases in point for this essential pluralism of classical sociology.

Following Bryan Turner's argument that the relationship between classical sociological reasoning and postmodern thought is characterized by continuity rather than divergence (Turner 1994, 198), the conceptualization of world society presented here is not in stark opposition to the argumentation of postmodern social theories. On the contrary, the postmodern critique of modernity is an inherent part of the self-referential social transformations which also characterize the globalization process. Postmodern theories reflect what Peter Wagner named the "second crisis" of modernity (Wagner 1994). In this crisis the ambivalences of modernity, the tension between individual liberties and social discipline, increased autonomy and rational mastery, experiences of contingency and the search for boundaries, have been radicalized by the post-modernity debate. The contemporary juxtaposition of cultural homogeneity versus cultural heterogeneity expresses the dissolution and reconfiguration of societal conventions and the pluralization of social practices which so far have characterized the social model of "organized modernity," this form of classical self-interpretation of "Western" capitalist society which Giddens and Beck have labelled "first modernity." This ordering character of organized modernity itself was a historical answer to the pervasive experience of contingency that is right in the center of the modern condition in general and the crisis-wracked modernization process in the second half of the nineteenth century in particular; and, according to Wagner, this "first crisis of modernity" formed the socio-historical context in which classical theories of modernity were written (Wagner 1994, 1–31).

To conclude, classical sociology, theories of reflexive modernity and postmodern theories should be interpreted as complementary rather than alternative interpretations of modern times. These corpuses of theory have their roots in the modern knowledge structures which developed in the course of the nineteenth century (see also Foucault 1994, 243). Even more important, this study assumes that the competition between rationalist and romanticist approaches to modernity and the social crises linked to the modernization process in general have also strongly impacted the evolution of Islamic and other non-European modernities. The French Revolution, the contradiction to Enlightenment by Fascism, or the universal relevance of normative concepts such as democracy and human rights have been discussed by Middle Eastern intellectuals not only as European ideas infiltrating Arab and Islamic culture. Rather, Muslim thinkers experienced and articulated these events and ideas as inherent and "authentic" parts of the social and intellectual transformations that characterized social life in the Middle East (cf. Nordbruch 2006).

To be sure, the rise of multiple modernities historically took off within the asymmetric power relations of colonialism. Many features of European origin —that is to say elements of French, British, Dutch, Portuguese or Spanish modernities—were undoubtedly imposed on the colonialized world. Yet this colonial imposition should not blind us to the fact that the historical reality of modernization in general has been a process of imposition, resistance, appropriation, innovation and borrowing in Europe and the rest of the world. Contrary to Edward Said's argumentation, the colonial situation in this more general sense did not only characterize the relation between Europe and the Orient. In its social dimension and as a form of center-periphery relationship the colonial situation was also an integral part of the internal developments of European and non-European societies. Conceptualizing modernity as an emerging abstract social whole, modernization is an all-encompassing process of socio-cultural evolution which has no precise origins in time or space. Hence it should not only be viewed in the historical framework of European expansion. Western imposition may be an important part of modern history but is far from being the whole story. The multiple modernities of the Muslim world and the West have been complementary features of the general emergence of modern society conceived here as world society. After these more principal reflections on globalization and modernity, I will now move on to the more precise conceptual construction of world society which is embedded in these foundational philosophical features of the modern paradigm.

World Society as a Sociological Construct

The puzzling, disparate, and uneven manifestations of globalization demand a conceptual frame of reference which is able to think together a large number of diverse and often contradictory phenomena as interdependent in their social origin. For the construction of this social whole behind globalization, this was my contention in the previous section, the following classical works on the sociology of modernity can serve as a theoretical foundation. Constructing ideal types of social processes such as democratization, monetization, formal rationalization, and stabilization of the social control of physical force, the classics conceptually grasped different traits of modernity that until today have dominated the various interpretations of the globalizing process. Even more important, the founding fathers of sociology and their works were an integral part of the very same process which they tried to comprehend. Chapter four, therefore, also will look more closely at the lives and works of Emile Durkheim and Max Weber.

Based on the sociological classics, globalization theoretically can be thought of as the historical emergence of a larger social whole that is utterly diverse and uneven in its visible manifestations. The global capitalist expansion through the logic of the self-expanding value (Marx), the world-wide dissemination of social forms based on formal rationality (Weber), the increasing differentiation of social relations (Durkheim), and the unplanned global process of civilization

(Elias) are all different classical perspectives on the emergence of this larger social whole, on the global advancement of modern society, here comprehended as world society.

In the following, I will base my definition of world society on the discussion of a number of different sociological concepts of society developed by classical and more recent sociologists such as Adorno, Durkheim, Elias, Habermas, Luhmann and Weber. Although these authors differ in perspectives and methods, their conceptualizations show lines of convergence which I will utilize for my own definition of society as world society. To a certain extent, all of them have an idea of society as a totality of complex social interrelations. Moreover, their theories of modernity refer more or less explicitly to the two essential dichotomies tradition/modernity and social/functional integration with which sociologists have addressed the nature of society as a process. In combining elements of these theories, I will construct an analytical framework for the understanding of historical trajectories of modernization. The section will end with a brief application of this framework to the experiences of Ottoman modernization in the nineteenth century.

The classical works of Durkheim and Weber already contain a notion of modern society as an abstract emerging unity not alien to the concepts of social emergence that are currently discussed in the social sciences (Sawyer 2004 and 2005). The early sociologists defined modern society in sharp contradistinction to traditional community types of the social, which they viewed as the "natural" forms of consociation harbouring culture, values and morality (Rammstedt 1988, 285). In defining society as a social fact, as an object distinct from and greater than the sum of its parts, Emile Durkheim tried to grasp this un-palpable modern social reality. In his definition, society first and foremost confronts us as the coercive structures of a transcendent moral, cognitive and symbolic order (Frisby and Sayer 1986, 36–49). This is precisely the notion of the social whole under whose constraints Geert von Innstetten, the central protagonist of Fontane's novel quoted at the beginning of this chapter, was acting. It was under the pressure of society's powerful quality as a moral order that Innstetten justified the duel in which he killed Major Crampas, the man who had had an affair with his wife more than six years previously. It was the moral codex of Prussia's aristocratic society that demanded his action. The irresistible power of societal norms made the duel inevitable, although Instetten considered it rationally as neither in his interest nor to his satisfaction. In his dedicated critique of late nineteenth-century Prussian society, Theodor Fontane fused patterns of the traditional habitus of a Prussian officer with the new societal concepts of a rising modernity. Fontane delivered a literary account on the contradictions of historical modernization processes in which historical reality can be understood as a patchwork of societal elements of both traditional and modern forms of consociation.

Emile Durkheim's fascination with society's transcendent facticity and objectivity drove him in the direction of a reification of social relations as *sui generis* objects of sociology.[13] Against this exaggeration of the autonomous character of society and the alleged bias of Durkheim toward defining society predominantly as a static, moral order, sociologists such as Norbert Elias and Theodor W. Adorno stressed the inherent procedural and relational nature of society. For them, society is a social process producing an ever-increasing functional connectedness of individuals in which all its members are entwined. However, this growing and increasingly imperceptible social interdependence takes on a certain kind of autonomy vis-à-vis its "members." In Adorno's definition, society is a mediated and mediating relationship between individuals, however, this relationship is neither the sum of individuals, nor an autonomous entity. Society is a relational category, it is a social unit "realized only through individuals" without being "reduced to them." Society is a concrete reality, yet a reality that only can be apprehended through theoretical abstraction. In Adorno's wording, society is a "real abstraction" (Adorno 2000, 38).

In light of this discussion about society, I preliminarily define world society as a conceptual construct based on the idea of a real totality of the social. World society gives expression to the global interconnectedness of individuals and social institutions based on a relational understanding of society as a non-linear and encompassing process of global social emergence. Modern society is world society with regard to a social structure where discourses and social practices cross-cut around the globe (Reckwitz 2006, 30). In conceptual terms, we can partly grasp the institutional dimension of this global social process through an ensemble of ideal types which are related to various empirical instances of the economic, political and cultural reproduction of social life. These ideal types reflect specific social functions, and they are constructed against the backdrop of the historical forms of modernization. Norbert Elias, for instance, has based his general conceptual models of the civilizing process on logical abstractions from the state-building process in France. Yet, ideal types such as the modern state, legal authority or capitalist economics have a tendency to represent abstractions of rather fixed results of social emergence. These conceptual elements of world society are basically derived from social structures or from comparatively highly stabilized "emergents" such as institutionalized social practices and semiotic orders (cf. Sawyer 2005, 220).[14] Consequently, there is a tendency to formulate them

---

13. In interpreting Durkheim as one of the first emergence theorists, Keith Sawyer criticizes this possibly too one-sided image of Durkheim's work. He points to the fact that Durkheim viewed society as emerging from the individual level, however, externalizing itself to a certain extent and therewith exerting causal power over individuals (Sawyer 2005, 103).

14. Sawyer defines five levels of social emergence: individual, interaction, ephemeral emergents, stable emergents, and the level of social structure. In this way, he presents a theoretical framework that intents to mediate between the individual and the structural level and to overcome the dominant methodological divides in sociology which appear in the dichotomies between agency and structure, as well as in structural and inter-action paradigms (Sawyer 2005, 225).

in a rather static way such as, for example, in the operationally closed models of Luhmann's systems theory.

In order to better grasp the process character of society, Norbert Elias suggested analyzing societal transformations against the background of a number of "elementary functions." Three of these elementary functions are basic in our understanding of society: the "economic" function of the provision of the material means of life; the "political" function of the control and management of the means of physical force; and the function of "orientation," the transmission and dissemination of knowledge. While all "societies" have to provide these functions, the specific ways in which they do it is under permanent historical change (Elias 1987, 227–231). Elias' elementary functions represent universal concepts that indicate the properties common to all social formations which we usually address as societies. They are generalizations of a more abstract nature, universal concepts serving as fixed points in an ever-transforming historical reality. Applying Elias' concept of elementary functions, the modern national state, for instance, would only be a historically specific form in which the political function of the control of violence has been achieved within a certain period of time.[15]

Another conceptual tool to grasp the procedural character of a rising global modernity is the classical dichotomy between tradition and modernity. The classics conceptualized modern society in sharp contrast to the direct personal relations on which local communities rest. In their eyes, society was first and foremost an indirect mediation of social (inter-)dependencies, a structural arrangement that is not directly comprehensible for either observer or observed. In Ferdinand Tönnies' categories, the rise of capitalist modernity thus can be interpreted as a successive move from *Gemeinschaft* (community) to *Gesellschaft* (society); from a social fabric characterized by direct, personal relationships to the predominance of a social unity of indirect, mediated forms of relations (Tönnies 1887).[16] In this way, modernization has been understood by juxtaposing two types of social units: community and society. Their ideal-typical polarity enables us to order empirical observations in describing them as processes of economic, political and cultural modernization, as historical moves from traditional to modern forms of consociation. From this perspective, we understand economic development as the transformation of socially embedded forms of material pro-

---

15. Throughout his work, Elias refers to a number of other forms of institutionalizing this "political" elementary function, such as tribes, tribal confederations, city-states, and patrimonial empires. It should be mentioned that in Elias understanding the construction of these universal concepts is not an aim of sociological research in itself. The elementary functions only provide "an auxiliary tool for the construction of process models" (Elias 1987, 226).

16. This is certainly a rather undifferentiated presentation of the relationship between these two ideal types of Tönnies and readers should be reminded that this relationship is not of a zero-sum nature. Moreover, Tönnies himself did not believe in the continuing dominance of modern society over community forms of consociations and perceived modernity as a passing phenomenon (Bickel 1988).

duction to the monetized and commercialized production of commodities for the capitalist market. Politically speaking, the institutions of the modern state, based on the legitimate monopoly of the use of physical force and Weber's principles of legal authority, replace traditional political units which rested on forms of traditional authority legitimized by kinship, genealogy or religion. In cultural terms, modernization is conceptualized as the establishment of a symbolic order in which rationally derived and principally open formal rules, concepts and norms take over the ordering functions previously held by religious, mythological or magic world views.

In Weber's sociology, the common denominator for the modernization of these three elementary functions is formal rationality, that is to say the regulation of "human action and institutions with abstract ethical demands and impersonal requirements" (Alexander 2005, 171). In his introduction added later to the essay collection of the *Protestant Ethic*, Max Weber described a whole set of modern institutions with "universal significance" whose common constitutive principle is formal rationalization: the sciences, the arts, law, and "the most fateful force in our modern life," modern capitalism (Weber 1930, xxxi). The principle of formal rationality is the central characteristic of modern institutions and the archetypical way in which Elias' elementary functions are structured in modern society. The formal rationalization of capitalist economic exchange, for instance, appears in forms such as double bookkeeping and the calculation of commodity-oriented production for a rational market. In the modern state, political authority is formally rationalized through the establishment of legally enacted procedures which elevate those who are authorized to issue collectively binding rules and commands. In terms of orientation, institutions such as schools and universities took over the tasks previously held by religious institutions, now producing and disseminating scientifically generated bodies of formalized secular knowledge.

While Weber stressed the core element of formal rationalization in modernity, Emile Durkheim emphasized processes of social differentiation.[17] From Durkheim's general approach in the *Division of Labour* (1964), this understanding of the dynamics of modernization as societal differentiation became a central feature of the sociology of modernity. In the twentieth century, many sociologists conceptualized modernization from this perspective as the spread of various patterns of functional differentiation. In its most rigorously argued version, modern systems theory, the emergence of modern society is understood as socio-cultural evolution, in which functional differentiation becomes the dominant mode of social differentiation. As a social process, modernization replaces the primacy of segmentation and stratification as the ordering principles of pre-modern forms of the social by social systems based on functional differentiation (Luhmann 1981, 187).

In a nutshell, systems theory conceptualizes modern society as an all-encom-

---

17. I will show in the fourth chapter of this book that the Weberian and the Durkheimian perspectives are not at all mutually exclusive but rather complementary ways of theorizing modernity.

passing global system of communication in which all world horizons are integrated as horizons of one communicative system. From this perspective, society can no longer be conceived as a corporate actor based on relations between individuals, but is observed as an all-embracing system of communications. Internally, society is differentiated by functionally defined subsystems such as politics, economy, law, education, science and religion. These subsystems operate according to their own distinct communicative codes and they are in this way clearly separated from their environment. The self-referential logic of these subsystems is based on specific binary codes which decide about the compatibility of communications. The legal system, for instance, operates with its specific code of legal/illegal, the religious system according to the binary dichotomy of transcendent/immanent. The selective mechanism of binary codes guarantees the operational closure of function systems—that communication is identified as juridical or religious—through a sharp distinction between systemic communication and communication in its environment (Luhmann 1986, 124 and 183). Given their relative autonomy and operational closure, none of these societal subsystems is able to represent society as a social whole, an assumption which renders the convenient fusion of society and national state obsolete. In Luhmann's eyes, modern society is world society because we can no longer speak of society in the plural (Luhmann 1990, 178).

According to the theoretical assumptions of modern systems theory, the all-encompassing unity of modern society is in itself based on diversity, on its internal principle of functional differentiation as modus of integration. Again, unity and fragmentation are essentially bound together. Following Luhmann's insight in conceptualizing modern society as world society, however, does not mean fully endorsing his theory of functional determination and operational closure. Similar to Durkheim's view, systems theory tends to exaggerate the apartness and distinctiveness of society. In Luhmann's theory, human beings are no longer a part of the social, but a part of society's environment (Luhmann 1991, 288). Yet, the global advancement of world society through functional integration does not render questions of social integration completely irrelevant. On the contrary, in applying different levels of analysis we can observe the friction between systemic integration and forms of social integration based on patterns of shared cultural meaning. Functional integration, characteristic to modern social systems, has been in strong tension with the cultural patterns of motivational integration of individuals and social groups. The functional logic of systemic patterns of action comes into conflict with meaningful social practices provided by local cultures (Geertz 1973, 145).

In historical terms, the transformation from the predominance of social to functional integration—modernization in its abstract meaning—was therefore first experienced and described as the painful destruction of traditional forms of life; as a disruptive force for cultural entities, and not as the establishment of a new social order. Jürgen Habermas discussed this transformation under the metaphor of "colonialization." According to him, in globally relevant functional processes such as bureaucratisztion and monetization, the coordination of social action by traditionally legitimized norms and values increasingly becomes replaced by the coordination of the consequences of social action through the abstract media of functional systems such as power, in the case of the political system, and money, in the case of the economy. In this way, Habermas interprets modernization as the global spread and dissemination of mechanisms of functional integration, as the separation of functionally integrated social systems from socially integrated life-worlds (Habermas 1986, 229–293). While the evolution of private law, for example, accompanied the institutionalization of money, the bureaucratization of political power happened through the public-legal organization of offices (Habermas 1986, 270). The institutionalization of these functional mechanisms, however, has been taking place only slowly and in an indirect manner.

Within the framework of world society suggested here, modernization can largely be understood from the theoretical vantage point of the global spread of functional integration, in Habermas' metaphorical words: as the "colonization of life-worlds by systems." Yet it would be wrong to perceive the global advancement of functional integration as a linear process in which only the functional logical of the social replaces all other forms of social integration. In an ongoing conflictive process, the functional imperatives of modernity have to be understood within shifting patterns of meaning which are based on the cognitive and normative structures of diverse cultural programs. Modernization is not a zero-sum game between community and society, but a reconstruction of societal integration under functional imperatives. Thereby, no radical break between tradition and modernity appears. Rather, tradition becomes incorporated in modern institutions and social practices. From this perspective, the different interpretations of globalization as either a process of homogenization or of fragmentation are a matter of the perspective of the observer rather than due to the nature of globalization itself. These interpretations depend largely on our application of functional or cultural approaches in understanding the social world (Geertz 1976). While globalization from a macrosociological perspective can be described as the institutional spread of functionalism, these formally isomorphic institutions of modernity are internally characterized by a vast variety of different social practices. Max Weber compared the intertwined nature of institutional macrostructures and their empirical reality of being a dense network of rather amorphous social actions with the concept of the state:

> When we inquire as to what corresponds to the idea of the 'state' in empirical reality, we find an infinity of diffuse and discrete human actions, both active and passive, factually and legally regulated relationships, partly unique and partly recurrent in character, all bound together by an idea, namely, the belief in the actual or normative validity of rules and of the authority-relationships of some human beings towards others. This belief is in part consciously, in part dimly felt, and in part passively accepted by persons who, should they think about the 'idea' in a really clearly defined manner, would not first need a 'general theory of the state' which aims to articulate the idea (Weber 1904, 99).

In reality the modern state is on the one hand an abstract and coercive macrostructure and on the other a network of interdependent social actions of everyday life. Modern statehood consists of historically developed and relatively stable institutional structures as well as culturally defined social practices. While the former give society isomorphic forms, the latter characterizes their social content of permanent interaction and ephemeral social groupings. Moreover, the functionally differentiated global political system has maintained forms of segmentation and stratification in its internal structures. Max Weber's ideal type of modern statehood, defined by the legitimate monopoly of physical force exerted over a territory and a people, combines forms of functional differentiation (monopoly of violence) with patterns of segmentation (territory, people). Historically, the organization of the international system as a "society of states" expresses the internal segmentation of the political system, whereas the Cold War division of First, Second and Third Worlds or post-Cold War tendencies toward US hegemony have reflected historical asymmetries of power through stratification. Looking at the historical development of world politics, the academic ideal type of modern statehood also corresponds, at least partly, to the institutional yardstick in the minds of political actors. In Weber's words: "the *practical idea* which should be *valid* or is *believed to be valid* and the heuristically intended, theoretically ideal type approach each other very closely and constantly tend to merge with each other" (Weber 1904, 99).[18] The isomorphic nature of world culture, as presented by the Stanford School, gives a stark expression of this correspondence between the scientific tool, the ideal type, and the normative idea of the state. Their conclusion that any political entity which assumes recognition has to take the path of national state building and is therefore the result of both contexts, that is, the structural power of the international system and the normative power of organizational models.

Modern state formation has been an integral part of the global modernization process structuring the elementary function of the control of physical force around the globe. In political terms, world society has become visible in an international society of states. The results of global state formation, however, have depended on the specific interface between the three dimensions of the state as an institution, a normative idea and daily social practices. The Ottoman experience shows in which way a mismatch of these dimensions caused the failure of a deliberate state-building project.

---

18. In declaring the ideal type as a construct of sociologists, Weber was following Kant's theoretical principle of non-correspondence between knowledge and reality. Yet this example of the state shows that the ideal type is far from being a "mental construct of the sociologists mind." Not only is it historical experience that serves as the departure point for the construction of ideal types, but the scientific construct can also find its way back among the normative ideas that guide social action. The relationship between abstract concepts, ideal types, and historical reality seems from this perspective rather to be of a circular nature.

The Ottoman reforms in the nineteenth century, the Tanzimat (1839–1878),[19] are a good example of the intersection of macro- and microsociological dimensions of modern state formation. In their attempt to reform the institutions of the Ottoman state, the empire's bureaucrats were guided by the then contemporary idea of the state, by a functionalist blueprint of political organization. In centralizing the state administration, monetizing the tax system, departmentalizing the provincial administration, and functionally differentiating the branches of government, to name just some of the administrative reforms, the Ottoman political elite tried to establish a modern state based on the formal idea of a system of legally rationalized authority (Jung 2001a, 40). The Tanzimat saw a reorganization of the fields of jurisprudence and knowledge production according to functionalist principles, establishing distinct systems of law and education. These reforms were largely an imperial project associating Ottoman politics with modernity and local resistance with ignorance and backwardness. This example shows that the rise of global modernity reproduced the center-periphery distinction on all societal levels from the international to the local site (cf. Makdisi 2002); and the Ottoman reformers had to struggle with similar forms of social resistance as, for instance, the authoritarian state-builders in Prussia.[20]

Contrary to the conventional narratives of the social sciences, the reformers of the Tanzimat followed a conscious strategy of modernization rather than conducting a hopeless attempt at importing "alien" European institutions. The Ottoman reforms show us a quite unique mixture of borrowing, innovation and reformulation of institutional patterns with global relevance. This is indicated not only by the very meaning of the term Tanzimat, a conscious "ordering" of society, but also by the Ottomans' efforts to construct a modern national identity for the empire's population. The opening of "national museums" in the second half of the nineteenth century is therefore just one example. Instead of only emulating Europe, the Ottoman bureaucrats rather explored ways "in which the Ottoman state could express itself as European" [read: "modern"] (Shaw 2003, 24). In introducing patterns of modern political institutions, the Ottoman state elite consciously applied the then contemporary templates of an emerging political order. They were attracted by these modern patterns of social ordering which developed into a globally accepted idea of statehood. Having the examples of Ottoman, Egyptian or Japanese state-building in mind, we should conceptualize

---

19. This periodization of the *Tanzimat* starts with the first reform edict, the *Hatt-i-Sherif* of Gülhane in 1839 and ends with the dissolution of the Ottoman Parliament by Sultan Abdülhamid II in 1878.

20. Prussian state formation was confronted with similar problems to those of the Ottoman reformers. The enlightened absolutism of the Prussian rulers in the eighteenth century did not directly reach the local level. In the countryside, state rule was transmitted by intermediaries that represented rather independent institutions of political authority in their domains. In the long run, however, the Prussian state makers were able to successfully monopolize the means of physical force and centralize state administration (cf. Spittler 1980).

modern state formation as a process of social emergence oriented toward a glob-ally shared set of institutions and guided by a common normative idea rather than thinking it exclusively from a point of origin in Europe. As part and parcel of the general globalization process, patterns of modern statehood simultaneously have exerted an increasing "gravity effect" on political actors on a global scale (cf. Urry 2003, 94). Viewing the rise of modernity through the lenses of the con-ception of world society presented here, the Ottoman reforms were an inherent part of modernization as a non-linear process of social emergence.

However, in the Ottoman example historical analysis also has shown the fac-tual mismatch between formal reforms and social practices, between the intro-duction of functional mechanisms and the resistance of culturally integrated life-worlds. Weber's "infinity of diffuse and discrete human actions" which translated Ottoman statehood into daily ruling practices did not correspond to the normative and organizational ideals that inspired the Empire's bureaucratic elite. In the broader context of international power politics and world market formation, the reform process failed from the perspective of the intentions of its initiators. In fact, Ottoman modernization resulted in the formation of a number of national states which themselves were modeled according to the very same dominant patterns of social order which the Ottoman reformers had in mind.[21] Moreover, the internal opposition to the Ottoman state-building project used the European stage for the advancement of their nationalist aspirations. The first Arab Congress, for instance, met on 18–23 June 1913 in Paris from where the Arab emigrant community had invited "the sons of the Arab nation" (Duri 1987, 288).[22] In the end the attempt at constructing a modern Ottoman state generated the formation of independent states in the Middle East and on the Balkan. The history of Ottoman decline was thus translated into various national narratives of successful state-building.

To sum up, world society is in the first instance a sociological construct which helps us to frame our understanding of historical processes such as the above example of Ottoman reform. Taking the macrosociological dimension of func-tional integration as its most abstract level, world society combines a multiplicity of analytical concepts to an imagined social order which is oriented toward con-crete historical material. In their systematic combination, these concepts—state, law, capitalist economy, education, religion, etc.—serve as both an encompass-ing analytical framework and a semantic reservoir for the description of global

---

21. To be sure, the dissolution of the Ottoman Empire was not the result of a mismatch between structural reforms and social practices alone. Rather, it resulted from the complex interplay among a variety of state and non-state actors with the larger struc-tural transformations of the economic, political and cultural conditions on which the Empire rested. I attempted to analyze this complex interplay in Jung (2001a, 28–58).

22. Although the invitation was directed at the "Arab nation" in general, most partici-pants came geographically from Syria and, besides the Arabs in exile, the congress factually was limited to Christian and Muslim Arabs from the Ottoman Empire (cf. Duri 1987, 288–294).

developments by the academic observer. In my conceptualization, world society is therefore first and foremost a tool of social theory. It serves as a means of reflection about social reality and does not claim predictive power. World society represents a heuristic framework generating research questions and ordering the complexity of empirical data rather than corresponding directly with historical facts. We can, then, understand the dynamics of global developments with the help of two leading binary differences: the paradigmatic dichotomy between tradition and modernity and the conflictive interaction between mechanisms of functional and social integration.

World society, religion and Islam

Contemporary concepts of religion have developed within the paradigm of modernity discussed so far. Within this development, the linear modernization theories of the 1950s and 1960s also heavily impacted on the social science debates about the relationship between religion and modernity. Through the lenses of a linear modernization process, they conceptualized this relationship as a zero-sum game: the more modern a society becomes the less religious it will be. From this perspective, modernization and secularization—conceived as a gradual but inevitable "disappearance" of religion on the societal and individual levels— were concomitant processes. This assumption has not only spread in the social sciences but also become a building block of the global discourse on religion and modernity. Even more, it attained the quality of a normative standard according to which a modern society had to be secular and therefore to relegate religion to non-political spaces (cf. Asad 2003, 182). The current debates about the "resurgence, revival, or return" of religion are deeply molded by this widespread equation of modernization with a particular but simplistic notion of secularization. For in order to view religion as coming back, it first has to disappear. Thus, this section will first look more closely at the conceptual relationship between modernization and secularization in the context of sociological theories. After briefly discussing three core approaches to defining religion, I will then present my own understanding of religion. This is inspired by both the sociological tradition associated with Peter Berger and Thomas Luckmann (1967), which perceives the sociology of religion as an integral part of the sociology of knowledge, and the more recent work of Peter Beyer, who applies elements of Luhmann's systems theory in analyzing religion within the context of globalization (Beyer 2006). The section leads to the conclusion that institutional secularization in the context of increasing functional differentiation contributed to shaping a distinctive field of religion which has made religious phenomena both more clearly observable and more limited in their societal reach. The possibility of a substantial definition of modern religion is thus in itself a result of increasing functional differentiation.

In emphasizing the secular character of modernity, the modernization theories of the 1950s and 1960s certainly did not completely deviate from the position of the sociological classics. There was a strong tendency among the classics to juxtapose modernity and religion. Although Weber's diagnosis of the disenchantment of the modern world does not necessarily imply a general and even linear disappearance of religion, he tended to grant religion only a relatively marginal role under the reign of modern rationalism. In Weber's interpretation, the modern disenchantment first and foremost meant an inner process of religious rationalization, doing away with all kinds of magical and ritual beliefs. In a similar way, the Durkheimian tradition has not entirely dismissed religion. Rather it perceived the institutionalization of "Christian values" as part and parcel of social integration in modern society. This tradition has viewed the content of these values, however, as becoming increasingly secular. Thereby it closely followed Durkheim's assumption that the integrative function of traditional religions will be replaced by a new type of secular solidarity which is based on the logics of modern "organic society" (Dobbelaere 2002, 83–84). Generally speaking, the paradigmatic dichotomies of the classics—traditional/modern; mechanical/organic society; *Gemeinschaft/Gesellschaft*—emphasized the overwhelmingly religious character of pre-modern forms of the social. Whereas modern society might provide religion with a societal niche, pre-modern communities were perceived as fully permeated by religious world views. Therefore, it is true that in classical theories of modernity, secularization represented a core feature of modernization, although not in the mechanical and linear meaning of a zero-sum relationship as the "scientist" modernization theories of the 1950s and 1960s put it.

In contemporary social science debates on religion, this assumption of an essentially secular modernity has increasingly lost its validity. Yet, as in the globalization debate, the theme of the "revival of the sacred" is often predicated on very simplistic readings of secularization, disregarding the historical course the development of the term has taken. The concept appeared for the first time at the Westphalian Peace negotiations in 1648. Then, secularization was exclusively a technical term for the economic expropriation of church property by the state. Only in the nineteenth century did secularization take on its political and cultural meaning of an inherent process of societal modernization, reflecting the historical experience of religious and social change in Europe (Matthes 1967, 74–84). In order to make sense of the role of religion in modern society, it is necessary to get a clearer picture of the various meanings that semantically have been lumped together in the concept of secularization.

Processes of secularization have been observed on societal, organizational and individual levels of analysis. From a macro perspective, the polarization of secular and religious spheres has been interpreted as a non-intended outcome of functional differentiation, structuring modern society according to relatively autonomous functional subsystems. This rather latent process of societal secularization, popularized in the catch phrase of the separation of church and state, has been accompanied by forms of organizational secularization as, for example, the bureaucratization and formal re-structuration of particular religions. Finally, secularization might occur on the individual level such as a decline of engagement with organized religion and the concomitant rise of new forms of religiosity or the emergence of non-religious systems of meaning (Dobbelaere 2002). While most of the proponents of secularization theories share the theoretical premise that secularization results from societal differentiation, they differ notably in their positions regarding the impact of this differentiation process on the relationship between religious and non-religious spheres, as well as on the intensity and forms of individual religiosity. In asking what has happened to religion, Philip Gorski discerned at least four different theses associated with the works of particular sociologists: disappearance (Auguste Comte); decline (Max Weber); privatization (Thomas Luckmann); and transformation (Talcott Parsons). Moreover, sociological literature often combines various elements of these four theoretical perspectives in newly defined hybrid forms so that there is not one single secularization theory but a family of quite different theories of religious change (Gorski 2000, 139–141).[23]

This picture of diversity applies likewise to the various critics of the secularization paradigm. In sharp contrast to proponents of the privatization thesis, José Casanova, for instance, observes a de-privatization of religion in modern societies. In a number of case studies, he points at the various forms in which religious organizations participate in public political discourse (1994). In Casanova's conclusion, the secularization of Western Europe is not the rule, but rather the exception in the rise of multiple modernities (Casanova 2001, 1057). Even Jürgen Habermas came out against views which conceptualize the relationship between modernization and religion as a zero-sum game. In light of the growing political influence of "religious orthodoxies," he declared, from the perspective of universal history, that the occidental process of rationalization is an exceptional path of modernization. Yet similar to Casanova's critique, Habermas still assigns the modern state a religiously neutral position. Also in his idea of a post-secular society, the return of religious argumentation into the public sphere is facilitated by the institutional separation of political authority and religion under forms of liberal statehood (Habermas 2005).

While Casanova and Habermas stress the ongoing validity of some institutional elements of societal secularization, in particular the constitutionally established "twin tolerations" between state and religion (Stepan 2000), representatives of rational choice approaches to religion declare the secularization theory in general to be a "product of wishful thinking" (Stark 1999, 269). In Rodney Stark's reading, theses of the decline or even disappearance of religion in modern Europe have been based on entirely exaggerated perceptions of Europe's religious

---

23. James Beckford identified six influential strands of social thought about religion and secularization which to a certain extent also overlap and intersect: 1) structural differentiation as a force of evolutionary change (Saint Simon, Comte, Spencer, Durkheim); 2) empiricist rejection of the plausibility of religion (Hume and the Scottish Enlightenment); 3) internal dynamics of secularization especially in Christianity (Weber and Troeltsch); 4) liberal visions of religious toleration (Locke and Mill); 5) Marxist critique of religion; 6) religious evolution in light of the realm of the unconscious of human beings (Beckford 2003, 35–39)

past. Thus, secularization theories have been built on a false "myth of past piety." In sharp contrast to this myth of a traditionally Christian Europe, according to Stark, the majority of medieval Europeans were almost completely ignorant of the basic features of Christian culture and the formal theological content of the Christian faith (Stark 1999, 257). Therefore, Stark suggests "carry[ing] the secularization doctrine to the graveyard of failed theories" (Stark 1999, 271).[24]

Today, scholars widely agree that the narrative of a linear decline of religion in Europe is a gross oversimplification of historical developments and social change. Not surprisingly therefore, the assessment of the role of religion in European modernization and state formation has been put under revision. Although the Christian Reformation set out as a religious movement, it soon lost its predominantly religious character (Greyerz 2000, 45). In the "Confessional Age" that followed the Reformation, the lines between religious and worldly authorities became entirely blurred and European state formation appeared first as the de-differentiation of church, state and society (Gorski 2000, 155). Moreover, the Reformation initiated a change less in the level of religiosity but rather in its specific character. In his analysis of ritual in early modern Europe, Edward Muir, for instance, interprets the Reformation as the starting point for a transformation from ritualistic and expressive forms of religiosity to more rationalized types of belief based on scripture: "The process of gaining access to the sacred shifted from experiencing the divine body through sight, touch, and ingestion to interpreting the scriptural world" (1997, 150).

What has been observable since the Middle Ages in Europe is a gradual rationalization of the Christian faith in which elements of magic, ritual and community have been replaced by an ethical, intellectual and more individual type of religiosity (Gorski 2000, 139–149). In this process of religious rationalization, however, a clear separation between revealed and empirical knowledge only began in the eighteenth century. The various forms of Christian confessions in post-Reformation times first remained as distinct ways of life rather than consciously followed systems of belief (Greyerz 2000, 36 and 68). The specific religious features of modern Christianity, often directly associated with the Reformation, are a rather late result of this religious rationalization process and closely linked to the reformulations of Christian faith under the impact of liberal Protestantism in the nineteenth century. The later chapters of this book will show in which way this Protestant revision of Christianity influenced disciplines such as sociology, anthropology and Islamic studies, as well as debates among orientalists and Islamic reformers. Furthermore, chapter six discusses the various ways in which elements of Protestant theology also became a part of the intellectual deliberations of Muslim thinkers. From this historical perspective, both Rodney Stark's

---

24. On closer inspection, Stark's theory of religious markets builds inherently on at least some assumptions of societal secularization. In defining competitive pluralism as a healthy environment for religion (Stark 1997, 17), his rejection of assumptions of religious decline are based on a societal structure in which the twin tolerations and therewith the legal and institutional separation of state and religion are granted.

critique of the myth of previous piety and the narrative of a linear religious decline are equally flawed. These assumptions rest on different and historically particular definitions of religion and on specific understandings of religiosity. In this sense, the different concepts decide about the respective trends observed.

Whereas the meaning of the term "religion" is apparently self-evident in public discourse, defining religion is a highly contested field in the social sciences and humanities. Indeed, from a scholarly perspective, it is far from evident what should be understood as religious and religion. In the sociology of religion two definition types have been prevalent so far: substantive and functional. Substantive definitions mostly rely on references to the supra-natural, to dimensions of human existence that transcend the empirical realm. Applying dichotomies such as sacred/profane, super-human/human or transcendent/immanent, they conceptualize religions as *sui generis* phenomena. As a distinctive realm of beliefs and social practices, substantive definitions construct religion as independent from the economic, political and social spheres of life. Functional definitions, in contrast, define religion within the framework of societal problem solving. They conceptualize religion as a means of social integration and systems of meaning, subordinating the religious sphere to society in general. While substantive definitions have a rather exclusive character, functional approaches tend toward inclusiveness, opening the meaning of religion in principle to all kinds of ideologies, institutions and movements that could provide for social integration, as well as for cognitive understanding and moral guidance, i.e. for orientation in Elias' sense.

In recent decades both functional and substantial definitions of religion have come under severe critique. This criticism is primarily directed against the allegedly unreflected cultural foundations on which these two sociological definitions of religion have rested. When Emile Durkheim, for example, defined religion as "a unified system of beliefs and practices relative to sacred things, that is to say, things set apart and forbidden" (Durkheim 1995, 44), he took the major building blocks of his definition from the historical development of Christianity. Contrary to Durkheim's generalization, some of the critics say, to many non-Christian religions the strict dichotomy between sacred and profane spaces seems to be rather alien (Matthes 1993, 23). Likewise, in medieval Europe the sacred and mundane worlds penetrated each other. The sharp distinction between the realms of the sacred and the profane is not a trans-historical universal attribute of religion. Rather it is the historical outcome of a particular process of religious rationalization that took off with the Christian Reformation (McGuire 2003, 129). Consequently, it is wrong to define religion as a transhistorical and transcultural phenomenon. We must understand religious symbols and institutions in dependence on their historical and social contexts of evolution (Asad 1993).

Together with more general theoretical shifts in the social sciences, this criticism has sparked new attempts to define religion differently from the functionalist and substantive approaches. On the one hand, polythetic definitions designate a whole class of attributes that could define religion. Instead of founding religion in a universal substance or function, polythetic definitions try to avoid sharp boundaries and to expand the concept of religion. They draw on Wittgenstein's idea of family resemblances and present clusters of religious attributes such as supernatural beings, salvation, rituals, the sacred, beliefs, ethics, traditions, priesthood, and mythologies. In order to qualify as a religion, a phenomenon has to share some of these attributes, but does not have to share all of them. On the contrary, according to polythetic definitions two phenomena that have none of the attributes in common with each other could nevertheless qualify within the whole cluster of attributes as religions (Hamilton 2002, 20–23).[25] On the other hand, constructivist approaches have made their inroads into the sociology of religion. They reject the assumption of religion being an anthropological or societal necessity, but view religions as socially and historically constructed phenomena which are "in a constant process of framing and re-framing." From a constructivist perspective, religion "is a social construct that varies in meaning across time and place" (Beckford 2003, 2 and 7).

Integrating religion in my theoretical framework of world society, I take these assumptions of constructivist approaches as my point of departure. In a theory of an emerging modernity religion also assumes a specific modern meaning. Modern religion is defined by its interrelatedness within the societal arrangement of world society as a whole. The essentialist image of Islam is therefore the result of a reframing and reinvention of Muslim traditions conditioned by the cognitive and institutional features of world society. It is a specific form of Islam whose features result from societal negotiations that should be understood against the conceptual background of religion as an abstract and universal dimension of world society. Talal Asad argued that there cannot be a universal definition of religion because this definition is itself a social and historical construct (Asad 1993, 29). Contrary to this radical constructivist position, I do claim that it is possible to apply a universal concept of religion within the analytical framework of world society. Like other isomorphic institutions of "world culture" (Meyer *et al.* 1997)—states, economies, education systems etc.—a generalized concept of religion which informs global discourses about religion also exists. Universality and historicity are not mutually exclusive. To be sure, the modern concept of religion is not transhistorical. But it represents the universalized idea of the religion of a specific epoch. The religious dimensions of multiple modernities find their reference point in this general concept, in an ideal type of modern religion. Even if the origin of this ideal type is in the Protestant reconstruction of Christianity, theoretically this particular historical origin does not undermine the validity of the concept as a means of transcultural negotiation about religion in the modern world. The universality of the concept is a matter of general recognition and not of its specific origin.

---

25. In this way, polythetic definitions open up for the classification as religious of new spiritual movements, forms of religious *bricolage*, and tendencies toward the individualization of faith.

Given this conceptual history, some elements of the substantive and functional definitions of religion might be quite useful within a constructivist approach. Making use of these sociological traditions does not necessarily mean endorsing their philosophical foundations. The idea of the universal concept of religion closely linked to both substantive and functional definitions can be related to the deist notion of Enlightenment thinkers, who explained different religions as the emanation of a "natural religion" (cf. Pals 1996, 6–7). Yet from this speculative philosophical origin these definitions have travelled into the legal, political and scientific frames of an emerging modernity. They became influential means of orientation in the modern world that have emancipated themselves from their own history of ideas.

In functionalist terms, the modern concept of religion is closely linked to the sociology of knowledge, viewing religion in terms of being a source of cognitive, normative and moral orientation. According to this tradition, the social function of religion has been related to moral codes, foundational world views and cosmologies. Religion is an inherent part of knowledge in its broader sense, which, manifested in traditions, institutions and languages, transcends individuals and provides them with societal meaning (cf. Luckmann 1963). In short, religion has frequently been associated with "the most basic self-evidences that inform our approach to the world" (Beyer 2006, 1). The tendency of the classics to generally conceptualize pre-modern social formations as inherently religious can be linked to the elementary function of providing orientation described by Norbert Elias. Religion was essential as a set of "meaningful frameworks for the apprehension of reality and of a set of moral constraints on social conduct" (Poggi 2001, 62). In the course of the modern transformations, however, this elementary function itself became increasingly differentiated. In modern society, different bodies of knowledge compete with each other, and meaning has lost its predominant foundation in revealed traditions. The previous unity of knowledge, ethics and aesthetics has been replaced by separated fields of communication and action, dominated by functionally differentiated specialists such as scientists, legislators and artists. The holistic religious world view, however, has been challenged not only by secular scientific knowledge and non-religious ethical systems, but also by other religions. Secularization in its societal dimension, the separation of state and religion, has engendered religious competition based on the constitutional precepts of religious freedoms. Consequently, the formation of the modern concept of religion as a clearly identifiable sector of society based on distinct features has to be seen in the broader context of functional differentiation as the dominant macrosociological pattern of world society. The analysis of religion must be embedded in a theory of society at large.

Regarding the combination of a constructivist perspective with the substantive approach in defining religion as a *sui generis* phenomenon, it makes sense to go back to systems theory. In Niklas Luhmann's concept of world society, religion is defined as one amongst many functional systems which are autonomous in terms of being self-referential (autopoetic) but not independent in their operations. It is precisely this operational closure of religion as a function system that sharply distinguishes it from the rest of society and furnishes it with a *sui generis* character. Modern religion has gained this autonomy at the expense of accepting the autonomy of other systems such as the state, education, the economy or law. In historical terms, the *Kulturkampf* ("cultural struggle") between the German state under Bismarck and the Catholic Church about education, political representation, and social services was an expression of this establishment of functionally defined domains in German society. Similar struggles have been observable in the Muslim world, where the traditionally religious learned, the *ulama,* have been in a continuous struggle with the state regarding control over juridical and educational institutions (cf. Zaman 2002; Zeghal 1999)

In European history, Christian religion achieved its modern form through this process of functional separation based on the operational distinction between salvation and damnation which materialized in the dichotomy between heaven and hell (Luhmann 1985, 12–13).[26] According to Luhmann, the generally self-referential nature of society, its communicative operational closure, causes a foundational paradox for the social to which religion refers. In God as the "centralized paradox" modern Christian religion has reformulated the paradox of self-reference as transcendence. With this exclusive linkage to the transcendent, religion differentiated in semantic and structural terms. Religion developed into a functionally defined subsystem of society while simultaneously losing its ability to support other areas of life (Luhmann 1985, 14). In this sense, the historical course of modernization in Europe provided the societal foundations for substantive definitions of religion which are based on the core feature of transcendence.

Peter Beyer further developed this Luhmanian perspective—"observing religion as one of several differentiated function systems"—in *Religion in Global Society* (Beyer 2006, 3). Beyer combines insights from both Roland Robertson's globalization theory and Luhmann's systems theory in order to analyze religious phenomena in the global context. In his theory of a global system of religion, Beyer observes religion as an emerging system of recursive and self-referential communication based on the general code of being "blessed or cursed" (Beyer 2006, 85). According to him, it is this communicative order of a specific circular system of signification and "not the conscious belief of human participants that makes a religion" (2006, 93). Beyer combines social constructivism with elements of functionalist and substantive approaches to religion that have gained their validity due to historical reasons, i.e. the very fact that the function system for religion "constructed itself more in a substantive way" (2006, 4). The classical ways of defining religion via substantive or functional approaches are therefore

---

26. Defining society through communication, Luhmann characterized each functional subsystem of society by a specific binary code that organizes the operational closure of the systems communication. The legal system, for instance, operates with the code legal/illegal, science with true/untrue, and economics with to have/ to have not. It is by these codes through which functional systems are sharply differentiated from their environments (Luhmann 1986).

themselves inherent parts of the historical construction of modern religion, involving both observers and the observed.

Internally this global system of religious communication is segmented into a variety of religions that derive their particular identities from very different and more specific codes and programs. The major "world religions"—Christianity, Islam, Hinduism, Judaism, Buddhism—are therefore different religious programs that represent relatively stable patterns of religious communication. These programs define what a particular religion is, and they are characterized by inner contestations over orthodoxy, orthopraxy, authenticity, and authority (Beyer 2006, 89). From a macrosociological perspective, the religious system evolved in conflictive boundary demarcations with other functional systems, developing its own specific code in excluding other fields of communication from its realm. Yet communications are not restricted to functional domains alone. On different levels of analysis—social interactions, organizations, and movements (2006, 51) —communication transgresses the systemic barriers of the structural setting of modern society; and it is on these intermediate levels on which religious, political, economic, scientific, and aesthetic communications mesh.

This section has shown that theories of secularization and modern definitions of religion closely intersect. Taking the classics' view of the, in principle, religious nature of pre-modern social institutions and life-worlds serious, only the rise of global modernity clearly differentiated the religious field from other social sectors. Religion in its distinct form is then itself an outcome of the functional differentiation of modern society. According to the German sociologist Georg Simmel, the idea of evolutionary progress applied to religion does not mean religion achieving a higher level of perfection, but that religion is developing into a more pure form of being exclusively religion (Simmel 1995, 113). It is this process of setting religion apart from other subsystems that has been discussed under the secularization paradigm. While this process has been interpreted as a marginalization of religion, it simultaneously made religious phenomena more visible, giving them the opportunity to define themselves as religious according to their observed autonomous logic. Now, the observer could define religion in a substantive way as a specific form of human communication and interaction with the supernatural. At the same time, sociologists could discuss the role of religion in relation to society at large and therewith define religion along functionalist lines. Substantive and functional definitions of religion are therefore complementary rather than contradicting in nature. From a macrosociological angle, institutional secularization and modern concepts of religion are inseparably intertwined.

The theory of secularization as a specific view on the functional differentiation of modern society therefore remains an important tool of social analysis. What was wrong, however, was to equate the functional separation of religion with its subsequent disappearance on societal and individual levels. In fact, as the discussion about so-called "post-secular" societies shows, we can even interpret secularization on the macrosociological level as an important condition for religious pluralism and the public "re-appearance" of religion in individuals and social movements. To be sure, secularization also has appeared on the individual level. The option to guide individual and collective actions entirely on the basis of non-religious bodies of knowledge, ethics and morals is a significant feature of modernity as a "secular age" (cf. Taylor 2007).[27] However, this option does not render soteriological ethics and the quest for salvation obsolete. On the contrary, also in a secular age religious motivations remain central to the lifestyles and actions of many individuals. Processes of increasing functional separation and of growing religiosity are by no means mutually exclusive.

For the purpose of this book, I will therefore rely on a definition of religion which takes its point of departure in the modern principle of functional differentiation. I define religion as a distinguishable discourse and field of social practices, as a global system of religion in Beyer's terms, within the overarching framework of a world society whose macrostructure is dominated by functional differentiation. In this definition, religion represents first and foremost a holistic body of knowledge based on changing interpretations of revealed and therefore to a certain extent extra-mundane traditions. On the macro-level, however, the holistic nature of religion remains in permanent tension with the principle of functional differentiation, leading to continuous social negotiations in maintaining boundaries to other social fields and in particular to secular forms of knowledge and morality. Moreover, the religious system is characterized by ongoing negotiation among and within the various different religious programs (read: globally acknowledged religions). The rise and spread of the essentialist image of Islam as a dominant interpretation of the Islamic religious program has taken place in this complex context of multi-leveled societal negotiations. The empirical chapters of this book will engage in a selective analysis of these complex negotiation processes over time. For the scholarly interpretation of these negotiations about the nature of modern Islam, world society represents my general theoretical framework, whereas the concept of an emerging global public sphere serves the analytical operationalization of my empirical investigation.

The Global Public Sphere: "Social Site" of World Society

The previous sections discussed the theoretical category of world society as an encompassing frame of reference for the analysis of globalization. In this theoretical context I understood globalization as the empirical expression of an emerging global modernity and I identified functional differentiation as the major structural force in shaping the macrostructures of society in a global dimension. In this macrostructure of modern society, religion has emerged as one amongst several distinct function systems. In a certain analogy to the global political system that has been internally structured by the historical formation

---

27. Although I agree with Taylor's argument regarding the character of the "secular age," I do not share his view that secular humanism and the "immanent order of Nature" are exclusive inventions of the West (Taylor 2007, 15).

of a multiplicity of national states, the global system of religion has appeared in form of a number of different mutually acknowledged religions character- ized through specific religious programs. The apartness of modern religion as a *sui generis* phenomenon is due to its operational closure as a function system. From a macrosociological perspective, the theory of institutional secularization —in Christian terminology commonly referred to as the separation of state and church—grasps this process of the differentiation and operational closure of var- ious functionally defined subsystems of modern society with a specific reference to religion. The formation of modern Islam, representing one internally highly contested religious program among other religions, took place in the course of this emergent structural transformation.

With its focus on social systems and macrostructures, however, this conceptu- alization of world society serves best as an outer theoretical frame of reference for the analysis of concrete instances of globalization. Functionalist theories focus on abstractions about the non-intended outcomes of multiple patterns of actions at the expense of their social meanings. Discerning the functions of social systems is an observer-dependent process, providing "convenient descriptors of how things appear to us" (Zeleny 1993, 21). Yet, many of the social phenomena which we usually associate with global developments are not located at this high level of abstraction but figure on various levels of analysis in between the ulti- mate poles of individual actors and of the totality of society as a systemic whole. Moreover, they are intimately linked to socially and historically constructed patterns of meaning—they refer to different cultures. The development of spe- cific religious programs, for instance, has taken place in between these poles as intense processes of societal negotiation and contestation. The evolution of modern religious programs has fundamentally to do with the construction and interaction of different systems of social meaning. In these processes the analy- ses of social structures and of human agency are mutually dependent yet dif- ferent perspectives. While structures frame and constrain social action, collec- tive and individual actors simultaneously constitute and re-constitute the social structures which, again, appear to them as outer constraints. Human agency is both coded by social systems and motivated by individual personalities (Alexan- der 1998, 214–215). Hence relatively stable cultural forms, organizations, social movements and patterns of social interaction represent intermediate levels of analysis between the polar ends of system and individual. It is on these interme- diate levels of analysis where we can observe the construction of knowledge and the social negotiations about Islam as a modern religion.

In order to reconstruct the formation of the essentialist image of Islam, I have to define the social arena in which this knowledge about Islam has developed. In borrowing from Theodore Schatzki's theory (Schatzki 2002), I perceive this arena as a "social site" that is composed of a changing and constantly evolving mesh of structural orders, culturally defined social practices and individual actions. For this social site, function systems are the most abstract social arrangements to which human agency relates. They form the isomorphic part of the modern order in which modern human coexistence takes place and in which the organizing power of culturally different but mutually interdependent social practices brought about the emergence of a global modernity as multiple modernities. These different cultural programs of the modern, however, have essentially developed through social processes in which human collectives attach meaning to a social reality that has been pre-structured by the formal rationality of societal systems. Multiple modernities are cultural programs making sense of the conflicting encounter between functional and social integration—or in Habermas' words the systemic colonialization of life-worlds. With my focus on the construction of knowledge, I delimitate this complex social site further to two essential dimensions, a societal stage of individual physical presence and of discursive exchanges. We can observe not only direct and indirect forms of social interaction, but also interlacing and overlapping discursive patterns of knowledge. I will claim that we have to understand the evolution of specific religious programs and their representations such as the essentialist concept of Islam within the analytical framework of this social site as an emerging global public sphere.

The application of concepts of the public sphere in the social sciences often refers back to the seminal work *The Structural Transformation of the Public Sphere* by Jürgen Habermas (1962; English translation in 1989). For Habermas, the public sphere forms a societal space of communicative political and social engagement. Linked to the concepts of discourse and reason, the public sphere provided the fundament for his normative theory of deliberative democracy (Habermas 1990, 38). Habermas developed the public sphere as a historical category specifically bound to the modern epoch, focusing on its liberal form as a communicative forum of society for criticizing and controlling state power (cf. Habermas 1962, 142; Luhmann 1970 and Koselleck 1979). Together with those of its conceptual relative, civil society, theories of the public sphere have also penetrated the field of Middle Eastern and Islamic studies. In particular with the advancement and spread of new communication technologies, there is a growing body of literature about new Arab and new Muslim public spheres.

Invoking Habermas' normative theory, many authors interpret the appearance of the internet, of satellite TV channels such as al-Jazeera or al-Arabiyya and trans-national Arab newspapers as a decisive break with the traditionally authoritarian structures of communications in which state authorities have dominated the Arab public by means of national state-controlled media. Thereby, technological innovation has been pictured as the driving force in establishing a discursive space transcending the previously rigorously controlled borders of Arab national states (cf. Eickelman and Anderson 2003; Lynch 2006). There is no doubt that the rapid change in communication infrastructure contributes to the transformation of Middle Eastern politics. Yet whether this new Arab public sphere will indeed become a discursive platform for the democratization of Arab polities remains to be seen. The role of the media in Middle Eastern politics has been far more ambivalent than the often all-too-easy association of these new media with democratic change would lead us to expect (Skovgaard-Petersen 2006).

Contrary to this focus on communication technologies, Reinhard Schulze's conception elaborates on the Muslim public sphere in emphasizing its historical dimension, emerging in the late nineteenth century together with the modern state. He defines Islam as a world culture whose social network has been communicated by religious symbols and which has transgressed geopolitical boundaries. In the debates of this Islamic public sphere, a secular discourse competed with an Islamic discourse about the building-up of a modern social and political order. Schulze conceives the Islamic discourse as based on a pool of vocabulary and signs derived from Islamic traditions, as a communicative template without having a definite content or necessarily being religious (Schulze 1994, 21–22). Thereby, the Islamic discourse increasingly became differentiated by traditional and various reformist voices. Indeed, a Sunni modernist thinker such as the Egyptian Azhar Sheikh Muhammad Abduh impacted not only Egyptian and Arab audiences. Facilitated by this Islamic communicative network, his ideas made their way throughout the whole Muslim World from Morocco to Indonesia and also resonated among learned circles of the Shiite clergy in Iran and Iraq (cf. Nakash 2003). *Al-manar,* the reformist journal edited by Abduh's disciple and biographer Rashid Rida, for instance, played a major role in the engagement of Southeast Asian Muslims in the reform movement. Published between 1898–1935, *al-manar* developed into a source of authority in religious matters that strongly challenged the traditional *ulama's* previous monopoly of religious interpretation (Burhanudin 2005).

In basing their concepts on larger cultural and religious groups, these works on Arab and Muslim public spheres transcend Habermas' focus on the political constituencies of national states. Yet they remain restricted to linguistically and religiously defined spaces of communication. Contrary to this segmentation of the public sphere, I claim that national European, Arab and Muslim forms of the public have emerged within a broader frame of reference. The internal linguistic and cultural fragmentations of the public sphere should not deceive us about its inherent global character. The history of world exhibitions is just one example that can illustrate this claim.

Beginning with the "Exhibition of the Works of Industry of all Nations" in London in 1851, the second half of the nineteenth century saw nine world exhibitions which represented accounts of universal developments in the fields of industry, technology, science, education and the arts.[28] These exhibitions were among the most important events of their time, attracted millions of visitors and "remain unsurpassed in their scale, opulence and confidence" (Greenhalgh 1988, 1). They were a "part of a unitary, though not uniform, landscape of discourse and practice that situated metropole and colony within a single analytic field" (Beckenridge 1989, 196). In a microcosm, these World's Fairs visualized a "single expanded world" (Celik 1992, 1), also visited by Muslim rulers from Egypt, Iran and the Ottoman Empire, as well as various intellectuals from the Islamic

---

28. London (1851), Paris (1855), London (1862), Paris (1867), Vienna (1873), Philadelphia (1876), Paris (1878), Paris (1889), Chicago (1893), see Haltern (1971, 2).

world (cf. Celik 1992, 32–49). In this way, these universal exhibitions perfectly symbolize the rise of a global public whose communicative interaction clearly surmounts national, cultural and linguistic boundaries.

To be sure, these spectacular events clearly mirrored the international power relations of the imperialist epoch and they provided a global arena for fierce competition between national states. In London in 1851, the event was launched as an integral part of British imperial consciousness and dominated by the politically and economically competing European powers. The colonized parts of the world were mainly represented by their colonizers. Even the exhibition of the Ottoman Empire was prepared with the assistance of Great Britain. The expositions tended to display the progress of Europe in contrast to the bizarre and picturesque rest of the world (Findley 1998, 38).[29] At the turn of the century, they became obsessed with evolutionary theories (Greenhalgh 1988, 100), visibly popularizing a central philosophy of history of the nineteenth century. Although these world exhibitions were thus molded by the asymmetric power structures of the international system, they nonetheless offered a stage of communication and social interaction that in principal involved humanity as a global whole (Haltern 1971).[30]

In my conception of the public sphere as a global social site, I view the public sphere as an emerging and encompassing social and communicative arena of global modernity. Like Habermas, I link my concept closely to processes of modern state formation and to the idea of the discursive nature of the public. Similar to Schulze, combining these three concepts—public sphere, modern state, and discursive structures—serves me to define the global public sphere as a specifically modern social site whose character is of a social rather than a technological nature. In emphasizing the role of the advancement of communication technologies, the more recent works on the new Arab and Muslim publics tend to turn the infrastructure of the public sphere into its prime mover, thereby disregarding its social content and historical depth.

While I share this linkage to modern state formation, I do not follow the mainstream literature, which conceptualizes the public sphere in Habermas' sense as an essential part of a liberal theory of democratic politics. The public sphere as a global social site has emerged in the context of local, national, and international power relations, which left deep marks on its communicative structures. Again,

---

29. Yet the reaction of non-Europeans to these bizarre representations also varied. While the envoy of the Ottoman sultan to the Eighth Congress of Orientalists in Stockholm, Ahmed Midhat, was amused about some of the expositions he saw at the Paris world fair in 1889 (Findley 1998, 38), Egyptian visitors were seemingly disgusted by the way their own country was represented (Mitchell 1989, 217). Apparently, a general solidarity among the colonized did not exist.

30. The exhibition was dominated by the two leading European powers Great Britain and France, with the various German states, as well as Russia and the United States, following as second in importance. Turkey and Egypt participated as two independent parts of the Ottoman Empire and received, together with Ali Bey from Tunis, a prize for their respective collections (Haltern 1971, 210).

the colonial situation in its various dimensions is reflected in the structures of this global public sphere. The formation of the global public sphere has been characterized by processes of exclusion and inclusion and has never lived up to the participatory and reciprocal claims of liberalism (cf. Peters 1994, 44–46). The world fairs are a good example of the inherent asymmetries of the global public. I, therefore, reduce the concept in my own usage to a mere analytical category and hardly refer to Habermas' work.[31]

Stripping the concept of its normative pretension, I define the global public sphere as an emerging social site that encompasses and transcends the political (states) and cultural (religions, ethnic groups, localities) segmentations of world society. In this way, it reflects the, in principle, borderless dimension of society as world society. It makes possible the unity of society in a multi-dimensional communication among the different cultural semantics of multiple modernities. Two distinct forms characterize this social site. On the one hand, it is the cognitive foundation and the operational stage for discursive interactions facilitating communication on a multiplicity of themes across historically and socially constructed borderlines. On the other hand, the global public sphere is also a field of direct and indirect social interaction with communicative technology and physical presence shaping ephemeral and more stable social interactions, organizations and movements.

The organization of the International Congress of Orientalists, for example, is one of the organizational features of the global public sphere with particular relevance for this study. In 1873, the French Professor Léon Prunol de Rosny organized and presided over the First International Congress of Orientalists in Paris.[32] Although primarily a forum for the understanding of Asia among European and American scholars (Chaudhuri 1982, 8), the series of congresses also included representatives of Asian countries right from the beginning. Looking at the lists of members for the first and second congress (London 1874), some individual scholars and institutional delegations from countries such as Algeria, Burma, Ceylon, China, Egypt, India, Japan and Turkey were also among the participants (CIO 1876 and Douglas 1876).[33] In particular India and Japan could

---

31. Habermas briefly addressed the actually ambivalent nature of the public sphere. He pointed to the manipulative dimension of a public sphere in which the media transmit a set of opinions in order to produce mass loyalty. He defined this as the plebeian form of a public sphere whose subject are the masses and the regulated, plebiscitarian-acclamative public sphere of industrialized dictatorships (Habermas 1962, 52). For a critical discussion of Habermas' theory, see Alejandro 1993; Calhoun 1997; Crossley and Roberts 2004; Dahlgren 1991; Marden 2003; McGuigan 1996; Peters 1994.

32. Léon de Rosny (1837–1914) was one of France's leading Japanologists working in the field of comparative linguistics, trying to show the linkages between Japanese, Pre-Columbian and European cultures through linguistic analysis (Léon de Rosny et les études japonaises en France, www.membres.lycos.fr, May 22, 2007).

33. In his diary, Ignaz Goldziher tells us that he met at the Orientalist Congress in Stockholm (1889) with a number of scholars, sheikhs and jurists from Algeria, Egypt and

match the numbers of representatives from some of the European countries at the two congresses, which in general were dominated by French, British and German scholars.[34] From 1873 to 1976, all in all 29 International Congresses of Orientalists took place, predominantly in Europe, with three congresses organized in Algiers (1905), Istanbul (1952), and New Delhi (1964).[35] At these congresses a new "scientific" understanding of the world, including Indian, Chinese, Japanese, Iranian and Arab cultures, was shaped through both texts and personal encounters. According to the uncritical conclusion of the Indian editor of the proceedings of the First International Congress of Orientalists, this series of congresses not only brought about a "more correct understanding of Asia" among European and American intellectuals, but was also "of service to the people of the East in understanding their own history and culture in their proper world perspectives" (Chaudhuri 1981, 8); a quote that to a certain extent testifies the appropriation of Western perceptions by the East.

From an analytical perspective, I structure the complexity of this global public sphere by distinguishing four different levels of observation: a cognitive deep structure; a field of general themes; a field of diverging and culturally differentiated semantics; and a microsociological level of social interaction. To be sure, these four levels are clearly distinguishable only as analytical categories. The mesh of the discursive and social patterns of the public sphere, however, is of a more holistic nature, that is to say that these four levels of analysis continuously interlace. They are presented here as categories of observation and not as directly accessible instances of historical reality. I construct my analytical device of the public sphere in borrowing from different cultural theories. Thereby I combine structuralism with hermeneutics, designing an analytical tool for a "robust cultural sociology" (Alexander 2003, 26). The following pages briefly present an ensemble of concepts that makes these analytical levels of the global public sphere operational as tools for social analysis.

I define the macro level of the global public sphere as a cognitive deep structure in accordance with Foucault's early concept of *episteme*.[36] This "archaeological" level represents the "unconscious" foundations of global bodies of knowledge. The *episteme* forms the cognitive historical *a priori*, the epoch-specific formative rules and regularities for the generation of knowledge, on whose implicitly applied order all my other analytical levels logically rest (cf. Foucault 1994, xi–xxii).

---

other Arab countries (Goldziher 1978, 119).

34. A note of caution is necessary here. The lists of participants of these congresses do not tell us anything about the factual participation of the individuals and organizations listed. Moreover, some participants from non-European countries probably were Europeans residing in these countries or indigenous colonial staff (cf. Fuchs 2002).

35. In 1976 the Congress was renamed and since then has taken place under the name of International Congress of Human Sciences in Asia and North Africa (Chaudhuri 1982)

36. Foucault used the term *episteme* only in *The Order of Things*. Later he replaced it by the term *archive*, in order to stress the historical and changing character of these cognitive deep structures (Sawyer 2002, 437).

Hence, this cognitive deep structure is the logical precondition for a global public sphere of cross-cultural communication. Foucault understands the *epistemé* as a "total set of relations," which "makes it possible to grasp the set of constraints and limitations which, at a given moment, are imposed on discourse" (Foucault 1989, 211). Different bodies of knowledge are then statements and concepts that have been systematized in discursive practices according to the rules of the *epistemé*. It is these discursive formations—systematic orders among objects, statements, concepts and themes (1989, 41)—that guarantee the unity of discourses about specific objects such as state, society, religion and consequently also about modern Islam.

In *The Order of Things*, Foucault defined the *epistemé* as the general structure of cognitive orders, which enable empirical knowledge and provide the common foundations for the diversification of the different branches of science. As historically distinct formations, the cognitive order of the Renaissance built on the principle of resemblance and that of classical times on classification, taxonomy and chronology. In modern times, a completely new *epistemé* emerged in which the human being moves into the centre as subject and object of knowledge (Foucault 1994). While Foucault focused on the specific cognitive orders inherent in ordering reality in a "scientific" way, my usage of the concept of *epistemé* is of a broader nature. I view Foucault's "human-centered subjectivity" of knowledge only as one feature of the cognitive macrostructure of modernity. My conception of a cognitive deep structure of the global public sphere refers more generally to the primacy of functional differentiation and the related systemic logic of functional integration of world society. Foucault's subject as bearer and agent of orders of knowledge is then only one specific element of the intertwined processes of modernization as social differentiation and individualization. That humans appear as "observed spectators" (Foucault 1994, 312) in the center of the knowledge-generating process must be understood in the broader context of the systemic nature of modernity. This central role of humans is part and parcel of a larger set of discursive practices through which society as a whole becomes apprehended by systematically interrelated but nevertheless sharply distinct concepts such as state, religion, science, law and education. From the perspective of modern systems theory, we can interpret Foucault's modern *epistemé* as an expression of the separation between the social and the individual, based on the distinction between communication and consciousness as their respective modes of operation. The category of world society in its abstract reading therefore also provides the conceptual landscape for understanding the modern *epistemé* of the global public sphere.

Consequently, it is also society as a global, functionally differentiated whole whose emergence has generated the general themes that can be discerned on my second level of observation. The various secularization debates are therefore a good example. They have articulated a great number of intertwined problems that arise from the transformative power of modern society. In terms of their conceptual organization, the various discourses around secularization deal with the complex relationships between state and religion, the validity of revealed versus scientific knowledge, the positioning of the individual vis-à-vis the community, or the competition between religious morals and formal norms and laws. These are just a few examples of the general themes that have entered the public debates within and between a multiplicity of local cultures. These themes have become socially relevant in a number of observable discourses revolving around their core problematics and anchored in the unconsciously applied rules of the modern *episteme*. Generally speaking, on this second level of analysis we can observe in which ways social actors try to comprehend the dissolution of traditional orders, the systemic colonialization of their life-worlds, and the inherent ambiguities and tension of modern pluralism.

These general themes of modernity are articulated in a multiplicity of concrete discourses which we can analyze on my third level of observation. While the first level, the modern *episteme*, represents "world culture" in its homogenous and isomorphic sense, the third level reflects the heterogeneous voices of multiple modernities. These multiple voices are discourses of a second order in comparison to what Foucault has labelled a discursive formation. These second-order discourses are specific forms of social practices that produce a network of representations in which cultural codes emerge. Reproduced through public discourses and social practices these cultural codes define possible forms of meaning (cf. Reckwitz 2006, 43–50). On this level, we can observe concrete cultures as unities of both mechanisms of control and systematic patterns of meaning. In terms of social control, cultures provide essential programs in governing human behavior (Geertz 1973, 44–46). As systematic patterns of meaning they are instrumental in constituting and communicating our understanding of the world. In this sense culture is a synthesis of meaning according to which social actors "interpret their experience and guide their action" (Geertz 1973, 145). According to Geertz, cultural analysis gives us an understanding of the intersection of human collectivity and individuality: "Becoming human is becoming individual, and we become individual under the guidance of cultural patterns, historically created systems of meaning in terms of which we give form, order, point, and direction to our lives" (Geertz 1973, 52).

From this perspective of cultural theory social life is permeated by meaning. The expressive, normative and constitutive dimensions of meaning are communicated by language, language defined as a part of the "wider gamut" of expressive gestures, symbolic forms, and social practices (cf. Taylor 1985, 265–269). Language and therewith discourses are an "irreducible part of social life," together with other concrete forms of the social such as institutions, organizations, and distributional schemes of resources and power relations (Fairclough 2003, 2). In order to make the various modern problematics apprehensible and communicable, social actors have to furnish them with meaning by articulating them within the linguistic, symbolic, narrative, and moral contexts of their life-worlds. It is on this concrete and more directly observable level of the public sphere where structural similarities become translated into social and cultural diversity. Thereby, meaning is both newly constituted by social interaction and already there in the form of more durable cultural patterns. The constitution and reconstitution of meaning by social actors takes place within and among established cultural environments which provide social actors with the necessary background knowledge to act.

Following the work of Charles Taylor, the understanding of social action is only possible in the broader context of meaning. Human beings live within given horizons of meaning that serve them as "backgrounds of intelligibility" (Taylor 1991, 37). A major part of this framework of meaning, according to Taylor, is the "moral ontology" of social groups, their ideas about moral obligations, and about the appropriate forms of life and dignity (1989, 26). Based on this hermeneutical approach to social life, people do imagine the above-discussed problematics and themes of modernity through culturally particular social imaginaries. These social imaginaries provide both self-transcending issues for the definition of individual identities and the implicit knowledge of values and social practices necessary for the common understanding of situations (Taylor 2002).

In a similar way, Pierre Bourdieu and Norbert Elias grasped the intersection of social structures and the individual with their concept of the social habitus. They defined the social habitus as a system of historically and socially constructed generative principles granting a frame in which individuality unfolds. Elias pointed out:

> ... each individual person, different as he or she may be from all others, has a
> specific make-up that he or she shares with other members of his or her society.
> This make-up, the social habitus of individuals, forms, as it were, the soil from
> which grow the personal characteristics through which an individual differs
> from other members of his society (Elias 1991, 182).

As a "generative grammar" of patterns of action the social habitus provides a reservoir of cognitive and normative resources to which individual strategies of action correspond (Bourdieu 1992, 33). Thereby, the social habitus is not a purely mental disposition, but the social order is also inscribed in the body, making it a mediator between physical and social spaces (Bourdieu 2000, 131).

The concepts of both social imaginaries and the social habitus, however, tend to conceptualize the implicit background knowledge of human beings, their particular culture, rather as a property of clearly demarcated social entities.[37] Consequently, they have certain difficulties grasping the, in principle, overlapping and interpenetrating nature of different cultural backgrounds. In *Truth and Method* Hans-Georg Gadamer emphasized precisely this interpenetration of cultural horizons as a methodological element not only of hermeneutical studies, but of the general hermeneutics of human life. In this "hermeneutic turn," hermeneu-

---

37. With regard to his communitarian political philosophy, Charles Taylor in particular
 gives the impression that different cultures form clearly distinguishable social groups,
 although he himself stated that another culture might not be viewed as totally unintelligible (Taylor 2002, 291).

tics were transformed from an interpretative method of understanding into the central mode of human existence. In dealing with the fundamental problem of historicism, that there are no subjects and objects of knowledge excluded from being regarded as historical and therewith contingent, Gadamer introduces the concept of horizon as a means of historical understanding. He defines the horizon as "the range of vision that includes everything that can be seen from a particular vantage point" (Gadamer 1993, 302). In order to understand a historical tradition, the observers must transpose themselves into the other situation, they have to discover the specific horizon of the observed tradition. This process starts out from the prejudices of the particular present of the observer's horizon. Yet no horizon is absolutely bound to the particular standpoint of its own present. The culturally closed horizon is an abstraction in the sense of an ideal type. Transposing oneself therefore means "rising to a higher universality that overcomes not only our own particularity but also that of the other" (Gadamer 1993, 305). The horizon is a moving category, and in understanding another horizon we do not enter into an alien world but rather we constitute a fusion of horizons within a larger interpretative whole.

It is my third level of observation on which we can detect this fusion of horizons, the ongoing interpenetration and reconfiguration of certain kinds of culturally framed background knowledge. The social imaginaries and social habiti of human beings are relatively stable cultural programs which we acquire through socialization. They provide us with evaluative and cognitive patterns of meaning to make sense of the world. However, they are neither fixed cultural structures, nor the emanation of sharply demarcated cultural totalities. Rather, they are stabilized but changeable bodies of knowledge and social practices whose various elements are compatible for individual and collective reconstruction. This applies in particular to the modern condition under which society as a global social whole provides the common frame of reference for multiple modernities. With regard to my analytical differentiation of the global public sphere, the construction of distinguished but mutually intelligible modern cultural programs is examined on this third level of observation, whereas the foundation for the principle intelligibility of various cultural horizons, the larger cognitive whole to which they refer, is given by the deep structure of a modern *epistemé*. In order to understand the fusion of horizons, we therefore have to apply both structural and hermeneutical perspectives. The two analytically distinct levels of deep structure and cultural practices, however, do not express a hierarchy. The *epistemé* is not the modern basis of various cultural superstructures. Rather these two levels relate to each other in a circular way, producing the contingent and often contradicting features of a globalizing modern world. The formation of different modern religious programs, for instance, with reference to an abstract functional system of global religion has been such a process of the reconstruction of historical traditions of knowledge in the context of the global public sphere. The modern image of Islam can thus be interpreted through a process of the partial fusion of Muslim and Western horizons with respect to a general modern *epistemé*.

This picture of an ongoing formative process of cultural programs brings me to my last level of observation, the microsociological level of individual action and inter-action. While individuality unfolds within given cultural contexts and their specific background knowledge, the constitutive structures of culture are themselves subject to the action and interactions of social agents. In order to understand the circular interrelations of structure and agency, Pierre Bourdieu linked his concept of the habitus closely to that of the social field. Based on the generative dispositions of the habitus, individual and collective actors follow subjective strategies of action that are adapted to the general conditions given by specific social fields. These fields demarcate social spaces as dynamic arenas of struggles for power and positions. While the social habitus of an actor provides the necessary background in terms of knowledge and practices, various forms of "capital"—social, economic, cultural—serve them as mutually convertible resources on which their respective power positions in the field rest (cf. Bourdieu 1986b, 1–6).[38] Social action takes place in these fields and is established "through the practical strategies of agents endowed with different habiti and quantities of specific capital" (Bourdieu 2000, 151).

The global public sphere consists of a multiplicity of fields, and actors move between fields applying varying strategies of action, using and appropriating different forms and quantities of capital. In this process, the applied background knowledge of individual actors resembles a patchwork of social habiti, providing them a certain flexibility to act according to specific fields and circumstances. In analyzing Ignaz Goldziher's studies on Islam, for instance, we have to take into account that his personal horizon comprised elements of different habiti associated with his positions as an internationally celebrated scholar of Islam, a member of Hungarian Judaism, a Hungarian nationalist, and a European intellectual. In a similar way, Muhammad Abduh, one of the major Arab representatives of Islamic reform, belonged to the field of the religious learned at the Azhar, acted as an Arab intellectual in the fields of Western scholarship, and in the political field he opposed as a convinced Egyptian nationalist both the Egyptian government and the European imperialist powers. Goldziher and Abduh contributed to shaping the modern image of Islam by acting according to the logics of several social fields. In these fields they maintained very different positions, depending on the respective particular power resources at their disposal. Contrary to the international status he received as a highly respected and leading scholar in

---

38. These forms of capital are accumulated power resources which in principle are mutually convertible. The various forms of capital can be derived from economic capital, but this conversion leads to transformation costs. Social capital is based on the aggregated resources which one derives from social networks and relationships of mutual acquaintance and recognition. Cultural capital exists in three forms: Firstly, in the embodied form of long-lasting dispositions of the social habitus; secondly, objectified in cultural artefacts and media such as writings, paintings, monuments, etc.; thirdly, in the institutionalized form of, for instance, academically acquired certificates (Bourdieu 1986b).

Islamic studies, in Hungarian academia Ignaz Goldziher was struggling against discrimination and marginalization because of his Jewishness. In the field of Islamic reform, Muhammad Abduh held a very strong position among Muslim intellectuals due to his double cultural capital based on both knowledge of modern sciences and Islamic traditions. However, being a representative of the colonized world, his position was far weaker in his interaction with European scholars and politicians. Toward the end of his life also his stance as a religious reformer in Egypt increasingly became precarious under the pressure by traditionalist and secularist forces.

These examples show that the formation of social imaginaries and social habiti is molded by power relations making the fusion of cultural horizons a process that by no means is based on equality. At the same time, we can discern the impact of power in its different forms between the poles of power as a social relationship and as a structural force. The former is based on the different access of social actors to relevant resources (cf. Poggi 2001), whereas the latter relates to an always-present web of inherent social controls exerted by a net-like anonymous form of organization (Foucault 1980, 98). While all actors are subject to the abstract power of the *episteme* as a discursive formation, the construction of specific cultural programs which can be observed on my third analytical level is subject to the opportunities and constraints of various forms of social power. It is in this way that imperialism has left deep marks in the confusion of modernization with Westernization, in the direct and indirect pressure to adjust emerging modernities to the historically specific cultural programs of Europe. The global public sphere is the social site on which these formative struggles about identity, knowledge, and world view take place. As an analytical device, the following empirical chapters will apply my multi-leveled scheme of the global public sphere in understanding the construction of the essentialist image of Islam.

With my concept of the global public sphere I refer, on the one hand, to an emerging reality, an indispensable part of globalization. I demarcate a public arena whose communicative processes cut across the functional differentiation of modern society and reconstruct the social whole in historically changing forms of segmentation and stratification. On the other hand, I employ the global public sphere as an analytical tool, characterized by four abstract defined levels of observation. This analytical distinction allows us to think the simultaneity of processes of cultural homogenization and fragmentation, one of the core puzzles of the globalization debate, by associating them with different levels of analysis: homogenization with cognitive deep structures and fragmentation with the multiple semantics of diverse cultural programs. Moreover, conceptualizing the global public sphere in four distinct levels of observation makes it possible to combine macrosociological analyses with the microsociological perspective of individual actions and biographical accounts.

4

State, Science, Religion and Islam:
Modern Europe between Positivism and Christian Apology

"Specialists without spirit, sensualists without heart; this nullity imagines that it has attained a level of civilization never before achieved"

(Max Weber)

This verdict on modern culture Max Weber passed at the end of his essay *Asceticism and the Spirit of Capitalism* (1930, 124). It aptly expresses the actual value judgment that permeated Weber's "tragic sociology" (Breuer 2006). In addition, the pessimist tone of this quotation shows the traces which the philosophies of Arthur Schopenhauer (1788–1860) and Friedrich Nietzsche (1844–1900) have left in his work. Max Weber certainly was an outstanding scholar and sociological genius. However, we should read his essays also as an extraordinarily reflected though nevertheless typical account of some of the major political, social, and cultural themes that had captured the public spheres of late nineteenth-century Germany and Europe. Weber's sociology deals with the then still palpable rift that the advancement of capitalist society created with regard to Europe's past; a rift which dominated public debates and which the sociological classics rationalized with the help of the conceptual dichotomy between tradition and modernity.

It was this fundamental societal change that preoccupied not only Weber, but the vast majority of nineteenth century intellectuals, transcending all national boundaries. The aristocratic and religious institutions of old Europe were fighting their death struggle against the modern state, capitalist market economy and the scientific world view. Nineteenth-century thinkers articulated this struggle through different, sometimes even cross-cutting semantics that ranged from positivist embrace to traditionalist rejection, from apologetic accommodation to romanticist critique. And it was this intellectual context within which the disciplines of oriental and later Islamic studies evolved. A short excursion might help to elucidate the kaleidoscopic nature of Europe's rising public sphere and the ways in which the different European intellectual milieus were interconnected by discursive structures and social relations.

In November 1868, Hermann Brockhaus (1806–1877) invited the twenty-four-year-old Friedrich Nietzsche for dinner. Brockhaus, an eminent orientalist scholar and son of the founder of the German publishing house Brockhaus, was married to the sister of the celebrated musician Richard Wagner (1813–1883). Having heard about Nietzsche's intellectual qualities and, even more important, the coming philosopher's interest in his music, Wagner asked his brother-in-law to make him acquainted with the philology student Nietzsche. Nietzsche, who was the favored student of Professor Friedrich Ritschl (1806–1876), a close friend of the Brockhaus couple, was delighted with this invitation and met at Brockhaus' home a comforting and intellectually stimulating atmosphere. In the philosophy of Arthur Schopenhauer, in particular in his philosophy of music, the circle soon found a common topic for the evening which became the departure point for almost a decade of close friendship between Friedrich Nietzsche and Richard Wagner.[1]

What has this episode of the lives of Nietzsche and Wagner to do with my study on the modern image of Islam? The answer is twofold: First of all, Friedrich Nietzsche's philosophy represents one of the intellectual foils against which generations of scholars in Europe and beyond have reflected on the rise of modern times. In particular, romanticist streams and intellectuals with conservative leanings have drawn on the work of Nietzsche. Even more important here, the "Nietzsche syndrome" was very closely linked to the debate about religion and modernity. With his "fight against Christianity" and Christian religious ethics which he perceived as a "resentment morality of pity" and as a rejection of life, Nietzsche profoundly contributed to the intellectual identity crisis that had captured late nineteenth century Europe (Rittelmeyer 1920). His philosophical essays became not only core readings for Europe's cultivated bourgeoisie but also for scholars in the rising field of comparative religion. The work of the philosopher-turned-student of theology and philology was a central source of theoretical and methodological inspiration in the development of various academic disciplines dealing with religion, amongst which were also orientalist and Islamic studies (Krech 2002, 293–311). It is therefore not surprising that Max Weber's sociology of religion contains various elements of Nietzschian thinking, in particular questions regarding the human condition in modern times. Although hardly referring directly to Nietzsche, Weber took his assistance seriously for posing the "right questions," and his sociology reflects some of Nietzsche's central ideas (Hennis 1988, 154).

In his own work, Nietzsche drew on the empirical and theoretical findings of the philologists and theologians of his time and he was engaged in criticizing their attitudes to modernity. One amongst them was the radically critical Protestant theologian David Friedrich Strauss (1808–1874). Initially fascinated by Strauss' biblical criticism, Nietzsche later exposed Strauss' affirmative stance toward the

---

1. This dinner and the way it was arranged is documented in a letter which Nietzsche wrote to his friend Erwin Rohde (1845–1898), who studied together with Nietzsche under Ritschl and became a professor of classical philology in Kiel, Jena, Tübingen and Heidelberg (Nietzsche 1902, 83–92).

scientific and utilitarian modern world view to his biting criticism. While Strauss was on the path of a de-mystification and secularization of the Christian faith, Nietzsche, together with Wagner, rejected both modern disenchantment and the religious ethics of Christianity. Representing the romanticist and expressionist critique of modernity, they were calling for the re-mystification of the world through a sacralization of the arts (Safranski 2005, 108).[2] Thematically, Richard Wagner's operas are dominated by the nineteenth-century critique of religion and society, aiming at a non-Christian and aesthetic form of salvation from the illnesses of modern times (Bermbach 1997, 212).

In 1835/36, David Friedrich Strauss published the "scandalous" *Das Leben Jesu* (The Life of Jesus), a book in which he applied the critical method to the New Testament. This publication made Strauss the best-known German theologian in Europe, and he triggered a Europe-wide life-of-Jesus debate that lasted until the 1870s. In this context, orientalist scholars took up the biographical approach to the Christian religion and began to contrast the life of Jesus with the life of Muhammad (cf. Motzki 2000). Despite their different theological positions, the numerous theological critics of Strauss viewed his book as an attempt to destroy Christian faith with scientific criticism (Graf 1982, 82–83). Indeed, Strauss, who started his career as a student of the Tübingen School under Ferdinand Christian Baur (1792–1860), was one of those Protestant theologians who paved the way for the "de-Christianisation" of Europe. In his last book, published in 1872, Strauss answered the question of whether we are still Christians simply with a straight "No" (Jung 2000, 61).

Among European intellectuals with positivist leanings, however, Strauss' destruction of the Christian faith was received with great enthusiasm. A good example of this positive reception is provided by the Catholic French intellectual and orientalist Ernest Renan (1823–1892).[3] In 1863, Renan published his own biography of Jesus, *Vie de Jésus*, a paradoxical construct of a romantic novel about a human Christ reflected through the scientific lenses of historicism. Renan refers to Strauss' "excellent" book as one of the major inspirations for his own work (Renan 1863, 223). A decade later, Renan wrote the introduction to a French translation of a collection of David Friedrich Strauss' later essays.[4] In his *Anti-*

---

2. Raymond Schwab has shown in which way Schopenhauer, Nietzsche and Wagner have underpinned their critical attitudes to modernity with orientalist stereotypes (Schwab 1950, 447–470).

3. Strauss' book was translated to French in 1840 by the well-known positivist philosopher Émil Littré (1801–1881), a trained philologist and close friend of the "founding father" of positivism, Auguste Comte. The English translation of Strauss by the novelist George Eliott (Mary Ann Evans) appeared in 1856. Having enjoyed a thoroughly evangelical childhood, her writings were a "conscious expression of positivism" and the "emblem of a generation distracted between the intense need to believe and the difficulty of believing" (Cashdollar 1989, 225 and 236).

4. *Essais d'histoire réligieuse et mélanges litteraires*, translated by Charles Ritter (cf. Graf 1982, 20, fn. 33). Moreover, Renan was engaged in an exchange of letters with the German

christ, Nietzsche refers to both Strauss and Renan. There he articulates his regrets for the enthusiasm with which he once welcomed Strauss' biblical criticism and he ridicules Ernest Renan's biography of Jesus. In particular Renan's "absurd" attempt to portray the "Galilean peasant" as both a genius and a hero made the French scholar a "mountebank" in Nietzsche's eyes (Nietzsche 1902, 397–398). Nietzsche's arguments with critical theology and the way in which this discourse involved wider circles of European intellectual life is just one example to illustrate the way the philosophical work of Nietzsche marks a discursive nodal point for nineteenth-century reasoning about religion.

Secondly, the dinner at Brockhaus' relates to my study as an exemplary starting point to understand the social web which knitted together European intellectuals of the nineteenth century. Nietzsche's host, Hermann Brockhaus, was an eminent Sanskrit philologist and one of the teachers of Max Müller (1823–1900), the Indologist who held the first chair in comparative religious studies at Oxford University.[5] In 1825, Brockhaus began his studies of oriental languages, first Semitic languages then Sanskrit. Between 1828 and 1835, he worked together with leading orientalists in Copenhagen, Paris, London and Oxford before he was awarded his PhD from Leipzig University in 1838. At Leipzig he then received a chair in oriental languages. Together with Heinrich Leberecht Fleischer (1801–1888), Brockhaus founded, in October 1845, the *Deutsche Morgenländische Gesellschaft,* the German Oriental Studies Association, modeled on the example of the French *Societé asiatique.* France was also the country in which the Arabist Fleischer received a good part of his orientalist education under Silvestre de Sacy (1758–1838), the founding father of French orientalism and one of the main targets in Edward Said's book. In the spirit of de Sacy, Fleischer later made Leipzig the philological center of German orientalism. There, he was the teacher of two of the foundational figures of modern Islamic studies, the German Arabist Martin Hartmann and the Hungarian Ignaz Goldziher. Goldziher arrived in August 1868 in Leipzig, three months before the above-described dinner party took place, with a more or less finished doctoral thesis in his suitcase. In Leipzig he took lectures in Arabic, Persian and Turkish held by Fleischer and Sanskrit grammar by Brockhaus. Both Fleischer and Hermann Brockhaus were members of his doctoral committee (Simon 1986, 35–39).

While from Hermann Brockhaus the social and intellectual threads lead us directly into the fields of oriental studies, Nietzsche's academic patron and facilitator of the dinner with Wagner, Friedrich Ritschl, marks an interesting link to Protestant theology. He was the cousin of Albrecht Ritschl (1822–1889), probably the most important Protestant theologian in nineteenth century Germa-

---

religious critic about the Franco-Prussian war in 1870, which Strauss had questioned about him in an article in the newspaper *Augsburger Allgemeine* (Euchner 1996, 50).

5. After studying Sanskrit in Leipzig, Max Müller continued his Sanskrit studies under Franz Bopp in Berlin and Eugène Bournouf in Paris, both orientalist scholars who made a strong impact on the work of Ernest Renan.

ny.[6] Deeply influenced by the Tübingen School, the intellectual environment in which also David Friedrich Strauss developed his thoughts, Albrecht Ritschl became a professor in systematic theology and the New Testament first in Bonn, then in Göttingen. In April 1869, the Scottish Protestant theologian and later orientalist, William Robertson Smith, traveled to Göttingen. He was seeking new knowledge about the historical and comparative method of higher criticism, the type of critical biblical studies in which Protestant German scholars excelled throughout the nineteenth century and which also made a profound impact on Ernest Renan. Smith was deeply impressed by the lectures of Albrecht Ritschl and his time in Göttingen laid the foundation for a life-long relationship between the two scholars (Black and Chrystal 1912, 110–112). Throughout his life, Robertson Smith kept in close contact with German theologians and orientalists such as Ritschl, Fleischer, Wellhausen and Lagarde, and his biographers tell us of the deep impression that Nietzsche's last book *Ecce Homo* once made on him (Black and Chrystal 1912, 535). His later works, in particular his *Religion of the Semites,* became foundational texts for disciplines such as comparative religion, anthropology, sociology, or Islamic studies. Emile Durkheim's sociology of religion, as we will see, was strongly influenced by parts of Robertson Smith's work.

To sum up, departing from Nietzsche's dinner with Wagner we are able to progressively chart an intellectual landscape that suggests the rise of a public sphere gradually expanding into a global dimension.[7] Albert Hourani indicated in which way the European and the Muslim public spheres were already closely interconnected in the nineteenth century (Hourani 1962).[8] The dinner at Brockhaus' is a

---

6. To my knowledge, there is no reference to any direct linkage between Albrecht Ritschl and Nietzsche, but one can assume that Nietzsche knew him and his theology well. Albrecht Ritschl was from 1852–1864 a professor in Bonn, where Nietzsche took up his studies in philology and protestant theology in the fall of 1864. At that time, the University of Bonn was fragmented by a quarrel among its professors, in which Friedrich Ritschl played a prominent role. Friedrich Ritschl, a classical philologist, left the University of Bonn for Leipzig, a move that his student Friedrich Nietzsche followed. Albrecht Ritschl had also not been on good terms with his cousin Friedrich for a couple of years before Albrecht Ritschl's move from Bonn to Göttingen in 1864 (Ritschl 1896, 13–15). Yet, as a student in Bonn, Albrecht Ritschl was in close contact with the family of his cousin, with whom he had a relationship characterized by deep friendship and affection (Ritschl 1892, 39).

7. In the nineteenth century, the gravity center of the global public sphere was in Europe, clearly reflecting the asymmetric center-periphery structures of the international system of imperialism. This also applies to the density of its exchanges, which decreased on leaving its European core. Yet, as the examples of the World's Fairs or the relationships of Muslim intellectuals with Europe show, a more global public sphere was observably in the making.

8. The coming chapters will more closely look at the ways in which this network of social interaction and intellectual interconnection went beyond Europe's borders and, directly and indirectly, integrated leading thinkers of the Islamic reform movement into one discursive context. Some of the better-known direct links within this global

good starting point for gaining an idea of the ways in which the rising global public sphere has been characterized by overlapping and interlacing social fields. In this context a network of scholars and public intellectuals generated some of the major ideas on religion and modernity in the nineteenth century. They represented various academic disciplines dealing with religious phenomena transcending national or disciplinary boundaries, combining a variety of positivist, apologetic and romanticist semantics. Most strikingly, this discursive weave of more-or-less scientific reasoning about religion also had a visible micro-sociological face. We can reconstruct a multiplicity of direct and indirect linkages between the young Nietzsche and his dinner partners, the four protagonists of this chapter—Renan, Smith, Durkheim and Weber—as well as some of the founding fathers of Islamic studies and leading figures of the Islamic reform movement.

Guided by my four analytical levels of the public sphere, this chapter will analyze the intellectual, social and political environment in which European scholars shaped the modern images of religion and Islam. Within this, the increasing functional differentiation of society represents the historical *a priori* on which these modern constructions rest. This formative deep structure is reflected on the second level of analysis in the general themes that characterized public debates and the scholarly works of the four personalities which will be examined here. Their basic ideas about state, science, and religion have spread in global society at large, providing a good part of the discursive formation on which later generations have comprehended the modern world. In this chapter, the most relevant of these general themes revolve around a cluster of four questions: the conceptual nature of modern religion; the ways in which different religions relate to each other, especially the three monotheistic religions Christianity, Islam and Judaism; the relationship between the modern sciences and revealed knowledge; and the evolution of religious systems from a historicist perspective.

It is my contention that the multiplicity of different answers to these questions is closely linked to some of the core thoughts of liberal Protestant theology. More precisely, I claim that the sociological, philosophical and orientalist discourses on religion were strongly inspired by the theological debates to which the controversial views of the Tübingen School of biblical criticism and the reception of David Friedrich Strauss' biography of Jesus had led.[9] Elements of this local Protestant revision of Christianity contributed to the construction of a universalized concept of modern religion. Since then, this concept of modern religion has more generally informed the global debate on religion and society. At the same time

---

public sphere, for instance, are the personal encounters and written exchanges Jamal al-Din al-Afghani had in Paris and Cairo with Ernest Renan and Ignaz Goldziher.

9. The younger Tübingen School refers to students of Ferdinand Christian Baur, as well as scholars inspired by Baur, who taught from 1826 Protestant theology at Tübingen University. Rather isolated by his colleagues, Baur focused on the historical reconstruction of early Christianity and applied the critical method to the New Testament. After the publication of Strauss' Life of Jesus, Baur distanced himself from his disciple, whose biblical criticism he viewed as too radical (Köpf 2002).

local cultures appropriated this concept, also particularizing it in taking it as a reference in the revision of their own traditions. In Roland Robertson's words, in the rise of the modern concept of religion, we can observe the universalization of the particular and the particularization of the universal. It is not so much biblical criticism as a method, as the Said controversy suggests, but its conceptual and philosophical impact on modern world views that has strongly conditioned the reinterpretation of religion in general and Islam in particular. For my own study, I have chosen Renan, Durkheim, Robertson Smith and Weber as paradigmatic individuals in this universalization process. Analyzing their lives and works gives an insight into which ways modern knowledge has been shaped and disseminated.

I will begin my inquiry with a more detailed analysis of the life and work of Ernest Renan. I did not select him because of his contributions to the field of Islamic studies, as they barely survived the turn of the centuries. Renan is relevant for the eminent role which his vociferous view on religion and Islam played in the European public debate. Eclectically combining semantics of positivism, Catholicism, biblical criticism and evolutionary philosophies, Ernest Renan is important as both a crossroads of various nineteenth-century ideas and a popularizer of them. From Renan we will move to Emile Durkheim by contextualizing Renan's thoughts in light of the power structures and cultural programs of nineteenth-century France. This second section provides us with the structural coordinates in which we have to interpret Renan's and Durkheim's works. The section on Emile Durkheim, then, will give us an insight into the emergence of major assumptions in the sociology of religion. In more trivial forms, these assumptions will reoccur in the ideas of the founding figures of Islamic studies we look at in chapter five.

The analysis of the life and work of Robertson Smith which then follows marks a crucial linkage between Protestant theology, oriental studies and the social sciences, as well as between Emile Durkheim and Max Weber. Although these two outstanding sociologists never referred to one another's writings, their lives and works largely overlapped, and particularly their concern for the sociology of religion was a major area of scholarly congruence between them. Section four, then, takes a glance at liberal Protestant theology in Germany, which was not only important for the works of Renan, Durkheim, Smith and Weber, but gave essential impulses for the construction of modern religious programs in general. The nineteenth century saw an enormous traffic of religious ideas among European countries and the USA, in which German universities played a central role. The construction of modern concepts of religion and of the modern image of Islam happened in close reference to the theological elaborations of Protestant thinkers; and it was first of all in Germany where this theological revision of Christianity took place. The chapter concludes by returning to sociology and an analysis of some basic concepts of Max Weber's sociology of religion and his analysis of Islam.

Focusing on these four paradigmatic figures, this chapter observes the intellectual environment of the late nineteenth century at all the four levels of analysis which I have associated with my analytical framework of a global public sphere. The following pages will discuss the general conceptual foundations and the central themes in whose context the semantics of orientalists and Islamic reformers evolved. The chapter will show how the general problematic of religion and modernity was translated into specific national, religious, ideological and scholarly semantics, generating modern knowledge on religion and Islam. In doing this, I try to make transparent the various interconnections between these semantics and the paradigmatic intellectuals related to them. In other words, this chapter substantiates my contention that the modern image of Islam emerged in an environment of increasing cultural interaction that we can conceptualize as the rise of a global public sphere. This public sphere has been grounded in a converging cognitive deep structure of modernity, generating specific problems regarding religion and negotiating them in different but mutually understandable semantics.

Ernest Renan: Orientalism, Romantic Positivism and the "Semitic Mind"

Edward Said declared Ernest Renan's *Système comparé et histoire générale des langues semitiques* to be the chief instance of the orientalist scientific project (Said 1978, 88).[10] According to the argumentation in *Orientalism*, Renan played a foundational role in the field of oriental studies, solidifying orientalist discourse through the scientific authority of the philological method. In Said's understanding, Renan was the systemizer in the orientalist project (1978, 130) who not only invented the idea of the Semitic, but was instrumental in giving the oriental subject matter its scholarly coherence (1978, 140). This prime role of Renan in Said's book sharply contrasts with his factual position in the intellectual history of nineteenth century Europe. To be sure, Renan was an orientalist, but at the same time he was a historian, a philologist, a philosopher, a novelist, a poet, an autobiographer and a moralist (Peyre 1969, 22; Lee 1996, 19). One of his biographers even called him a "mixture of prophet, visionary, reformer and spiritual leader" (Wardman 1964, 212). In writing on religion, history, philosophy, and modern life, as well as the social and political problems of France and Europe, Renan was able to win the largest audience among educated Europeans of a living French author in the second part of the nineteenth century (Robertson 1924, 1 and 29).

Reducing Ernest Renan to the ideal type of an orientalist is therefore a grave misjudgment of his intellectual role. In Renan's work, orientalist studies in Edward Said's sense are comparatively marginal. He wrote his doctoral thesis on Ibn Rushd (Averroes) under the supervision of the French philosopher Victor Cousin (1792–1867), an educational reformer and famous scholar in European philosophy, yet with no erudition in oriental studies (Renan 1866, x). Apparent-

---

10. Ironically, it was precisely this book by Renan that Ignaz Goldziher refuted in his early book on Hebrew myths (Goldziher 1876). Yet it was Goldziher who did the foundational work for the discipline of Islamic studies whose "orientalist" representatives Said puts in line with Renan.

ly, Renan's dissertation did not make a very strong impact on the scholarly specialists among his orientalist contemporaries (Irwin 2006, 167).[11] This applies to a certain extent also to his studies on Semitic languages, in particular his *a priori* thesis on the Semitic mind. In this thesis Renan repeated the so-called Indo-European hypothesis which became very fashionable in eighteenth and nineteenth century Europe. This hypothesis bestowed the polytheistic culture of Indo-Europeans with a progressing character, whilst declaring the monotheistic Semites to be immobile in time and space, hardly able to contribute to universal historical progress (Olender 1992, 12). What Said designated as the chief instance of orientalism was actually nothing more than a popular truism in nineteenth century thinking that had even seized the world views of some Muslim intellectuals.[12]

In its rather crude version, very few specialists in the field endorsed Renan's thesis about the non-mythological and stagnant "Semitic mind." Many of the leading scholars in mythology, religious studies and Hebrew strongly criticized Renan's thesis: Abraham Kuenen (Leiden), Ignaz Goldziher (Budapest), Heinrich Ewald (Göttingen), William Robertson Smith (Cambridge), and Max Müller (Oxford) were only the most prominent of these critics (Robertson 1924, 33). In reviewing Renan's *Histoire du peuple d'Israël* in 1887, the Protestant theologian and orientalist Robertson Smith rejected Renan's hypothesis of natural monotheism as a "relic of unhistorical deism" that "grafted on a strict Roman Catholic education." Instead of being a scholarly work, Renan's analysis of the Old Testament was in Smith's evaluation a mere product of the imagination in which the author "bends facts to suit his hypothesis" (Robertson Smith 1887, 613).[13] Renan's more lasting scholarly contributions to the orientalist disciplines might be found in epigraphy and archeology, in particular in his compilations of Phoenician inscriptions that he collected on his archaeological mission to Lebanon and Palestine in 1860–1861. Later, through Renan's initiative, they found their way into the *Corpus Inscriptionum Semiticarum* (Dussaud 1951, 9).[14] The grand academic project of his life, however, was the seven volumes of his *History of the Origin of Christianity*, for which his philological knowledge provided the most important means (Peyre 1969, 14).

If Said's portrait of Renan as a leading orientalist is essentially biased, pre-

---

11. In a letter to Theodor Nöldeke on 9 November 1911, Ignaz Goldziher, for instance, described Renan's book on Averroes as a study completely devoid of details, remaining in the general (Simon 1986, 354).

12. We will later discuss in which way the Indo-European thesis also became a theoretical axiom among intellectuals of the Islamic reform movement, in particular in Muhammad Abduh's defense of Islam (cf. Haddad 2005).

13. It should be mentioned that Edward Said himself refers to this article as a "savage attack" on Renan (Said 1978, 235).

14. The Académie des inscriptions et belles lettres decided in April 1867 to publish the *Corpus* on the initiative of Ernest Renan, who worked toward re-launching the project after his return from the Levant in 1861 and perceived it as his most beloved achievement (Lozachmeur 2007).

senting him as a scholar systematizing orientalist thinking and giving it disciplinary coherence is utterly flawed. There is an overwhelming consensus in the literature on Renan that the man and his work present us with a "tissue of contradictions" (Roman 1992, 6). His writings were described as pieces of "reflecting poetry" based on a bewildering blending of romanticism with positivism (Michaelis 1913, 9). Renan's thoughts were inspired by a plethora of different sources such as Scottish Moral Philosophy, Cousin's philosophical eclecticism, Franz Bopp's comparative grammar, German biblical criticism, Herder, Goethe, Fichte, Lamartine, Pascal, Michelet, Hegel, Comte and orientalists like Bournouf and Étienne Quatremère, whose "erudition in Orientalist studies" made a deep impression on the young Renan (Renan 1936, 211; cf. Blinkenberg 1923). In light of this patchwork of influences, Robertson's conclusion aptly describes the character of Renan's work: "No discipline could have made him a solidly systematic thinker" (Robertson 1924, 120). On the contrary, the lack of any system was the main characteristic in Renan's writings (Blinkenberg 1923, 83). Edward Said used elements of Ernest Renan's life and work for his construction of an ideal type of orientalist. This ideal type—immersed in texts, devoid of experiences with the real Orient and pre-occupied with a racist and male-chauvinist justification of Western colonial domination—has survived in its uncritical application through Said's epigones.[15] In this way, Said did disservice to his own cause, distracting us from a better understanding of the emergence of the stereotypical and essentialist image of Islam. A closer look at Ernest Renan's life and work will prove that he actually did play an important role in this process, yet in a quite different way than Said would have had us believe.

From Catholic Priesthood to Republican Intellectual: Life and Work of Ernest Renan

Ernest Renan was born at Tréguier, a village on the coast of Brittany, on February 28, 1823. His family was of a humble social background and his early childhood was strongly molded by the traditional Catholicism of Brittany. In this milieu, the talented boy seemed irrevocably dedicated to ecclesiastical life, making his way through the institutions of Catholic education where he impressed his teachers with an exceptional industry and achieved a number of school prizes. In 1838, his extraordinary talent helped him to acquire a scholarship from Abbé Dupanloup, who later became the Bishop of Orleans, and the fifteen-year-old Renan left Tréguier to study theology at the Catholic seminaries of Saint-Nicolas-du-Chardonnet, Izzy, and Saint-Sulpice in Paris. On his way to Catholic priesthood, Renan

---

15. A good example of this blind borrowing from Said is Wendy Shaw's references to Ernest Renan. In her otherwise interesting thesis on museums in the late Ottoman Empire, Shaw claims that orientalist scholarship developed "on absence" and refers to Renan as a typical representative of this kind of scholarship which "could do this without setting eyes on the regions they studied" (Shaw 2003, 64–65). Contrary to this claim, Renan not only traveled through Palestine and Lebanon for one year, but also traveled, together with his wife, to Egypt, Syria, Asia Minor and Istanbul from December 1864 to June 1865 (Wardman 1964, 94–96).

underwent a deep crisis of faith which eventually led him to leave Saint-Sulpice and the Catholic Church in 1845. He took up a teaching position at the "Pension Crouzet" and in April 1847 was awarded with the Volney prize for his essay on Semitic languages. In October 1849, he went to Italy on a government mission to classify historical manuscripts previously inaccessible to French scholars. Back in Paris (1850), he worked at the Department for Oriental Manuscripts of the Bibliothèque National and completed his doctoral thesis in philosophy in August 1852.

In 1856, only 32 years old, Renan became a member of the Académie des inscriptions et belles lettres. After his return from Lebanon and Palestine, he was appointed to the Chair of Hebrew, Chaldean and Syriac at the prestigious Collège de France. However, due to the uproar around his inaugural lecture in February 1862, Renan was suspended from his chair only four days later, and the forthcoming publication of his Vie de Jésus (1863) made his reinstatement impossible.[16] In June 1864, his chair appointment was finally cancelled by ministerial decree (Wardman 1964, 84). For the coming years, Renan was left to live by his pen before regaining his chair after the breakdown of the empire in November 1870. In 1878, he was elected to the Académie française, and in June 1883, he became appointed administrator of the Collège de France. Although he remained for most Catholic clerics a sort of "Antichrist"—in 1871 Pope Pius IX declared even him to be "the European blasphemer" (Robertson 1924, 81)—Renan enjoyed high prestige and influence in French and European intellectual life and was a celebrity in the eyes of the French public (Wardman 1964, 169). Ernest Renan died on October 2, 1892, at the age of 69, and he received a state funeral in Paris (Euchner 1996, 46–49; Lee 1996, 277–279; Robertson 1924, 1–39; Wardman 1964).

The literature on Renan unanimously points to the "religious crisis" of his youth when understanding his work on the individual level. Although eventually taking place at the seminar in Saint-Sulpice, the process leading to his crisis must have started a couple of years before, possibly when he studied at Izzy. While studying, his philological approach to the Bible became at odds with the Catholic dogmas about the Christian revelation (Lee 1996, 68). At Saint-Sulpice, these crossroads of scientific proof and revealed truth were epitomized in Renan's most popular teacher, Le Hir. Coming from Brittany like himself, Renan found in Le Hir his ideal of the combination of being both a scholar and a saint. The exact philological method of Le Hir and his knowledge about the biblical criticism of German Protestant theology filled Renan with total enthusiasm. It was the example of Le Hir that made Renan a convinced and critical philologist (Renan 1936, 210). Renan fully engaged in studying Hebrew, as this was the necessary key to a sound understanding of the Christian scriptures. In addition, he learnt German, the language of the most sophisticated critical exegesis of the

---

16. Renan's suspension was instigated by the Catholic establishment, which was scandalized by the following passage on Jesus Christ of his inaugural lecture: "a man so great that, although in this place everything ought to be judged from the standpoint of positive science, I should not wish to contradict those who, impressed by the unique character of his achievement, call him God" (quoted in Robertson 1924, 38).

Bible in his times. In this way, Renan achieved the scholarly means for analyzing the Bible thoroughly, coming to the conclusion that the Holy Scriptures resemble other antique texts in being full of contradictions, historical inaccuracies and factual mistakes. With the rise of this insight, Renan's belief in the doctrinal edifice of Catholicism and in the supernatural origin of the Christian revelation disappeared (1936, 218).

In sharp contrast to his adored teacher, Le Hir, who was able to combine scholarly work with deep belief in the dogmas of Catholic orthodox theology, Renan could not stand the conflict between the two truths. He was not able to live the contradiction of modern scholarly knowledge and orthodox belief in harmony. The incompatibility of scientific and revealed truth led in him to psychological crises (Renan 1936, 202). Rejecting the supernatural claims of Christianity, he felt to make a decision between modern scholarship and Catholicism. In leaving the priestly seminar and subsequently the Catholic Church in 1845, Renan embarked on his life-long mission of reconciling reason and faith, the latter without doctrines and belief in the supernatural. Based on his striking "capacity for cherishing religious sentiment alongside of intellectual disbelief" (Robertson 1924, 12), he developed a philosophy of history in which science came to play a divine role (Michaelis 1913, 101).

L'Avenir de la science (The Future of Science) is the manifesto of Renan's divination of science, penetrated by an air of optimism in the ordering and moral power of the scientific organization of humanity (Robertson 1924, 22–23). Written from autumn 1848 to spring 1849, as a full book it was not published before 1890. Due to its challenging character to all orthodoxies, Renan's friends Thierry and Burnouf counseled him against its publication. The publication of *L'Avenir de la science* more than forty years after it was written shows the inherent consistency of Renan's world view, besides all the contradictions and the rampant eclecticism that otherwise characterizes his work (cf. Michaelis 1913, 10). The preface to the 1890 publication is an explicit testimony to this continuity in Renan's thoughts. He presents the late publication of the book as a new confirmation of the fundamental ideas which had molded his thoughts since he left the priestly seminar in Saint-Sulpice. In its content, the book expresses what replaced the ruins of Catholicism in Renan's life, and he declares the progress of reason to be his religion (Renan 1890, II–III). However, by 1890 the optimism of his youth had waned. He had experienced progress in political and social affairs as weak and the destruction of his supernatural beliefs was followed by the erosion of the scientific idealism of his youth. Nevertheless, he maintained his belief in science as the only possible means to better the lot of humanity (1890, xix).

L'Avenir de la science was a deification of science in which from an evolutionary perspective the civilizational role of Christianity was replaced by the modern sciences (cf. Peyre 1969, 34–36). The reverse process, the secularization of Jesus Christ, was to a certain extent the inner logic of Renan's most successful book, *Vie de Jésus*. Published in 1863, it soon became the most popular biography of Christ ever written. Within six months, more than 66,000 copies had been printed, and by the end of 1864, the book had already been translated into a dozen languages (Baird 1992, 376). The publication of *Vie de Jésus* catapulted Renan from the more restricted world of scholarship far out into the public sphere of general readers in Europe. With fifteen editions in thirteen years, a number of popular reprints, and because of its poetic style, the book soon achieved the status of a classic in French literature (Robertson 1924, 40). Again, the scholarly reputation of this successful work remained weak. The Protestant milieu in Germany, basically the fertile ground for the production of a whole series of Jesus biographies, was not very impressed by this first "Catholic" version. For them, Renan substituted theology by a kind of poetry which despite its rejection of any form of supernaturalism nevertheless had traces of piety associated with Roman Catholicism (Nowak 1998). The academic deathblow to Renan's *Vie de Jésus* was dealt by Albert Schweitzer. In his seminal book on the history of life-of-Jesus research, Schweitzer called Renan's book a terrible example of "Christian arts," a tasteless piece of work without any methodological justification in the field of historical criticism (Schweitzer 1913, 180–192). Renan's popularity, however, was enormously enhanced by the book and the avalanche of protest-publications it had stirred. It is not Renan as a philologist and orientalist, but as the author of *Vie de Jésus* who resonated most in Europe's public spheres.

In the first chapter—"Place of Jesus in the History of the World"—Renan acquaints his reader with his scholarly *a priori*. Religion is presented as an anthropological constant differentiating humanity from all other living species. The Indo-European hypothesis is introduced, telling us that the Indo-European and the Semitic races have basically shaped humanity. In so doing, the glory of the Semitic race was "having made the religion of humanity" (Renan 1863, 29). However, according to Renan Judaism resembled nothing more than a confused mixture of clear views and dreams. Only in Jesus Christ these confused ideas "found at last their interpretation in the incomparable man, to who the universal conscience has decreed the title of Son of God" (1863, 35). Christianity developed in the Semitic environment of oriental cults, emerged from Judaism, but stripped away its Semitic bonds and immersed itself completely in the Indo-European milieu of the Greek and Roman Worlds (1863, 2). But according to Renan, it was only Jesus Christ, the absolute idealist, the greatest son of man ever borne (1863, 227), who could initiate this move. In severing his bonds with Judaism, he proclaimed the universal rights of man and founded the "religion of humanity, established, not upon blood, but upon the heart" (1863, 124).

For Renan, Jesus was "a ghost from the past but also a lost friend" (Lee 1996, 188). He designed the personality of Christ according to his own creed. Renan very closely identified with the historical Jesus, although his portrait of Christ is in fact "pure Romantic stereotype" (Pitt 2000, 93).[17] On the one hand, Jesus was the naïve peasant of Galilee, "a man of the people who had no idea of politics"

---

17. Following Pitt's interpretation, Renan paralleled his own idealized childhood in Brittany with Jesus' in Nazareth and Christ's departure from Judaism with his own separation from the Catholic Church (Pitt 2000, 89).

(Renan 1863, 83). Rooted in the "gentle and peaceable society" of Galilee, he lived in perfect harmony with a country which had not yet been affected by civilization in the Greek and worldly sense. His idea of the Kingdom of God reflected this terrestrial paradise (1863, 92). On the other hand, Jesus was an astonishing genius who dreamt of a great social revolution (1863, 84). He shrewdly concealed the true sources of his strength, his superiority over the people, and let them believe in the revealed character of his power in order to satisfy their ideas (1836, 97). Renan's Jesus was both a representative of romantic primitivism, of "the cult of the noble savage" (Manuel 1962, 10), and a man of reason who could spark the evolutionary progress of humanity toward modern rationalism. He was not the founder of a dogma and he did not aim at a "religious book containing a code and articles of faith" (1863, 157). In Renan's eyes the miracles of Jesus were "a violence done to him by his age," a concession forced from him by the dominant popular conceptions of his times (1863, 144). Being a stranger to all refinements of theology, Jesus was the founder of religion as the undogmatic pure spirit, making Christianity almost a synonym with religion: "In this sense we are Christians, even when we separate ourselves on almost all points from the Christian tradition which has preceded us" (1863, 221).

In his biography of Ernest Renan, Harold Wardman concludes that Renan created an alternative to Christianity in a "messianic religion of progress with himself as its God" (Wardman 1964, 212). In his proneness to self-conscious aestheticism, his romanticist, universal ideal of humanity becomes dissolved into its opposite, absolute individuality, into Renan himself (Blinkenberg 1923, 203). In viewing the revelation of God in the world, Renan was convinced of the necessity of bringing scientific and religious world views in harmony once again. In his idealism, Renan tried to reconcile positivist science and religious belief in a new synthesis of a religion of humanity (Ritter 1865), which, however, evolved out of Christianity and, in Renan's eyes, had Jesus Christ as its unchallenged foundational figure. Although Renan renounced the dogmas, institutions and rites of Catholicism, his apostasy remained incomplete, since he still "regard[ed] Christianity's foundation as the most important event in history and its founder as history's noblest product" (Lee 1996, 269). Renan combined a speculative philosophy of history, an evolutionary process of the unfolding of the human mind, with an understanding of Christianity as "pure religion." He purged the Christian revelation of miracles, superstitions and all kind of supernatural pretensions, choosing the course of radical Christian rationalism (cf. Olender 1992, 77). In this sense, he was an apologist of religion and of the absolute supremacy of Christianity in the history of the human mind (Nowak 1998, 76). It is from this perspective that we must understand his work as an orientalist and the way in which he portrayed Islam.

The Continuation of the Semitic Tradition: Renan on Islam

Typically for his generation, Renan found his way into orientalism from theology. Aiming at a philological exegesis of the Bible, he became a scholar of Semitic languages, excelling in Hebrew, however, according to his own judgment, remaining mediocre in Arabic throughout his life (1936, 210). His scholarly knowledge of Islam predominantly rested on two sources: The reading of contemporary secondary sources such as the Muhammad biography by the German orientalist Gustav Weil (1808–1889) or Caussin de Perceval's (1795–1871) History of the Arabs (Dussaud 1951, 197)[18] and the observations he made in Egypt and the Levant, in particular, the situation he experienced during 1860–1861 when he traveled under the protection of French troops in Lebanon and Palestine in the aftermath of the Druze rebellion. In addition, Renan's pejorative picture of Islam built on the well-known sample of inherited anti-Muslim stereotypes then prevalent in Europe. It was this combination of his general reputation as a scholar of religion, as a prime representative of French nineteenth-century literature and his authority of "having been there" rather than any kind of orientalist erudition which gave him enormous power in spreading the essentialist image of Islam in Europe.

In his scandalous inaugural lecture in February 1862, Renan already stressed the "deadliness of Islam to civilization" (Robertson 1924, 38). His world success, Vie de Jésus, disseminated this negative image further. Although this book contains only a few references to Islam, these are all of a strongly denigrating and stereotypical character. In his general fight against traditional religion, Renan declares the prophecy of Muhammad to be a result of epilepsy rather than divine revelation (Renan 1863, 143). In his eyes, Islam everywhere bears "something sordid and repulsive with it" (Renan 1863, 37). Contemplating the beauty of Galilee, Renan states that this "country [has] now become sad and gloomy through the ever-impoverishing influence of Islamism" (1863, 56). In a passing sentence, Renan points to the opposite role to Christianity which Islam has come to play in his theory of human history. While Jesus laid the foundations for the rationalist and sensualist break of Christianity with the Semitic mind, he interprets Islam as "a sort of resurrection of Judaism in its exclusively Semitic form" (1863, 121). Neither Jews nor Muslims have ever understood Jesus' "delightful theology of love" of "the God of humanity" (1863, 62). Furthermore, he sharply distances Galilee and its "energetic, brave, and laborious" people (1863, 56) from the theological and canonical culture of Jerusalem. According to Renan, Jerusalem was dominated by the religious fanaticism and pedantry of the Pharisees, following the "purely barbarous, un-mitigatedly absurd" science of the Jewish doctors, which was "denuded of all moral elements" (1863, 117). For Renan, the

---

18. Gustav Weil (1843): *Mohammed der Prophet, sein Leben und seine Lehre: aus handschriftlichen Quellen und dem Koran geschöpft und dargestellt* (Muhammad the Prophet, his Life and Teaching: based on and presented according to handwritten sources and the Koran), Stuttgart: Metzler. Gustav Weil was a Professor for Oriental Languages at the University of Heidelberg and best known for his translation of Thousand and One Nights. Armand Pierre Caussin de Perceval (1847-48): *Essai sur l'histoire des Arabes avant l'islamisme, pendant l'époque de Mahomet et jusqu'à la réduction de toutes les tribus sous la loi musulmane* (An Essay about the History of the Arabs before Islam, during the Epoch of Muhammad and until all the Tribes were subjected under Muslim Law), Paris. Caussin de Perceval was a Professor of modern Arabic at the Collège de France.

Pharisees were Jewish predecessors of the "empty science" that was later taught by the Muslim learned. From Renan's evolutionary historical perspective:

> The Jewish scribe, proud of the pretended knowledge which had cost him so much trouble, had the same contempt for Greek culture which the learned Mussulman of our time has for European civilization, and which the old Catholic theologian had for the knowledge of men of the world. (1863, 118)

In a nutshell, this citation contains the role of Islam in the edifice of Ernest Renan's evolutionary theory of history in which religion in its supernatural and transcendent form has remained a severe obstacle to the progress of human rationalism. From this general perspective, the differences between Catholicism, Judaism and Islam are only of a relative nature. Yet while with its founder Jesus Christ, Christianity bears the seeds for an escape from the "Semitic" confines of superstition and supernaturalism, Jews and Muslims remained prisoners of the religiously dominated Semitic mind. In introducing monotheism, the Jewish prophets at least did an undeniable favor to mankind (Renan 1883a, 205), laying the foundations for the establishment of the universal, "pure religion" by Jesus Christ (Renan 1863, 226). The establishment of Islam, however, led to a strengthening and continuation of the Semitic tradition by Muhammad, who himself, according to Renan, remained to a certain degree a Jew (1883a, 216). In Renan's philosophy of history, Judaism formed only a preliminary foundation for human civilization and Catholicism turned up a blind alley, an epiphenomenon of "real Christianity," whereas Islam represented the most direct religious threat to rational science and philosophy.

In his well-known lecture "Islamism and Science," Renan reiterated this world historical role of Islam as the religious counterpart to secular civilization and progress. Stressing the apparent inferiority of Muslim countries in his time, Renan began his lecture with a cascade of denigrating statements about Islam. Following his view, Muslims have "the most profound disdain for instruction, for science, for everything that constitutes the European spirit." Islam as a religion turns the believer into a "fanatic," into a believer foolishly proud of holding the absolute truth and completely incapable of acquiring new knowledge. Conversion to Islam eradicates all differences between people, producing the "intellectual nullity" and "decadence" observable in the countries governed by Islam (1883b, 85). The whole lecture is an attempt to prove the incompatibility of Islam with the modern world and to show the audience that the previous flourishing of science and philosophy under Muslim rule was not due to the Islamic religion but an achievement of other forces against it: "Do not let us honor it then for what it has been unable to suppress" (1883b, 98). In addressing a French audience predominantly concerned with the internal political struggles of the Third Republic, Islam turns into a synonym for orthodox religion and supernatural beliefs in general:

> Western theology has not persecuted less than that of Islamism; only it has not been successful, it has not crushed out the modern spirit, as Islamism has trodden out the spirit of the lands it has conquered. (1883b, 98)

We easily can translate the title of Renan's lecture "Islamism and Science" into "Religion and Science," taking Islam as the foil against which to discuss the harm that orthodox religion could do to science and human progress. To be sure, given Renan's socialization in the Catholic milieu of Brittany, as well as his apologist mission of reconciling positivist science with a kind of "secularized" and sensualist Christianity, he certainly was at ease in choosing Islam as his prime target. Nevertheless, his lecture on Islam and science must also been understood as a vocal petition to further curtail the worldly and ecclesiastical powers of the papacy in Rome, for a strict separation of state and church, and for the promotion and implementation of national state education, which finally took place in France under the Ferry Laws in 1905. This reading of Renan's work, abstracting from the literal meaning of its words, is based on the context of the political and cultural structures of nineteenth century France and Europe. Only within the context of this intermediate level of analysis can we come to a sound interpretation of Ernest Renan's often extremely puzzling thoughts.

Ernest Renan and the Struggle for a Secular Republic in France

There is no doubt that we can find many traces of orientalist stereotypes and racist, even anti-Semitic ideas in Renan's work.[19] Consequently, Renan might be read as giving a moral justification for the colonial domination of European states over the Muslim world. However, this reading of his work is out of context. Renan was socialized into an intellectual milieu dominated by the "Prophets of Paris," thinkers such as Turgot, Condorcet, Saint-Simon, Fourier and Auguste Comte. From their perspective, "Europe was the chosen continent, France the chosen people, and Paris the mount from which the new gospel had to be delivered" (Manuel 1962, 5). The widespread belief of European intellectuals in their civilizing mission was a deeply ingrained part of their social habitus. This feeling of European superiority was self-evident, hardly calling for any moral or political justification. Thus Said's portrait of Renan is not only extremely reductionist, but also based on the historical context and normative pretexts of the American university in the 1970s. The importance of Renan lies not in his oriental scholarship but in his prominent function as a public intellectual and in the eclectic and broad character of his work, making him "the complete mirror of his time" (Lee

---

19. Labeling Ernest Renan an anti-Semite is contested terrain. That his work contains anti-Semitic tendencies is without doubt; however, these are often contradicted by positive statements about the civilizational achievements of the Jews. Regarding his concept of race, at least the late Renan used it not in the static or even biological meaning which became widely disseminated in the late-nineteenth century, but as a historical and linguistic category (cf. Euchner 1996; Hoffman 1988; Renan 1882 and 1883a). Personally I would tend to support Shmuel Almog's conclusion that Renan was a "gifted popularizer" who "without being an out-and-out anti-Semite" or an "avowed racist", nevertheless "played a significant role in the creation of racial anti-Semitism" (Almog 1988, 273).

1996, 52). Ernest Renan was a man in transition in a century in transition. From the micro-sociological starting point of his life and work we can reconstruct the more general environment of power and knowledge in which the modern understanding of religion and Islam was shaped.

In analyzing Renan's dramas, published in the years 1878 to 1886, Paul Michaelis detected the most eminent topics of his time: "God—World—Science—State" (Michaelis 1913, 87). In the dress of antiquity, Renan articulated questions such as the relationship between science and religion, the existence of God, the role of the Church, moral questions about poverty, progress and education, and the political order of France and its relationship to Germany (Michaelis 1913, 123). Embedded in a philosophy of history as human progress (Gore 1970, 289), Renan's literary work dealt with the inner logic and the competition among the emerging functional subsystems of state, science, religion and education. Renan constantly raised the four questions which I mentioned in the introduction to this chapter: the modern role of religion, its historical evolution and relation to secular knowledge, as well as the relationship among religions. In so doing, his work was driven by the search for a holistic synthesis of the increasingly differentiating social reality epitomized in his confession to "systematic eclecticism." Renan finds himself in a position between the major intellectual streams of nineteenth-century France: Catholic traditionalism, modernist positivism, anti-modernist romanticism and a form of Christian apology which tried to reconcile modern and religious world views. While the transformation of society generated the major questions of his work, these different intellectual streams offered the essential semantics to answer them within the particular cultural context of France. In the contradictory image of Renan's personality and work we can detect different social imaginaries of his time, combined in Renan as an individual, however, biographically spread along his course of life.

From this theoretical perspective, the puzzling simultaneity of the scientist, believer, poet, romantic and moralist, as well as the changing political attitudes that have characterized Renan's life, become understandable. In principle, Renan's political conviction rested on his belief in the advantages of the enlightened governance of an educated elite. This conservative political aristocratism, however, was mediated by actual political events. Therefore, he could appear from time to time as a supporter of the empire, of a constitutional monarchy or of the republic (Gore 1970, 295). While the young Renan found himself among liberal intellectuals in the immediate aftermath of the revolutionary events of February 1848, he soon made his peace with the empire after 1852 (Peyre 1969, 12–13). Germany's defeat of France in 1871 and the subsequent German annexation of Alsace-Lorraine changed his opinion about the national state, moving from a dynastic and more organic conception of the nation to the "elective principle" of his famous *Qu'est-ce qu'une nation?* (Roman 1992, 16). In this lecture at the Sorbonne, Renan defined the nation as a spiritual unity which is based on forms of historically developed solidarity, rejecting nation-building by variables such as race, language, religion, common interests or geography (Renan 1882). Apparently, Renan came to accept the functional autonomy of the national state and reconciled his "Romantic individualism" with the fragmented reality of modern times (cf. Pitt 2000, 80).

On a more abstract level, Renan's work was deeply molded by the positivist world view that dominated the intellectual life of France during his lifetime. However, this kind of positivism should not be confused with the narrow technical meaning the concept has taken on in the twentieth century. Nineteenth century positivism was not a "value-free" scientific method. On the contrary, in the "myth of science," positivism was the expression of an inner-worldly faith in human welfare and progress in replacing traditional religion by rational science (LeGouis 1997, 28). It was an encompassing world view with a strong moral if not almost "religious" connotation. In fighting against theological world views, positivism spread throughout Europe and the Americas, also resonating among modernist Muslim intellectuals, in particular among the bureaucratic elite in the Ottoman Empire. The Ottoman reformer Ahmed Riza (1859–1930), for instance, resigned from his position as minister of education in 1889 and went to Paris. There, he stayed for six years, coming to the conviction that only education and science could save his country. Ahmed Riza returned to the Ottoman Empire as a convinced positivist and was a leading member of the Committee of Union and Progress, an important faction in overthrowing Sultan Abdülhamid in the so-called Young-Turk Revolution of 1908 (Berkes 1964, 306).[20] In the nineteenth century, positivism developed into a large variety of different forms, shaped by their respective social, cultural and political environments. The common denominator of these variants of positivism (1798–1857) was to replace irrational belief in religious revelation by a rational faith in modern science (Plé 1996, 447).

Taking its departure in the writings of Auguste Comte, the self-image of positivism emerged for the first time in France and focused on science as an entirely new model of comprehending the world (Plé 1996, 111). The main theme of this positivist self-image, its belief in human progress and material betterment, attained widespread acceptance in France and abroad during the second half of the nineteenth century (LeGouis 1997, 15). Influenced by English utilitarianism, Pantheism and German romanticism, not even French positivism ever expressed a coherent or uniform stream of thought, but was a multi-faceted phenomenon. This explains the confusion regarding Renan's positivist leanings. On the one hand, his secularist apology of Christianity and his rejection of systematic thinking put him at a certain distance to mainstream positivists of his time. In L'Avenir de la science, Renan sharply distances himself from the "negative rationalism" expressed by Comte (1890, 65). Yet in contradiction to this explicit distancing of himself from Comte, L'Avenir deeply breaths the spirit of the positivist deification of science. Renan's rejection of metaphysics, his confidence in betterment through applied sciences and his belief in a new synthetic age based on scientific

---

20. I will elaborate more on the ideological background of Ottoman modernism and how it paved the way to the Kemalist Turkish Republic in chapter six.

knowledge are inherent parts of the positivist gospel of his time. Moreover, his three periods of the evolutionary development of the human mind strongly resemble Comte's law of social evolution from the theological through the metaphysical to the positive stage of humanity (Blinkenberg 1923, 188–190).

Related to Auguste Comte's ideas, the semantics of positivism were an essential part of the nineteenth century public sphere. Positivism was "discussed and argued about in scholarly quarterlies, on the popular lecture circuit, from college lecterns, and from church pulpits" (Cashdollar 1989, 6). Given his struggle against Catholicism, Renan was most commonly seen in close connection to Comte among his readers in the Anglo-Saxon world (1989, 199). Without being a positivist in the Comtean sense, Renan probably did more to spread Comte's ideas than any of his true followers (Michaelis 1913, 141). The actually pantheist character of his concept of science as self-realization of the divine in the world disappeared behind the broader confrontation between positivist and Christian world views (cf. Pitt 2000, 81). And so did the romanticist traits of his ideas which were related to his readings of German literature, especially his encounter with Goethe and Herder while studying Catholic theology in Saint-Sulpice (Renan 1870, 21). Both Pantheism and romanticism of a rather Protestant origin had seemingly penetrated Renan's thoughts.[21]

The positivist program of science and rationality was countered by religious traditionalism and the semantics of Christian apology. In order to defend Christianity against the scientific and political assaults of positivist and liberal ideologues, as well as materialist and pantheist philosophies of history, nineteenth century theologians developed a broad range of apologetic literature. In this process, Christian apology moved between the extremes of traditional and fundamentalist rejection to attempts at full reconciliation of Christian beliefs with modern science (cf. Zöckler 1907). While ideological opponents, positivists and Christian apologists nevertheless shared a similar concern. Behind the public confrontation between these two mutually hostile semantics was a deeply felt anxiety about the uncertainties which were created by the modern social transformation. Deeply sensing modern contingency, positivists and Christian apologists were desperately searching for a comforting scheme for certainty and social order (LeGouis 1997, 231).

In France, positivism produced a rich diversity of thought in which ideas of progress, in particular scientific progress, became the "guiding spiritual force." As the work of Renan aptly shows, this belief in progress came close to a metaphysical deification of history and to the deterministic opinion that the laws of historical progress can be discovered by the methods of modern science.

---

21. Ernest Renan's romanticism closely resembles what had been called "liberal romanticism": "The religion of the liberal romanticist is a Protestantism which has broken down into a quasi-pantheistic kind of deism. His sense of divine immanence has almost wholly submerged his sense of divine transcendence, and he likes to think of God, man, and nature as interfused in one great cosmic harmony. He believes in natural goodness, the moral sense, the inner light, the powers of genius" (Fairchild 1941, 337).

Although some Christians concurred in several of these ideas, mainstream Catholics rejected this notion of progress outright. For them, history did not reveal evolutionary laws of progress, but the laws of God and the path toward salvation. While in Protestant environments such as England and Germany various compromise philosophies emerged, the Catholic Church increasingly became intransigent in terms of doctrine and world view. The doctrinal resistance of Catholicism culminated in the declaration of the infallibility of the Pope (1870) and the famous Syllabi of Pius IX (1864) and of his successor Pius X (1907). In these two Syllabi they condemned modern religious errors such as pantheism, absolute rationalism, socialism or liberal protestantism, as well as the institutional separation of state and church. In France, this Catholic "intolerance" was matched by a strong anti-clerical stance and a similar ideological intransigence on the side of positivist thinkers. The life and work of Ernest Renan is the perfect example of an individual caught between these increasingly incompatible semantics about modernity (cf. Charlton 1963).

However, this discourse on modernity with the help of a variety of different semantics was not only an intellectual enterprise. The knowledge of history, state, education, science, religion and Islam that intellectuals like Ernest Renan produced evolved within historically concrete power relations. Within this, the colonial situation was only one dimension of the crucial linkage between power and knowledge. To be sure, the political, economic and cultural hegemony of Europe strongly impacted the communicative structures of the global public sphere. In order to participate in its debates, non-European intellectuals had to conform to a high degree to the discursive patterns that had been established by Europeans. Otherwise, their voices would not have been heard. Yet the structural power of this discursive formation did not exclude the construction of non-European semantics and cultural programs. On the contrary, like European intellectuals non-Europeans developed their own semantics to grasp and debate the modern condition related to different historical trajectories, popular narratives and religious traditions. In this sense, the French experience was also of a very particular nature and conditioned by various sets of international, European and national power relations.

From a theoretical point of view, Renan and the different intellectual milieus in which he acted were constrained by the emerging macro-structures of modern society. Two essential social transformations related to Norbert Elias' category of elementary social functions must be highlighted in this context. On the one hand, we can observe a rapid differentiation of the elementary function of orientation. The all-encompassing institutional, moral and cognitive unity of European Christendom eventually gave way to a plurality of world views and moralities, both secular and religious, creating both competition and uncertainty among their social representatives.[22] Moreover, the clergy, previously holding a quasi-monopoly over the means of orientation, was severely challenged by

---

22. McLeod convincingly differentiates Christianity from Christendom. The latter he defines as "a society where there were close ties between the leaders of the church and those in positions of secular power, where the laws purported to be based on Christian

scientists, lawyers, school-teachers, university professors, secular intellectuals and lay advocates of religion who defined their own roles with direct referene to the internal logics of new societal subsystems such as science, law and education. In this complex societal process, the Christian religion was not only relegated to a sub-system of society, but also confronted with increasing internal fragmentation. Through new interpretations of its traditions and a general tendency to move from organized religion to privatized forms of Christianity, religious pluralism became not only a character of its environment but of Christianity itself. The question of Christian identity across its confessional demarcation lines was raised again. In the construction of Christianity as a modern religious program, we can observe a gradual move of the center of belief from the Holy Bible to the exemplary individuality of Christ himself (Schröder 1996, 1–10). The proliferation of life of Jesus publications in the nineteenth century is just one instance of this doctrinal development.

On the other hand, the elementary function of the control of physical force attained its modern form in the territorial national state based on the rule of law and representative institutions. Since the French Revolution in 1789, political life in France was mainly structured by the transformation of absolutist state power into a representative setting of constitutionally defined governance. Between the French Revolution and the death of Ernest Renan in 1892, France experienced eight political regimes – three monarchies, two empires and three republics—based on fourteen different constitutions (Müller 1999, 153). The country was torn apart by conflicting political factions, went through a severe famine during the Franco-Prussian War and was shocked by the internal violence around the bloody suppression of the Paris Commune in 1871, which left more than 30,000 people dead (Bloch 1972, 36). In the Third Republic of France (1870–1940), the government changed on average every eight months and the only stabilizing factor in French politics during the second half of Renan's life was the bureaucracy (1972, 48). This bureaucracy, together with the urban bourgeoisie, was also the stronghold of various forms of positivist ideology against which stood a coalition of royalists, aristocrats and the Catholic Church. In the early Third Republic of France, "the conflict between republicans and conservatives was largely an ideological one over the place of the Church in French society" (Jones 1999, 21). In this historical setting, the erosion of Rome's political power went along with the strengthening of the theological and doctrinal position of the Pope, leading to the declaration of the infallibility of the Pope as the ultimate and only center of authority in the Catholic Church (Schatz 1990 and 1992). Thus, the affiliation with positivism or Christian apology was as much political positioning as an intellectual choice.

This brief, theoretically guided sketch of nineteenth century developments in France indicates the myopic nature of Edward Said's view on the nexus between power and knowledge under which oriental studies evolved. To be sure,

---

principles, and where, apart from certain clearly defined outsider communities, every member of the society was assumed to be a Christian" (2003, 1).

the colonial expansion was part and parcel of this nexus, but it did not entirely capture the political mindset of European intellectuals. On the contrary, Renan's imaging of religion and Islam was intimately linked to the struggle between modern science, the intransigent position of the Catholic Church, and the impact Catholic officials had on French public policy, especially on education, and his own career. Most probably, it was the intransigence of Catholic orthodoxy in fighting historical and philological criticism which spurred Renan to become an apostate who nevertheless tried to salvage religion against the encroachment of modern disbelief. At the same time, he defined religion as inner-worldly in contradistinction to the modern Christian program based on transcendence. Pure religion, in Renan's sense, was free of traditions, orthodox teachings, supernatural claims and superstitious rituals. He considered all orthodoxies as enemies to this religion of humanity, and in Renan's eyes Islam with its continuation of the "Semitic mind" only was the purest representative of orthodox religion.

As mentioned before, Ernest Renan was not a systematic thinker and his scholarly achievements were not to last for very long. Instead, he played an eminent role in disseminating and popularizing concepts and ideas related to Europe's nineteenth-century encounter with modern society. Public intellectuals like him were instrumental in shaping new social imaginaries, in embedding modernity's general themes into the historically particular narratives of everyday life and, in so doing, in shaping forms of public understanding with respect to the otherwise incomprehensible nature of the abstract reality of a functionally integrated modernity. In abstracting from this public generation of knowledge, it was the task of sociology to elaborate the new cognitive conceptual apparatus for the apprehension of modern life. Nineteenth-century sociologists constructed the "scientific foundations" from which later public debates about themes such as secularism or religious differences could unfold. To a large extent, they laid the cognitive foundation, the conceptual toolkit, from which our general themes about religion have emerged and to which the rising semantics of multiple modernities refer. Within the French context, Emile Durkheim represents one of the leading early sociologists whose work shaped many twentieth-century debates on modernity and religion in Europe and beyond.[23] It is to him we turn now.

Emile Durkheim: Anomie, Solidarity and Secular Education

Some of the central doctrines and concepts of Emile Durkheim's sociology entered the canon of given knowledge of the social sciences.[24] Even more important as a body of knowledge on modern society it also has trickled down to society at large, representing a popularized form of academic knowledge whose

---

23. In chapter six we will meet Durkheim again with respect to Ottoman and Egyptian intellectuals who drew on his concepts or even studied under him.

24. Durkheim's work impacted on the social sciences far beyond the disciplinary boundaries of sociology. He found a critical reception in so diverse disciplines such as linguistics, psychology, ethnography, anthropology and history (Müller 1999, 166–167).

origin is no longer to be traced back. With his positivist leanings, Durkheim has frequently been portrayed as the methodological antipode to the interpretative approach of Max Weber. While Weber's methodology assigned an active role to both observers and actors, Durkheim insisted on the passive role of the observer. In contrast to Weber, he separated meaningful action from the sociologist's subject matter, which he defined by the externality and coercive nature of social facts (Mitchell 1931, 115). In Durkheim's own words: "Sociological method as we practice it rests wholly on the basic principle that social facts must be studied as things, that is, as realities external to the individual" (Durkheim 2002, xxxvi). Durkheim advocated the use of measurable empirical data and expressed "his impatience with unfounded and unverified theories of his day" for which Renan's variant of the Indo-European hypothesis is a good example (cf. Smelser 1976, 41). Regarding the sociology of religion, the methodological difference between Weber and Durkheim translated into two traditions: the Weberian tradition, analyzing religion on the individual level of human agency, emphasizing it as a factor of motivation; and the Durkheimian, focusing on the macro-level of "total societies," viewing religion as a means of societal integration (Luhmann 1985, 5).

The methodological antagonism between Weber and Durkheim partly reflects the impact of the very different academic cultures in Germany and France. In Germany, French positivism was largely received as a threat to the holistic ideal of education as cultivation (*Bildung*) promoted by Germany's intellectual elite. They viewed the field of "learning as personal self-fulfillment through interpretive interaction with venerated texts" (Ringer 1992, 2). In contrast to advocates of German historicism and interpretative scholarship, the republican intellectuals in France adhered to some form of positivist outlook, and the strong German sense of historical decline—resonating in Weber's "specialists without spirit" —was almost absent amongst them (Ringer 1992, 249). However, in their empirical work, Weber and Durkheim resembled one another in various ways. Even more important, their sociological interest revolved around the same problems, similar to the cluster presented in the beginning of this chapter. They both were deeply concerned with the ambivalence of modern society. The sociologies of Durkheim and Weber developed in a general climate of deeply felt social crisis, and Durkheim's "social realism," defining the social as social facts, was as much a methodological position as a solution to this crisis and its particular French circumstances (Jones 1999, 9).

Born in 1858, Emile Durkheim was an intellectual representative of the establishment and consolidation of France's Third Republic. He experienced the struggles between monarchists and republicans, Catholic clericalism and anti-clerical movements, and rising industrial capitalism and collectivist ideologies (Hayward 1960, 129). His formative years saw the Franco-Prussian war, the subsequent annexation of his home region Alsace-Loraine by Germany and the bloody confrontation between the young republican state and the Paris Commune. The crisis-laden consolidation of republican rule accompanied Durkheim's academic career, and his political world view attained a profound consciousness of the disintegrative forces of modern life. The sociology of Durkheim is permeated by a deep sense of a "moral crisis," the anomic situation which modernity creates in dissolving traditional moral orders without simultaneously establishing a new form of solidarity (Harms 1981, 394–395). Flavored by the particularities of French political and intellectual life, Durkheim's sociology is therefore an original expression of the first crisis of modernity (Wagner 1994), setting his generation apart from the more optimistic world views of their intellectual predecessors such as Ernest Renan.

The theme of social dissolution, of egoism and anomie was pervasive in nineteenth-century French thought (Lukes 1985, 195), expressed through the cliché of solidarity. Solidarity referred to the idea of replacing post-revolutionary anarchy by a program of social reconstruction in which scientific knowledge should play a key role (Hayward 1960). Whereas sociology could deliver the scientific insights for this reconstruction, public education was expected to provide the institutional means for the establishment of a new moral order. In Durkheim's eyes, secular, rational public education was a major means of remedying the evils of contemporary society (Mitchell 1931, 121). The new form of solidarity was a liberal, secular, republican kind of civic morality that should be transmitted through the public education system (Lukes 1985, 77 and 111). Durkheim was an exponent of the sociological strand of France's solidarist tradition, which reached a certain "apotheosis" in his work (Hayward 1963, 205). He was not only a sociologist, but also a leading educationist of the Third Republic who was deeply involved in the secularization of French education (Debesse 1973).

Being a convinced rationalist, Durkheim did not like Ernest Renan. He had no sympathy for Renan's romantic celebration of science and progress as a surrogate theology and he disliked his aristocratic cult of the genius (Lukes 1985, 71). Nevertheless, we can detect a number of themes and theoretical ideas in Durkheim's work which to a large extent also occupied Renan's thoughts. First of all, Durkheim shared a general anxiety about the uncertainties of modern life and that the inevitable decline of traditional religion might lead to a moral void. He gave a sociological explanation for this tendency and pointed to the institutionalization of a new moral order based on individualism instead of the rigid collective orders of traditional communities. In a different form, Renan's idea of a "religion of humanity," in general deeply rooted in French thinking from Rousseau to Saint Simon and Comte, also resonated in Durkheim's thoughts, yet in a non-theological and more skeptical way. Secondly Durkheim shared with Renan a concept of history as progress toward a more self-conscious, rational and scientific world view. However, Durkheim conceptualized this philosophy of history as a process of socio-cultural evolution from primitive to more sophisticated forms of the social. He rejected the prophetic and self-evident notions of previous theories of progress without giving up his belief in the superiority of the modern scientific world view. Making "the social role and historical development of morality" his central theoretical interest (Lukes 1985, 227), the role of religion in social life became a crucial concern of Durkheim's work.

Sociologist and Educator: Life and Work of Emile Durkheim

Emil Durkheim was born on April 15, 1858 in Epinal, a mid-sized provincial town in the French Department of Alsace-Lorraine. Coming from a family with a religious background, his father being a Jewish Rabbi in the eighth generation, Durkheim's early education was also directed toward the rabbinate. However, his move from Epinal to Paris led to his break with Judaism. His education at the prestigious Lycée Louis le Grand and later at the École normale supérieur (ENS) marked decisive steps toward becoming a religious agnostic. Possibly under the influence of his co-students Henri Bergson (1859–1941), the later French philosopher, and Jean Jaurès (1859–1914), a leading republican and socialist politician in the Third Republic, Durkheim began to view traditional religion as a form of morality that "has to be substituted by a positive scientific moral" able to suit modern needs (Lukes 1985, 44). After entering the ENS in 1879, Durkheim's life and work was characterized by three interrelated goals. In scholarly terms, he pursued the analysis and theoretical explanation of modern society. With regard to education, Durkheim was a driving force behind the establishment of sociology as an independent academic discipline in France. Finally, he was preoccupied by the idea of developing a new kind of modern moral that could provide French society with a new cohesive form of solidarity (Müller 1999, 150–151).

Durkheim passed his last competitive examinations at the ENS in 1882, and he took up a number of teaching assignments at provincial state secondary schools (Peyre 2007). In 1885, he received a scholarship to visit Germany. Since the Franco-Prussian war, anxiety had risen about the superiority of German scientific education, which was conceived as a central element in causing the French defeat. Studying in Berlin and Leipzig, Durkheim was especially interested in the psychology of Wilhelm Wundt (1832–1920), who was quite fashionable in France at this point of time (Lukes 1985, 90). Moreover, he studied the organicist theories of Albert Schäffle (1831–1903), an economist who was involved in shaping parts of Bismarck's social welfare legislation in 1881–1882. Durkheim intensively followed the discussion around Germany's historical school of economics and the so-called *Kathedersozialisten* (socialists of the chair) who were searching for political solutions to the pressing social questions of the time. For Durkheim, these German economists were significant in their recognition of the ethical dimension of economic phenomena and their insistence on the historically contingent character of these ethics (Jones 1999, 194–195). This school also had a profound impact on the young Max Weber, who in the late 1880s began to engage himself in the *Verein für Sozialpolitik* (Association for Social Politics), an influential social lobby organization of academics close to the *Kathedersozialisten*. Apparently, the content of Durkheim's readings during these years—by authors such as Knies, Menger, Schmoller, Roscher—closely reflected the theories and methods which Max Weber discussed in his methodological writings. Again, the two eminent sociologists shared academic interests, which makes their "mutual unawareness" if not deliberate neglect of each other's works even more surprising (cf. Tiryakian

1966). Returning to France in 1886, Durkheim published two articles on his studies in Germany. Dealing with German higher education and the works of a variety of Germany's social scientists, these articles contributed to his appointment to a lectureship in education at the University of Bordeaux in 1887 (Jones 1999, 182–183; Müller 1999, 152).

In Bordeaux, Durkheim was soon promoted to a full professorship, now holding the first French chair in sociology. In 1896, he founded the *Année Sociologique*, a sociological journal that was published over twelve years and became a major forum for the "Durkheim school." Before receiving a call to the Sorbonne in 1902,[25] Durkheim wrote three of his four major books in Bordeaux. His dissertation *De la division du travail social* (The Division of Labour, 1893) laid out his general theory of social evolution and the analysis of the structural features of modern society. In 1896, *Les règles de la méthode sociologique* (The Sociological Method) followed. This book became the methodological foundation for the Durkheim school. Finally, he published *Le suicide* (Suicide, 1897), an empirical investigation into a social phenomenon that he linked to the problem of anomie in modern society. Here, Durkheim explained suicide as resulting from the coercive power of social forces (Peyre 2007), as "the individual antithesis of social solidarity" (Lukes 1985, 206). In 1912, now full professor at the Sorbonne, Durkheim published *Les formes élémentaires de la vie religieuse* (The Elementary Forms of Religious Life), which became the only book translated into English during his lifetime. The Elementary Forms is a key text for Durkheim's sociology of knowledge, his theory of morality and his sociology of religion. He explains the origins both of our fundamental cognitive concepts and of moral orders as being socially constructed. Religion is of a social nature and human categories of thought originate in collective ritual practices (Joas 1993, 269). In the following years, Durkheim continued to teach, write and engage in the reform of public education. Then, the First World War came to him as a shock. Suffering from ill health and under attack from nationalist circles, the death of his son, who was killed at the Balkan front in 1916, dealt him a final blow. Durkheim died in November 1917 (Peyre 2007).

For my own study, the general thesis of *De la division du travail social* and the conceptualization of religion in *Les formes élémentaires de la vie religieuse* are the most important parts of Durkheim's work. The Division of Labor represents the theoretical framework in which Durkheim's work is firmly grounded. Besides its particularly French connotations, for instance its focus on differentiation and individual integration, it reflects many of the general assumptions that characterized the thinking of classical sociologists. Durkheim developed a theory of social evolution from "mechanical" to "organic" societies. In light of the general theme of classical sociology, the conceptual dichotomy between tradition and modernity, and the specific French discourse on solidarity, Durkheim analyzed modernization as the gradual transformation from mechanical to organic forms of solidarity. At the same time, his underlying question was: "how is it possible

---

25. Durkheim became a full professor at the Sorbonne in 1906.

that the individual becomes more autonomous and at the same time more dependent on society" (Hayward 1960, 135).[26]

For Durkheim, modern society is generally characterized by the increase of social differentiation in all spheres of life. In an analogy to organisms, he defines modern society as an organic society composed of socially specialized institutions which together form a dynamic whole, yet a social whole which is more than its individual elements (Harms 1981, 396). Contrary to highly differentiated modern society, the social structures of mechanical societies are predominantly characterized by segmentation, only knowing a rudimentary degree of the division of labor. This difference of social structure is reflected in very different forms of social cohesion. Mechanical solidarity rests on the *conscience collective,* a rather rigid consensus of moral, religious and cognitive beliefs that provides conformity in social conduct. Organic solidarity, however, emerges from the moral validation of the division of labor in which the abstract individual becomes the central idea of a morality of cooperation (cf. Giddens 1972, 1–10).

Reflecting the social structures of organic society, this new form of solidarity is "rendering the individual sacred." In the modern moral order, the autonomy of the individual is of the highest moral value, "justifying individual freedom and rights" (Lukes 1985, 199). During the political crisis that was triggered by the Dreyfus affair Durkheim explained his theory of individualism in a short essay in the *Revue Bleue.* In 1894, Alfred Dreyfus (1859–1935), a French officer of Jewish descent, was sentenced to lifelong deportation for false charges of spying for Germany. Together with other republican intellectuals, Durkheim protested against the verdict, which supposedly had an anti-Semitic background. They called for a retrial and eventually Dreyfus was rehabilitated in 1906. In the course of the Dreyfus affair, the liberal values of the Third Republic came under sustained attack by the political right and a fierce debate about the rights of the individual and the nature of French patriotism emerged (Pickering 1984, 15). In attacking the public campaign in support of Dreyfus, Ferdinand Brunetière (1849–1906), a conservative Catholic intellectual and member of the Académie française, denounced the humanistic individualism of this group of republican intellectuals as "the great sickness of our times" (Lukes 1969, 169). In his essay, Durkheim responded to Brunetière's accusations. He distanced himself from the narrow utilitarianism of "Spencer and the economists" and linked his type of individualism to Kant and Rousseau. The essay stressed the supra-individual origin of this variety of individualism which in Durkheim's sociological explanation emerges from the functional division of labor in modern society itself. Organic solidar-

---

26. The German sociologist Georg Simmel in his *Sociology* (first published in 1908) also posed the question of the interrelation between individualization and the emergence of ever bigger and abstracter social forms. In particular, in chapter ten Simmel points to the relationship between the increasing division of labor and the formation of the modern individual, as well as the emergence of two kinds of individualism: "individualism of equality" (*Gleichheit*) and individualism of "difference" (*Ungleichheit*) (Simmel 1992, 814).

ity is grounded in the plurality of differentiated social functions, resembling a "unity in diversity" where individual gifts ought to meet the functional demands of modern society (Hayward 1960, 139). Based on the autonomy of reason and freedom of thought, individuals get their dignity from humanity in general. This kind of universal moral individualism, the "cult of man," is therefore a fully social phenomenon, reflecting society as an abstract moral order (see Lukes 1969, 171–182).

In historical terms, however, the increasing division of labor is not a linear move from mechanical to organic solidarity. In principle, Durkheim saw two reasons why the progressive weakening of the *conscience collective* has not been accompanied by the simultaneous establishment of a morality of cooperation. First, he pointed to "pathological" developments in the division of labor itself. In real society, individual gifts and societal demands often do not match. Durkheim interpreted the political conflicts, economic deprivation and social disorder he could observe as a consequence of this deviation of the historical conditions of organic society from its normal status. Preoccupied by the idea of social cohesion, Durkheim analyzed contemporary society through the dichotomy of normal versus pathological forms of the social, almost completely disregarding the role of social power relations (Lukes 1985, 131). Second, in Durkheim's eyes, organic society tended to neglect the emotional basis of moral orders. While mechanical societies experienced a regular vitalization of their moral orders through the effervescence of social gatherings, organic societies were confronted with a gradual de-vitalization of their moral fundaments, contributing to the proliferation of anomie and suicide (Shilling and Mellor 1998, 197).

The Representation of Society: Durkheim on Religion

At first glance, the persistent and burning importance of religion in Durkheim's work comes as a surprise (Pickering 1975, 3). Why does a convinced agnostic with a strong anti-clerical attitude constantly refer to religion? It was not only the Durkheim of *Les formes élémentaires,* but the young Durkheim for whom the social function of religion played an important role (cf. Wallwork 1985). In *De la division du travail social* Durkheim defined the role of religion through the theoretical lenses of both functional differentiation and socio-cultural evolution:

> ..., if there is one truth that history teaches us beyond doubt, it is that religion tends to embrace a smaller and smaller portion of social life. Originally, it pervades everything; everything social is religious; the two words are synonymous. Then, little by little, political, economic, scientific functions free themselves from the religious function, constitute themselves apart and take on a more and more acknowledged temporal character. God, who was at first present in all human relations, progressively withdraws from them; he abandons the world to men and their disputes. (...) This regression did not begin at some certain moment of history, but we can follow its phases since the origins of social evolution. It is, thus, linked to the fundamental conditions of the development of societies, and it shows that there is a decreasing number of collective beliefs and sentiments

which are both collective enough and strong enough to take on a religious character. (Durkheim 1964, 169–170)

In primitive communities, so the argument goes, religion and the social are
synonymous, whereas in modern organic societies religion becomes marginalized by the increasing differentiation of social functions into relatively autonomous realms such as state, economy, the arts, law and science. Religious experience represents the unconscious structures of social life from which our moral
and cognitive categories and our understanding of the world emerge. Therefore,
the analysis of "primitive religion" holds the key for our understanding of the
evolution of modern society and its secularized form of integration through organic solidarity (Müller 1999, 162–165). These theoretical assumptions provided
the fundament for Durkheim's sociology of religion and his study of the elementary forms of religious life. He viewed religion as "that primitive social phenomenon from which all other social phenomena subsequently emerge" (Lukes
1985, 240). The analysis of religion itself provides us with a sound understanding
of the secularized modern world. The origin of the new moral of cooperation,
the secular religion of humanity, can be traced back as evolving from primitive
religion through a process of increasing social differentiation. "While the primitive Gods were present in all human relations, the Christian God withdraws from
the world" (Wallwork 1985, 209). Religions become more general with the rising
complexity of society, leading to the final modern stage of the cult of the individual. In this way, the sociology of religion is not only an academic enterprise,
but also provides a justification for the secularization of modern education and
science. Durkheim's focus on religion is thus congruent with the central policy
concerns of the Third Republic during his lifetime.

The general theory of religion which Durkheim presents in *Les formes élémentaires* is only one facet of his sociology of knowledge and morals. The book is an
inquiry into the social nature of our categories of understanding (Worsely 1956,
14). In a revised form it takes up the evolutionary idea of Auguste Comte that
mankind has moved from theology via metaphysics to science (Lukes 1985, 445).
Religious speculations are the predecessors of scholarly reflections about nature,
man and society. In their nature—making the world intelligible—religions are
not different from the language that the modern sciences employ. Also religions
represent a system of ideas explaining the world (Durkheim 1995, 611–613).
Religions, moral orders, world views and the sciences represent social realities,
and are of social origin. Thus religious rituals and beliefs are not *sui generis* phenomena, but socially conditioned. Their explanation must be based on social and
secular terms, the principle of the sacred is nothing more than the self-awareness
of society in a hypostatic and transfigured form (Durkheim 1995, 495).

The explanation of Durkheim's interest in religion lies in the intellectual and
political contexts of his time. In scholarly terms, Durkheim was in the pervasive
grip of the evolutionist theories of the nineteenth century and fascinated by the
concepts about primitive societies discussed in the fields of comparative religion
and anthropology. In particular the idea of totemism as the most primitive reli-

gion lies at the heart of his later studies on religion (Lukes 1985, 454). Yet in spite of his scholarly insights, his denial of religious claims to truth and his personal agnosticism, Durkheim's thoughts about morality and social order also were molded by the nostalgic tendencies of the late nineteenth century. Accordingly, not only did modern Europe evolve from Christendom, from a world completely penetrated by religion, but this Christian world was also a respectable unity of faith, morality and reason. Together with the conviction that religion was a "dying social force," this ideal picture of pre-modern Christendom was behind Durkheim's "secret longing for the ideals and aspirations of a much earlier period than his own" (Pickering 1984, 441). Politically, Durkheim's academic work is embedded in both the struggle of the republican state against the conservative, Catholic establishment and imperial competition in international politics. This is apparent in his interest in morality and in his search for a substitute for societal cohesion that religion supposedly provided to humanity in more primitive stages of socio-cultural evolution.

In defending modern individualism against his conservative critics, Durkheim tells us that the "religion of humanity" is not less imperative than those traditional religions it will replace. However, this modern "religion" is now an individualistic religion in which man is at the same time both God and believer (Durkheim 1898, 173–175). In light of the anomies of modern society, only this kind of individualistic religion can ensure the "national unity of the country," and it is the secularized state system of education that has the task to preach it to the nation. In the religion of humanity resonate the threats of both societal anomie and an imperialist explosion as it occurred in 1914. Even more important, there seems to be a hidden linkage behind Durkheim's concept of an individualistic moral of cooperation to the ideas of liberal Protestant theology. In his short essay in the *Revue Bleue* Durkheim locates the origin of his individualistic morality in the individualist spirit of Christianity. The agnostic descendent of a Jewish Rabbi family confronts his predominantly Catholic opponents with the conclusion: "It is thus a singular error to present individualist morality as antagonistic to Christian morality, quite the contrary, it is derived from it" (Durkheim 1898, 179). Like Renan's pure religion, Durkheim's theory of a religion of humanity resembles the theological idea of Christianity as a historically peculiar religion but with an inherent universal potential as advocated by the German Protestant theologian Albrecht Ritschl (Buss 1999, 268). Pickering tells us that there are only a few references to Protestantism in Durkheim's work and he emphasizes the rather cold attitude of Durkheim toward Protestant forms of Christianity (Pickering 1984, 435–439). However, in his idea of an emergent individualistic morality, sociological evolutionism seems to merge with ideas from liberal Protestant apology, the latter conceptualizing modernity as a form of unfolded Christianity. This crossroads of sociological and theological ideas, in Durkheim's case an example for the implicitly applied discursive elements of the public sphere, is most clearly epitomized in the life and work of William Robertson Smith.

William Robertson Smith: Orientalist by Default

In the literature on Durkheim, the intellectual encounter between the French sociologist and the Scottish Protestant theologian and orientalist William Robertson Smith plays a very prominent role. Durkheim's reading of Smith's *Lectures on the Religion of the Semites* is closely associated with the French sociologist's shift toward more in-depth studies on culture and religion, moving his focus from a general sociology of modernity to a modern sociology of knowledge (cf. Müller 1999, 162). In declaring the reading of Smith and "his school" of religious history a revelation, it was Durkheim himself who stressed the crucial role of Smith in his work (Pickering 1984, 61). However, what indeed was "the flash of insight that Durkheim received from reading Robertson Smith"—the relationship between religion and ritual, the role of totemism, the evolutionary perspective, the social origin of religion etc.—still remains open (Pickering 1984, 67–69). That Durkheim's *Les formes élémentaires* seems to be "permeated by Robertson Smith's principal ideas" (Warburg 1989, 55), therefore, might be due to both his reading of Robertson Smith and the general concepts of religion under whose influence Durkheim and Robertson Smith wrote.

For our study here, the connection and convergence of ideas between Durkheim and Smith is important because of the extraordinary influence these two scholars exerted on the study of religion in general. Durkheim's work impacted the social sciences far beyond the disciplinary boundaries of sociology, and he found a critical reception in such diverse disciplines as linguistics, psychology, ethnography, anthropology and history (Müller 1999, 166–167). Robertson Smith was a dominant figure in the discipline of comparative religion. His fundamental idea of the social origin of religion became a constitutive element for religious studies in the social sciences and the humanities (Warburg 1989, 41). In short, Durkheim and Smith, a sociologist and a theologian, were central sources for modern knowledge on religion. Even more important, in trivialized forms their concepts traveled far beyond the realm of academic disciplines, molding public perceptions on religion and modernity at large.

Reconciling Modern Scholarship and Christian Faith: Life and Work of William Robertson Smith

William Robertson Smith was born on 8 November 1846 in Keig, a parish in the historic county of Aberdeenshire, Scotland. His father, previously the headmaster of a school, had recently been ordained a minister in the Free Church of Scotland. The Free Church was a conservative, evangelical offshoot of the National Church of Scotland which had left the National Church after ten years of conflict in May 1843. William was the oldest son of seven children who were brought up in a household in which "religious studies, the sciences, mathematics and languages were fields for daily discussion" (Beidelman 1974, 3). Due to his bad health and economic problems, Smith was taught at home by his parents before entering Aberdeen University in 1861. There, his performance was outstanding, in particular with regard to mathematics and the classical languages of theology. At the age of twenty, Robertson Smith entered the New College in Edinburgh, pursuing his major interests in natural science and biblical studies. At New College, his Hebrew teacher, Andrew Bruce Davidson, who was also versed in the methods of biblical criticism, made a profound impact on Smith. With his position of "believing criticism," viewing the critical historical and philological study of the Bible as a necessary foundation for the Christian faith, Davidson gave Smith's peculiar scholarly career its fundamental direction (Black and Chrystal 1912, 77).[27] In 1867, Smith wrote his first essay in the field of biblical scholarship in which he already dealt with the central problem of his future works: "Was the history of Israel the history of God or just any history"? (Rogerson 1995, 116). For Smith, the answer must be found in the resolution of the contradictory aspects of revealed and unvarying truth and the historical particularity in which divine prophecy had appeared (Beidelman 1974, 6).

In his search for knowledge, Robertson Smith visited the continent, in particular Germany, several times. In comparison to the elementary achievements of biblical studies in Britain, German scholarship of the Old Testament was enormous (Rogerson 1995, 138). As early as 1865 Smith took up lessons in German. In May 1867, he paid his first visit to Germany. His interest in German scholarship was entirely driven by his theological studies. He learnt Hebrew and German as a "preparation for his ecclesiastical life." Perceiving the Tübingen School and Richard Rothe in Heidelberg as far too rationalistic, Smith eventually decided to study in Bonn, where he found himself in a completely different religious environment than he had experienced before. In Bonn, there were more Catholics than Protestants, and among the latter both doctrinal divergence and religious indifference were widespread. For a number of German theologians, theology was nothing more than an "abstract science" (Black and Chrystal 1912, 84). However, Smith did not endorse this radical approach, and in correspondence from his second trip to Germany, in July 1869, he called David Friedrich Strauss an infidel (Black and Chrystal 1912, 60 and 85–88). On this second visit, Smith made the acquaintance of Albrecht Ritschl in Göttingen, whose lectures he described as the most impressive experience of this summer in Germany (1912, 111). Finally, in 1872, Smith studied Arabic under Paul de Lagarde (1827–1891), who had succeeded Heinrich Ewald as chair of Oriental Languages at Göttingen University.

These experiences in Germany, the encounter of sincere faith with rationalistic theology based on historicist and philological methods, shaped Smith's scholarly life. He became a Protestant apologist for whom the scientific study of the Bible did not contradict the message of Christ. On the contrary, being a convinced biblical critic and a "fervent evangelical" at the same time, Smith was committed to bringing modern scholarship into the "service of theology" (Rogerson 1995, 147–149). His interest in Semitic languages and the cults of pagan Arabia

---

27. In combining sincere faith with historicist scholarship, the role of Davidson for Smith shows clear parallels to the impact Le Hir had on Ernest Renan.

was driven by this very same motive: to understand better the message of the Bible, especially the divine revelation contained in the Old Testament, through comparative studies of Semitic religions. Believing in the supernatural and sub-scribing to almost all traditional Presbyterian doctrines (Glover 1954, 24), Smith utilized his Arabic studies as a means of proving wrong the more radical forms of criticism such as the Tübingen and Leiden Schools. In sharp contrast to them, Smith insisted on the special character of the revelation of the Old Testament and rejected the view that it merely represents another form of Semitic religion (Rogerson 1995, 85).

After his return to Edinburgh, in May 1870, Smith was elected successor of Professor Sachs, the previous holder of the chair of Hebrew and the Old Testa-ment at the Free Church College in Aberdeen. He took over the chair and was ordained a minister of the Free Church in November 1870, a requirement for his new academic position (Beidelman 1974, 7; Black and Chrystal 1912, 123). Yet his passion for biblical criticism soon gave his career an unexpected twist. In 1875, Smith's article "Bible" appeared among others by his pen in the ninth edition of the *Encyclopedia Britannica*. The editor had chosen him for a number of articles because of his excellent knowledge in the fields of biblical criticism and Semitic studies. As a pioneer of higher criticism in Scotland, Smith was specifically asked to reflect in his biblical entries the international standard of this new critical approach (Beidelman 1974, 13). Smith's articles gave a precise and well-informed overview of the ways in which the modern critical schools interpreted the Holy Scriptures. In the religious world of the Free Church, however, the Holy Bible was an "unimpugnable authority" and considered as "an infallible divine guidance" (Cheyne 1995, 33).

The mere idea, expressed in Smith's articles, that the Bible should be inter-preted as any other historical book was unbearable for the conservative estab-lishment in the Free Church. Smith's critical approach touched the very foun-dation of the dogmatic Protestantism of his contemporaries and especially the theological principles of the Free Church itself. "The inerrancy of the Bible was so intimate a part of their religious thought and life that a denial of it seemed to threaten the destruction of faith itself" (Glover 1954, 16).[28] Soon after the pub-lication of "Bible" rumors about Smith's "heresy" were circulating, leading to public agitation against him and his views. Under this rising public outcry, the Church felt compelled to take up seriously the case of Robertson Smith (Tul-loch 1876–1877, 545–547). Confronted with these accusations of heresy, Smith reaffirmed his Christian faith. At the same time, he reiterated that the critical method provides a better understanding of the Bible and demanded a formal accusation against him by the Church. In 1877, Smith was suspended from the

---

28. This notion of the Bible as the authoritative, infallible word of God was closer to the Catholic interpretation of Scripture than to the early Reformation doctrines them-selves. From the late seventeenth century onwards, however, this interpretation gained influence in Protestant theology and was later identified as distinctively Prot-estant (Glover 1954, 15–16).

college at his own request and eventually, in 1881, formally removed from his chair (Beidelman 1974, 19–22).

Having unsuccessfully applied for a chair in mathematics in Glasgow, Smith accepted the co-editorship of the *Encyclopedia Britannica* soon after his dismissal from the Free Church College. He moved to Edinburgh and published his *The Old Testament in the Jewish Church* (1881) and *The Prophets of Israel* (1882). In 1883, he was appointed as a Reader in Arabic at Cambridge University, where he became an elected fellow of Christ's college (1885), University Librarian (1886) and eventually holder of the Sir Thomas Adam chair of Arabic in 1889 (Shiel 1995, 79–84).[29] At Cambridge, Robertson Smith became an orientalist scholar, however, remaining a Protestant theologian and Christian apologist at heart. In 1885, he published a series of lectures under the title *Kinship and Marriage in Early Arabia*. The book dealt with J.F. McLennan's general thesis that male kinship had been preceded by female kinship and corresponding laws of marriage and tribal organization. In the preface, Smith tells the reader that he wants to collect and discuss the available evidence for the genesis of the kinship system in Arab society at the time of Muhammad. In order to construct a hypothetical picture of the Arab social system "consistent with all the Arabian facts" (Smith 1903, xiii), Smith invited several internationally known colleagues to contribute to this book, an invitation to which the orientalists Wellhausen, Nöldeke and Goldziher responded very positively (Black and Chrystal 1912, 483). Ignaz Goldziher contributed to the first and the new edition in 1903, of which he also did the proof-reading and added numerous notes. In his diary, Goldziher lamented that Robertson Smith published important results about Arab family law before he himself was able to do so (Goldziher 1978, 113).

By far the most influential book by Robertson Smith, however, became his *Lectures on the Religion of the Semites*. First published in 1889, it must be conceived as a classic in comparative religion that not only impacted so strongly on Emile Durkheim, but on a wider range of European anthropologists, psychologists, sociologists and theologians. Smith aimed with this book at illuminating the evolution of Judaism and Christianity from more ancient Semitic religious traditions (Warburg 1989, 44). Strongly influenced by his friend McLennan and the critical method of Julius Wellhausen and Abraham Kuenen, Smith framed an evolutionary religious history in sociological form, making him "the founder of the modern sociology of religion" (Beidelman 1974, 31–35 and 68). After his dismissal from the chair at the Free Church College, Robertson Smith did not change his academic direction. He remained a theologian and continued unswervingly in his mission to reconcile Christian faith with modern scholarship. At Cambridge, however, he did so in excelling in orientalism, the "auxiliary field" of Christian theology, and in the emerging disciplines of sociology and social anthropology (Rogerson 1995, 13). In addition to his principal preoccupation with Christian

---

29. His move to Cambridge was facilitated by the testimonials of a number of German Professors—Nöldeke, Wellhausen, Lagarde and von Kremer—emphasizing Smith's outstanding skills in Arabic (Black and Chrystal 1912, 464–466).

theology, Smith traveled the Middle East several times. Between his first trip to Cairo in 1878 and his last stay in Egypt in 1890, Smith visited Palestine, Syria, and the Arab Peninsula, as well as Algeria and Tunis (Shiel 1995, 85). In March 1894, William Robertson Smith died of spinal tuberculosis, at the age of only 48.

Orientalist and Christian Apologist: Robertson Smith on Islam

Robertson Smith became an orientalist by default. The common theme through his life and work was his sincere Christian faith. Already in his first essays, he declared criticism to be a means of gaining knowledge that never "can take from us our personal fellowship with God in Christ." For Smith, this fellowship with a divine personality did not stand in contradiction with the modern world and his apologetic purpose was rooted in the "immediate certainty of Christian faith" (Smith 1869, 134). While Durkheim conceptualized the rise of modernity as a process of socio-cultural evolution, Smith framed the evolutionism of his time in religious categories. Yet they shared the general approach of conceptualizing history as religious evolution from primitive to more rationalized forms. Smith's inquiry into the Old Testament was an attempt to show "the changing form and the permanent substance of prophecy" (Smith 1871, 266). In the Bible, "God and man meet" (Smith 1881, 18), and modern criticism is the instrument for distinguishing between the "accidental and the essential, the human conjectures and the divine truth" in the Holy Scriptures (1881, 5). Therefore, Smith saw no discordance between modern science and faith, and for him "every new progress in biblical study must in the end make God's great scheme of grace appear in fuller beauty and glory" (1881, 29). The Old Testament, as well as the old Semitic religions before, were "preparations for Christ," the manifestation of divine unity through variable historical circumstances. The general history of progress is synonymous with the development of "God's plan of revelation and redemption" (Smith 1876, 347). The nineteenth-century notion of evolutionary progress permeated Smith's religious world view (Whitelam 1995, 181) and he defined history in terms of a possible scholarly reconstruction of the "objective process in which God was at work" (Rogerson 1995, 152).

For Smith, the study of pre-Islamic Arabia became a comparative necessity in understanding God's plan of salvation through a hermeneutical process. He perceived Judaism, Christianity and Islam as "positive religions," as the conscious teaching of the faith by "great religious innovators" (Smith 1903, 1). Smith, however, saw the origins of these positive religions in older, unconscious religious traditions. Like Renan, Smith conducted Semitic studies in search of the spiritual roots of Christianity. Implicitly applying the distinction between tradition and modernity, Smith defined in his *Lectures on the Religion of the Semites* traditional religion as a holistic, unconscious religio-social order based on the mythological understanding of fundamental ritual practices; a definition not far from Durkheim's description of "mechanical solidarity." In this "rude form," according to Smith, religion was a collectively binding moral force (1903, 53), and in tribal Arabia the "influence of religion over conduct was of no little use in the slow and difficult process of the consolidation of an orderly society out of barbarism" (1903, 64). In declaring the Semitic rites to be the rudest and most visibly primitive in character, Smith combined his theological reason for the recourse to tribal Arabia with a "scientific" evolutionary approach (1903, 338).

Given his apologetic mission, Smith's relatively negative attitude toward Islam does not come as a surprise. As a liberal and critical Protestant, he perceived the Islamic religion of the Hejaz as a form of "organized hypocrisy" (Smith 1880–1881, 493). In contrast with the intimacy of his own relationship with Christ, he perceived the Muslim worshipper's relationship with God as being remote in character. Therefore, Muslims could not adequately address God through the language of prayer and Muslim devotion deteriorated into a system of "formalism and vain repetition" (1880–1881, 511). While nineteenth-century Protestant religious individualism was the standard against which to measure Muslim religiosity, Smith judged the role of the Koran according to his own dedication to historical criticism:

> The Koran is the bulwark of all prejudices and social backwardness in the East. I am far from saying that no progress can be made by Mohammedan people, but it is indispensable to progress that a freer attitude be taken up towards the Koran, and the best means towards this is a better knowledge of the ethics and religion of the Western nations. (1880–1881, 568)

In this way, in Robertson Smith's judgment of Islam, the historicist scholar and the Protestant apologist converged with the colonial habitus of the British intellectual. Consequently, he confused Arab resistance against Ottoman rule with the longing of the tribes of the Arab Peninsula for a European civilizing mission under British supremacy. In political terms, Smith concluded: "The idea is certainly gaining ground that England is the country whose protectorate would be most acceptable and most fruitful in good results" (1880–1881, 495).

As with Ernest Renan, William Robertson Smith is not so important for my study with regard to his achievements in oriental studies. The core element of Smith's work, his theory of sacrifice based on Semitic religions, is no longer accepted by anybody in the field (Warburg 1989, 51). Yet he represented a nodal point in the network of nineteenth century scholarship on religion and Islam. In terms of influence and inspiration, Robertson Smith closely knitted together the intellectual milieus of Victorian Great Britain, positivist France, the Netherlands and Germany. In particular, he transferred the central ideas of Germany's most eminent Protestant theologians—Heinrich Ewald, Richard Rothe and Albrecht Ritschl—to a British readership and more indirectly also made them a part of Emile Durkheim's sociology. In a letter from 1890, Smith explicitly mentioned the three German theologians as the "leading influences" of his career (Black and Chrystal 1912, 534–535). Robertson Smith introduced core concepts of Germany's liberal Protestant theology into the conceptual apparatus of emerging disciplines such as anthropology, sociology or Islamic studies. This applies not only to the concept of modern religion as a combination of rationalized ethical subjectivity with belief in supernatural revelation, but also to the view of human history in evolutionary and religious terms, developing from primitive via monotheistic religions to a form of secularized Christianity. As with Renan, the life and work of William Robertson Smith is a crucial crossroads of ideas, which strongly suggests taking a brief look at the arts of higher criticism in Germany. Smith's work indicates the impact of Germany's Protestant intellectual milieu on both the modern concept of religion and the development of oriental studies. Moreover, this excursion into German Protestant theology will lead us directly to the sociology of religion of Max Weber.

Protestant Theology and Biblical Criticism in Germany

In the introduction to *Orientalism,* Edward Said admitted that his book does not do justice to the contributions of German orientalists and the impulses in oriental studies generated by the "revolution in Biblical studies" in the eighteenth century (Said 1978, 17). Indeed, the disciplinary development of oriental and Islamic studies can barely be understood without taking into consideration the impact of Protestant theology on the theoretical perspectives of the social sciences and humanities. The examples of Ernest Renan and William Robertson Smith have aptly shown the roles which Christian belief and theology played for European scholars in engaging in orientalist disciplines. Moreover, we have already seen in which ways the scholarly conceptualization of religion in modern society borrowed from the ideas of liberal Protestant theology. This section will therefore present some of the core ideas of the liberal Protestant revision of Christianity. We will look more closely at four internationally important German theologians whose works critically discussed the historicization of the Bible by the Tübingen School and who profoundly impacted the works of Renan, Smith and Weber: Heinrich Ewald, Richard Rothe, Albrecht Ritschl and Julius Wellhausen. Moreover, these theologians were more or less closely connected with the discipline of oriental studies.

The construction of the modern program of Christianity took place on a heavily contested religious field and in close connection with the formation of the subsystems of politics, economics and science. The theological discussion, therefore, was conditioned by issues such as the relationship between church and state, pressing social questions and the scientific world view. In the Catholic world, orthodox and traditionalist positions under the leadership of Rome remained dominant throughout the nineteenth century, whereas in the Protestant parts of Europe Lutheran orthodoxies, liberal theologies and various new religious movements, often joined together under the label of a "Christian awakening," competed in defining the right position of the Protestant confession in the modern world. This broad range of competing forms of religious apologies, however, converged in one general point of view: the role of the Christian faith in preventing modernity from sinking into chaos and barbarity (Graf 2004, 173). This moral concern about the modern order was shared by many secular intellectuals in principle, although they no longer believed in the ethics of Christianity.

From the eighteenth century, Protestant theologians and various religious lay movements spearheaded the transformation of organized Christianity into forms of religious privacy (Schröder 1996, 1). The nineteenth century saw an increasing subjectivation of both religious semantics and Christian faith, emphasizing the religious experience of the self (Graf 2004, 171). In theological terms, this transformation was accompanied by the move from the authority of the Bible to the exemplary role of Christ, the model and origin of Christian faith (Schröder 1996, 232). With the revealed nature of the Holy Scriptures the dogmatic system of orthodox Protestantism also crumbled. Robertson Smith closely followed this move in viewing the living God and not doctrines as lying at the heart of religion (Rogerson 1995, 277). From this perspective, individualistic experience and the religious model in Jesus Christ became the essence of Christianity, strongly juxtaposed with the "fatalistic" piety of Muslims subject to the almighty of God. Moreover, the entirely non-political and spiritual nature of Christ was contrasted with the image of Muhammad as a dogmatic statesman and law-giver.

This subjectivation of the Christian faith was compatible with the "historicist spirit" of the nineteenth century, the awareness of the historical relativity of human history and men. This philosophical position, an application of Enlightenment criticism against its own universalist pretentions, provided the foundation for the various forms of romanticist ideas as well as hermeneutics as a scientific method for the humanities and the social sciences (Schnädelbach 1984, 33–65). The theological revision of Christianity and the historicist approach came together especially at German universities. Most German theologians of the nineteenth century followed the source-critical premises of Germany's historical school and its mentor Leopold Ranke (1795–1886) (Lessing 2000, 35). This combination of theology and history made German universities centers of biblical criticism, "the literary and historical study of the Bible with the object of determining the composition, the dates, and the authors of its various books" (Glover 1954, 18). In particular the source-critical analysis of the Old Testament, proving the incompatibility of the Mosaic origin of the Pentateuch with historical practice (Nicholson 1998, 5), shattered belief in the revealed nature of the Bible and consequently in the very foundations of traditional Christianity.

Theologian and Orientalist: Heinrich Ewald and Julius Wellhausen

Heinrich Ewald and Julius Wellhausen represent two generations of leading German scholars of biblical criticism who also contributed a lot to the establishment of oriental studies. Born in 1803, Ewald received his education and spent most of his professional life in Göttingen. There, he studied theology in combination with classical and Semitic philology, becoming Professor in Oriental Languages in 1827. In 1837, he was dismissed because of his role among the "Göttingen Seven," a group of professors who protested against the abolition of the constitution in the Kingdom of Hanover. From 1838–1848, Ewald taught philosophy and theology in Tübingen, eventually coming back to Göttingen, where he died in 1875. Heinrich Ewald was one of the most prominent philologists and biblical scholars of the nineteenth century, "described as 'one of the greatest critical Old Testament scholars of all time'" (Nicholson 1998, 7). In 1855, Ernest Renan also published an article which was based on Ewald's work and which formed the foundation stone of his five volumes of *Histoire du peuple d'Israël* (Hoffmann 1988, 47). Ewald represented the traditional linkage of theology and oriental studies, but he strongly supported the idea of the establishment of independent orientalist disciplines and was a founding member of the *Deutsche Morgenländische Gesellschaft*. In contrast to Fleischer's exclusive focus on philology in Leipzig, Ewald established in Göttingen a school of oriental studies that applied a historical-comparative method whose perspective went beyond the mere fixation on texts and grammar. This historical perspective made him particularly interesting for scholars who already excelled in philology who were looking for an interpretative framework for oriental cultures (Mangold 2004, 95–100).[30]

In his biblical studies, Ewald criticized the view of Moses' authorship of the first five books of the Bible, the Pentateuch. He supported the "Supplementary Theory," arguing that a basic source runs through the Pentateuch, but later was supplemented by other sources (Nicholson 1998, 7). His analysis of the Old Testament influenced generations of European scholars and represents "a milestone" in biblical scholarship "that time has not been able to remove" (Vries 1968, 55). In his theological position, Ewald fought against both Protestant Orthodoxy and rationalist schools, in particular the Tübingen School, whose representatives he considered as atheists (Ebach 1982, 695). For Ewald, the historical reconstruction of the Bible was a means of providing evidence of a divine direction in history, confirming sincere belief in God (Rogerson 1995, 93). It was certainly this apologetic approach which found Robertson Smith's wholehearted acceptance. Smith had already been introduced to Ewald's thoughts at the New College in Aberdeen by his preferred teacher, Andrew Bruce Davidson, who had once studied under Ewald at Göttingen University (Rogerson 1995, 115). Later, Smith built lasting working relations and friendships with Ewald's successor, Paul de Lagarde, and one of Ewald's most prominent disciples, Julius Wellhausen.

Nineteenth-century research on the Pentateuch found its climax in Wellhausen's work (Nicholson 1998, 11). Born in 1844, Wellhausen grew up in an orthodox Lutheran parish in Hameln. In 1862, he reluctantly took up his theological studies at Göttingen University, where the illustrious Heinrich Ewald immediately captured his full attention (Kratz 2003, 527). Despite Ewald's very difficult personality, Wellhausen held him in high esteem throughout his life (cf. Wellhausen 1901). He even called him "our father" in a letter to Robertson Smith (Smend 1995, 231). In his work, however, he took a different direction. At Göttingen, Wellhausen also was a student of Albrecht Ritschl, who had a very problematic relationship with Ewald (cf. Ritschl 1892, 300), but high expectations regarding Wellhausen (Ritschl 1896, 121). Ritschl made Wellhausen familiar with the Grafian thesis on

---

30. Apart from Wellhausen and Robertson Smith, Ernst Nöldeke, who held a chair at Strasbourg, also viewed himself as a disciple of Ewald (cf. Fück 1955, 167).

the Pentateuch, and Wellhausen became a leading representative of this variant of the Documentary Thesis. The Documentary Thesis dealt with the Pentateuch as a literary corpus employing source-critical methods. It focused on the historicity of the Pentateuch's documents and authors, claiming that their origins were clearly separated by time, style and religious outlooks. According to the thesis, several redactors gradually combined these documents later, projecting their perspective into them in an anachronistic way (Nicholson 1998, 29). The Dutch scholar Abraham Kuenen largely followed Wellhausen, and the Kuenen-Wellhausen thesis was definite in abolishing the view "that Israel's sacred books were the product of divine revelation" (Vries 1968, 10).

For Ewald and Robertson Smith, the critical method was a scientific means of proving the divine direction in history, whereas Wellhausen left the path of Christian apologetics. In the struggle between Germany's Chancellor Bismarck and the Catholic Church, the so-called German *Kulturkampf,* Wellhausen emphatically sided with Bismarck and the secularist demands of the Prussian state (Ess 1980, 42). In April 1882, he resigned from his chair in theology at the University of Greifswald, which he held since 1872. In a letter to Robertson Smith, he announced his resignation in 1881 with the words:

> I do not care about my church, that is the difference; therefore I am voluntarily resigning from a state appointment which is linked to the church. I do not believe in the possibility of the resuscitation of the stinking corpse, which is called the orthodox, and even the liberal German Protestant church.
>
> (quoted in Smend 1995, 241)

After his resignation, the Prussian Minister of education appointed Wellhausen as extraordinary professor in Semitic languages at the University of Halle. In 1885, he moved to Marburg before succeeding Paul de Lagarde at Göttingen in 1892 (Kratz 2003, 527). Already during his last years at Greifswald, Wellhausen began to study manuscripts in Arabic which he had collected in Leiden, London and Paris. It was Ewald who aroused his interest in Semitic philology and after his resignation from theology, Wellhausen continued his career predominantly as Arabist. Applying the same source-critical method, he analyzed pre-Islamic and early Islamic sources in historical analogy to the Old Testament.[31] Wellhausen explained his transition from the Old Testament to the Arabs with the intention of finding the Semitic "savage" to whom the prophets addressed the Thorah (Wellhausen 1882, 5). His Arabic-Islamic studies, however, were not merely in the service of his biblical studies, but soon developed into a significant field of their own. Based on the thorough education in Hebrew and Arabic he received from Ewald, Wellhausen was perfectly prepared to apply his historical-philological method to Arabic sources. He strictly focused on texts, trying to reconstruct historical processes directly based on these written sources. In his interpretation of early Islamic history, Wellhausen emphasized the "political history" of Islam

---

31. The work of Wellhausen was predominantly based on the early historiography of Islam and not on religious texts such as the Koran and the Sunna.

and the role of Muhammad in Medina (Rudolph 1983, 121). Even more important, Wellhausen spread this idea of the "political nature of Islam" globally, through his article on Muhammad in the *Encyclopedia Britannica*, in which he wrote: "The Koran is Mohammed's weakest performance. The weight of his historical importance lies in his work of Medina" (Wellhausen 1883).[32]

In spite of his break with the church, Wellhausen and Robertson Smith remained close friends. As editor of the *Encyclopedia Britannica*, Smith commissioned nine articles from him between 1881–1888, whose fees alleviated Wellhausen's financial strains (Smend 1995, 229). Moreover, Smith continued to make Wellhausen's work known in Great Britain and described his two volumes on the *History of Israel* as "the most important book on the subject" (Rogerson 1995, 85). Apparently, it was not the critical approach to the Bible as such, but the religious standpoint of scholars and their social context that determined the nature of their reconciliation of science and faith. While Ewald and Smith remained sincere Christians throughout their lives, Wellhausen and Renan could not reconcile the antagonism between modern science and traditional faith.

Modern Culture as Advanced Christianity: Richard Rothe and Albrecht Ritschl

The relationship between Protestantism and modern life was also at the centre of the theological work of Richard Rothe and Albrecht Ritschl, however, more with regard to dogmatic questions than biblical criticism. Richard Rothe, born in Posen 1799, studied theology in Heidelberg, where he attended Hegel's philosophy lectures in 1816/17. He later taught in Wittenberg, Bonn and Heidelberg (Wagner 1998, 436). Rothe's work is characterized by a theology of Christianity without a church. For him, the church was a dying institution from whose confines Christianity had to liberate itself. Inspired by Hegel's philosophy of the state, he conceptualized modern culture as the unification of the Christian faith with an, in principle, universal constitutional state, yet a state that should not implement dogmas of the Bible or the Reformation, but whose legislation should be based on the moral maxims of Christianity (Dörfler-Dierken 2001, 66).[33] Rothe's theology was deeply molded by the Enlightenment, which he saw as a higher level of Christianity. In his construction of a philosophy of history in which the Reformation marks the transition from Christianity's ecclesiastical to its political and moral phase in modern culture, he saw modernity as Christianity in its unity of a religious, political and moral community (Wagner 1998, 438). The allegedly secular culture of modernity was for him in fact a higher stage of Christianity (Dörfler-Dierken 2001, 60).

---

32. In chapter five, I will elaborate more on Wellhausen's contributions to Islamic studies in the context of the development of oriental studies in Germany.

33. The role of the state in Rothe's theology also reflected the close relationship between church and state in Germany. Liberal Protestant theologians at German universities were state employees who were afraid of rising monistic and mystical religious movements, as well as emerging Protestant sects at the fringes of the country's state churches (cf. Hübinger 1994, 310).

According to Rogerson, Rothe was the German who did most to shape Robertson Smith's theology. Smith met Rothe shortly before his death (1867) in Bonn and was deeply impressed by him and his *On Dogmatics* (Rogerson 1995, 83–85). Rothe interpreted the Bible not in a normative but in a historical way. The norms of the Holy Scriptures do not express the eternal will of God, but they are historically contingent narratives demanding a hermeneutical interpretation (Dörfler-Dierken 2001, 52). "If dogmas do not make sense of religious experience in the light of modern knowledge of the Bible and the world, then they are anachronistic impositions from the past ages, puzzles that prevent rather than assist faith" (Rogerson 1995, 89). Given Rothe's piety and commitment to the Reformation, this unity of modern knowledge and faith was an apologetic position that Smith enthusiastically embraced. From this theological position, biblical criticism was the necessary handmaid of Christianity based on the subjective commitment to God through Christ (Rogerson 1995, 93). Orthodox Protestants viewed Rothe's theology as a form of only thinly disguised secularism (Cashdollar 1989, 388), whereas the liberal theologian Albrecht Ritschl called his speculative ideal of a unity of Christianity and state as a "fairytale from our scientific childhood" (Ritschl 1896, 42). Although Rothe had constantly been for Ritschl an important partner for intellectual exchange, their theological positions sharply diverged in many aspects.

Albrecht Ritschl was born in March 1822 in Berlin. His father was a pastor and later protestant bishop of Pomerania. In 1839, Ritschl began his studies in theology at the University of Bonn, where his elder cousin Friedrich Ritschl, the academic mentor of the young Nietzsche, taught philology. He later studied in Halle, briefly with Rothe in Heidelberg and eventually moved to Baur in Tübingen, the center of Germany's rationalist school. Having been a private lecturer in Bonn since 1846, Ritschl was appointed extraordinary professor in theology in 1852. Finally, he received a chair in theology at Göttingen University in 1864, where he met with Robertson Smith (Schäfer 1998). Already as lecturer in Bonn, Ritschl had distanced himself from the radical criticism of the Tübingen School, aiming at "a theology for the present age that still represents the essence of Christianity" (Rogerson 1995, 81). Like Ewald and Rothe, Ritschl had an overall vision of the presence of God's will in history. His contemporary theology was re-oriented toward the Reformation, in particular its theory of justification, and he rejected metaphysical, speculative and mystic approaches. Distancing himself from the traditional Protestant orthodoxy and from pietistic movements, Ritschl tried to develop his theology on strictly historical foundations. Accordingly, he interpreted the Holy Scriptures first of all as documents on the historical evolution of the Christian faith. In his view the Bible had to be interpreted and did not "interpret itself," as traditional Protestant exegesis claimed (Lessing 2000, 33–39).

Given this historicity of the Bible, Ritschl also found "the essence of Christianity" in Jesus Christ. In his Christology, Ritschl emphasized the role of Jesus Christ as founder of a religious community. As part of the community the believer knows God through Christ. With the appearance of Christ, the search for salvation in the Kingdom of God lost its particularistic notion, in the Old Testament bound to a specific nation, and became universal. In this manner, Christianity is the ultimate theological form of monotheism, eventually leading to a moral community that transcends all ethnic and social boundaries (Rohls 1997a, 773–775).[34] In Ritschl's philosophy of history, God's will to form a community with and among humanity was already visible in the Old Testament but finally became manifest in the person of Jesus Christ.[35] Justification, then, means the acceptance of individual sinners in the community with God and salvation is a collective process, rather than being based on an individual relationship between believer and God (Schäfer 1998, 229).

Ritschl interpreted Christ's divine role as the moral vocation of the historical Jesus. This vocation was to realize the Kingdom of God, and Jesus Christ followed it with total obedience. The will of God was revealed in the vocation of Christ, and the Christian believers find justification in their experience of morally dealing with the world. The Christian ethic is therefore far from any ascetic rejection of the world, but characterized by the believers' staunch will to follow their vocations in daily life (Rohls 1997a, 780). Ritschl tried to reconcile Lutheran tradition and the living conditions of a modern middle class. His theology is an ethics of life in which justification and faith are related to community and social practice (Nipperdey 1988, 69). Inspired by Immanuel Kant's practical philosophy, Ritschl conceptualized the Christian believer as working for the Kingdom of God in fulfilling the duties of everyday life (Hübinger 1994, 172). As the next section will show, Ritschl's theology has several points of reference to important elements of Max Weber's sociology of religion.

In conclusion, the clash between scientific and religious world views runs through this sketch of higher criticism and Protestant theology in Germany. The reconciliation of modern science, in the broader German sense of *Wissenschaft*, and religion was the central theme with which these theologians struggled. Within this, the scientific world view was synonymous with historicism, and philology appeared as the appropriate means to understand the course of history. For theologians, these structural constraints converged in the method of biblical criticism and the historicization of the Bible. While most theologians succeeded in subordinating modern science to faith, some of them turned toward positivist agnosticism on the way. Julius Wellhausen and especially David Friedrich Strauss might be good examples of the latter. Ironically, both Christian apologist and positivist semantics helped in the end to establish functionally separated spheres of scientific and religious communication and therewith the relatively autonomous societal subsystems of science and religion. With regard to the topic of this book, these developments are relevant in four points.

---

34. A similar concept of Islam as the ultimate and universal form of monotheism we will discuss in chapter six in the work of so different Muslim thinkers as Muhammad Abduh and Sayyid Qutb.

35. A way of rationalizing history, which in a more romanticized form already appeared in Renan's biography of Jesus Christ.

Firstly, the modern revision of the religious program of Christianity heavily impacted the construction of modern religion in general. Biblical criticism strongly contributed to the rationalization, individualization and spiritualization of the Christian program that has been occurring since the eighteenth century (Rohls 1997a, 693). As a result, modern religion has become conceptualized with the help of elements such as revealed systems of ethics and beliefs, orientation toward salvation, concern with the supernatural, and based on religious experiences. Gradually, religion lost its all-encompassing character shrinking into a body of knowledge that is based on revealed but not mutually intelligible sources. Secondly, from a modern point of view, Christian eschatology has turned into a philosophy of history, scientifically reconstructed as a process of socio-cultural evolution. Consequently, modern culture could be interpreted as an evolutionary result of religious history with Christianity as its ultimate stage. For apologists, modernity was in the end the universalization of Christianity, while secularists interpreted Christianity as the last step toward a secular culture of humanity. Thirdly, the academic discipline of Islamic studies developed in this thematic context, embedding its disciplinary discussions in this broader discourse on religion and modernity, as well as applying the historicist methods of Protestant theology to Islamic sources. Finally, in a secularized version, the theological concepts and process models of rationalist and liberal Protestant theologies re-emerged in the conceptual apparatus of sociology. Durkheim's move from mechanical to organic solidarity, his functional definition of religion, and his individualist humanism are cases in point. Even more visible are the traces of Protestant theology in the work of Max Weber, who will be the last protagonist in this chapter.

Max Weber: Religion, Islam and the Culture of Modernity

In his programmatic methodological essay *Objectivity in the Social Sciences*, Weber tells us that our cognitive interest in social phenomena arises "from the specific cultural significance" which we attribute to them. It is from this epistemological perspective that he defined the social sciences as cultural sciences (Weber 1904, 64 and 67). His methodological reflections soon found their empirical expression in the first two essays of the *Protestant Ethic* from 1905, which were also foundation stones for Max Weber as a sociologist (Küenzlen 1980, 10). Hence, in trying to understand Weber's interest in religion and Islam, I follow his own methodological path and turn first toward the more general political, cultural and social milieus in which Max Weber lived. It is the specific cultural and political context of Germany at the turn to the twentieth century out of which Weber's culturally significant questions about religion grew.

The encyclopedic knowledge of Weber and the scarcity of references in his work make it difficult to precisely trace back the multiple sources of his complex thoughts. Therefore, ongoing controversies revolve, for instance, around Weber's concept of asceticism and its primary roots in the philosophies of Nietzsche, Schopenhauer or rather in Protestant theology, in particular the theology of Albrecht Ritschl (cf. Breuer 2006, 45; Kippenberg 1993; Treiber 1999; Tyrell 1990). There is no doubt that all three influenced Weber's work and the socio-cultural milieu to which Weber belonged. Before the First World War, Germany could be characterized, among others, by four relatively separate social and intellectual milieus: Catholics, Social Democrats, Conservative Protestants and Cultural Protestants. Although he considered himself to be religiously "unmusical," Weber nevertheless reflected in his world view many of the ideas prevalent among Cultural Protestants.[36] They represented Germany's liberal Protestant educated middle classes (*Bildungsbürgertum*) with their affinity for social innovation and the liberation of the individual through education. In theological terms, Cultural Protestants such as Ernst Troeltsch and Adolf von Harnack attempt a synthesis between the traditions of the Reformation and the ideals of modern culture. The liberal credo of Germany's Cultural Protestants was, on the one hand, directed against the stifling influence of traditional orders, manifested in a pronounced anti-Catholicism; on the other hand, they perceived the increasing industrialization and bureaucratization of social life as a threat to individualism. Based on the emphatic concept of an autonomous individual, the semantics of Cultural Protestants revolved around core ideas such as national reform, reflective scientific world view, civil religion, bourgeois emancipation, ideal historicism and civic self-organization. They attempted to reconcile religious experience with modern culture through scientifically guided education, at the same time claiming universality for their interpretation of Christianity from an evolutionary perspective (Hübinger 1994, 307–310).

The previously discussed ideas of Germany's liberal Protestant theology apparently resonated deeply in the world view of Cultural Protestants. To a certain extent, this applies also to Weber's sociological investigation of the universal dimension of Europe's Christian, capitalist and legal cultures. While writing his methodological essays and parts of the *Protestant Ethic,* Weber was a member of an intellectual circle called "Eranos." Eranos was founded in Heidelberg (1904) by the Theologian Adolf Deismann (1866–1937) and the philologist Albrecht Dieterich (1866–1908).[37] Besides Max Weber, prominent scholars such as the theologian Ernst Troeltsch (1865–1923), the philosopher Heinrich Wilhelm Windelband (1848–1915) and the Jurist Georg Jellinek (1851–1911) participated in its gatherings with the purpose of discussing the history of religion and religions. In scholarly terms, the members of Eranos could be associated with two strands of religious studies. On the one hand, they represented the school of comparative religion related to Hermann Usener (1834–1905), a philologist who attempted to

---

36. The term Cultural Protestantism refers to the common denominator of shared values among Germany's educated middle class, rather than to religious belief. A Cultural Protestant may or may not have been a sincere believer.

37. Ignaz Goldziher made the acquaintance of Dieterich in Heidelberg where he spent two days before attending the retirement of Theodor Nöldeke in Strasbourg in March 1906 (Goldziher 1978, 249).

emancipate religious studies from theology. On the other hand, some of its members were associated with the "history of religions" school (*Religionsgeschichtliche Schule*) among Germany's Protestant theologians, the latter analyzing the historical development of Christianity based on comparative and historical critical methods (Treiber 2005).

This linkage between sociology and Protestant theology was epitomized by the personal and intellectual friendship between Max Weber and Ernst Troeltsch. Since 1896, Weber and Troeltsch had been in close contact and "hardly any scholars had such intense mutual communication and scholarly interaction" (Graf 2006, 219). Through Troeltsch Weber became familiar with theological literature and he adopted Troeltsch' critical stance toward Lutheranism. Probably the *Protestant Ethic* would never have been written without this intensive dialogue between the two scholars (Mommsen 2006, 9). Against this background, some parts of Weber's sociology of religion could be read as an indirect conversation with his theological interlocutors (Graf 1987, 145). After a brief overview of the life and work of Max Weber, this section will sketch out his approach to religion. In particular it will look at some of the sociological concepts in Weber's sociology of religion and their relationship to Protestant theology. Then we will move to Weber's fragmentary analysis of Islam and the image that the German sociologist disseminated about the Muslim religion.

From National Economy to the Sociology of Religion: Life and Work of Max Weber

Born in 1864 in Erfurt, Max Weber grew up in a family of eight children that exposed him to both liberal German nationalism and Protestant religiosity. His father was a Doctor of Law and a politically active member of the National-Liberal Party, which supported Bismarck and his anti-Catholic and anti-Socialist policies. While the father was religiously rather indifferent, Weber's mother was a relatively orthodox Protestant. In addition, his cousin Otto Baumgarten and his uncle Adolph Hausrath were theologians with whom the young Weber frequently discussed religious matters (Honigsheim 2000, 100). In 1869, the family moved to Berlin, where his father became a city advisor and later a deputy in the Prussian Chamber and the German Reichstag. Weber received his secondary education at the local grammar school in Charlottenburg, which he completed with readings in philosophy, history and the German classics. His main intellectual impulses, however, he may have gained through the large circle of famous personalities who frequently visited his parents (Käsler 1988, 3). Between 1882 and 1886, Weber studied law, national economy, agrarian history, philosophy and theology in Heidelberg, Berlin and Göttingen. In 1889, he received his PhD and in 1891 his habilitation, which was a study on Roman agricultural history.

Max Weber's education took place during the foundational phase of the German national state. The young Weber witnessed the *Kulturkampf* between the Prussian state and political Catholicism (1872–1887), as well as the aggravation of the "social question," which was accompanied by the rise of the Social Democrats and Bismarck's response of formulating anti-Socialist laws (1878–1890). Not surprisingly, the social impact of capitalism evolved into a central theme of Weber's work when he became Professor for National Economy at Freiburg University in 1894. In his inaugural lecture at Freiburg in May 1895, Weber described the economic decline of the Prussian aristocracy. While Germany's aristocrats were not willing to give up power, the German bourgeoisie was not yet able to take it over (Mann 1992, 413–414). Weber declared himself a representative of this bourgeoisie; a bourgeoisie, however, which was lacking "the political maturity to assume the direction of the state" (Weber 1895, 21). Focusing on the East Elbian agricultural situation, Weber gave a vehemently nationalistic speech with even social-Darwinist undertones. He later confessed that he "aroused horror" among the audience by "the brutality of his views" (Weber, Marianne 1975, 216). Weber perceived the ruling power of the Imperial dynasty and the Prussian aristocracy as an utter anachronism. At the same time, he considered the political leadership of the working class as incompetent and dangerous for the national interests of Germany. His lecture was therefore a call upon Germany's middle class to assume political leadership and to socially and politically unify the country based on secular German nationalism. Yet behind the political issues of the day, his inaugural lecture already contained the central question which, according to Wilhelm Hennis, explains Max Weber's work: the inquiry into the fate of humankind (*Menschentum*) under the conditions of modernity (Hennis 1988, 147).[38]

To a certain extent, the development of Weber's work expresses Germany's changing public discourse based on the continuation of this above-mentioned central question. Since 1880, the theme of a "cultural crisis" gradually replaced the dominance of the social question in Germany's public sphere. Around 1900, the relationship between religion and modern culture became a fashionable topic among intellectuals and a central concern of the social sciences and humanities (Bruch *et al.* 1989, 11–13). Although he did not give up political economy as a field of his studies, Weber's move from a lawyer and national economist to a sociologist reflects this general intellectual development. In biographical terms, this shift from studies on trade, agriculture and national economy to culture and religion was also accompanied by Weber's severe illness. In 1896, Weber received a call to succeed Karl Knies on the chair in political economy at Heidelberg University. Teaching at Heidelberg, Weber showed first signs of mental and physical exhaustion in autumn 1897, leading to several nervous breakdowns. Between 1899 and 1902, he was more or less exempted from teaching, and in October 1903, after having resumed his scholarly work, in particular his methodological studies, Weber finally resigned from his teaching post and remained an honorary professor at Heidelberg (Käsler 1988, 10–13). Until summer 1919, when he took over the chair of Brentano in Munich, Weber did not hold an official teaching post at a German university. In early June 1920, Max Weber fell ill with pneumonia and died on June 14 in Munich.

---

38. In his lecture, Weber defined political economy as a science concerned with human beings that should be concerned with the "quality of human beings" under specific social, economic and political conditions (Weber 1895, 15).

In the field of the German university, Max Weber represented the "modernist" stream, as his inaugural lecture in Freiburg clearly demonstrated. The status of these typically German cultural elite of university professors was based on educational qualifications, for which reason Fritz Ringer defined them as "mandarins" (Ringer 1969, 5). While the German mandarins in general shared a pronounced "pessimistic attitude toward modern social conditions," the modernists among them distinguished themselves from the conservative majority in their response to the modern transformation. In contrast to the conservatives, the modernists did not believe in any possible escape from the modern condition. Consequently, they dissociated themselves from the Wilhelmian political and social establishment and strongly criticized the predominance of Prussia's agrarian and military aristocracy in German politics. Although not completely at home in the liberal camp, the modernists supported moderate social reform and believed in progressive cultural and educational programs (Ringer 1969, 133).

In a unique way, Weber expressed his modernist attitudes in a blend of scholarly virtues and being a convinced German nationalist and a sharp political commentator. In terms of academic works, the writings after his illness gave him a worldwide reputation and made him a founding father of sociology. In this period his major methodological works appeared, his theory of social action, his sociology of the state, his legal sociology and the three volumes on the sociology of religion. In addition, he engaged in public debates, as partly documented in his political writings (cf. Weber 1994). It is impossible to present here the ambiguities and "explosive contradictions of his work" (Dahrendorf 2006, 576). To a certain extent they might reflect Weber's elusive attempt to mediate between modernity's competing philosophies of romanticism and rationalism. In Max Weber's work and personality, we can find various elements of these contradictory facets of modernity (Breuer 2006, 272). Yet behind the enormous complexities of his work, we can nevertheless detect a number of concepts and models which have influenced modern reasoning on religion more generally. Even more important, they also became part of the conceptual background knowledge of Islamic studies.

The "Spirit of Capitalism:" Max Weber on Religion

In their difficulties to define religion, it almost became a convention among contemporary sociologists to refer to the opening phrase of Weber's sociology of religion in *Economy & Society*. There, Weber rejects defining religion "to say what it is" (Weber 1978a, 399). Yet Weber only refuses to give a substantive definition of religion. As a matter of fact, his texts provide us with several defining elements close to functionalist explanations of religion. In the context of the theodicy problem, for instance, religion appears as a means of mastering suffering, injustice and the contingencies of fate (1978a, 519). In particular for the underprivileged classes, religions provide salvation and redemption (1978a, 490–492). Structured as collectively shared belief systems, religious ethics represent a "cosmos of obligations" which serve as moral guidance (1978a, 430). In systematizing "all the manifestations of life," religions are a major source for the development of particular world views and ways of life (1978a, 451). Weber also apparently associates religions with what Elias would later regard as the elementary function of orientation. Religious programs help us to understand the world, to rationalize our complex experiences as part and parcel of a "meaningful cosmos" (Weber 1915a, 281).

Quite like Durkheim, Weber deals with religion as a part of the sociology of knowledge. However, the functionalist tone of the above-cited sequences does not have any methodological implications. Weber rejects the idea, for instance, that religions are only derivations or reflections of particular social circumstances (1915a, 269–270). For Weber, religion is not a mere ideal emanation of the social whole. In concordance with his general definition of sociology, he approaches religion as a particular type of social action. The explanation of the social, therefore, must start by the specific meaning which the believers associate with their actions (1978a, 399). With this methodological prerequisite, Weber defines religion as an autonomous but not independent realm of social action, a concept of religious autonomy that can be traced back to his early engagement with liberal Protestant theology (Graf 1987, 124). Weber views both religiously and magically motivated actions as rational and, in principle, worldly oriented forms of action (Weber 1978a, 399).

Encompassed by the concept of salvation, the goals of religious actions basically refer to two dimensions. Firstly, religious action aims at the transformation of specific states or conditions of being, for instance, the dispensation from sufferings such as illness, economic deprivation and suppression. Secondly, they are directed toward the transcendental realm. Salvation thus attains two forms. Predominantly it is oriented toward this-worldly aims but it also can postpone the this-worldly transformation into other-worldly redemption. Then, salvation will be achieved in a "state of nonbeing," in the "union with a divinity," or in "permanent bliss in a heaven." The distinctiveness of religious action lies therefore not so much in its ends, but rather in its means and in the specific kind of actors with "whom actors believe they interact." Religious action interacts with supernatural forces and the religious realm is linked to the ordering of relations among them and human beings (Sharot 2001, 22–23). In short, religious action has its origins in the individual experience of the "irrationality" of the world (Kippenberg 1993, 364).[39]

In Weber's sociology two very different perspectives appear simultaneously and in a rather abrupt way. While he insists on a certain form of "methodological individualism," comprehending the social from the perspective of individual actors, a large part of his writings deal with social macro-structures and analyzes the systemic logic of the social (Breuer 2007, 358). This double perspective also

---

39. Interestingly, Weber relies in this on the result of the very process he tries to understand. The experience of the irrationality of the world is only a late product of the rationalization process. He himself points to it when he tells his reader that only in a fully disenchanted world events just take place but not without having any meaning in themselves (1978a, 308).

characterizes his sociology of religion. In particular his theory of the historical development of religion is a form of structural history underpinned by certain evolutionary ideas. Although Weber disliked the evolutionism of his time, in his work we can find various elements of the evolutionist theories so prevalent among the religious studies of his contemporaries. As with Durkheim or Robertson Smith, Weber also presents us a history of religious evolution (Küenzlen 1978, 220). Cases in point are evolutionary moves such as from naturalism to symbolism (Weber 1978a, 403), from orgies to sacraments (Weber 1915a, 278) or from ritualistic to ethical religions. Weber took up the idea of an inherent development of religion, while changing this concept decisively. He transformed the theory of an inherent evolutionary logic of religious development into a general evolution of human rationality (Küenzlen 1978, 226). From this angle, the secular modern world has religious origins. The tragedy of religion is, however, that in the process of increasing rationalization that basically emanates from its own sources, religion has taken a direction toward dissolving itself (Küenzlen 1980, 126). I will briefly illustrate this central assumption of Weber's sociology of religion with reference to the *Protestant Ethic* and his essay *Zwischenbetrachtung*.

The enormous resonance found by Weber's essays on the *Protestant Ethic* has been a singular instance in sociology. Published in 1905, they have remained a part of the standard textbooks for sociological freshmen around the globe. The controversy about his thesis began immediately after publication and has continued into our days. The "Weber thesis" on capitalism has left the narrow confines of scholarly discourses and become a core issue in the global debate about religion. It turned into an acknowledged but also heavily criticized theme in the global public sphere. Yet under this process of dissemination, interpretation and trivialization of the Protestant Ethic thesis, Weber's argumentation has been buried under splinters of popularized knowledge about the relationship between Protestantism and modern capitalism. Therefore let us briefly go back to the original sources.

In the *Author's Introduction*, written for the publication of the collected essays on the *Protestant Ethic* in 1920, Weber formulates the problem, method and aim of his investigation as follows. After a long description of the peculiarities of modern "European" capitalism he states "the origin of the Western bourgeois class and of its peculiarities" as the central issue behind his essays (Weber 1930, xxxvii). Within this, capitalism is not only a form of economics, but an encompassing, extremely rationalized and systematized way of life; a way of life, with ascetic and life-negating traits that have developed into a fateful structural power in a global dimension. Given this "irrational" but coercive nature of modern capitalism, its mere coming into existence is a miracle and required an enormously strong force as its midwife (cf. Tyrell 1990 and Weber 1930, 38). Fully in line with other early sociologists, Weber discovers this social power in religion, in the past one of the "most important formative influences on conduct." His aim is to inquire into the "influence of certain religious ideas on the development of an economic spirit." Yet Weber points to the methodological fact that dealing with the connection between modern rationalism and Protestant asceticism is nothing more than analyzing only "one side of the causal chain" (1930, xxxix). Weber was well aware of the role of material structures and socially conditioned interests in the rise of European capitalism. What he found in Protestant asceticism was not the "independent variable" causing modern capitalism, but a religious ethic that could play the "switchman" for putting future social developments on track (Weber 1915a, 280).

In the second essay, *The Spirit of Capitalism* (1905), Weber constructs an ideal type of the capitalist habitus with reference to the empirical example of Benjamin Franklin (1706–1790). Franklin was an ideal example because his peculiar ascetic ethic arose in a social environment that was distinctively pre-modern (1930, 13–19). His "utilitarianism," therefore, could not reflect the material structures of his social environment in Pennsylvania (1930, 36). Weber juxtaposes the capitalist spirit with traditionalism, the attitude "to live and to earn as is necessary" and not to earn "more and more money" (1930, 24). In Calvinist ascetics, he identifies the specific religious force which was able to break through the wall of traditionalism. This particular case of Calvinist ascetics Weber apparently took from Albrecht Ritschl, however, in a re-interpretation of Ritschl's rather hostile and critical analysis of forms of Christian asceticism (cf. Treiber 1999).[40] In the Protestant Ethic, Weber turns the very specific and historically accidental social practice of a religious minority into an essential part of modern culture. Separated from its religious roots, this social practice became a major ethical feature in the everyday life of the masses (Breuer 2007, 35).[41] Weber's argument is the universalization of a religious particularism into a secular ethic of global relevance that was entirely stripped of its local religious origin.

From Weber's evolutionary perspective, the rise of the spirit of capitalism is a part of the general development of rationalism in which he perceived Protestantism as a stage prior to "the development of a purely rationalistic philosophy" (1930, 37). The fundamental philosophy of history and idea of socio-cultural evolution in Weber's sociology of religion becomes most transparent in an essay published in 1915. Parts of this essay *Zwischenbetrachtung* appeared in English under the title *Religious Rejections of the World and Their Directions* (Weber 1915b, 323–359). In this complex and densely written text, Weber deals with "the motives from which religious ethics of world abnegation have originated and the directions they have taken" (1915b, 323). These directions are linked to the already mentioned thesis of religions' inherent tendency to rationalize their ethics and world views. Weber defines the sociology of religion therefore as a part of the sociology of rationalism (1915b, 324). In the *Religious Rejections* he tries to understand

---

40. See also Weber's references to Albrecht Ritschl in his essay *The Religious Foundations of Worldly Asceticism* (1930, 210).

41. This emphasis on the ethics of everyday life is also a part of Charles Taylor's definition of the modern condition, in which he points to the moral affirmation of ordinary life in modern ethics. There is no reference to Albrecht Ritschl or other Protestant theologians in Taylor's book, so he apparently took this idea from Max Weber (Taylor 1991).

religious rationalization through the prism of the theodicy problem. The rationalization process is a reaction to the awareness of the "unbridgeable tensions" between religious ethics and the world (1915b, 358). From the unity of magical world views, two forms of religious practices for achieving salvation result: asceticism and mysticism. While in the first form the believer takes an active stance toward the world and feels like a tool of God, the second is a contemplative form of religious action in which the individual "is not a tool but a 'vessel' of the divine" (1915b, 325). Both forms can attain an inner-worldly and an outer-worldly direction, and it is the particular inner-worldly form of asceticism that proves itself through action within the world (1915b, 326). It is precisely this form which Weber detected in Calvinist Puritanism, "the rational mastery of the world" (1968, 248).

Weber tells us that the directions of religiosity lead from ritualism to ethical absolutism, from magic belief to sublimation by knowledge and from social embededness to individualization. He judges the level of rationality of religions according to which degree they have divested themselves of magic and systematically rationalized their ethics; and "the most characteristic forms of Protestantism have liquidated magic most completely" (1968, 226). In this, Weber did not agree with the mainstream in the field of comparative religion and he denied any time sequence from magic world views via religion to modern science. He did not see in magic and the concept of animism the origin of religion. The radical disentanglement of magic and religion in Protestantism was for Weber historically exceptional, because although not identical, religious and magical beliefs can amalgamate and do so in most cases. The disenchantment of the world is thus not only due to the consequent rationalization of religious beliefs but also to the disempowerment of magic (Breuer 2007, 13–23).

From the theoretical perspective which I developed in chapter three, the *Religious Rejections* could also be read as an analysis of the autonomization of religion vis-à-vis other modern function systems. Weber discusses the relationship between religion and the world by juxtaposing religious ethics with the ethical demands of other spheres of social life. The formalization of love and brotherhood by ethical religions is in sharp contrast to the formalization of exchange in the economic field, which becomes visible in the critical attitude toward money economy by ethical religions (1915b, 327–333). The political sphere is characterized by its own logic of the formalization of bureaucratic domination. States come into conflict with the ethic of religious brotherhood. Moreover, as "communities of war," states compete with religious communities in giving meaning to the existential question of death (1915b, 333–340). The inherent logic of arts turns the esthetic sphere into a means of providing this-worldly salvation and pushes religion more toward the transcendental realm (1915b, 340–343). Finally there is the intellectual sphere, where tension with religion is greatest. This tension rests on the "unavoidable disparity among ultimate forms of images of the world," the struggle between rationalist and revealed knowledge. Religion claims "to unlock the meaning of the world not by means of the intellect but by virtue of a charisma of illumination" (1915b, 352). The rise of modern science with its rational empirical knowledge pushed religion decisively in the supernatural and, from its own logic therefore, "irrational realm." The substance of religion, human search for salvation (1915b, 353), increasingly becomes alienated from all other spheres of life and the essence of religion appears to be found in otherworldly relationships and concerns (1915b, 357). In the language of Luhmann or Beyer, a religious system emerges whose communication has been reduced to the binary code of immanent/transcendent or blessed/cursed. In competition with the formation of other function systems, the social relevance of religion has been enormously limited but simultaneously it became more autonomous and gained a pronounced visibility.

In *Wissenschaft als Beruf* (Science as Vocation) Weber referred to this functional differentiation of modern society using the metaphor of polytheism:

> Today the routines of everyday life challenge religion. Many old gods ascend from their graves; they are disenchanted and hence take the form of impersonal forces. They strive to gain power over our lives and again they resume their eternal struggle with one another. (Weber 1917, 149)

Behind Weber's investigation of modern rationalism, we can observe a theory of differentiation, reminding us of Durkheim's theory of the marginalization of religion in his *Division of Labor*. However, Weber subordinated social differentiation to the dominant theme of formal rationalization. The so-different "gods" of politics, law, economics, education, science and the arts, the functionally separated inner logics of social systems, rest on the more general fundament of formal rationality. Formal rationality, however, is this disenchantment that the intellectualization and rationalization of the world brought about. It is the belief in mastering all things by rational calculation with no mysterious and incalculable forces coming into play. In its final consequence, disenchantment is the reliance on calculation and technical means; it is a purely instrumental ethic which, apart from its formal nature, has no meaning (1917, 139).

In terms of the individual, formal rationalization tends to produce these "specialists without spirit and sensualists without heart" as quoted at the beginning of this chapter. In modern culture the "ultimate and most sublime values have retreated from public life" (1917, 155). For Weber, modernization did not lead to a new form of organic solidarity. He did not share Renan's or Durkheim's optimism of a rising religion of humanity, nor did he believe in the reconciliation of modernity with the Christian faith like Robertson Smith. According to Weber's diagnosis of modern culture, remaining religious inevitably implies making an intellectual sacrifice, which Weber himself was not willing to make. He therefore suggested that each individual should find and obey his or her own demon, meeting the "demands of the day," in human relations as well as in their work (1917, 156). Ironically, this individual ethic of the religiously unmusical Weber reminds us closely of Albrecht Ritschl's "Kingdom of God," the realization of the Christian revelation in following the duties of everyday life. Weber's secular ethic can hardly hide its Protestant roots.

"A Religion of World-Conquering Warriors:" Weber on Islam

In contrast to the empirically rather poor work on religion done by Emile Durkheim, Max Weber's work included some reflections on Islam in his sociology of religion. Together with Buddhism, Christianity, Confucianism, Hinduism and Judaism, Islam represents for Weber one of the major religions (*Kulturreligionen*) which aside from Judaism all developed into "world religions." However, in Weber's work there is no independent and coherent study on Islam. Rather we are confronted with scattered fragments appearing in his sociologies of religion, domination, law and the city (Schluchter 1987, 11–20). Weber's interest in Islam was subordinated to his general interest in religious rationalization and, more specifically, in the peculiarities of the rise of European modernity. From his universal historical approach, the non-Christian religions served as a means of comparison to answer the question of the unique features of Western capitalism and the related phenomena of formal rationalism in Occidental culture. Hence, his studies on Islam were also guided by the question of which ways the exceptional historical development of Western culture and institutions could be explained.

This "Eurocentric" nature of Weber's work has found its criticism in the literature about Max Weber and Islam (see: Huff and Schluchter 1999; Rodinson 1966; Turner 1974; Paul 2003). Bryan Turner, for instance, criticized Weber for "ignoring Muslim self-descriptions" and therewith deviating from his own program of a sociology of understanding (1974, 38). According to Turner, Weber's thesis that Islamic patrimonialism prevented the evolution of capitalist preconditions such as "rational law, a free labour market, autonomous cities, a money economy and a bourgeois class" built on a too-narrow source basis (1974, 2).[42] Other scholars perceive Weber's general question as inadequate for the field of Islamic studies. Research on Islam, according to Jürgen Paul, should not be guided by European peculiarities, but directed toward the specific traits of Islamic societies in their own right (Paul 2003, 113–114). In particular, scholars of Islamic studies doubt the applicability of the Weberian conceptual apparatus, and they question the validity of Schluchter's suggestion of viewing Weber's Eurocentrism from a heuristic perspective, that is to say, of basing comparative studies on ideal types that have been derived from the European social experience (Huff and Schluchter 1999, 58).

In spite of the critical stance of Islamic studies toward Weber's ideal types, Joseph Schacht showed the heuristic utility of Weber's sociology of law in analyzing Islamic law already in the 1930s (Schacht 1935). Indeed, not the origin but the heuristic value of Weber's concepts decides their applicability in cross-cultural studies. From my own theoretical position, a Weberian approach to Islam makes sense without doubt. Problematic is not the conceptual apparatus of Weber, but the sources and assumptions on which he built his reflections on Islam. Based on the knowledge of Islamic studies of his times, Weber gives his reader a very stereotypical and, at least on first reading, essentialist image of

---

42. With regard to Islam, this section will show that Turner's criticism of Weber's source basis is fairly justified. For a brief critique of Weber's sources regarding China, see Hung (2003).

Islam. He strongly draws on the dichotomy between occidental and oriental culture, and in empirical terms, his sociology reflects many of the popular prejudices of the nineteenth-century discourse on Islam (Turner 1974, 140).

In distinguishing Islam from other major religions, Weber emphasizes the role of Arab warriors as social carriers of the faith. In the introduction to his three volumes of the sociology of religion, Weber mentions the Muslim religion only twice. There, he defines Islam as "a religion of world-conquering warriors, a knight order of disciplined crusaders" (1915a, 269). According to Weber's interpretation, the prophecy of Islam was directed to warriors (1915a, 285). To be sure, Weber defines Muhammad first as a clear representative of ethical prophecy. In Mecca, Muhammad represented an ethical prophet "who has received a commission from god" and "demands obedience as an ethical duty" (1978a, 447). Yet soon after his arrival in Medina, the "pietistic leader" from Mecca turned into the power-holder of Medina. From this point in time, Islam lost its qualities as an ethical religion of salvation; a position we later will find again in Ignaz Goldziher's work. The pristine religion of Mecca with its tendency to withdraw from the world, Weber continues, was transformed into a "national Arabic warrior religion." Now, Muhammad and the subsequent Khalifs commanded holy war and the political and economic subjugation of the infidels. Instead of "unique salvation," the religious promises became associated with the idea of an "Islamic paradise" for those killed in holy war (1978a, 473–474).[43]

The development of Islam into a warrior religion, so Weber, strongly impacted the social habitus of Muslims. Their strong belief in divine predestination did not result in the same ethical rigorism as that of Christian Puritans. Rather it developed into a form of fatalism and into a complete obliviousness of the self "in the interest of fulfillment of the religious commandment of a holy war for the conquest of the world" (1978a, 573). The Islamic belief in predestination was not "rational" in the sense of the Puritans' which called for an ethical rationalization of the individual's conduct in everyday life. Instead, the ethics of Islamic warriors largely exerted external and ritual demands, leading to the specifically fatalistic characteristics which the belief in predestination assumed in the religious world view of the Muslim masses (1978a, 575). Moreover, "the role played by wealth accruing from spoils of war and from political aggrandizement in Islam is diametrically opposed to the role played by wealth in the Puritan religion" (1978a, 624). Although Islam shares some features with Calvinism and Puritan sects, such as the belief in an almighty God, the "proof of the believer in predestination," i.e. the specific form of inner-worldly asceticism, did not play a part in Islam (1930, 185, fn.36). In Weber's eyes, Islam was never really a religion of salvation. Ancient Islam did not know "an individual quest for salvation," and there was no mysticism. The religious promises pertained to status in this world or to the sensual paradise of the holy warrior. Therefore, the distinctive religious obligations in Is-

---

43. Here Weber follows the general, popularized narrative of the orientalist interpretation of early Islam of his times.

lam and its chief ordinances were of an essentially political nature (1978a, 635).

In imaging Islam as the violent religion of Arab warriors without separating worldly and outer-worldly affairs (read: politics and religion), Weber strongly confirmed some of the well-known orientalist stereotypes. Presumably influenced by Julius Wellhausen, he presents Islamic history as a form of political history driven by a national-religious Arab awakening. From this perspective, a similar rationalization of religious ideas as in some branches of Protestantism was impossible. In addition, Weber saw the rationalization of Islam as also constrained by the "irrational" nature of Islamic law and by the structure of the Islamic city. Regarding these two subjects, it seems that Weber drew especially on Snouk Hurgronje's work.[44] In his reflections on the Islamic city, Weber directly builds on parts of Hurgronje's two volumes on Mecca. Weber takes Mecca as an example of the Arab city, which he defined as a typical clan town (1978b, 1231–1232). Empirically, Weber refers to parts of Hurgronje's first volume in which he describes Mecca in the sixteenth and seventeenth centuries (Hurgronje 1888, 110–120). In this way, Weber based his analysis of the Muslim city not only on a very exceptional case (cf. Paul 2003, 123), but he also constructed his ideal type on secondary sources about a specific period in the history of Mecca. Indeed, given the roles in Islamic history that have been played by cities such as Baghdad, Cairo, Cordoba, Damascus, Kairouan or Istanbul, the selection of Mecca seems awkward, only to be justified by the "religious prejudice" that the typical Islamic city must be found at the place of the origin of Islam.

In his sociology of law, Weber describes Islamic law as a typical form of "sacred law." In bodies of sacred laws, religion exercises a "stereotyping effect on the entire realm of legal institutions and social conventions," treating "legal prescriptions in exactly the same manner that they treat ceremonial and ritual norms." Based on revealed sources and substantial rationality, sacred law "constitutes one of the most significant limitations on the rationalization of the legal order and hence also on the rationalization of economy" (1978a, 577). According to Weber, at least in theory there has been no single sphere of life "in which secular law could have developed independently of the claims of sacred norms" (1978b, 818). In fact, and here Weber follows the then contemporary orientalists like Goldziher and Hurgronje, the schools of Islamic jurisprudence (*fiqh*) were essential in interpreting the sacred norms and adjusting them to changing historical needs. Yet this right to legal interpretation (*ijtihad*) was supposedly extinguished around the thirteenth century. From then onward, Islamic law became inflexible and basically fixed. Islamic jurisprudence declined into the teaching of routinized recitation of fixed sentiments and the arbitrary formulation of legal judgments (1978b, 819–820). Islamic law was therefore exerted as "*Kadi*-justice," a form of jurisdiction that "knows no rational 'rules of decision'" (1978b, 976).[45]

---

44. Regarding Weber's interpretation of Islamic law and its relationship to the work of Hurgronje and Goldziher, see Johansen (1999, 46–51).

45. It has to be mentioned that Weber used the concept of "*Kadi*-Justice" not only in refer-

The complex of problems in Max Weber's sociology of religion shows close affinities with the central questions of Protestant theologians in the late nineteenth century. Beginning with the *Protestant Ethic*, Weber's sociological research agenda represents a specific version of the investigation into the significance of Christianity for the emergence of the modern world. Weber extended this question to a broader research program, analyzing the cultural significance of religious world views in general. His fragmented studies on Islam have to be seen within this context. Weber's work is implicitly based on an evolutionary thesis according to which the rational culture of modernity is a consequence of the immanent tendency to rationalize religious beliefs. Yet formal rationality is not a necessary result of socio-cultural evolution. On the contrary, the secular spirit of capitalism is the accidental outcome of the transformation of a very peculiar religious ethic. It is the non-intended outcome of Calvinists' and Puritans' search for salvation, i.e. for the inner-worldly confirmation of their divine predestination. From this perspective, indeed, Weber did not analyze Islam as a religion in its own right, but with the purpose to show the difference to and historical peculiarity of the trajectory which European Christianity has taken. Moreover, in comparison with the increasing rationalization of Christianity, the development of Islamic doctrine and law appears to have been a decline.[46] However, this "Eurocentric" bias of Weber's research program does not render his general questions obsolete for the study of Islamic history as Paul suggested (cf. Paul 2003, 113). Islamic ethics and Muslim belief have both been confronted with the formal rationalization of everyday life, and Weber's central question about the position of the ethical personality in modern culture has also informed the moral debates among Muslim intellectuals.

While Weber's general concepts and basic questions are not obsolete, his analysis and description of Islam are. Not only do they represent the knowledge of his times, but they do so in a very narrow and selective way. Despite his sociological approach, explaining religious phenomena as socially conditioned, Weber's representation of Islam confirms many essentialist stereotypes. In his writings, Islam appears as a rigid but not rationally applied system of sacred norms in which religion and politics are joined together. With Muhammad's flight to Medina, a unity of state and religion was formed, turning the previous ethical message of salvation into an ethics of war.[47] In this way, Weber makes the typical association of Islam with violence and characterizes the Muslim believer by the fatalistic attitude of the divinely inspired warrior. Already in 1896, the Brit-

---

ence to Islam, but as a general concept for juridical processes which lack any form of rational calculability.

46. To be sure, Weber himself had a quite ambivalent judgment about this rationalization process and would not have used progress and decline in a normative sense as some of his interpreters might have done.

47. Here, Weber seems to follow a thesis with which we will deal in the following chapter and which was shared by a clear majority of orientalist scholars at the end of the nineteenth century.

ish orientalist Thomas Walker Arnold (1864–1930) presented a rather different interpretation of Islamic history. In his *Preaching of Islam*, Arnold rejects the then dominant orientalist image of Islam as a "political religion." Following the distinction between the missionary and non-missionary religions of Max Müller, Arnold explains the global spread of Islam as the result of its "missionary spirit." Not warriors but preachers and traders carried the faith peacefully "into every quarter of the globe." For Arnold, Islam was essentially an ethical religion of salvation, and he underpinned his interpretation with quotations from both Meccan and Medinian Surahs of the Koran (Arnold 1896, 4–6).[48]

Weber apparently did not take this alternative interpretation into consideration. In his fragmented analyses of Islam, he represents the Muslim religion in sharp contrast to the modern program of Protestantism with its non-violent ethics of the autonomous subject searching for salvation through peaceful engagement in the world. The plurality of Muslim self-interpretations and the different trajectories of Islamic history disappear behind a religion defined by a narrow interpretation of the circumstances of its origin. Moreover, his picturing of Islam as the violent religion of an Arab national awakening was deeply molded by the prevalent concepts of European nationalism in the nineteenth century. In the *Protestant Ethic*, Weber analyzed a very specific development within Christianity in a comparative perspective, whereas in his studies on Islam he reduced actual historical complexities to a political and religious unity. Max Weber's interest in Islam was driven by his goal to explain the peculiarities of the historical development of Christianity. Although different in its direction, this interest Weber shared with Ernest Renan and William Robertson Smith.

Conclusions: Constructing Modern Knowledge on Religion and Islam

This chapter started with the young Friedrich Nietzsche's dinner party at Leipzig. Departing from this small gathering at the house of Hermann Brockhaus, I tried to trace some of the discursive and social structures that characterized the European core of an emerging global public sphere. In intellectual and personal terms, the network around Nietzsche served as an illustration of the nature and as an exemplary individual nodal point of the global public sphere. His critique of Christianity marked a crossroads of European reasoning about religion and modernity influenced by and impacting on a multiplicity of academic disciplines such as anthropology, comparative religion, oriental studies, philology, philosophy, psychology, sociology and theology. Departing from Nietzsche, we looked more closely at four crucial intellectuals and their scholarly and cultural milieus—Renan, Durkheim, Robertson Smith and Weber. In analyzing their lives and works, the public sphere appeared as an historically ever-expanding field of overlapping discursive and so-

---

48. In 1913, Arnold's book was published in a second edition which shows its continuing relevance for the field of Islamic studies. Snouck Hurgronje, for example, critically refers to him in his popular book on Islam (Hurgronje 1916b) and in a letter to the German orientalist Nöldeke from October 1924 (Koningsveld 1985, 330).

cial circles embroiled in a web of general themes which were articulated in different but mutually intelligible disciplinary, national and philosophical semantics.

Central among these general themes was the role of religion with respect to modern science, in the comprehensive meaning of the German term *Wissenschaft*, education and the state. The public and scholarly debates were driven by the ambiguities, ambivalences, anxieties and uncertainties of Europe's intellectuals with the modern condition. In the context of massive social transformations, they sensed a certain moral crisis and were looking for new forms of solidarity and civic morality or calling for the resurrection of religious—that is to say, Christian — values. Theoretically speaking, these debates revolved around the increasing dominance of functional differentiation in demarcating relatively autonomous spheres of communication and social action. The firmer establishment of modern society as world society, the global spread of functional social systems as the primary differentiation of the social, was conceptualized in juxtaposing religion—often equated with "traditional society"—with the autonomous social logics of other function systems. In institutional terms, this can be observed in the struggle between state and church, whereas in the realm of ideas we see a clash of scientific and religious world views.

The four protagonists of this chapter were deeply embroiled in this negotiation process and contributed enormously to the modern understanding of religion. In intellectually borrowing from Protestant theology, they were shaping a new understanding of religion in modern society. In comparing different religions, they constructed general concepts of religion within a framework of an evolutionary history of religions. In doing so, the antagonism between modern science and religion was a central theme in their works. All of them applied the means of modern scholarship in order to deal with this conflict between scientific and religious world views. Yet, while Robertson Smith was at ease with reconciling religion and science from the position of a Protestant apologist, Emile Durkheim dissolved religion in a form of agnostic secular humanism. Max Weber, in contrast, took the antagonism between worldly and revealed knowledge for granted, proclaiming an eternal struggle among different spheres of value. In a peculiar blending of ideas, Ernest Renan solved the problem in re-interpreting the history of Christianity as the evolution of an inner-worldly religion based on the ideal model of the perfect individuality of Jesus Christ. Imaging Islam against the backdrop of their general concepts of religion, our protagonists pictured the Muslim religion as an apparent double antagonist. On the one hand, Renan, Smith and Weber confront us with ideas of a rather unchanging Islam remaining in opposition to the specific dynamic rationalism of the modern world. On the other hand, the history of Islam seems to reverse the evolutionary tendency of a progressively rationalizing Christianity to a history of stagnation and decline. In short, Islam is presented as an opposing pole to the civilizing dynamics closely associated with the development of Christianity.

At the individual level of analysis, Renan's combination of positivism, romanticism and poetic Christianity, Weber's tragic sociology, Smith's scientific Christian apology or Durkheim's sociological search for organic solidarity show the broad range and combination of attitudes possible between the outer semantic poles of radical positivism and Christian apology. They express various combinations of ideas in their biographical patchworks. The implicit and abstract unity of world society turns into a unity of difference on the individual level, permanently negotiated through competing semantics and narratives. Perceived from the more abstract level of general themes, however, the differences of these four intellectuals do have a common denominator with respect to the conceptualization of religion under the impact of historicist and evolutionary constructions of human history. There is no doubt that in this general reconfiguration of religion, Christianity was the explicit or implicit model for what can count as a religion (cf. Beyer 2006, 117). Yet it is important to stress that the model was not Christianity as such. Rather, it was the specific ways in which Christianity itself has been reshaped in the nineteenth century, in particular under the impact of philological analysis, biblical criticism and liberal Protestant theology. Moreover, this chapter has shown the various ways in which the different intellectual milieus around Renan, Durkheim, Smith and Weber were related to the controversies about the theological thoughts which emanated from the Tübingen School, whether in mere discursive forms such as in the case of Emile Durkheim, or via chains of social relations as it holds true for William Robertson Smith and Max Weber.

Ironically, the apologist attempts to make Christianity more rational contributed, in the end, to pushing religion further into the transcendental realm of interaction with the supernatural. Modern religion ultimately was conceptualized as faith, as individually experienced belief in supernatural forces. In short, in the structural context of functional differentiation, religion emerged as a more autonomous and therewith clearly visible but at the same time much more limited social sphere whose outer-worldly orientation often has been equated with irrationality. In light of these reductionist tendencies of modernization, orientalists and sociologists have conceptionalized Islam as a holistic unity trying to resist modern differentiation. In the modern image of Islam, this resistance is epitomized in presenting Islam as an inseparable unity of religion and politics, as an all-encompassing way of life. In light of the Protestant reconstruction of Christianity, western scholars turned Islamic traditions into an ideal type of traditional religion, fiercely opposing the rationalizing, individualizing and spiritualizing tendencies of the modern Christian program. Chapter six will analyze the reconfiguration of modern Islam by thinkers of the Islamic reform movement who acted both within and against these very same discursive structures of the global public sphere. We will then see in which ways leading Muslim intellectuals were an integral part of the discursive and social production of knowledge on a global public sphere that in this chapter we observed from its European core.[49]

---

49. Given my theoretical perspective of an emerging modernity, this core is defined by means of power rather than of evolutionary origin.

In the end, what does this chapter tell us with regard to the field of the sociology of knowledge? Within the complex framework of an emerging global public sphere, publicly accepted knowledge seems to be produced and spread in a circular and not in an accumulative way, increasingly integrating a large variety of social and discursive settings. Moreover, the various centers of knowledge production are permanently moving in geographical and institutional terms. Modern knowledge on religion was developed in colonial offices, national and international literary circles, and French, British or German universities, thereby molded by the distinct variants of French positivism, Victorian evolutionism, or German liberal Protestantism. It was synthesized and put into "scientific" categories by sociologists and again disseminated among different scholarly disciplines and the broader public. In this way, Weber's ideal types drew on the scholarly output of philologists, theologians and historians. Turned into conceptual apparatuses of sociology, these ideal types were subsequently spread among scholars who were working in the very same disciplines on whose findings these ideal types once built. In Weber's abstraction of the warrior religion, Wellhausen's image of Islam found its way back from sociology into the field of Islamic studies, here serving further scholarly rationalizations of Islam.

In this circular process, many details disappear, leaving only some reductive core thoughts which public discourses take up and establish as truths. The so-called secularization theory in its crude and popular form is a good example of this way of the dissemination and popularization of knowledge. This complex of taken-for-granted assumptions about religion in modern society has served as a foil to interpret Islam as fundamentally different in perceiving religion and state as inseparably joined together in the Muslim world. In the course of these circular processes, knowledge is fundamentally changing its character and once heavily contested interpretations of reality turn into popularly accepted truths. First established as axioms of common knowledge, these truths serve as relatively stable points of reference in public debates. The next chapter will look more closely at the role of Islamic studies in the creation, dissemination and popularization of knowledge, more specifically of contemporary knowledge about Islam.

5

"Islam as a Problem:"
The Formation of Islamic Studies

"...Islamic Studies in the sense of an increasingly developing independent discipline remains the creation of the two friends Goldziher and Snouck Hurgronje."
(C.H. Becker)

In his obituary on Ignaz Goldziher, the German orientalist C.H. Becker
emphasized the foundational roles which the Hungarian Goldziher and his Dutch
colleague and friend Christiaan Snouck Hurgronje played in the formation of
Islamic studies as an academic discipline. It is generally acknowledged that the
scholars were pioneers in the modern research on Islam. Moreover, Goldziher
and Hurgronje formulated the central problematic and core rationale of the new
discipline: As a scholarly problem, Islam has to be addressed as a "cultural whole
from its religiously determined starting point" (Becker 1922a).[1] Moreover, they
were both particularly interested in the Islamic legal traditions, thus giving the
new discipline and the Western approach to the religion of Islam a specific trait
(cf. Humphreys 1995, 209 and Krüger 2000/2001, 304). Goldziher and Hurgronje
did this in following scholarly different paths. Ignaz Goldziher's work was mostly based on texts which he predominantly analyzed in his study in Budapest.
Snouck Hurgronje, in contrast, as versed in Arabic literature as Goldziher, gained
much of his knowledge through participant observation and as an advisor to colonial politics in Dutch East India. What is important, however, is that the studies
of these two scholars converged in a single direction. In this way, they built the
foundations for Islamic studies and gave the discipline its coherence.

Like Nietzsche with regard to modern reasoning on religion, Ignaz Goldziher and his work represent a nodal point in oriental studies and beyond. From
remoteness in his study in Budapest, we can trace a global network of scholars
and Islamic reformers, a web of exchange about Islam, which perfectly illustrates

1. This "cultural turn" at the beginning of Islamic studies seems to mirror the general,
    strong turn toward culture and religion which characterized the European intellectu-
    al milieu, particularly in Germany, at the turn of the centuries and which we discussed
    together with Max Weber's shift to sociology in the previous chapter.

the concept of a rising global public sphere. Goldziher bequeathed to us a compilation of 13,700 letters from 1,650 persons, literally putting him in contact with every reputable scholar in philology, oriental studies and the history of religion of his times (Simon 1986, 15). Over decades he was regularly in correspondence with leading orientalists such as Fleischer, De Goeje, Snouck Hurgronje, Theodor Nöldeke or Martin Hartmann. Goldziher's first major book *Der Mythos bei den Hebräern* (Mythology among the Hebrews and Its Historical Development, 1876) was an explicit critique of Ernest Renan's Arian-Semitic thesis. In a letter to Goldziher, Renan thanked the young scholar for his critique which he said he would take "into most serious account" (quoted in Conrad 1999, 149). Later, Goldziher met Renan personally on his visit to Paris in 1885 (Goldziher 1978, 108). Upon Renan's death in 1892, Goldziher gave an extended obituary speech for the Hungarian Association of Science of which Renan had been a foreign member (Conrad 1999, 154).[2] Goldziher was also in close contact with William Robertson Smith. In 1892, he spent one week at Christ's College in Cambridge, where he intensively discussed matters of oriental and critical biblical studies with Robertson Smith. Goldziher later edited the second edition of Smith's *Kinship in Arabia,* and after Smith's death Goldziher was offered his Cambridge chair in Arabic studies.

Although a Hungarian Jew, Goldziher was also in close contact with the German and Dutch circles of liberal Protestant theology. In 1904, for instance, Goldziher was invited to the World's Fair in St. Louis. There, he gave the keynote lecture on "Muhammedan history" at the Congress of Arts and Science. Most probably Ernst Troeltsch and Max Weber were among his audience.[3] Goldziher undertook the long journey to the United States together with the German liberal Protestant theologian Adolf von Harnack (1851–1930), who was one of the most influential figures in framing German policies of science and education (Müller 1991, 147). In his theological work, Harnack was profoundly influenced by the historical school and the theology of Albrecht Ritschl. Due to his historical-critical method and insights, he distanced himself from Lutheranism and came under criticism from both orthodox and liberal theologians. Harnack's writings also impacted the work of Max Weber, who knew him from the *Evangelisch-Sozialer Kongress* (Protestant Social Congress), a Protestant organization taking up the social question

---

2. Also in his book on the history of Arab grammar, Goldziher critically departs from Renan's *Histoire general et système compare des langues sémitiques* and the thesis that Arab grammar was not formed under foreign influence (Goldziher 1994, 4).

3. Max Weber and Ernst Troeltsch attended the St. Louis World's Fair together as a part of their journey through the United States. Georg Stauth alluded to the idea that Weber might have been a silent listener to Goldziher's lecture (Stauth 2000, 211). Given the relationship between Weber and Harnack, this allusion makes even more sense. Weber must have known Goldziher and, given his interest in comparative religion, it is very likely that he attended Goldziher's lecture. However, in the official list of academic participants at the World's Fair, Weber's name does not appear, in contrast to those of Ernst Troeltsch and Adolf Harnack, who both also gave lectures at the congress (Rogers 1906).

from the perspective of religious ethics, the president of which Harnack served from 1902–1912 (cf. Swatos and Kivisto 1991, 352). In a letter to Theodor Nöldeke, Goldziher tells us about his pleasure at having traveled together with Harnack and about the intense discussions the two scholars had on the long way to the United States (Simon 1986, 267–269).

Ignaz Goldziher's intellectual and social life was tightly knitted into the network of orientalists, sociologists and theologians with whom we dealt in the previous chapter. In addition, he had numerous direct and indirect relations with Muslim intellectuals. Although Goldziher only spent six months in the Middle East (1873–1874), he was able to establish important lifelong friendships with a number of prominent Muslim intellectuals. For instance, he regularly met with al-Afghani during his stay in Cairo and saw him and other exiled Egyptians on his later visit to Paris. During a four-month study period at the Azhar, Goldziher immersed himself in the world of Islamic scholarship, meeting with leading Sheikhs of Egypt and their students at this center of Islamic learning and at private gatherings (Patai 1987, 70–72). In Damascus, Goldziher became friends with Tahir al-Jazairi, an important Syrian representative of the Islamic reform movement.[4] Al-Jazairi viewed Goldziher "as much of a friend as he did Muhammad Abduh." He generally perceived the studies and text editions of some orientalists as "a useful service" to Islam (Escovitz 1986, 29).[5] Al-Jazairi's follower, the journalist and later Minister of Education in Syria under the French Mandate, Muhammad Kurd Ali, continued this relationship and visited Goldziher in February 1914 in Budapest (Goldziher 1978, 282). Another example is Muhammad Iqbal. Although the Indian reformer did not know Goldziher personally, he apparently knew his work and was in direct contact with Martin Hartmann.[6]

These examples suffice to illustrate the role of Ignaz Goldziher in the social and intellectual networks that connected Western studies on Islam with the Islamic reform movement. Later in this chapter we will return to Goldziher's life and work. To this point, Goldziher has served as a paradigmatic example of the role of individuals in constructing knowledge within the coordinates of an emerging global public sphere. The network of direct and indirect ties around him clearly indicates in which ways the construction of modern knowledge about religion and Islam was embedded in structures of intellectual exchanges already tran-

---

4. Tahir al-Jazairi was born in Damascus in 1852 and should not be confused with Abd al-Qadir al-Jazairi the leader of the Algerian insurrection of 1830 who also was a leading member of the Syrian reform movement after having left France to Damascus. Tahir's father Salih al-Jazairi was participating in the insurrection and belonged to this group of Algerians who were exiled to Syria.

5. In a similar way, Rashid Rida acknowledged the work of Western orientalists with regard to their research on early Islam and on the fundaments of Islamic belief (quoted in Fähndrich 1988, 184).

6. In his diary, Goldziher mentions a meeting with Thomas Arnold, Iqbal's teacher and mentor, whom he met together with William Robertson Smith at the London Congress of Orientalists in 1892 (Goldziher 1978, 149).

scending European borders. The emergence of Islamic studies, in this sense, can be viewed as an instance of globalization that can be analyzed through the conceptual lenses of the theoretical framework of world society presented above. Discussing the formation of Islamic studies as a distinct academic discipline, this chapter will focus on the life and work of four scholars who were crucial for the construction and dissemination of modern knowledge on Islam. Goldziher and Snouck Hurgronje on an international level and Hartmann and Becker on a more German national level mark the turning point in the disciplinary development of oriental studies: the discovery of Islam as an independent field of academic research (Haarmann 1974, 57).

This chapter takes up the academic construction of the modern image of Islam. It investigates the societal and cognitive conditions which have framed the Western scholarly understanding of Islam in the context of global modernization. I will interpret the evolution of the field from two angles. Firstly, there is the macro-sociological framework of progressing functional differentiation combined with the international power relations of imperialism. In this structural context, Islamic studies have evolved as a sub-discipline of the humanities within the larger system of modern science. Secondly, a number of individuals influenced the form and the content of the new discipline, laying the foundations for imagining Islam as both a coherent subject of academic research and a religion in the modern world. They did so in rather unconsciously basing their work on concepts which were derived from the cognitive deep structure of modernity. These concepts and the related themes were discussed in the previous chapter. Now, we turn to four founding figures of Islamic studies whose interpretations of Islam are a result of both the implicitly applied modern *epistemé* and their own historically contingent personal motivations. These individually different motivations to study Islam were clearly influenced by colonialism and by the scholarly environment of biblical criticism. However, this influence was rather different from what Edward Said proposed. The legitimization of colonialism was the least motivation for their studies and biblical criticism meant much more to them than merely serving as a reservoir for methodological tools. Finally, this chapter will argue that in spite of the scientific professionalization and consequent historicization of Islamic studies, the works of these four founding fathers of the discipline nevertheless contributed to the discursive dominance of the essentialist image of Islam.

We will begin with the institutionalization of Islamic studies as an academic discipline in Germany. The German development is significant, as the German language was "the paramount vehicle for Orientalist scholarship" during this early phase of the establishment of Islamic studies (Conrad 1993, 110). For Suzanne Marchand, German orientalists were even "the pacesetting European scholars in virtually every field of oriental studies between about 1830 and 1930" (Marchand 2009, xviii). The four scholars in this chapter all published in German and were closely affiliated with the German university system.[7] After this brief

---

7. At that point of time, German universities were still very small. In 1871, only eleven

glance at institutional history we will move to the biographical aspect. This move first brings us back to Ignaz Goldziher. He devoted almost his whole adult life to the study of Islam although it was only very late that Goldziher found professional recognition as a scholar in his own country, Hungary. In the third section we will look at the life and work of Christiaan Snouck Hurgronje, who as a professor in Leiden and as a colonial advisor in Dutch East India was engaged in both researching and administering Islam. From these two founding fathers of Islamic studies we move to C.H. Becker and Martin Hartmann, two scholars, closely connected to Goldziher and Hurgronje, who tried to establish modern Islamic studies in Germany before World War I. The chapter will conclude with an analysis of the way in which the works of these scholars were embedded in the broader intellectual and political contexts of their times and took part in shaping modern knowledge on Islam.

From Oriental to Islamic Studies: The Emancipation of an Academic Discipline

The emergence of Islamic studies as a distinct academic discipline is one particular element in the general rise of modern science as a societal sub-system. From the theoretical perspective of world society, the formation of Islamic studies represents an instance in the global spread of functional differentiation, more precisely, in the establishment of science as a global system of communication and social action. Historically, we can observe the evolution of modern science as two different but mutually dependent processes. On the one hand, the global system emerged through the establishment of national scientific communities, to a certain extent mirroring the evolution of global politics by national state formation. On the other hand, the national fields of modern scholarship were characterized by increasing internal differentiation into disciplines and sub-disciplines. This internal differentiation generated specific forms of scientific communication that again transcended the narrow realm of the national state. Due to growing specialization in all fields of research, scholars had to develop professional ties beyond their national scientific communities. The disciplinary differentiation of national science became an incentive for international collaborations on both the personal and the organizational level, the latter expressed in the increasing number of international congresses, means of publication and professional associations. A case in point was the compilation of the *Encyclopedia of Islam,* an enterprise of a truly transnational nature (Goldziher 1897). With regard to Islamic studies, C.H. Becker mentioned in 1912 the emergence of five new journals focusing on the Muslim world as a proof of the firm establishment of the new academic discipline. Since the foundation of the French journal *Revue du Monde Musulman* in 1906 the young discipline had witnessed the launching of *Der Islam, Orientalisches Archiv, The Moslem World, International Review of Missions* and

---

universities had more than 500 students. The three biggest universities—Berlin, Leipzig and Munich—grew above 5,000 students until 1914, eleven other universities, then, had between 2,000 and 5,000 students (Wokoeck 2009, 47).

Mir Islam (Becker 1912, 531–533). The academic biographies in this chapter clearly demonstrate this globalization of science in the meaning of a rapidly growing global interconnectedness of scholarly work. Islamic studies developed first in national contexts, however, from its beginnings characterized by the fluidity of social, discursive and cognitive links which interconnected Western scholars and Muslim intellectuals as actors in an increasingly global public sphere.[8]

This section will look more closely at the formation of Islamic studies in the German context. In reference to the above theoretical sketch, I will analyze the rise of Islamic studies in Germany as the formation of a national community of scholars on Islam in an increasingly globalizing context. The German experience displays the major general features of the evolution of the discipline of Islamic studies in Europe. In organizational terms, we can first observe the emancipation of oriental studies from theology and then its internal differentiation into sub-disciplines such as Indology, Semitic languages, Assyriology or East Asian studies. The formation of Islamic studies was, then, a result of new methodological and socio-political developments.[9] Methodologically, the introduction of the theoretical approaches and conceptual tools of history, anthropology, comparative religion and sociology loosened the close linkage between Semitic philology and Islamic studies. In this way, the disciplinary evolution of the social sciences and humanities contributed to the dissolution of the classical and encompassing concept of oriental studies as a branch of non-European philology. Politically, the imperialist power struggle of the late nineteenth century gradually made research on modern Muslim societies a topic which was not only politically important but also economically viable because of the provision of state subsidies for research on Islam. Although a late-comer in colonial politics, these developments were clearly visible in Germany and undoubtedly facilitated the promotion of modern Islamic studies by C.H. Becker and Martin Hartmann.

On the individual level, we can observe the formation of Islamic studies in the occurrence of a shift in careers from theologians to philologists and then to distinct scholars of Islamic studies. The latter began to supplement their knowledge based on the study of texts with their personal experiences in the Muslim world from extended study tours and professional assignments in colonial administrations. The paradigmatic example among the founding fathers of Islamic studies is Christiaan Snouck Hurgronje. He combined theological and philological education with ethnographic and sociological methods while serving in both the educational and the colonial administrative systems of the Netherlands. Regarding these developments on the organizational and on the individual level, German

---

8. For a more detailed analysis of the emergence of modern science through the lenses of systems theory, see Stichweh (1984 and 1996).

9. In the foundation of independent university institutes for oriental studies, Germany was a comparative latecomer, probably due to the fact that oriental studies did not play a role in the education of teachers. Apart from the first seminar in oriental studies in Jena which was founded in 1837, 21 institutes were opened between 1894 (Heidelberg) and 1929 (Berlin) (Hanisch 2003, 58).

scholarship and the infrastructure of the German university became central in shaping modern Islamic studies.[10] In the intellectual milieu of the German universities the scholarly discourses of various disciplines not only overlapped, but they also became places of academic pilgrimage for young scholars from Europe and beyond.

In the early nineteenth century, oriental studies in Germany was still the domain of theologians. At that point of time an orientalist was primarily a university teacher who combined the exegesis of the Old Testament with knowledge of Hebrew and Arabic (Mangold 2004, 48). In contrast to this clear subordination of oriental studies to theology in Germany, the French National Assembly established in March 1795 the École Speciale des Langues Orientales Vivantes in Paris. At this institute for oriental languages, three professors taught Arabic, Turkish, Crimean Tartar, Persian and Malay as subjects independent from the disciplinary bonds of theology. Related to the spirit of the French Revolution and the country's colonial interests, the École developed into a "secular" institute of oriental studies. In particular the École's chair in Arabic and prime target of Edward Said's critique, Antoine Isaac Silvestre de Sacy, attracted students and scholars from all over Europe, making the École the center of European scholarship in the field. For decades, his Arab grammar, first published in 1810, and his anthology of Arab texts formed the basis for Arab studies in Europe (Fück 1955, 140–157). In the years from 1810 to 1840 around twenty Germans studied in Paris, who then exported the philological know-how of de Sacy to Germany (Mangold 2004, 66). Among these German students was Heinrich Leberecht Fleischer (1801–1888), who not only firmly established oriental philology at Leipzig University, but was also a leading figure in gradually moving the center for oriental studies from France to Germany.

Fleischer became probably the most popular teacher of Arabic in nineteenth century Europe. Focusing on the formal side of philology, he taught scores of young European scholars, making Leipzig into the "Mecca" of Arabism. When Ignaz Goldziher joined his class in 1869, he and his eleven fellow students represented six different nations (Fück 1955, 171). The four protagonists of this chapter were all connected with the Leipzig school of Arabism. Fleischer had first studied theology at Leipzig University under theologian and orientalist Ernst Friedrich Karl Rosenmüller (1768–1835) (Preissler 1990, 25). In 1824, he went to Paris for four years and became de Sacy's favorite student. Fleischer adored de Sacy and completely identified with de Sacy's approach of pure philology. It was not Ernest Renan, as suggested by Edward Said, but Heinrich Leberecht Fleischer who continued de Sacy's work and elevated his formal philological approach to the scientific standards of nineteenth century oriental studies. In contrast to Renan, Fleischer was not interested in comparative linguistics and did not apply

---

10. The importance of Germany in the rise of modern Islamic studies is also expressed in the fact that the Hungarian Goldziher wrote his academic publications almost all in German and the Dutch Hurgronje published at least a substantial part of his work in German.

any theories related to Franz Bopp's (1791–1867) comparative grammar. As early as in grammar school, he developed a specific interest in Semitic languages and began to teach himself Arabic (Goldziher 1904, 190). Unfortunately, Fleischer did not manage to visit the Arab world personally, but he was in constant contact with Arab intellectuals. Besides his meeting with Rifaat al-Tahtawi (1801–1873) in Paris,[11] he was in regular correspondence with Butrus al-Bustani and other Arab reformists in Beirut (Goldziher 1904, 198).[12] In his *Oriental Diary*, Ignaz Goldziher mentioned the almost "religious" reverence with which the Christian-Arab scholars around Bustani referred to the German Arabist (Patai 1987, 109). For Fleischer, there was no principle dichotomy between East and West. Convinced of Europe's scientific primacy, however, he viewed oriental culture as dormant, fossilized by the power of tradition. Therefore, it was Europe's mission to awaken the Orient and help oriental societies to modernize (Karachouli 1994, 178–182). Like many European intellectuals in the nineteenth century, Fleischer's world view was deeply molded by the colonial habitus of Europe without himself actively supporting or defending colonial policies.

Fleischer's appointment at Leipzig (1835) marked the eventual break-through of the scientific philological approach to oriental studies in Germany. He was the founding father of scientific Arabic philology in Germany (Brockelmann 1922, 3). With his rationalist philology, Fleischer influenced the disciplinary differentiation and methodological consolidation of oriental studies, although its final emancipation from theology did not take place before the end of the century (Mangold 2004, 151).[13] In this process, oriental studies took its example from classical philology, which had attained a leading position in the formation of the modern scientific system of the humanities. Fleischer was also a driving force in developing the necessary infrastructure for the establishment of oriental studies as an academic community of communication. From 1843, he contemplated the organization of regular meetings among German orientalists, which eventually

11. The Egyptian religious scholar Tahtawi was the Imam of the first Egyptian study mission to Europe. Between 1826 and 1831 he lived in Paris where he also was in regular contact with orientalist scholars such as de Sacy. After his return he wrote a well-known book about his stay in Paris which also was translated into Ottoman Turkish (Hourani 1962, 69–70).

12. Butrus al-Bustani (1819–1893) was a leading figure in the Christian-Arab Awakening throughout the nineteenth century (cf. Sharabi 1970, Chapter IV).

13. Most of the students at Fleischer's institute for Arabic studies in Leipzig were theologians who continued to view Arabic as an auxiliary language for biblical exegesis. Regarding the prominent role of theology it is important to mention that theology was the option for students with a modest or poor socio-economic background, who were not able to study the expensive subjects of law and medicine. Moreover, the theological faculty was responsible for the education of school teachers whose number rose significantly throughout the nineteenth century (Wokoeck 2009, 44). From this perspective, the emancipation of oriental studies from theology was also "supported" by theology in making oriental studies feasible (cf. Wokoeck 2009, 218).

led to the foundation of the Deutsche Morgenländische Gesellschaft, DMG (German Oriental Studies Association) in 1845 (Preissler 1990, 33). Thereby, he took similar organizations in France, Great Britain and the United States as his example. At the same time, he launched the publication of a journal, *Zeitschrift der Deutschen Morgenländischen Gesellschaft (ZDMG),* which would serve both as a forum for disciplinary discussions and for the dissemination of scholarly research to a broader public (Brockelmann 1922, 12).

In Fleischer's work, we can observe major patterns behind the internal differentiation of science as a modern social system. Under the roof of the department for philosophy, he introduced methodological distinctions and a disciplinary specific problem complex that distinguished oriental studies from theology as well as classical philology. With the foundation of the DMG and its journal, he built up the necessary infrastructure for the consolidation of a national scientific community of orientalists. At the same time, his teaching connected scholars from all over Europe, and the openness of the ZDMG to articles in languages other than German provided a nationally established platform of communication reaching far beyond the borders of Germany. Moving its centre from France to Germany, oriental studies did not lose its international character. On the contrary, the German scholars of the nineteenth century did not work independently, but their studies were a European affair with an in principle global dimension (cf. Paret 1968, 15). On the individual and organizational level, German orientalists were closely interconnected with an emerging global community of scholars, they were part and parcel of the formation of science as a global system and the dissemination of their work occurred throughout the global public sphere.

Looking more closely at the educational and topical background of its members, the history of the DMG also shows its transitory role in this process of the internal differentiation of the modern system of science. In the decades of Fleischer's engagement, oriental studies still appeared as one field of studies, encompassing a broad variety of languages, cultures, historical periods and geographical locations (Brockelmann 1922, 3). Yet this perceived unity soon disappeared under the impact of a progressive disciplinary differentiation. In this process, theoretical and methodological innovations, the attempt to systematize disciplinary knowledge and the increasing specialization of scholars played decisive roles. In Göttingen, the second important school of oriental studies in Germany, Heinrich Ewald criticized Fleischer's and de Sacy's exclusive focus on grammar and linguistics. Ewald rejected the idea of "pure philology," but promoted philological knowledge as a means for the interpretation of texts (Mangold 2004, 99). Some of his more prominent followers, especially Theodor Nöldeke (1836–1930) and Julius Wellhausen, tried to combine philological with interpretative skills. In doing so, they applied the historicist methods of German biblical criticism to the field of oriental studies and gave the discipline a new direction.

As we saw in the previous chapter, Wellhausen came to Arab and Islamic studies from theology. However, in working on early Islam, Wellhausen was not much interested in religious matters. On the contrary, he saw Muhammad's historical importance not in his prophecy but in his "political" activities. Based on the differentiation of Muhammad's role in Mecca and Medina, he introduced the paradigm of Muhammad as "statesman" and contributed strongly to emphasizing the theme of Islam and politics in Western scholarship (cf. van Ess 1980, 43). Both Wellhausen and Nöldeke based their studies on classical literature. Yet, while Wellhausen was more an interpretative historian, Nöldeke understood himself primarily as a philologist, although with a strong interest in and a good understanding of historical problems (Becker 1932, 46). He combined his Semitic studies with Persian and Turkish, becoming famous as a linguist, editor and translator of classical texts. With his dissertation about the history of the Koran written in 1856, Nöldeke already made a lasting contribution to the emerging field of Islamic studies. For an extended version of this study he received an award from the Academie des inscriptions et belles-lettres in Paris, and its German edition, *Geschichte des Korans* (1860), became a standard reference for the critical investigation in the historical chronology of the chapters of the Koran (Fück 1955, 218). After his graduation in Göttingen, Nöldeke went first to Vienna and then to Leiden (1857–1858). There began his lifelong friendship with the Dutch orientalist De Goeje, a teacher of Snouck Hurgronje, and he was in touch with the circle of liberal Protestant theologians around Abraham Kuenen (Hurgronje 1931, 248). From 1864 to 1872, Nöldeke was a professor at the University of Kiel, before taking up his chair in oriental studies at the newly founded *Reichsuniversität* in Strasbourg.[14]

Theodor Nöldeke certainly was one of the most important orientalists of his time. He made Strasbourg into the third center of oriental studies in Germany, where he received students from all over Europe and the United States. Although a master in the interpretation of texts, in his teaching Nöldeke focused on the precise philological handling of original sources (Mangold 2004, 90). He wanted his students first and foremost to become versed in the large field of Semitic languages. Whoever was not able to study directly with him was at least familiar with his writings. Thus it is fair to say that from the 1860s all orientalists became followers of Nöldeke (Hurgronje 1931, 277). To a certain extent, he continued Fleischer's attitude of stressing the importance of exact philology in oriental scholarship. In a letter to Ignaz Goldziher, however, he underlined how much he owed to the inspiration of his teacher Heinrich Ewald and that he was happy not to grow up under the philological narrowness of Fleischer. By transforming exact philology from being a purpose in itself into a means of sound interpretation, Wellhausen and Nöldeke opened the field of oriental studies to historicist criticism and to approaches inspired by the social sciences and humanities. Based on their work on early Islam the study of Islamic history and its driving forces

---

14. The *Reichsuniversität* in Strasbourg was founded after the Franco-Prussian war in 1870 and the subsequent annexation of Alsace-Lorraine by Germany. Established as a "model university" by the imperial government of the Reich, the university was a part of Germany's efforts to strengthen the cohesion between Alsace and the Reich. In order to fulfill this "cultural mission" the humanities and cultural studies played and important role at the *Reichsuniversität* (Hanisch 2003, 5)

moved into the center of interest for the next generation of orientalist scholars who were to become the founding generation of Islamic studies proper.

When examining the careers of individual scholars, the emergence of Islamic studies can largely be associated with these processes of internal differentiation and disciplinary specialization. In order to understand the establishment of Islamic studies as an autonomous discipline of research and education, however, we also have to look at the historical-political context. The developments in Germany are therefore again good examples. Inspired by religious and romanticist ideas, the older generations of German orientalists pursued their studies in the rather detached environment of the humanist German university. Their studies gained societal legitimacy with reference to the hegemonic role of Germany's middle-class intellectuals (*Bildungsbürgertum*) and their humanist attitude to education. Soon after the foundation of the German national state in 1871, however, the Islamic world also became a matter of political and economic concern for Germany. During the short period of German colonialism (1884–1914), the knowledge of orientalist scholars was of public interest (cf. Gründer 1985). In the context of imperialism, the establishment of Islamic studies in Germany was closely linked to Berlin's political affiliation with the Ottoman Empire. In 1882, Germany resumed its military collaboration with Istanbul. The signing of an Ottoman-German trade agreement (1890), Emperor Wilhelm's visit in Jerusalem (1898), and the granting of a concession to Germany to build the Baghdad Railway were further steps in the political and economic collaboration between the two empires. In this, Germany's oriental politics were guided by four publicly shared motives concerning what the Ottoman Empire represented: a source of raw materials; a market for German goods; a territory of strategic depth in imperial competition; and a field for Germany's cultural mission, as a subordinated partner in German world politics (cf. Schöllgen 1981).

Germany's imperial policies were reflected in the foundation of the Seminar for Oriental Languages in Berlin (1887) and the Colonial Institute in Hamburg (1908). The latter even became the example for the foundation of what is now the School of Oriental and African Studies (SOAS) at the University of London in 1916 (Mangold 2004, 235). The foundation of the Seminar for Oriental Languages in Berlin was a joint initiative of Chancellor Bismarck and the Prussian government, predominantly driven by political and economic interests. In contrast to the humanist character of German universities, the Seminar was an institute of "applied sciences" (Hartmann 1912, 614). Financed by the Prussian state and the German Reich, its primary task was to train German diplomatic staff in oriental languages. In addition, the Seminar was open for non-diplomatic students in order to support German economic interests in the East. Moreover, it developed into a place of higher education whose teaching program comprised not only oriental languages but also courses on legal, cultural, economic and political affairs (Mangold 2004, 226–236). To a certain extent, the establishment of the Colonial Institute in Hamburg occurred as a critique of and in competition with the Seminar in Berlin (Hanisch 2003, 44). Not a university at the time of its foundation, the Colonial Institute was more oriented toward the combination of teaching and research with the intention of becoming a foundation stone for the establishment of Hamburg University. The academic profile of the institute was decisively shaped by its first director C.H. Becker (Mangold 2004, 246). Both institutes opened the discipline of oriental studies in Germany for new fields of research, making the modern Islamic world an independent subject of academic analysis for the first time.

In light of the Said controversy, German scholarship was not so much an exception in comparison to that of Britain and France. Rather, Germany was a latecomer with regard to the relationship between colonial politics and the scientific investigation of the Orient. Late nineteenth century imperialism, the political embroilment of the Ottoman Empire in European power politics, and the anti-colonial idea of Panislamism form the specific historical context in which Islamic studies evolved. Processes of internal disciplinary differentiation were thus facilitated by political and economic interests. Yet, Said significantly exaggerated the impact of these interests. Looking at Germany, they were just one variable among many in a complex setting of disciplinary and societal developments. Empirically this is supported by the fact that only a minority of the graduates from the Berlin Seminar for Oriental Languages found employment in Germany's colonial administration (Mangold 2004, 234). Furthermore, the differentiation of oriental studies into a large variety of distinct sub-disciplines of the humanities even increased after the explosion of European imperialism in the First World War.

The German example shows rather in which ways the colonial condition contributed to the rise of contemporary Islamic studies. The older generation of orientalists such as Fleischer, Ewald, Wellhausen or Nöldeke, normally did not have the opportunity to travel or work overseas. They pursued their studies within the confines of the ivory tower of Germany's humanist universities, focusing on texts and the history of early Islam. At the same time, the complex of problems behind their studies mirrored the essential themes of nineteenth-century reasoning about modernity. In sharp contrast to this generation of primarily philologists, many of the teachers in the Berlin Seminar, for instance Martin Hartmann, had first-hand knowledge from living and travelling in the Islamic world. Their interest in contemporary Muslim affairs was as much driven by personal experiences and political world views as supported by political and economic interests. Still anchored in the philological tradition of orientalist studies, this new generation of scholars continued the shift in focus from philology to interpretative methods by applying them more and more to contemporary questions. In doing so, however, they also took over some of the general categories and standards with which their predecessors interpreted Islamic history.

Crucial in this respect were the impact of scientific rationalism and the often unconscious application of the categories of political history writing on this tradition. In the work of Nöldeke and Wellhausen, for example, this impact is reflected in a critical attitude toward religious orthodoxies in general and in the tendency to study Islam not as a religious practice but from the angle of dogmatic and political developments. For Edward Said, Theodor Nöldeke's "dislike of the Orient" and "love of Greece" resulted from the "substitution and displacement" which the Orient experienced in the work of orientalists (1978, 209). Blinkered by his own thesis, Said failed to notice that Nöldeke fundamentally questioned the positive role of religious beliefs. C.H. Becker refers to a letter from Nöldeke in which he expressed his doubts about whether religions have not harmed humanity more than benefited it (Becker 1932, 515). In his letters to Ignaz Goldziher and Snouck Hurgronje, Nöldeke several times describes the Koran and the Bible as fantasies. He calls himself an "orthodox heathen" and repeatedly refers to Islamic rationalists such as Ibn Rushd (1126–1198) or Ibn Tufail (1105–1185) as philosophers who in reality were far detached from "true Islam." Nöldeke associated true Islam with Sunni orthodoxy in general and with the purist interpretations of the Hanbali and Wahhabi schools in particular (cf. Simon 1986, 253–256 and Koningsveld 1985).[15] In 1894, he told Goldziher that as a young man he had been accidentally drawn into Koranic studies, but now he was no longer able to understand these worlds of religious dreams (Simon 1886, 191). Nöldeke's appreciation for Greece had nothing to do with Said's thesis of substitution and displacement, rather it was a strong vote against the religious values of Christianity and Judaism. He was equally denigrating of orthodox Muslims, Christians and Jews.[16] Born into the Protestant household of a school director, Theodor Nöldeke soon became a staunch rationalist and agnostic with a strongly antagonistic attitude toward religion.

In the late nineteenth century, modern knowledge of Islam was disseminated through the lenses of positivist rationalism and the semantics of political history writing. An excellent example of presenting Islam in this way is the article *Mohammedanism* by Julius Wellhausen, published in the ninth edition of the *Encyclopedia Britannica*. Wellhausen tells his audience that Muhammad had a "thoroughly practical nature" and "knew how to utilize Islam as the means for founding the Arabian commonwealth." Hence, according to Wellhausen, by becoming mixed up with practical considerations, almost from the very beginning Islam lost its religious ideality and received the political nature it has ever since re-

---

15. This attitude to associate "true Islam" with Wahhabism might be related to the important role which the idea of "survivals" played in nineteenth century evolutionary anthropology. According to this idea, anthropologists can understand past "primitive" cultures in studying still existing remnants of this social past. From this perspective, the culture of the Arab peninsula was perceived as containing surviving patterns of the social conditions under which the Islamic revelation took place. Consequently, Islam as practiced there could be interpreted as the most pristine existing form.

16. In February 1884, he responded to the theses of I. Singer's book *Sollen die Juden Christen werden?* (Should the Jews become Christians?). In a letter to Singer, Nöldeke turns against the association of religion and politics and refutes the idea of the existence of a Jewish nation. At the same time, Nöldeke does not claim that Jews should become Christians but they should discard their "oriental religious rites," which prevent them from becoming modern Europeans of Jewish faith (Nöldeke 1884).

tained (Wellhausen 1883, 552). In Medina, "the prayers took the form of military exercises" and the mosque was turned into "the great exercising ground of Islam." In Wellhausen's eyes, not the preaching of God's revelation, but the founding of the Muslim state was the Prophet's greatest achievement. According to his interpretation, Islam as a religion did not attract the Arabs. It was mere material success which turned them into Muslims. Assuming Muhammad's prophecy to be a pretext for the establishment of his power, Wellhausen concludes that "the politician in him outgrew the prophet more and more" (1883, 553–561).

To be sure, Wellhausen based his interpretations of early Islam on original sources, however, mainly on the texts of Arab historians that were written in the three centuries after the Prophet's death. These texts basically reflected the imperial struggles and social conditions of the patrimonial empires of this epoch (cf. Paret 1930). Even more important, Wellhausen's highly praised imaginative and synthetic writing style was grounded in the concepts and themes which we analyzed in the previous chapter as the nineteenth century's intellectual encounter with modernity. The voice of *Mohammedanism* aptly reflects this embeddedness of Wellhausen in the specific cognitive framework of late nineteenth century Europe and the particularities of Germany's political history. From this perspective, he interpreted Muhammad's chief achievement in "his Bismarck-like unification of the Arabs" (Marchand 2009, 188). As a well-versed historian, he was not unaware of the historical determinedness of his work. He himself pointed out the anachronistic tendencies of his picture of the Prophet and early Islam which was guided by modern notions such as the separation between religion and state (Wellhausen 1883, 561). Recalling Max Weber's selective reception of Wellhausen's work, however, I do have the suspicion that even the most enlightened readers of *Mohammedanism* did not take much notice of these anachronistic tendencies in Wellhausen's way of imaging Islam. They all were hostages to the implicitly applied background knowledge of their times.

This historically conditioned selectiveness in the reception of the results of oriental and later Islamic scholarship has also leveled out many elements of critique with which Goldziher, Hurgronje, Becker and Hartmann continued the work of their predecessors. These four founding fathers of Islamic studies proper were firmly rooted in the historical tradition conveyed by Nöldeke and Wellhausen. However, in comparison to the work of their teachers, their writings were much more molded by the often only implicit application of concepts and theoretical assumptions from disciplines such as anthropology, comparative religion and sociology. The key concepts and process models of classical modernization theories framed the studies of this new generation of scholars on Islam and at the same time they reinforced and revised the features which classical orientalists handed down to them.

Ignaz Goldziher: "Religious" Devotion to the Study of Islam

Ignaz Goldziher was born in 1850 in Székesfehérvár (Stuhlweissenburg), a provincial town with an ethnically mixed population some 50 km from the Hungarian capital Budapest. His father was a Jewish tradesman and Goldziher's ancestors had moved from Hamburg, Germany, to Hungary. Ignaz Goldziher grew up in an environment characterized by a high appreciation of knowledge, Jewish traditions and humanist values. From his early childhood, religion played an important role in his life. In his diary, Goldziher tells us that he was raised with Jewish self-confidence and in tolerance toward other religions. He lived in close contact to Christian children, even attending church services together with them. His father tutored his son intensively in Hebrew. As a child, Goldziher immersed himself in Jewish religious literature, and parallel to his school education he was taught in Jewish theology and philosophy. At the age of five, Goldziher began to read the Bible and at eight he received his introduction to the Talmud (Goldziher 1978, 18). From then on, his youth consisted in studying in a daily routine which gave him night rest from only midnight to five in the morning (Patai 1987, 15). In 1862, the twelve-year-old Goldziher published his first book on the history of prayers in Judaism, criticizing "orthodox exaggerations" (Haber 2004, 76). As Goldziher put it in his diary, his Jewish identity soon developed into the "pulse of his life" (Goldziher 1978, 33).

Due to economic problems, the family moved to Pest in 1865.[17] His father, a traditional trader in leather, could no longer compete against the growing industrialization of the economy and economic hardship accompanied Goldziher's youth. In his father's view a career as a scholar would be Goldziher's escape from this situation of economic deprivation. After arriving in Budapest with his "private library" of 600 volumes, Ignaz Goldziher enrolled at Budapest University in the winter of 1865/66, attending courses in philosophy, linguistics, and classical and oriental philology (Goldziher 1978, 24–25). Here, he became a student of Ármin Vámbéry (1832–1913), at this time an internationally known Turkologist and oriental traveler (Haber 2006c). Vámbéry introduced his enormously talented student to the Hungarian minister of culture, Baron József Eötvös, who granted Goldziher a scholarship in order to facilitate his subsequent studies in Berlin, Leipzig, Leiden and Vienna. In 1868, he departed for Germany, first to Berlin and in 1869 to Leipzig. In Berlin, at the *Hochschule für die Wissenschaft des Judentums* (Higher Institute for Jewish Studies), Goldziher met Abraham Geiger (1810–1874) and Moritz Steinschneider (1816–1907), who were both representatives of the German Jewish reform movement and scholars with an interest in oriental studies. In addition, Heymann Steinthal (1823–1899), a comparative linguist and philosopher of religion, introduced him to the work on comparative methodology of the Oxford professor Max Müller (Waardenburg 1962, 12).

In Leipzig in 1869–1870, Ignaz Goldziher received his firm training in Arabic under Fleischer, which formed the indispensable philological basis for all of his later works (Desomogyi 1961, 10). His excellence in Arabic was proven by the fact that Fleischer quickly assigned him to teach the basic language courses, a position

---

17. Pest was one of the three cities (Buda and Óbuda) which in 1872 were merged into the Hungarian capital Budapest (cf. Haber 2004, 75).

for which his fellow students named him the "little Sheikh" (Skovgaard-Petersen 2001b) Yet, Goldziher did not follow Fleischer's exclusively philological path. Rather, he was interested in the historical dimension of languages. Influenced by German historicism, he adopted the ideas of Alfred von Kremer (1828–1889), an Austrian diplomat and orientalist who aimed at writing a cultural history of Islam.[18] In 1871, Goldziher spent six months at the University of Leiden, where he not only engaged in oriental studies under Dozy and De Goeje, but was strongly attracted by the university's liberal Protestant theologians. The scholars around Abraham Kuenen made Leiden one of the most important centers of biblical criticism. In his diary, Goldziher described this encounter with the orientalists and theologians at Leiden as an experience that was in many ways decisive for his future career, making Islam and the method of biblical criticism the two pillars of his academic work (Goldziher 1978, 50). In the same year, however, Baron Eötvös died. Thus Goldziher lost the most important political advocate in his career, who had promised him a university chair upon his return. Back in Hungary, the new minister of culture did not offer him the expected professorship. Instead, he furnished Goldziher with another scholarship, this time to travel the Middle East.

On September 15, 1873, Goldziher embarked a steamer on the river Danube, bringing him to Istanbul from where he continued to Beirut, Damascus, Jerusalem and finally Cairo. Sent by the Hungarian Ministry of Religion and Education to collect texts and to study Arabic dialects, the young scholar gained far more from his journey than just this (Conrad 1993, 112). In retrospect, he described his aim as to immerse himself in Islam and its sciences. He desired to become a part of Muslim scholarship and to learn about the motivating forces that transformed the "Judaic cult of Mecca into the colossal world religion of Islam." Moreover, Goldziher wanted to analyze the impact of this religious system on society and morals (Goldziher 1978, 57). Apart from a short trip as a travel guide for Jewish teachers, which brought him again to Cairo in 1896, this study tour was his only direct experience with the world of Islam. In personal terms, Goldziher viewed it as the happiest period of his life, as his "Muhammadian Year" full of "honor, glory and light" (1978, 50). This splendid "year" ended after six months, however, when he was called back to Budapest, where his father lay on his deathbed.

With his return to Budapest in April 1874, Goldziher's life underwent a dramatic change. The professorship in Semitic philology had gone to Péter Hatala (1832–1918), a Catholic theologian whose qualification as an orientalist was based on his three years of experience as a missionary in Palestine. In publicly criticizing the infallibility of the Pope, Hatala raised a scandal which was only contained by transferring the theologian to the faculty of arts. For Goldziher, however, began a 30-year-long ordeal. In January 1876, he became the secretary

---

18. The work of Alfred von Kremer, especially his *Geschichte der herrschenden Ideen des Islam* (History of the Leading Ideas in Islam, 1868), made a profound impression on the young Goldziher. Goldziher found the direction for his own research in Kremer's approach of analyzing Islamic history from a universalist perspective as a history of ideas (Simon 1986, 31–33).

of the Neolog Jewish community of Pest, a position he held for over 30 years until he eventually succeed Hatala on the chair in Semitic languages in 1905 (Simon 1986, 49–51).[19] In these thirty years, Goldziher lived two lives. On the one hand, he was the deeply frustrated secretary of the Jewish community who hated his job and the people surrounding him. Goldziher experienced his daily work as slavery and as a constant humiliation. In June 1892, he called his birthday a day of mourning and he looked back on his life as a time full of grief, insult and misfortune (Goldziher 1978, 140).[20] On the other hand, there was the world-famous scholar who already at the Orientalist Congress in Stockholm (1889) received a gold medal for his scholarly work, an award given to him and Theodor Nöldeke under the applause of the leading scholars in the field by the Swedish King Oscar II (1978, 119).

It was under the hardship of his job as a secretary that Ignaz Goldziher wrote most of the scholarly works which so decisively contributed to shaping the modern discipline of Islamic studies. While enduring his ordeal by day, the nights and his vacation were spent on academic work, leaving him only around six weeks a year for writing (Goldziher 1978, 93). His first major book, *Der Mythos bei den Hebräern,* still dealt with Judaism and was not a success. In particular among the Jewish community the book was perceived as an affront to the sacrosanct nature of the Bible and thus not well-received. In Hungary, hundreds signed a petition in protest against Goldziher and demanded that he be removed from his position as secretary of the Jewish community (Conrad 1999, 148). Goldziher's celebrated works on Islam, then, began with a series of conference papers in 1881. In 1884, *Die Zahiriten* appeared, a pioneering study on Islamic law in which Goldziher for the first time applied his historical-critical method to classical Arabic sources. He developed his evolutionary perspective on the history of Islam further in the two volumes *Muhammedanische Studien* (Muhammedan Studies), published in 1889 and 1890. In these two books, dedicated to his friend Snouck Hurgronje, Goldziher masterly applied his critical method to the large corpus of Islamic traditions, showing in which way the political and religious quarrels after the death of the Prophet are reflected in the Sunna, the collected traditions about the Prophet (Ritter 1922). According to C.H. Becker, the Muhammedan Studies represent Goldziher's masterpieces, opening a new epoch for orientalist studies (1922a, 506). In 1910, he published a series of six lectures, *Vorlesungen über den*

---

19. The Neolog congregation represents a relatively conservative position in the Jewish reform movement which maintains the authority and importance of the Halacha, the Jewish legal tradition. In contrast to Orthodox Judaism, however, the Neolog school of thought not only accepts the historical critical analysis of traditional texts but also perceives them as being beneficial in religious terms. In this way, the Neolog congregation positions itself between Orthodoxy and more radical reform movements.

20. Contrary to the impression one gets from Goldziher's diary, this secretary position was, in fact, quite powerful. Together with a staff of ten, Goldziher was managing the affairs of Europe's largest Jewish congregation and was responsible for its "manifold religious, educational, medical, charitable, cultural, and social activities" (Patai 1987, L 30).

Islam (Lectures on Islam) which he originally prepared to hold in the United States upon an invitation of the "American Committee for Lectures on the History of Religions" (Goldziher 1910a, VII). Although Goldziher himself perceived them as "light," these lectures represent a synthesis of his previous works on the historical developments in Islam and were highly applauded in the scholarly world. His last major book was published shortly before his death in 1920. *Die Richtungen der islamischen Koranauslegung* (Directions of Islamic Koran Exegesis) represent an erudite history of Koranic exegesis (*tafsir*), based on a vast selection of original sources. As in the "Muhammedan Studies," Goldziher shows how the interpretations of the Koran were conditioned by the social and historical contexts in which they were written. Besides these major works, Goldziher published numerous articles and book chapters in various languages and on a multiplicity of subjects such as Arabic poetry, literary history or linguistics. A great number of these essays in German have been collected in six volumes by Joseph Desomogyi (1967–1972).

Against this background, it is not surprising that most scholars in the field agree with the German orientalist Richard Hartmann, who called his Hungarian colleague a pioneer in the religious and historical understanding of Islam and the real creator of Islamic studies as a discipline based on its own methods and problems. In particular the historical critical analysis of the Islamic traditions about Muhammad, the *hadith,* Richard Hartmann viewed as the crown of Goldziher's work. Goldziher's critique of the *hadith* radically changed our understanding of the history of Islam (Hartmann 1922). This judgment is supported by the impressive range of honorable awards Goldziher received during his life. He was a member of the Royal Asiatic Society in London, the Société asiatique in Paris, the Deutsche Morgenländische Gesellschaft, the Finno-Ugarian Society in Helsingfors and the Academies of Science of Prussia, Bavaria and Amsterdam. During his ordeal as a secretary, Goldziher was offered amongst others professorships in Cambridge, Heidelberg, Königsberg, Prague and Strasbourg. He rejected them all and continued his humiliating work as secretary of the Jewish congregation until he eventually succeeded Hatala at Budapest University in 1905.

A Crossroads of Islamic Studies and Religious Reform

Goldziher's biography is a history of both success and failure. On the one hand he was the internationally celebrated scholar of Islam and the founding father of an academic discipline in which his works have been relevant until today. At the same time, Goldziher was a Hungarian Jewish intellectual who sought a third way for Europe's Jews between assimilation and Orthodoxy. In doing so, he remained a "marginal man" in Hungary's national academic system throughout his life (Haber 2006a, 10). With his diary, we have an authentic source about the lifelong struggle in which Goldziher generated his knowledge on Islam. Directed to his wife, his children and his closest friends, Goldziher's diary represents a means of self-reflection and a valve for the continuing humiliations which he experienced in his daily life. Becoming a historical document by accident, the diary questions the narrative of the harmonic assimilation of the Hungarian Jewry (Haber 2006a, 223). Before the

First World War, approximately 900,000 Jews lived in Hungary, 65,000 of them in the Jewish quarter of Budapest where Goldziher worked as a secretary (Pietsch 1999, 9).[21] The "Golden Age" (1867–1919) of the Jewish-Hungarian synthesis began in 1867, when the Jewish community was granted political and legal equality. Religious parity, enabling mixed-marriages, followed in 1896. In a country with many minorities, the emancipation of the Jews was closely knitted into the striving of the relative majority of Hungarians for political and cultural domination. In this context, Goldziher was first and foremost a Jewish Hungarian nationalist and then an international scholar. His strong nationalist feelings might also explain why he remained in Hungary until he eventually obtained a professorship at Budapest University. On May 16, 1902, Goldziher wrote in his diary that he perceived publishing his work in Hungarian as a duty ranking higher than his success on the international academic stage (Goldziher 1978, 231). The alliance between Jews and Hungarians, however, ended with the First World War. At Versailles, Hungary lost two thirds of its population and three fifths of its territory. The results of the war rendered the Jewish-Hungarian symbiosis politically irrelevant and dramatically changed the position of the Hungarian Jewry. In the year of Goldziher's death, the Jewish community was declared an ethnic minority, marking the eventual failure of their assimilation process (Haber 2006b and 2006c).

Like Ernest Renan, Max Weber or William Robertson Smith, Ignaz Goldziher was confronted with the diverging functional imperatives of religion and science in the political framework of the formation of the modern national state. This confrontation with the structural imperatives of modern society profoundly marked his life and work. However, since he belonged to Europe's Jewish minority, Goldziher's struggle with modern society took place within a very different environment. For him religious reform and political emancipation were inseparably joined together. At the same time, Goldziher was a pronounced adherent to a "universalist agenda of liberal religious reform" and a convinced Hungarian nationalist (cf. Conrad 1993, 127). In analyzing his life and work, we have to take "the challenge posed by the modern world to the situation of Jewry in central and eastern Europe" as our starting point (Conrad 1999, 169). For Goldziher, the modernization of the Jewish religion was the key to national integration without assimilation. Therefore, he strongly rejected political Zionism as an ideology that in his eyes wrongly turned religion into an ethno-political marker. This motive of achieving a merger between Jewish reformism and Hungarian nationalism was already apparent in the background of his study tour to the Middle East. On this tour, Goldziher wrote a travel diary reflecting his mood and objectives, as well as his encounters with Muslim life and Islamic scholarship. Begun while under quarantine in Istanbul, this diary has no addressee and was most probably motivated by the loneliness and homesickness he apparently felt during the first

---

21. In 1869 the whole Jewish population was about 44,890, in 1910 it had grown to 203,687 (Pietsch 1999, 34).

phase of his journey (Conrad 1990).[22]

The first pages of Goldziher's diary express mostly his nationalist sentiments and the chauvinist attitude with which Hungarian nationalists viewed southeast Europeans and Turks. In September 29, the day he was freed from his quarantine, Goldziher describes Istanbul as a depressing, corrupt and "bakshish hunting" site (Patai 1987, 97). The Bulgarians, Wallachians and Turks he so far had met are all presented in stereotypical denigrating terms. This applies to a certain extent also to the Christians and Jews he encountered in Istanbul and later on in Beirut, Damascus and Jerusalem. While he calls the Christian missionaries "religious swindlers," Protestant Arabs appear to him to be a degeneration of the "original Arab race" (1987, 110). In Damascus, Goldziher is disgusted by the "*galuth* (exile) physiognomies" of the local Jewish community whose bonds to European Jewry he views in the shared character of "external decay" and "inner hollowness" (1987, 13). Observing the ritual practices of traditional Christians and especially of Orthodox Jews, the religious reformer Goldziher despises them as mean "religious rabble" (1987, 127). Given this critical attitude toward the ritualistic observance of Christians and Jews, the diary is conspicuously silent with regard to Muslim religious practices. Muslim ritual observance does not appear, at least not in the notes conveyed to us.

In Goldziher's oriental diary we meet Muslim Arabs almost exclusively as cultivated and rationally minded friends who strongly appreciate his excellent knowledge of Arabic and the Islamic traditions. In Cairo, Goldziher immersed himself in Muslim scholarship at the Azhar and once even participated in Islamic prayer at a mosque dressed up like a Muslim. In retrospect, he wrote that his mode of thought and state of mind in Cairo was entirely Muslim and that he sincerely believed in the prophecies of Muhammad. The firm Jewish believer wanted to raise the standard of his own religion to the same high level of rationality he found in Islam (Goldziher 1978, 71). In his attitude to Islam, Goldziher presents a fusion of emotional romanticism with an absolute rationalist belief in modern science. Although very different from Ernest Renan, Goldziher's personality was also a complex and hybrid mixture of social patterns which we can analyze through such general nineteenth-century dichotomies as tradition/modernity or religion/science. Putting his veneration of pristine Arab-Islamic culture together with his frequent attacks on the European style of modernization in Beirut and Cairo, the oriental diary tells us something about the young Goldziher's disenchantment with modern European life. In his younger years, this eminent scholar of Islam also projected onto the Orient the kind of authenticity he considered to be lost in Europe. In Islam, he was looking for purity and unspoiled spirituality (Haber 2006a, 136). The study of Islam became the scholarly form in which he expressed his lifelong search for a universalist agenda of liberal religious reform. In his scholarly devotion to Islam we can observe the value attitudes of Europe's Jewish middle class, viewing the search for knowledge as both

---

22. This travel diary, which was published in English by Raphael Patai (1987), is therefore quite different from the diary which Goldziher began to write in 1890. It is a very personal document not envisaging wider circulation (Conrad 1990, 110).

a cultivated bourgeois practice and a religious duty (Haber 2006a, 59–60).

Ignaz Goldziher was a man at the crossroads of Jewish, Muslim and Christian reform. His life was socially and intellectually embedded in these nineteenth century movements of religious reconstructions. Their concepts guided his Islamic studies and within six years (1868–1874) some of its most eminent representatives—Abraham Geiger (Berlin), Jamal al-Din al-Afghani (Cairo) and Abraham Kuenen (Leiden)—crossed his ways. Contrary to Edward Said's interpretation, Goldziher's studies on Islam should not be seen as stemming from Silvestre de Sacy. Rather, Goldziher's frame of reference was the Haskala, the European Jewish reform movement or the "Jewish Enlightenment." Studying under Fleischer at Leipzig Goldziher only acquired the philological skills for his research that was driven by his personal engagement in religious reform. Emerging in the eighteenth century, the Haskala was a rather heterogeneous religious and intellectual movement challenging the values, lifestyles and world views of the traditional Ashkenazi society in Europe. It was one path in the modernization of European Jewry whose center became Germany. Yet it contained a double message of threat and hope. It threatened the deep-rooted religious heritage of the Jews while promising them they would leave their ghettos. A new intellectual elite, the leaders of the Haskala confronted the rabbinical Orthodoxy and gradually eroded their monopoly of knowledge and social guidance. Similar to liberal Protestants and Islamic modernists, these Jewish reformers aimed at a rejuvenation and regeneration of Judaism in light of modern ideas (cf. Feiner 2004, 1–20). In searching for a third way between Orthodoxy and assimilation, Ignaz Goldziher perfectly represented the core rational of this movement and closely followed the example of Abraham Geiger.

Born in 1810, Geiger became a central figure of the Haskala's second generation. He grew up in a rather traditional and fully observant Jewish family which clearly destined him for the rabbinate. In 1829, he took up studies in classical and oriental philology at Heidelberg University, however, increasingly developing interests in philosophy and history. Encouraged by his teacher, the Arabist Georg Wilhelm Freytag (1788–1861), Geiger participated in a contest in 1832 which enquired into the thematic relationship between Judaism and the Koran. His dissertation *Was hat Mohammed aus dem Judenthume aufgenommen?* (What did Muhammad borrow from Judaism?) earned him not only the prize, but also his doctorate from the University of Marburg (Geiger 1902). Some decades later, Theodor Nöldeke expressed his appreciation of this early work by Geiger as being a classic in its approach to comparative religion and in dealing with the origins of Islam (Lassner 1999, 103–105).[23] However, not orientalist studies but Jewish reform became the passion of his life. In the historical context of the scientifically guided Protestant revision of Christianity, Geiger viewed Judaism as being in utter stagnation. For him, historical criticism of the sacred texts was a means of both destroying the authority of rabbinical Orthodoxy and "preserving an

---

23. Geiger and Nöldeke corresponded with each other (see Wiener 1962).

inner emotional connection with the Jewish legacy." From this perspective, Geiger maintained the balance between scholarship and religion throughout his life, being active as both a scholarly critic and a rabbi serving his congregation (Meyer 1988, 91).

In viewing historical knowledge as the "essential prerequisite for reform," Geiger was deeply influenced by the work of the radical Protestant theologians of his time. In particular David Friedrich Strauss made a strong impression on him, and he applied the critical method of the Tübingen School to rabbinical texts.[24] Like William Robertson Smith, Geiger followed the apologetic path and historicized the sacred texts of Judaism in order to reconcile modern knowledge and divine revelation. So seen, the Talmud was then a document of the spiritual evolution of Judaism not representing antiquated dogmas but containing a universal message for humanity perfectly suited to meeting the challenges of modern times. With this interpretation, Geiger was simultaneously fighting against Jewish Orthodoxy and defending his faith against Christian theologians such as Julius Wellhausen, who perceived Judaism as incompatible with modern life (Meyer 1988, 203). He perceived Jews not as a people in the ethno-national sense, but as a religious community that "had become estranged from its own inmost self." In Geiger's view, by concentrating on ritual externals, Judaism had lost access to its very essence (Meyer 1988, 97).

In Abraham Geiger's thoughts we can easily discern the general themes that characterized the intellectual discourse of nineteenth century thinkers about religion, science, history and faith. For Goldziher, Geiger's writings were a "revelation" and he later applied Geiger's concepts of religious reform and his text critical method to his own fields of interest, analyzing and interpreting the large corpus of Islamic traditions (Goldziher 1978, 33, 123). On his study trip to Germany, Goldziher made himself more acquainted with the ideas of the radical Tübingen school of Protestant theology, which had had such a lasting impact on Geiger. In his diary, Goldziher mentions that he began to understand Abraham Geiger better through the works of Ferdinand Christian Baur and David Friedrich Strauss which he studied while in Berlin in 1868 (Goldziher 1978, 39). In this way, the all-penetrating ideas of historicism, cultural evolution, religious rationalization and social differentiation became the cognitive fundament on which Goldziher's Islamic studies rest. In the introduction to his first book, "Mythos," he refers to this intellectual background and the inspiration by authors such as Max Müller, Abraham Kuenen, Heinrich Ewald, Theodor Nöldeke or Steinthal (see Goldziher 1876, Introduction). He conceptualizes religious history as an

---

24. In his biography of Geiger, Max Wiener leaves it open how strongly Geiger was influenced by Strauss and Renan, associating this view with Christian critics of Geiger (1962, 62). His son, Ludwig Geiger, tells us about the critical linkage between Geiger's work and the Jesus biographies of Renan and Strauss. While he perceived Strauss as "hyper-critical," he disapproved of Renan's rapture. In his eyes, the work of both was characterized by the mere absence of knowledge about Palestinian Judaism in the time of Christ (Geiger 1910, 187).

evolutionary process of rational progress toward pure monotheism, as a living source of morality and truth (1876, xxiii). Indeed, the intellectual background of Goldziher's work cannot be understood in a Saidian way, which traces it back through Fleischer to Silvestre de Sacy. The image of Goldziher's Islam is intimately linked to categories developed by Strauss and the Tübingen School transmitted to him via various intellectual encounters in whose center stands the Jewish reform movement around Abraham Geiger (Conrad 1993, 144).

"I call my monotheism Islam:" Ignaz Goldziher on Religion and Islam

His biographers mutually agree that Ignaz Goldziher was a deeply religious man. Even more, they assume behind his restless studies a strong religious impulse with a Jewish core. Throughout his life, Goldziher remained a sincere believer and his children grew up in a religious atmosphere, however, characterized by the idealistic interpretation of the Jewish traditions of their father (cf. Goldziher 1978, 111). His diary contains numerous references to the importance of religious Jewish literature for Goldziher. On December 31, 1893, he wrote that his studies had their foundations in Judaism. Yet although Goldziher perceived Jewish texts to be pure, in his view those who were involved in the modern study of Judaism were "street urchins, sales agents, moneybags and liars" devoid of any idealism. According to Goldziher, in choosing Islamic studies, he made a great sacrifice, but he had been compelled to turn his back on this disgusting community of Jewish scholars with whom he did not want to keep company (Goldziher 1978, 167–168). For Goldziher the essence of Judaism was a universal ethical message strongly opposed to all forms of scholasticism and ritualistic worship. His religiosity had an eminent emotional meaning (Haber 2006a, 55) and he aimed at "a fusion of pristine Judaism with modernity" (Conrad 1999, 154). Robert Simon called this ethical ideal a "bourgeois society concept of religion," an intimate and individual practice of private life (Simon 1986, 129). Apparently, Goldziher's religiosity closely resembled the core elements of the Protestant revision of Christianity. Indeed, as much as Goldziher fought against conversion as a way to Jewish assimilation, he simultaneously reconstructed "his Judaism" in the same direction in which Protestant Christianity had developed. With his ideal concept of a pure religion, he interpreted the Jewish faith along the paths of rationalization, individualization and spiritualization which Protestant theology had taken.

It was apparently in the context of his hatred against the Jewish establishment in Europe that Goldziher turned his scholarly interest toward Islam. In his enthusiastic youth he even declared Islam to be his monotheism (Patai 1987, 71). Goldziher's monotheism closely resembled the modern concept of religion which evolved in the nineteenth century. Concerned with the supernatural and quests for salvation, his concept of religion differentiated between its universalistic, humanistic inner ethics and its external, historically contingent forms. Accordingly, he constructed Islam as an originally un-dogmatic religion whose beginnings did not know rules of ritual and whose "really religious" circles were critical of any dogmatic fixations (cf. Goldziher 1914). Consequently, he could open the study of revealed Islamic sources for critical historical examination without jeopardizing their revealed content. Similar to the way in which his contemporaries studied the Pentateuch, Goldziher showed that the absolute majority of Islamic traditions represent anachronistic projections of later concerns onto the times of Muhammad (Goldziher 1886, 365). In the second volume of the *Muhammedan Studies*, he transferred the method of biblical criticism as he had learnt it from the Tübingen School, the Leiden School around Abraham Kuenen, and Julius Wellhausen to the analysis of the *hadith*. While the Sunna refers to the traditions in general, the *hadith* contains orally transmitted religious or profane stories about the Prophet and his companions, most of which were written down during the second and third century after Muhammad's death (Goldziher 1890, 3).[25] At this time, jurists and theologians developed the thesis of a "second revelation" that implied the equality of the Koran and the traditions in their quality as revealed sources (Goldziher 1910b, 95–97). Goldziher developed a typology of the *hadith* according to the different purposes it supposedly served. In particular during the political struggles of the first centuries of Islamic history, political traditions supported the incumbent rulers or their opposition, justifying either political quietism or the right to revolt. The third century saw an increase in "prophetic traditions" in which Muhammad foresaw the future of Islamic empires or specific cities such as Ceuta or Fes (Goldziher 1890, 130). In addition, there appeared numerous *hadith* with pious narratives or ethical instructions by the Prophet (1890, 153). In Goldziher's analysis, every political and intellectual stream of Islam found its expression in the form of the *hadith* (1890, 131). Not surprisingly, this proliferate production of traditions raised various forms of critique. However, the classical Islamic critique of the *hadith* never took the form of a hermeneutical examination of the traditions' content. Instead, Muslim scholars focused on the reliability of the chain of traditionalists who transmitted the *hadith*. Consequently, the Muslim critics failed to see the striking anachronisms of many traditions (1890, 149).

Goldziher approached the study of Islam with the very same concepts and the same historicist perspective that characterized his early works in the field of Jewish studies. In a letter to Nöldeke in April 1904, he described this method as the integral part of his "philological consciousness" (Simon 1986, 265). From this perspective, he emphasized the "receptive character" of Islam. The essential message of Islam, Goldziher defined with reference to the Protestant theologian Schleiermacher as a strong feeling of dependence on an omnipotent god. Yet also in Goldziher's analysis Muhammad did not preach new ideas, but an eclectic composition of religious ideas of Christian, Jewish and other provenances

---

25. According to Goldziher, the writing down of the canonical *hadith* literature began in the second century after Muhammad. In the beginning, it was accompanied by serious disputes about whether these oral traditions should not be an object of memorization alone and, therefore, should not be written down. In later years, however, the compilation of written traditions became almost a pious act and we know of at least six important collections that are relevant up to present times (cf. 1890, 203–267).

(Goldziher 1910a, 2–3). According to Goldziher, throughout history, Islam has undergone a massive transformation in assimilating new ideas and in adjusting to various historical and social circumstances. Ignaz Goldziher presents us a quite ambivalent image of Islam. On the one hand, it depends absolutely on an omnipotent but merciful God. When he was in Mecca teaching this message, the ascetic Prophet was captured by dark and eschatological ideas. Drawing on his eclectic and superficial knowledge of other religions, Muhammad perceived himself as being a link in a chain of biblical prophets. His prophecies were first and foremost of a negative nature, calling the Meccans to get rid of their "barbarian," pagan traditions in light of the coming Last Judgment (1910a, 12). On the other hand, Goldziher tells us that it was in Medina where Islam truly was born (1910a, 8). Not the Meccan period of divine revelation, but the Medinan decade of worldly strife gave Islam its characteristic contours. Here the "suffering ascetic" was transformed into the "statesman and warrior," giving Islam its character of a warrior religion (1910a, 27). Due to this historical development, the transcendental God was drawn into worldly affairs, with his mercifulness increasingly, but not completely, being replaced by the power of revenge (1910a, 24).

To be sure, in contrast to Wellhausen and Weber, Goldziher did not view the image of a warrior religion as being the core feature of Islam. For him, the turn to violent and worldly affairs was a mere consequence of its historical development. Moreover, it was a precondition for its success among the Arabs. In Goldziher's eyes, neither the personality nor the message of Muhammad at Mecca could capture the hearts and minds of the Arabs. In the first volume of his "Muhammedan Studies" he explains this struggle between Arab traditions and Muhammad's teachings. In Goldziher's view, given the strong resistance of the community to his message, Muhammad's great achievement was the very fact that Islam spread and was finally accepted by the Arabs (1889, 12). He is the "reformer of the Arabs" and this became manifest under his leadership in Medina (1910a, 4). In discussing the first volume of the "Muhammedan Studies," Theodor Nöldeke agreed with Goldziher regarding the difficulty of judging Muhammad as a Prophet, whereas his "political talents" were beyond debate (Simon 1985, 180). In religious terms, Goldziher viewed Islam within the same divine context as the other monotheistic religions. Yet its historical development he interpreted as a progressing distortion of the inner religious idea leading to orthodox legal and dogmatic systems. Islamic history, therefore, appears as the compromising of Islam's revealed ethical content; a theme which we will meet in chapter six again in Islamic reformist and Islamist thought.

One of his last students, Joseph Desomogyi, described Ignaz Goldziher as a scholar and sincere religious believer who wanted not only "to harmonize religion and science, but also the three monotheistic religions with each other" (1961, 14). To a certain extent, the founding father of Islamic studies appears to be an apologist in whose life and work the Jewish, Islamic and Christian reform movements converged. Without questioning the inner ethics of their revelation, he treated divine scriptures, in particular the Koran and the Sunna, as textual sources for the analysis of historical developments. For Goldziher, the historical critical method was not only an instrument of scholarly work, but also a means to distinguish between "true religion" and historical accidents. In line with his religious ideals, Goldziher viewed the emergence of the *fiqh*, Islamic jurisprudence, as a fatal degeneration of religious life, in which the quibbling religious jurists became victorious over their critics (1910a, 45 and 70). The same stifling orthodoxification he discerned in Islamic theology (*kalam*) in which the man of reason eventually succumbed to the dogmatic traditionalists.[26] In his religious world view, Islamic history represented a history of stagnation and decline, a perspective widely shared by Islamic reformers such as al-Afghani and Abduh, or al-Jazairi, with whom he was in personal contact. In the last chapter of his *Die Richtungen der Islamischen Koranauslegung*, Goldziher analyzed the contemporary Indian and Egyptian reform movements in emphasizing the modern and apologetic nature of their Koran interpretations. In his analysis, these religious movements proved the Western prejudice wrong that there is an incompatibility between Islam and modern culture (1920, 310). This historicization of Islam's traditions would also allow Muslim intellectuals to be able to re-interpret Muhammad's message according to the challenges and needs of modern times. Ignaz Goldziher was therefore confident that also Muslim scholars will profit from the findings of critical Western scholarship on Islam, from a discipline of Islamic studies whose contours he had largely shaped (1906, 517).

Christiaan Snouck Hurgronje: Researching and Administering Islam

Christiaan Snouck Hurgronje was born the son of a Calvinist priest on February 8, 1857, in the village Oosterhout in the Netherlands. There and in the neighboring town of Breda he went to school until he passed his entry exam to university in June 1874. As did so many orientalists in the nineteenth century, Snouck Hurgronje began his academic career by studying theology.[27] In September 1874 he joined the theological faculty at the University of Leiden. There, he enthusiastically read the very popular writings of the Tübingen School, as he mentioned in a letter to the German orientalist Enno Littmann in November 1926 (Littmann 1936, 446). Protestant theology in Leiden was shaped by Abraham Kuenen. Together with the German theologian and orientalist Julius Wellhausen, Kuenen was considered the leading European scholar in the critical analysis of the Old

---

26. It should be mentioned that Goldziher refused to view the Muatazila, the so-called rationalist movement, as being made up of men of reason. For him they were rationalists in the sense that they introduced reasoning as a means of acquiring religious knowledge. At the same time, however, they were extreme dogmatists who relentlessly persecuted their opponents (Goldziher 1910a, 114).

27. In most of the literature about Christiaan Snouck Hurgronje, the authors follow the Dutch convention not to use his second family name Hurgronje but his middle name Snouck as short form. I decided to use Hurgronje as he appears in the reference list of this book.

Testament. Following the "Grafian hypothesis," he analyzed the Bible by employing source-critical methods.[28] Abraham Kuenen himself remained a sincere Christian believer throughout his life. His work, however, made a strong contribution toward putting into question the Bible as a source of divine revelation.

In April 1878, Snouck Hurgronje took his exam in theology and renounced his priestly career. For him, there was no scientific progress in the circular reasoning of theology (Littmann 1936, 446). He continued his studies by choosing Semitic philology under M.J. de Goeje and Reinhard Dozy, taking with him the analytical tools of biblical criticism. In November 1880, he submitted his doctoral thesis on the history and rites of Islamic pilgrimage to Mecca, *Het Mekaansche Fest* (Hurgronje 1880). Written under the supervision of De Goeje, Hurgronje analyzed all available sources on the *hajj*, pointing out the pagan origin of the Islamic pilgrimage. Soon afterwards, Hurgronje went to Strasbourg, where he continued his studies in Arabic and Aramaic with Theodor Nöldeke, who was a personal friend of his Leiden teacher de Goeje. From that time, Nöldeke and Snouck Hurgronje remained in close contact, as their intensive correspondence shows (Koningsveld 1985). Returning to the Netherlands in October 1881, Hurgronje became a lecturer in Islamic studies at the training institute for colonial administrators in Leiden, a post which he held until 1887. During this period of time, he published various studies on Islamic law. This subject he chose against the will of his academic teacher but with the support of Ignaz Goldziher, with whom he engaged in an intensive exchange of letters (Fück 1955, 232).

In 1884–1885, Hurgronje made his famous trip to Mecca, where he undertook theological and juridical studies, as well as intended to participate in the Islamic pilgrimage, the *hajj*. In August 1884, Hurgronje arrived in the Red Sea port of Jiddah, from where he left to Mecca in February 1885. He spent almost six months in Mecca before an official order called him back in August 1885, shortly before the *hajj* started in September (Bousquet 1957, XV).[29] In Mecca, Hurgronje presented himself as the Muslim student Abdel Ghaffar, and he joined the circle of followers around Sheikh Ahmad Zayni Dahlan (1817–1886), at that time the highest representative of the religious learned, the *ulama*, of Mecca (Freitag 2003, 42). Later, Hurgronje published a number of studies on the history and social realities of the holy city which were based on his observations as well as on the written and oral sources provided by Dahlan. Most prominent among these publications are

---

28. Karl Heinrich Graf (1815–1869) claimed in 1866 that parts of the Pentateuch related to the Levitical Law had not been written before the fall of the kingdom of Judah and therefore of later origin than Deuteronomy.

29. After his return, Hurgronje explained in an article in the German newspaper *Münchener Allgemeine Zeitung* that his departure from Mecca was due to an intrigue by the French consul in Jiddah. In July 1885, Hurgronje was mentioned in an article in the French magazine *Temps* which reached the Ottoman authorities. The article presented him wrongly as a Western scholar who was in Arabia to collect antiquities and not to study Islam, the purpose with which Hurgronje himself had justified his stay in Mecca (Hurgronje 1885).

the two volumes on Mecca which Hurgronje published in the years 1888–1889 in German.[30] In the second volume, he added a chapter on the living conditions of Indonesians in Mecca, in particular about the small colony from Aceh in northern Sumatra. This first study on the Acehnese marks the starting point for his later research and administrative duties in the East Indies.

In 1889, Snouck Hurgronje entered public service as an "unattached official" in Batavia. For two years, he studied Indonesian Islam on Java and other parts of the archipelago (Littmann 1936, 448). In 1891, he declined a chair at the University of Leiden and instead accepted the appointment as "Adviser for Eastern Languages and Muhammedan Law" to the Dutch colonial administration (Wertheim 1972, 322). Hurgronje served the colonial administration in the East Indies until 1906. For his first task in government service, the Dutch authorities sent him to Aceh in order to study the role of Islam in the ongoing war in this northern province of Sumatra. As with his study on Mecca, Hurgronje again "went native" and settled from July 1891 to February 1892 in Aceh, analyzing the daily life of the Acehnese by participant observation. During this stay he collected data on the culture, religion, language, politics, and economic relations of the Acehnese, which he subsequently published in two books (Hurgronje 1906a and 1906b). They contain a detailed description of the social conditions in Aceh, embedded in general reflections about Islam. Hurgronje's study touches a multiplicity of subjects such as architecture, literature, arts, popular games, daily social practices, political authority, legal orders, the distribution of land, as well as religious beliefs and ritual practices. Together with his study on Gajo (1903), these two volumes on Aceh are paradigmatic in the emancipation of modern Islamic studies from the domination of philology that at this point of time still characterized the field of oriental studies. In combining desk studies with extensive field work, Hurgronje strongly contradicts the stereotype of Edward Said's orientalist who only knew the East from immersing himself in classical texts. Moreover, Hurgronje combined philological with historical hermeneutics and opened the field of Islamic studies for the application of concepts from the emerging social sciences.

In the two volumes about the Acehnese, however, it is not only the scholar who speaks to the reader. The study was also a "piece of counter-insurgency research" (Wertheim 1972, 323). Already in the introduction, Hurgronje addresses the reader in his capacity as adviser to the colonial administration acting in the larger interest of the Dutch state. He strongly criticizes previous colonial

---

30. As mentioned in chapter four, these two books later served Max Weber as sources for his analysis of the Islamic city in *Economy and Society*. Given the extraordinary status and political remoteness of Mecca in Islamic history, so my argument in chapter four, it is most likely that Weber was following an "orientalist impulse" when choosing Mecca. Even Snouck Hurgronje pointed out that in political terms Mecca "became a remote territory with a steadily decreasing significance" (1916a: 314). Moreover, the political economy of the town was entirely conditioned by the *hajj*, the Muslim pilgrimage and therefore a complete exception with regard to all other Islamic cities (regarding Mecca's economy, see also Hurgronje 1887, 54).

policies which for all too long had been designed by an ignorant majority in the Netherlands. Had it not been for a series of disastrous insurgencies, The Hague would not have understood that it was important to bring Aceh into the "community of civilized nations." Yet this necessary modernization of Acehnese society had to be based on a consciously derived Islam policy (Hurgronje 1906a, vii–xvii). According to Hurgronje, in deriving this policy, in particular the doctrine of *jihad*, of "holy war," with which the local *ulama* mobilized the resistance of the population against the colonial administration, should be given serious consideration. Only if the Muslims were to give up this "mediaeval doctrine" would they be able to assume their place among the developed societies.[31] According to Hurgronje, it was the historical mission of the Netherlands to guide the Acehnese in this reform process. In order to achieve this goal, it was first instrumental to win the war in Aceh. Snouck Hurgronje viewed this victory over a politicized form of Islam as the precondition not only for the modernization of the country, but also for developing closer ties between the Dutch government and the Muslim population of East India in general (Hurgronje 1906b, 351).

In his thoughts and actions, Snouck Hurgronje represents a European intellectual oriented toward secular and liberal values. In terms of foreign policy his attitude reflected both the colonial habitus of the Europeans' feeling of superiority and the historical context of imperial power struggles. Politically, he aimed at shaping a geographically divided but politically unified Dutch state in Europe and South-East Asia. Following the general move of Dutch colonialism from economic exploitation to the safeguarding of territories, Hurgronje's vision was to firmly integrate the population and the territories of East India into the Dutch state. This merger of political and scholarly interests was apparent already in Hurgronje's doctoral thesis on the *hajj*. These interests were closely related to the Netherlands' then contemporary public debates. In 1873, Hurgronje's predecessor in Batavia, K.F. Holle (1829–1896), had already undertaken a government-sponsored investigation into the social consequences of the *hajj*. He concluded that the returning pilgrims were "instigators of fanaticism" who should not be appointed to positions in the colonial administration (Steenbrinck 1993, 76–79). Apparently, when Hurgronje chose the topic of his dissertation, studying Islamic pilgrimage was not only of scholarly interest, but also a matter of high political relevance.[32]

---

31. In the second volume, Hurgronje continues: "The passion for religious war which is so deeply rooted in the teaching of Islam is more marked among the Acehnese than among the majority of their fellow-believers in other lands, who have come by experience to regard it as a relict of a bygone age" (1906b, 337).

32. In this context, we might also find the answer to Bousquet's "open question" as to why the Dutch government financed Hurgronje's trip to Mecca in 1884 (Bousquet 1957, xv). However, in contradiction to the public discourse on the political significance of the pilgrimage, Hurgronje emphasized that most of the pilgrims had never played a political role and that only a minority of Indonesian students in Mecca had become affected by Panislamist ideas (Hurgronje 1911, 272).

In 1906, Hurgronje's teacher De Goeje resigned from his chair at Leiden University. Having rejected previous offers such as Robertson Smith's chair at Cambridge or a professorship in Malayan language and literature at Leiden, Snouck Hurgronje accepted the offer to succeed De Goeje. From 1906–1927, he taught at Leiden and continued in his function as an adviser in Islam politics to the Dutch government. In this role, he often took a very critical stance toward official colonial policies, never hiding his convictions. Apart from his *Lectures on Islam* (1916b), the publication of a series of lectures he held in the USA, all his major scholarly publications appeared before 1906. Later, he continued to write short academic pieces and to comment on contemporary Islamic affairs, such as the Young Turk Revolution in 1908, to which he was an eye witness (Hurgronje 1909). These shorter writings were collected by A. J. Wensinck and edited in six volumes under the title *Verspreide Geschriften van C. Snouck Hurgronje* between 1923 and 1927. Christiaan Snouck Hurgronje died on June 26, 1936 at the age of 79 and his funeral was a quiet affair. In his will, he specified that only his doctor and friend Professor van Calcar was permitted to accompany him on this last journey (Littman 1936, 458). In order to analyze his thinking on religion and Islam, it seems appropriate to put the close connection between Snouck Hurgronje the scholar and the colonial advisor at the beginning and to start with his strategy of dealing with Islam in the Dutch East Indies.

A Crossroads of Islamic Studies and Colonial Politics

The goals of Hurgronje's Islam policies in Indonesia were twofold. First of all, he aimed at immediately suppressing the religiously mobilized resistance in Aceh. Secondly, he wanted to firmly integrate the colonies into the political and social reality of the motherland. For Hurgronje, to curb the insurgency in Aceh was the first and necessary step to achieve his long-term goal of eventually securing the political loyalty of Indonesia's population to the Netherlands.[33] In replacing colonial exploitation by a development strategy, the living standard of the indigenous population was expected to gradually rise to that of Dutch society. With these aims, Snouck Hurgronje was completely in line with The Hague's new colonial policies, the so-called "ethical politics" as the journalist Pieter Brooshoof branded the revision of Dutch colonial strategies in a booklet in 1901.[34] In the context of the Aceh War (1873–1903) the Dutch government decisively revised its colonial policies in East India. Due to the pressure of liberal forces at home and the pervasive situation of "uncontrolled violence" in the colonial dominions, the political elite in the Netherlands adopted a strategy of deliberate colonial state-

33. Hurgronje explained the relationship between military coercion and modernizing policies as follows: "For we must always recollect that reason, education and other similar influences gain no hold upon the self-esteem of Mohammedans until they find themselves opposed to irresistible force. Such is the tendency of their doctrine and their practice entirely accords therewith" (1906a, 170).

34. *De ethishe koers in de koloniale politiek* (The Ethical Course in Colonial Politics).

building justified as a "civilizing mission." At the end of the eighteenth century, the Dutch territories in the East Indies did not form a colonial empire, but rather resembled a set of widely scattered trade outposts (Tagliacozzo 2000, 90). From the mid-nineteenth century onward, however, mere policies of economic exploitation were gradually replaced by elements of colonial state formation. Now, it was the Dutch civilizing mission to modernize the colonized, who gradually were to be elevated to the level of Dutch civilization. In so doing, the architects of the new ethical politics aimed at strengthening the ties between colony and motherland against internal and external threats (Vlekke 1945, 179). Snouck Hurgronje was a central figure in this process of colonial state formation, and "he left a whole school of followers" in the Office of Native Affairs who adhered to the ideology of ethical politics (Steenbrinck 1993, 91).

The attempt of The Hague to centralize and modernize the colonial administration of Dutch East India sparked various forms of local resistance against colonial rule. This resistance the Dutch government tended to identify with Islam in general, increasingly viewing religion to be a political force that undermined its state-building project (Waardenburg 1988, 572). The proselytizing influence of Islamic political ideas raised anxiety in Batavia and The Hague, making Panislamism "one of the most pressing topics" among Dutch policy makers and colonial administrators (Tagliacozzo 2000, 87). Yet in the framework of ethical politics, the Muslim population of the East Indies were no longer perceived as heretics and enemies of the Christian faith. They now represented the underdeveloped and religiously indoctrinated inhabitants of a colony which under the guidance of the motherland had to be elevated to the level of contemporary European civilization (Steenbrinck 1993, 76).

In order to accomplish this political vision, Hurgronje tried to utilize the political, religious and social realities which he discovered through his scholarly analysis of Acehnese society. Although he viewed the politicization of Islam as his major challenge, he strictly rejected the widespread assumption that Islam would provide the central if not only source of political loyalty among the Acehnese. Hurgronje detected two important social institutions which decisively limited the political influence of Islam in the various local forms of customary law on the one hand, and the authoritative position of East Indies traditional aristocracy on the other. In comparing the formal rules of Islamic law with the legal practices of the Acehnese, he came to the conclusion that the *ulama* could only partly and temporarily impose the normative order of Islam (Hurgronje 1906a, 15). The aristocracy was merely paying lip service to the *ulama* and Islamic norms. In reality, they continued to administer justice in accordance with local traditions (1906a, 6). Consequently, the traditional indigenous political elite viewed the empowerment which the *ulama* enjoyed in the course of the ongoing insurgencies as a direct threat to their own political and economic privileges (1906a, 160).

Based on these observations, Hurgronje concluded that the colonial administration should utilize the power of the traditional order in its struggle against the religiously mobilized anti-colonial resistance. The aristocracy and local customs could be turned into weapons against forms of regional and Panislamic agitation.[35] Hurgronje later presented the Islam politics of the Netherlands in detail in a series of four lectures (1911). Theoretically, he based his strategic thoughts on two social dichotomies. On the one hand, he differentiated between deeply rooted local customs and the normative claims of a transcendent religious order. Although presented in the form of almost sacred and unchangeable traditions, customary law was a quite flexible and dynamic institution alongside Islamic law (1906a, 10). The legislators of the colonial administration could use this flexibility and legitimacy of customary law in their fight against the normative power of Islamic law. On the other hand, Hurgronje called for the separation of religion from politics when dealing with Islam. In "purely" religious matters, political authority should remain neutral (1911, 269). While the colonial administration should grant complete individual religious freedoms to the Acehnese, Batavia should at the same time answer any propagation of Islam as a collective political ideology with full military repression (cf. Benda 1972, 88). In his writings, Hurgronje does not really define what "purely religious" matters are. In my interpretation, he implicitly employs a definition of religion that derives its conceptual coordinates from nineteenth-century liberal Protestantism. In advocating individual religious freedoms, he put his emphasize on "religious privacy," applying a concept of religion in which faith is individualized into a matter of personal experience and belief (cf. Schröder 1996).

In addition to the implementation of this divide-and-rule strategy, Hurgronje strongly suggested building up of a modern system of education (1911, 288). Taking Dutch education as its model, this new education system was to primarily incorporate the younger generation of the traditional political elite. In light of their social competition with the religious elite, Hurgronje viewed these young aristocrats as the Netherlands' natural allies. In educating them according to Western scientific principles, so Hurgronje's assumption, they would loosen their ties to Islam and thus could be convinced of supporting the colonial state-building project (Steenbrink 1993, 89). Similar to Durkheim's educational program in the Third Republic of France, Hurgronje's colonial educational strategy was aiming at creating a new spirit among the younger generations of Indonesians. By means of modern education, a new form of solidarity between colonizers and the colonized was supposed to replace collective identities based on Islam with a nationalist ideology of the "greater Netherlands."

Regarding their short-term goals of pacifying the colonial territories, Hurgronje's Islam policies were rather successful. The colonial administration was able to stop the war in Aceh, and the general security situation in East India improved considerably at the beginning of the twentieth century. In the long term, however, the ethical politics of the colonial administration failed. Political Islam, a rather nascent movement during Hurgronje's service in the colonies, developed

---

35. To be sure, Hurgronje's position was not entirely new. However, he was able to apply scholarly principles to underpin a point of view which since the mid-nineteenth century spread among the bureaucrats in Batavia (Lapidus 2002, 660).

into a political force which played an important role on Indonesia's way to independence. Ironically, the modern education system established by Hurgronje turned into a breeding ground for Indonesian nationalist and Islamic revivalist ideas (Steenbrink 1993, 88; Lapidus 2002, 661–666). In some circles, the ideas of Islamic reform and Indonesian nationalism merged, contributing to the imagination of Indonesia as both a political and religious community (cf. Laffan 2002 and Noer 1973). Why did Hurgronje's religious policies not achieve their long-term goal, the strengthening of political relations between colony and motherland?

First of all, Hurgronje's strategy was characterized by internal contradiction. Within the logic of his own theoretical assumptions, the instrumentalization of Indonesia's traditional social institutions only could serve as a transitory means of reform. In the long run, the continuing modernization of society had to undermine the power position of the aristocracy and the influence of customary institutions in their ability to contain political Islam. Secondly, and for our study more important, Hurgronje underestimated the dynamic role of religious forces and the possibility that his modernizing policies might be accompanied by a renewed empowerment of religious groups and institutions. In the end, it was Islam in both its orthodox and its reformist forms that stood in strong opposition to Hurgronje's desire for the unification of colony and motherland. The separation of religion and politics in administering the Muslims of East India could therefore only serve as a temporary measure. In order to achieve his long-term goal, Hurgronje's strategy should have aimed at rendering Islam completely irrelevant as a force in the region's social and political life. Apparently, he calculated that the containment of Islam by the forces of tradition would gradually be replaced by the secularizing influence which the new generation of graduates of the new education system would exert on society (cf. Benda 1972). This miscalculation with regard to the roles of traditional, religious and genuinely modern social forces, as well as Hurgronje's ambivalent position toward Islam, were most probably rooted in some basic assumptions held by the intellectual spirit of nineteenth century Europe.

The Islam politics of Snouck Hurgronje were implicitly predicated on an almost complete confusion of modernization, secularization and Westernization. For Hurgronje, the relationship between religion and modernity appeared to be a zero-sum game. From this perspective, religion in general and Islam in particular could not play any conducive roles in the modernization of East Indies society. This said, however, it would nevertheless be wrong to label Hurgronje as an "enemy of Islam" (Reid 1990, 38). Throughout his life and work, orthodox religion as well as racist Western attitudes of superiority found his strong criticism. However, he perceived religion as "the most conservative factor in human life" (Hurgronje 1916b, 138). For him, to be a Muslim and to be modern were not necessarily contradictions, but a modern Muslim had to get rid of Islamic traditions, in particular as they are systemized in Sunni orthodoxy and the canons of Islamic jurisprudence. In Mecca and in Aceh, Snouck Hurgronje presented himself as a Muslim and he was, although almost in secrecy, married to two women from the Indonesian aristocracy. There is still a dispute whether Hurgronje's identity as

Muslim was due to a genuine conversion or a means in his process of going native (cf. Freitag 2003, 54–55). In judging him according to his biography and writings, I see very little of a man with a strong religious identity, but rather a staunch secularist who perceived religion as a strictly private matter.

Looking more closely at Hurgronje's political strategies and scientific works we find them permeated by barely reflected elements of the evolutionary theories of the nineteenth century. In line with some of the thoughts held by Robertson Smith and Durkheim, he conceptualized cultural history along evolutionary steps. Accordingly, religious life develops from primitive stages toward a scientific world view in which religion has lost its social power and becomes an individual means of dealing with existential contingencies. He had no doubt that modernization would render the normative system of Islam obsolete. In his *Lectures on Islam*, Hurgronje clearly expressed these evolutionary ideas:

> …the irresistible power of the evolution of human society…is merciless to laws
> even of divine origin and transfers them, when their time is come, from the
> treasury of everlasting goods to a museum of antiquities. (Hurgronje 1916b, 150)

Both his theory of religious and social evolution and his confidence in the transformative power of modern, secular education mirror elements of the grand theories of nineteenth century thinkers such as Auguste Comte (1798–1857), Charles Darwin (1809–1882), or Herbert Spencer (1820–1903) and the more systematic way in which Emile Durkheim developed them further. Snouck Hurgronje did not apply these theories consciously or in a systematic way. On the contrary, they featured as an undeliberated cognitive framework, as a form of implicitly applied background knowledge, in his world view. Hurgronje and his colonial policy strategies are therefore a good example of the ways in which academic theories trickle down into the conceptual apparatus of society at large and shape the thoughts and action of individuals. In Hurgronje's eyes, modern Indonesia was neither an Islamic society nor could it ground its institutions in indigenous traditions. Indonesia had to follow the historical example of Europe, and it was the historical mission of the Netherlands to facilitate this way.[36]

"The Mufti of Dutch Imperialism:" Snouck Hurgronje on Religion and Islam

Contrary to Snouck Hurgronje's expectations, Islam has continued to play an important role in Indonesian politics. None of Hurgronje's long-term visions

---

36. There is no doubt that Hurgronje sincerely believed in his political strategy and the "ethical" mission which he pursued, while he fully identified with the Netherlands' colonial policies at the same time. In 1915, he expressed his conviction that the establishment of the new education system would render powerless the trust of the population in institutions such as the caliphate or holy war and that the colonies were visibly on their way toward becoming a modern society (1915a, 283). In a letter to Ignaz Goldziher, the German orientalist and teacher of Hurgronje, Theodor Nöldeke, asked his Hungarian colleague and friend whether he thought that Hurgronje still believed in the fantasy of unifying Indonesians and the Dutch in one state (Simon 1986, 412).

came true. His colonial strategy could not prevent the separation of the colony from the motherland, and since the Netherlands finally accepted Indonesia's independence in 1949, the modernization of Indonesian society has not been accompanied by the retreat of religious forces. What does this failure of the "mufti of Dutch Imperialism" (Wertheim 1972, 321) tell us about his concepts of religion and Islam? As a scholar, Hurgronje called for a systematic historicization of Islamic studies. Already more than one hundred years ago, Snouck Hurgronje sharply differentiated between what he perceived as the dogmatic, mediaeval Islamic traditions and the social practices of Muslims, standing in contrast to the still influential tradition of rather essentialist Western scholarship on Islam. This distinction, apparent in his colonial policies in the attempt of playing out Islamic law against customary rules, he introduced into the discipline of Islamic studies. In Hurgronje's eyes, the dogmatic character of Islamic law formally ruled out all kinds of reform, whereas the legal practice in Muslim countries factually applied a variety of sources, customary and legislation by political authorities in order to administer justice (Hurgronje 1906a, 95). Generally speaking, Hurgronje detected a huge gulf between the ideal character of Islamic law and the social practices of everyday life (1907, 454). Similar to Ignaz Goldziher, he analyzed Islamic history as the result of a complex mixture of assimilative and transformative processes. In so doing, he reconstructed the dogmatic system of Islam from texts, in particular religious and legal sources, while he gained his knowledge on the social practices through participant observation and historical critical analysis. Academically, Hurgronje aimed at establishing a discipline of Islamic studies based on the method of historical criticism and free from cultural philosophical speculations. Moreover, he was one of the first scholars in the field to decisively open the discipline for the study of the modern Islamic world.

Nevertheless, the historian Hurgronje also did so selectively, relying on a number of conceptual predispositions which he did not reflect upon. These undeliberated assumptions not only characterized his colonial policies but also entered his scholarly work. For instance, like many orientalists, Snouck Hurgronje was convinced that the real history of Islam was a "political history" which began with the merger of religion and politics after the Prophet's exile to Medina (Hurgronje 1899, 1924). In Medina, in Hurgronje's view, "the words of God became in almost every respect different from what they had been at first" (1916b, 37). Moreover, he also interpreted Islamic history in terms of stagnation and decline. Although he did not view Islam and modern thought as fundamentally incompatible, he diagnosed a "petrification of spiritual life" that made it difficult for Islam to accommodate modernity (1916b, 154). From this perspective he passed the verdict that "the treasuries of Islam are excessively full of rubbish that has become entirely useless; and for nine or ten centuries they have not been submitted to a revision deserving that name" (1916b, 139). Together with this picture of a stagnant politicized religion, his emphasis on the legal traditions of Islam had a decisive influence on shaping the modern image of Islam as a "law religion." He identified in religious law a kind of historical constant in Islamic history. From this perspective, Hurgronje conceptualized orthodox Islam as a total system of legally fixed religious and social duties, relatively resistant to the change of time.

On the one hand, we can detect in Hurgronje's approach the conceptual influence of thinking in holistic systems as it appears in nineteenth-century theories such as in organicist biology, philosophical systems of argumentation or in the broad range of holistic cultural theories. On the other hand, Jacques Waardenburg was probably right in associating Hurgronje's emphasis on Islam as a normative order with his Calvinist background. Hurgronje, whose religious socialization took place under the dogmatic structures of Dutch Calvinism, presumably conceptualized Islam as a systematic normative order of belief which was quite familiar to the way in which he himself experienced traditional religion (Waardenburg 1962, 273). What is important here is that, although Hurgronje historicized Islamic practices, his presentation of Islamic traditions as a fusion of religion, law and politics impacted heavily on the way in which Islam has been understood in the twentieth century. He contributed to the holistic and essentialist image of Islam according to which Islam represents a counter-model to the functional differentiation of modern societies. And it is this image which has informed the debates about Islam, modernity and democracy until today.

His political strategy in Dutch East India was basically built on the very crude assumption of an intrinsically secular modernity. From this perspective, modernization and secularization—conceived as a gradual but inevitable "disappearance" of religion on the societal and individual levels—were concomitant processes. For Hurgronje, this crude version of the secularization theory was not only an analytical device, but also a normative standard according to which a modern society had to be secular. Consequently, it was the task of modernizing policies to relegate religion to private spaces. Based on this assumption, Hurgronje's suggestion of separating religious and political spheres in colonial politics was an important step in modernizing the colonies. Once relegated to non-political spaces and in competition with the secular knowledge which was being spread by the new education system, Islam increasingly would lose its societal relevance. In the same way that science replaced the religious knowledge of Calvinism in Hurgronje's own biography, the scientific world view was to have replaced Islam in Indonesia as well.

In viewing traditional religion as an obstacle to modernity, Hurgronje aptly represented a major stream of European thought of his times. Moreover, his attitude toward religion showed deep traces of the liberal Protestant revision of Christianity as took place in Leiden under his theological studies. In the course of the nineteenth century, strong anti-clerical and anti-religious positions, as well as schools of liberal Protestantism, brought Dutch Calvinism into the defensive. Yet it was in particular Catholicism and the papacy in Rome which became a generally despised enemy for large numbers of Europe's intellectuals. With the victory of Ultramontanism, the syllabus of Pope Pius IX against the modern world and the confirmation of the anti-modern stance of official Catholicism at the First Vatican Council (1869-1870), the Roman church became the role model for the incompatibility of traditional religion with the modern world (cf. Schatz 1992). This general attitude is mirrored by the frequent analogies between Islam and Catholicism throughout Hurgronje's work.[37] This anti-clerical and anti-Catholic attitude was also an inherent trait in the world views of C.H. Becker and Martin Hartmann, the German orientalists whose generally very close relationship to Hurgronje only was disturbed by the impact of the First World War.

Martin Hartmann and Carl Heinrich Becker: The "German Jihad" and Islam as Area Studies in Imperial Germany

On November 14, 1914, the Ottoman Sultan Mehmet V (1909–1918) declared a "holy war" (*jihad*) against the Entente nations.[38] Only two weeks before, the Ottoman Empire had entered the First World War on the side of the central powers, Germany and Austria. Given the close collaboration between Great Britain, France and Russia, the Ottomans main enemy for the past two centuries, as well as its pronounced fear of isolation, the Ottoman government supposedly had not much of a choice. Imperial Germany seemed to be the only European great power willing to join forces with the empire on equal footing (Zürcher 1993, 117). The declaration of *jihad* was an attempt to rally both the Arab Muslims of the empire and Muslims in Russia and the colonial territories of Great Britain and France to the central powers' cause. In Istanbul, the proclamation of *jihad* was followed by an organized demonstration moving to the German embassy where the crowd was received by the German ambassador to the Ottoman Empire, Baron Hans Freiherr von Wangenheim. In light of this "enthusiasm" for the cause of the central powers, Wangenheim wired to Berlin his concerns about the unleashing of religious passions. In his eyes, Berlin should not have all-too much confidence in the success of this Ottoman *jihad,* which in his opinion was not likely to make a major impact on the Muslims under colonial rule. Indeed, Wangenheim was to be proved right, the "holy war sentiments" of this proclamation day soon fell flat and did not resonate much in the greater Muslim world (Trumpener 1968, 117–119).[39]

While the Sultan-Caliph was not able to stir up a holy war, the episode caused a serious dispute among the international community of orientalists. At the center

---

37. Hurgronje himself tells his readers that he had constantly pointed out the specifically "Catholic instinct" of Islam (1899, 130). At several points in his famous lectures on Islam, he compares the "petrification" of Islamic spirituality by the Sunni Orthodoxy with Catholic dogmatism (1916b, 87, 154). Furthermore, he identifies the *ulama* and Islamic law as "the spiritual authority in Catholic Islam" (1916b, 129). In these analogies, I found two different elements to which Hurgronje refers to. On the one hand, he compares the universal claim of Catholicism with Islam. On the other hand, he uses Catholicism as a cipher for orthodoxification and dogmatism by the consensus of the religious learned.

38. For an English version of the proclamation, see Lewis (1975).

39. As we will see in the concluding chapter, at the same time Rashid Rida tried to convince Great Britain to support his idea of an Arab empire.

of this clash was an exchange of statements between Christiaan Snouck Hurgronje and C.H. Becker. Like most foreign observers, Hurgronje suspected Berlin of being behind the proclamation of this *jihad* and that German orientalists were involved in Germany's religious policies (cf. Hagen 2004, 145). In his article *The Holy War "Made in Germany"* Hurgronje expressed his disappointment that his "esteemed colleague, Professor C.H. Becker at Bonn" also seemed to be "swept away by the incredible Jihad-craze, which at present possesses German statesmen" (Hurgronje 1915a, 274). Although Becker previously called Panislamism and the "solidarity of Islam" a phantom, he now supported a war propaganda invoking an atavist mediaeval religious doctrine, a "politico-religious mixture of deceit and nonsense" only resonating—if at all—among the uneducated lower classes of Muslims (1915a, 283). Viewing Becker, together with Martin Hartmann, as the "chief representative of the science of Islam in Germany" (1915a, 279), Hurgronje vehemently criticized Becker for participating in and supporting this attempt to unleash a religious fanaticism that could also harm the successful educational work of the Netherlands in Dutch East India (1915b, 291).

From a scholarly perspective, Hurgronje ridiculed the idea that Muslims would rally behind the Ottoman ruler for a holy war. According to Hurgronje, the "usurpation" of the caliphate by the Ottoman rulers had been barely endorsed, and many Muslim regions such as those in Asia and Africa had never been in touch with the supposed center of Islam in Istanbul. The title of Caliph did not add any political authority to the Ottoman Sultan beyond the territories he could conquer with the power of his armies (1915a, 265). The widespread European concerns with Panislamism were based on the "absolute misunderstanding of the caliphate as a kind of Mohammedan papacy" (1915a, 267). In Hurgronje's analysis, "Panislamism cannot work with any program except the worn-out, flagrantly impracticable program of world conquest by Islam," an idea that, according to Hurgronje, had "lost its hold on all sensible adherents of Islam" (1915a, 266). While he attacked Becker, Hurgronje quoted Martin Hartmann at length in order to support his argumentation. In particular he cited a number of Hartmann's denigrating statements about Turks and the Ottoman Empire which were intended to underline the German orientalist's factual contempt for precisely this kind of Islam the German government was now trying to use in its war strategies (1915a, 276–279).

The German reply came swiftly. In a letter from January 1915, Becker asked Hartmann to leave him the right to respond to Hurgronje's accusation. With Becker as the main target of Hurgronje's article, Hartmann agreed but asked him to do so as soon as possible. Like Becker, he viewed Hurgronje's criticism as a violation of Dutch neutrality in the war, but defended Hurgronje by pointing out his personality. Hartmann explained Hurgronje's "quick-tempered" and "sometimes malicious" character as being due to his supposedly unhappy childhood (Hanisch 1992, 82–83). In a similar vein, Theodor Nöldeke and Ignaz Goldziher discussed Hurgronje's sharp and personal attack with indignation. While the Hungarian Goldziher called upon his German colleagues to see this affair only as a political dispute among scholars and friends, Nöldeke had his doubts about whether he would be able to forgive Hurgronje this "unacceptable attack." Although critical with regard to the proclamation of *jihad*, Goldziher and Nöldeke agreed that the German and the Ottoman governments should have the right to use all means to win this "struggle for existence" (Simon 1986, 373–376). In his response to Hurgronje, Becker argued in a similar direction. He conceded that Hurgronje rightly pointed to the unique character of this *jihad* in which Muslims and non-Muslims were fighting side by side for Islam. German scholars were also aware of the conditions for *jihad* in the traditions of Islamic law, but why not employ a possibly effective means in times of existential war (Becker 1915, 288)? In setting Germany's Islam policies in the context of Europe's imperialist power struggle, Becker criticized the unrealistic scholarly character of Hurgronje's argumentation. For Becker this was not the time to argue from the position of an armchair scholar who was erudite in Islamic law, but to take real politics into consideration. In the historical context of imperialism, Panislamism was not a medieval doctrine, but a modern anti-colonial political ideology for whose emergence colonial powers such as Great Britain shared the responsibility. The Ottoman proclamation of *jihad* was as such not a call for a holy war, but a sign of national awakening among Asian peoples under an already out-dated religious bond (1915, 298). In this context, Germany had accepted that the empire was using the idea of *jihad* as a political means; however, this was by no means a holy war made in Germany (1915, 301).

In retrospect, it looks as if all the protagonists in this affair were both right and wrong. There is ample documentation that the idea of using the Islamic institution of *jihad* had indeed been developed in Berlin. There, Max von Oppenheim created the *jihad* idea at the Information Unit for the Orient (*Nachrichtenstelle für den Orient*) in the German Ministry of Foreign Affairs (Schwanitz 2003). However, C.H. Becker's role in this process seems to have been exaggerated by Hurgronje. The two German proponents of applied Islamic studies, Becker and Hartmann, certainly acted in the environment of political circles close to the Information Unit.[40] Similar to Snouck Hurgronje, both of them saw "a natural political component" in their academic work and they supported the *jihad* strategy on political grounds (cf. Hagen 2004, 154). Yet neither Hartmann nor Becker belonged to the inner circle out of which the strategy emerged. Becker probably did know about the agreements between the German Emperor and the Ottoman Minister of War, Enver Pasha, but he apparently had no detailed knowledge of Oppenheim's plans (Schwanitz 2003, 31). This assessment is further strengthened by the fact that, from a scholarly perspective, Becker and Hartmann would not have endorsed this holy war idea either. Like Hurgronje, they perceived the *jihad* as a remnant of traditional Islam which would not survive in the modern world. For them, the idea of religious war in modern times seemed to be a contradiction in terms. Given the rise of Jihadist Islamist ideologies in the second half of the twentieth

40. Martin Hartmann translated the Fatwa that was issued in order to justify the proclamation of *jihad* into German and mentioned in the introduction that it was not known what exactly had taken place (Hartmann 1916, 2).

century, this conviction held by the founding fathers of Islamic studies seems to have been proven wrong. The following sections will show the origin of this perception. Furthermore I will discuss the ways in which the prevalent theories on religion and modernity, as well as the individual political opinions of Hartmann and Becker, molded the image of Islam which they spread through their academic and popular writings in the German public and beyond.

Martin Hartmann: "The Islamic Danger"

Martin Hartmann was born on December 9, 1851, in Breslau, today Wroclaw in Lower Silesia, Poland. His father was a Mennonite preacher and the family of four children lived under relatively strained economic conditions (Hanisch 1992, 14). First educated by his father at home, Hartmann later attended the local grammar school for six years. At seventeen, he took his high school exam and entered university, first studying theology in Leipzig and Breslau, then Arabic at Leipzig University under Heinrich Leberecht Fleischer (Hanisch 2000, xviii). From Fleischer he received his solid training in Semitic languages, which enabled him throughout his life to base his studies on original sources. In 1874, he submitted his doctoral thesis on "pluriliteral forms in Semitic languages" (Kramer 1989, 284). However, in contrast to Fleischer, who was obsessed with philology, Hartmann increasingly focused his academic interests on the contemporary Muslim world.

In 1874, Hartmann went to Adrianople, working as a private tutor before moving on to Istanbul in March 1875, where he enrolled in an apprenticeship for a career as dragoman, a translator for Middle Eastern languages. A year later, Hartmann got an appointment as dragoman at the German consulate in Beirut, where he stayed from 1876 to 1887. From Beirut, he was able to observe regional politics and the rising Arab discontent with Ottoman rule. It was at this time that he became familiar with Arab nationalism, the "idea of Arabism" (*der arabische Gedanke*), which he later perceived as the politically most important cultural factor in the region (Hartmann 1908, 30). As the dragoman of the German Consul, however, his job was not to comment on regional politics but to facilitate the daily affairs of the consul in Turkish and Arabic. During his work in Beirut, Hartmann engaged in studying local Arabic dialects and he traveled to various places in Syria, research activities in which he luckily enjoyed the support of his superiors at the consulate. In 1880, he published an Arabic phrasebook for travelers, which was based on the vernacular language of the Beirut market. Most probably due to his excellent knowledge of both classical and colloquial Arabic, Martin Hartmann was appointed lecturer in Arabic in autumn 1887 at the newly opened Seminar for Oriental Languages in Berlin. Hartmann remained in Berlin until his death in December 1918 (Fück 1955, 269; Kramer 1989, 284–285).

During his first years at the Seminar, Hartmann still focused on philological topics. He published studies on popular songs in Syria and the Libyan desert, and he analyzed the rhythm and meter of Arab, Kurdish and Hebrew poetry. In addition Hartmann wrote short articles on Arab coins, geographical subjects, names, and local cults (see the bibliography in Jäschke 1941, 115–121). Given the character of his early works, which were more closely related to the classical fields of German orientalism, Hartmann most probably considered a career in the German university system. Toward the end of the century, however, he increasingly took up the then contemporary issues, first with his work on the Arab press, then with studies on Islam in China and Central Asia.[41] At the same time, he promoted the idea of supplementing the language teaching at the Seminar with courses on "realities" (*Realien*), on issues related to the modern culture, politics and economics of the Muslim world. His promotion of this idea had, from 1888, created constant conflict between Hartmann and Eduard Sachau (1845–1930), the director of the Seminar, who strongly opposed this innovational approach (Hanisch 1992, 18). In spite of this opposition from Sachau and other influential German orientalists, Hartmann continued to advocate the scientific study of the modern history of Islam and to complement philology with the theories and methods of the social sciences and humanities. His insistence on disciplinary development and change together with his difficult personality and often unacademic and popular writing style might have been the main reasons why Martin Hartmann was denied a university career. In 1910, he eventually succeeded in establishing courses on modern Islam at the Seminar in which he could teach the history, religion, law, and economics of the Muslim world (Hartmann 1912, 614). Two years later, in 1912, he was one of the founding members of the "German Association for Islamic Studies" (Deutsche Gesellschaft für Islamkunde) with its journal *Die Welt des Islams.* In terms of academic reputation, however, Hartmann's pioneering role in Islamic studies remained officially unrecognized.

In his rather critical obituary on Martin Hartmann, C.H. Becker acknowledged Hartmann's path-breaking approach to Islamic studies (Becker 1920). Going against the orientalist consensus that the contemporary conditions of this "petrified Islam" were not worth studying, Hartmann became the first German scholar to intensively deal with issues such as state-building, political conflicts and cultural developments in the modern Muslim world. In doing so, he not only opened the eyes of the younger generation of German orientalists such as Becker, but was also an important disseminator of knowledge on Islam in the broader German public. Yet as he did so he strongly colored his analyses with his own emotional and arbitrary value judgments. A paradigmatic example of Hartmann's approach to disseminate general knowledge about Islam is his book *Der Islam: Geschichte—Glaube—Recht* (Islam: History—Belief—Law), which appeared in numerous editions after first being published in 1909. The book was directed toward the general reader and Hartmann was perfectly aware of the generalizations and simplifications on which it was built. In a letter to Ignaz Goldziher, he admitted that he was writing the book in a general mood of fundamental criticism of Islam whose principle errors increasingly appeared to him in a more precise way. Although afraid the book might become "grist to the mills of sanctimonious

---

41. While working at the Seminar in Berlin, Hartmann was constantly expanding his fields of interest and also traveling various Muslim regions in North Africa, the Ottoman Empire, Central Asia and China.

Jewish and Christian clerics," he nevertheless had to document in it some of the "facts which are devastating for Islam" (Hanisch 2000, 266–267). In Hartmann's opinion, the religion of Islam was nothing more than another example of the anachronistic resistance with which all religions impede social progress and why he decided to leave the Church at the age of 53 (Hanisch 2000, xx). He concluded that "hatred against the unbeliever is as essential to the true Moslem as the hatred of the Roman Catholic Church against all heretics" (Hartmann 1899b, 18). In a similar vein, Hartmann wrote to Goldziher in March 1911 that the "Islamic danger" is the same as the "Roman, the Greek-Orthodox or the Protestant-Positive danger" of perceiving other believers as heretics (Hanish 2000, 380).[42] Yet what is Islam in Hartmann's work?

In the preface to *Der Islam,* Hartmann stresses the historical importance of Islamic law in understanding contemporary developments in the Muslim world such as the Young Turk Revolution (1908) or the Iranian Constitutional Revolution (1909). Based on original sources, his book was intended to give the reader an insight into the historical role of religious law, the *sharia,* which allegedly determines the whole life of a Muslim. However, the *sharia* should not be confused with the rule of law.[43] In fact, as Hartmann pointed out, Islamic history had been dominated by a state of lawlessness which in the end destroyed all Islamic states (Hartmann 1909a: III-V). Hartmann's handbook on Islam starts with the life of Muhammad and Arab society as its departure points. He describes the tribal Arabs as "jealous, disloyal and mendacious thieves," living in a constant war of everybody against everybody (1909, 13, 2). In this environment, Muhammad was initially rather an odd searcher for knowledge and enlightenment, who, in a state of "mental illness," received his revelation in which he combined Christian and Jewish motives. According to Hartmann, Muhammad was not a dogmatic thinker, but a poet and later an organizer. Ironically, continues Hartmann, Muhammad's success in Medina became the death of his religion. With his move from Mecca to Medina, the Prophet exchanged the search for knowledge with the striving for power. In Medina, Hartmann concludes, the era of Islam found its starting point (1909, 4–16). Consequently, he presents the spread of Islam as a violent process of military expansion, driven by the dogmatic belief in the duty to fight against non-believers (1911, 49). In a chapter on the Islamic constitution and administration, Hartmann tells the reader that the Islamic state does not know the state of peace and that Muslims do not openly declare war, but start it with "insidious attacks" (1911, 74).

Looking at the religious scriptures, Hartmann describes the Koran as a book of slogans, as a document of Muhammad's military campaigns rather than a presentation of a concise system of religious beliefs (1909, 31, 63). The Muhammad of

---

42. The term Positive Protestants, in this context, most probably refers to the rising fundamentalist movements in American Protestantism (cf. van Ess 2003, 105).

43. In another book published at the same time, Hartmann described the *sharia* as a "dogmatically sanctified world view which is embodied in a detailed system of law" (1910, VI).

the traditions, as presented by the Sunna and in the *hadith*, is a "caricature," due to the fact that these traditions were fabricated by a "bunch of swindlers" (1909, 38-39). In building on these sources, Islamic law has become petrified, it moves in circles making any evolution of new law impossible (1909, 82). It is individualistic in its nature, does not contain an idea of the state, and due to its religious nature, the *sharia* makes any kind of social progress impossible (1909, 77). Therefore, the Islamic state is synonymous with stagnation. As in Catholicism, there is no separation of "church and religion" in Islam because the religious idea has permeated the entire social life of the Muslims (1907, 858). This all-encompassing religious character of Muslim society also excludes a harmonization of Islam and modern science. Similar to Ernest Renan, Hartmann asserts that the Arab sciences were not an achievement due to Islam, but against its repressive character (1911, 82). Against this background, Hartmann interprets the modern Muslim reform movements of his times as searching for "salvation from a fruitless tradition" (1911, 49). Muslims are "yearning for culture and education," they are longing to join the family of civilized nations (1911, 83).

Regarding the political future of Muslim states, Hartmann suggests two options. Either they reject the "culture of the Franks," i.e. the Europeans, and remain in their current state of decay, in which case the days of political independence for the rest of sovereign Muslim states are numbered. Or they embrace the Franconian culture unconditionally, growing under the hand of this culture toward a new and powerful life. The latter, Hartmann tells us, is compatible with the Koran and Sunna, as the moral and mental decay of Islam is the result of centuries of bad government (1900a, 65). For Hartmann, modernization in the Muslim world can only succeed against Islamic traditions and following a national path—as Arab, Indian or Turkish awakenings—under European supervision (cf. Hartmann 1909b). On the one hand, Hartmann confronts us with the image of an unchangeable dogmatic Islam based on Islamic law. His writings reflect some of the core findings of the works of Ignaz Goldziher and Snouck Hurgronje, yet, presented in an often unacademic and very popular voice. In these popularizations of Islamic studies, Hartmann combined scholarly knowledge with deeply entrenched stereotypes and the general conviction of Europe's cultural superiority. On the other hand, he believed in principle in the potential of reform in Islam. At the same time, he identified the application of biblical criticism to the Koran as one of the crucial preconditions for the elevation of Muslim societies to the level of civilized peoples (1911, 85). In Martin Hartmann, we again discern a scholar of Islamic studies whose anti-clerical and anti-religious attitudes conditioned the way in which he was imaging Islam. Hartmann did not despise Muslims, but he hated Islam in its form as a revealed body of orthodox traditions. While Muslims could modernize, Islam in this form of a religion could not.

In the literature on Hartmann, we read that he promoted approaching Islamic studies from a sociological point of view (Fück 1955, 272; Haarmann 1974, 62; Kramer 1989, 287). Yet Hartmann was not a sociologist. In conceptual terms his work is poor. The short chapter *Gesellschaft als Summe D. Gesellungen* (Society as a Sum of Consociations) is one of the few theoretical elaborations in his work in which he classifies human relationships into consociations of blood, language, professions, and imaginations (1909c, 187). The "sociological method" of Martin Hartmann was rather the uncritical application of a number of widespread modernist concepts of his times. One of these crude conceptual truisms is his evolutionary view on religious history. From this perspective, the Muslim world could achieve the level of "contemporary civilization" if the Muslims got rid of their religious traditions. Europe has shown the way and it is this way all peoples must follow in order to live a modern life. In general, Martin Hartmann's writings are a peculiar blending of actual scholarly erudition regarding historical and linguistic details with the striking inconsistencies of both his political opinions and his constant value judgments. Whereas he narrates the spread of Islam as a history of military expansion, at the same time he admires *Preaching Islam* by Thomas W. Arnold, a book written precisely against this dominant narrative of the violent Islamic expansion (1900a, 41). In *Islam and Modern Culture* we learn that "true Islam" is reflected in both the ruthless exertion of power and the complete submission to despotic rule (1907, 864). At the same time, Hartmann describes Islam as democratic in essence (1899a, 7). In his book *Der Islam*, we find a lot of factual information about essential features of Islam combined with the image of a stagnant holistic system, whereas in *Strassen durch Asien* (Roads through Asia) Hartmann strongly criticizes the essentialist dichotomy between East and West by Rudyard Kipling (1900b, 87). His swift generalizations follow his shifting mood and political opinions, which combined socialist and anti-colonial attitudes with a strong sense of European cultural superiority. In light of his letters and the judgment of his biographers, the striking inconsistencies in Martin Hartmann's work were most probably a result of his rather erratic personality. Although he was a pioneer of modern Islamic studies, Hartmann contributed largely to the confirmation of popular stereotypes regarding Muslims, and especially Turks. In his analysis of the Egyptian press, for instance, Hartmann characterized the Egyptian as "in a high degree indolent, frivolous, aimless, changeable, servile" (1899b, 3). Yet in particular his frequent denigrating remarks on Turks, the "inferior scum of East Asia," whose aggressiveness could only be stopped by the "energetic resistance of the Teutonic world" (1909a, 60–61), emphasized the negative image of the Turk cum Muslim so prevalent among the European populace.[44]

---

44. In the introduction to his "Un-political Letters from Turkey," Hartmann calls himself a genuine friend of the Turks who nevertheless uses bold language in criticizing them. Traveling Turkey for 40 days after the Young Turk Revolution (1908), Hartmann compared this event to the French Revolution, indicating how far the Turks were still away from being able to join the family of civilized nations. Only if they discarded their orthodox Islamic world view and their imperial ambitions would the Turks be able to modernize and to achieve the social and political standards of contemporary civilization (1910, iii–viii).

Carl Heinrich Becker: The Historical Unity of Christian and Muslim Cultures

In sharp contrast to Martin Hartmann, Carl Heinrich Becker came from a wealthy family of Germany's pre-First World War commercial and academic bourgeoisie. He was born on April 11, 1876, in Amsterdam, where his father was one of two leading managers of the local branch of the banking house Rothschild. Having spent his early childhood in Amsterdam, Becker and his family went back to Germany in 1882, settling in Frankfurt (Wende 1959, 12). After finishing grammar school in Frankfurt in 1895, Becker studied theology for one semester in Lausanne, and then continued his studies at the universities of Heidelberg (1895–1897; 1898–1899) and Berlin (1897–1898). He had begun to learn Hebrew at school already and develop his interest in the Old Testament and related theological questions. In Heidelberg he complemented theology with the study of Semitic languages under the Assyriologist Carl Bezold (1859–1922), who also supervised Becker's doctoral dissertation on Ibn Jawzi. After submitting his dissertation in 1899, he returned to Berlin where he studied Arabic and Persian under Martin Hartmann (Müller 1991, 22). In August 1900, Becker embarked on a journey which brought him via Paris, where he attended the World's Fair, to Spain, and further on to Cairo. In Egypt he took lessons in colloquial Arabic, immersed himself in the study of Arabic manuscripts and traveled several times to Upper Egypt and once to Khartoum in Sudan. In April 1901, he returned via Istanbul, Greece and Italy to Germany, before he undertook another trip to Egypt and Syria in December 1901. On this second trip to Egypt, Becker met with the reformer and then Great Mufti of Egypt Muhammad Abduh and attended lectures at the Azhar University in Cairo (Ritter 1937, 177; Wende 1959, 19–20).

C.H. Becker received his major scholarly formation in the academic milieu of Heidelberg. There, he not only undertook most of his studies, but also taught courses in philology, Semitic languages and Islamic history between 1902 and 1908. In winter 1906/07, Becker started a well-attended series of lectures on modern Islam, indicating his interest in freeing oriental studies from the confines of philology (Wende 1959, 21). Moreover, he apparently participated in the academic gatherings of Eranos, the interdisciplinary scholarly circle on religious history around Max Weber that was discussed in the previous chapter, and attended lectures by Dieterich, Troeltsch and Gothein, as well as the academic *jour fix* which took place on Saturdays at the house of Max Weber (Ritter 1937, 176).[45] In July 1906, Becker was awarded the title of extraordinary professor at Heidelberg University, probably facilitated by the fact that the Indian Muslim Reform University in Aligarh offered him a chair in Arabic. Becker

---

45. The only reference to Becker's presence at Weber's is the short essay *Carl Heinrich Becker als Orientalist* by his follower Hellmut Ritter (1937). Marianne Weber does not mention Becker in her portrait of Max Weber's life, a fact which might indicate the comparatively low status of Becker in Heidelberg's scholarly hierarchy of that time. I therefore strongly doubt Bryan Turner's assumption that Weber "almost wholly" relied on the work of Becker in his studies of Islam (Turner 1974, 16). Rather, it was the works of Wellhausen, Hurgronje and Goldziher on which Weber's study built.

rejected the offer from India and remained in Heidelberg until his appointment at the new Colonial Institute in Hamburg, where he took up a position as Professor for the History and Culture of the Orient in autumn 1908. While Heidelberg was foundational for Becker's scholarly outlook, he himself described his time in Hamburg (1908–1913) as the most important period for his further career (Müller 1991, 59).

With its emphasis on the historical development of the modern Muslim world, the chair in Hamburg was an ideal position for Becker. In his letters to Karl Rathgen (1856–1921), a well-known economist and professor at the Colonial Institute who strongly supported Becker's appointment, Becker expressed his delight about the profile of this chair. With its focus on culture and political history, the chair precisely corresponded to the idea which he himself had proposed in the past years. A professorship in modern oriental studies that was free of the philological apparatus of classical Semitic studies could deal with contemporary Islam, integrating studies on the oriental question, the history of Turkey or Islam policies in Dutch East India (Müller 1991, 64–65). This new emphasis on current Islam politics Becker clearly reflected in his work when he began to write more about the impact of Islamic law and culture on colonial policies, in particular on the German colonies in Africa. He perceived the Colonial Institute to be a model university for teaching and researching in world politics, and he conceptualized colonial studies as an ideal combination of disciplinary academic research and applied sciences.[46] This concept, however, also generated resistance among his conservative critics, who still adhered to the Humboldian ideal of Germany's classical universities (Müller 1991, 81–98). Due to indecisiveness regarding the transformation of the Colonial Institute into a model university in Hamburg, which had arrived at a stalemate, Becker accepted a chair in modern oriental studies at the University of Bonn in 1913 (Wende 1959, 34). In Bonn he continued his scholarly and administrative struggle for the establishment of the discipline of modern Islamic studies until he left the academic world for politics. In 1916, he took up a position in the Prussian ministry of culture, where he first became permanent secretary in 1919 and served as minister in 1921 and from 1925 to his resignation in 1930. From September 1931 to April 1932, Becker traveled through Japan, China, Dutch East India, Iran and Syria as a member of an educational mission of the League of Nations. His desired return into academia, however, was prevented by his premature death in February 1933, at the age of only 57 (Ritter 1937, 179, 184–185).

While holding the chair at the Colonial Institute in Hamburg, Becker launched the publication of *Der Islam,* a new journal focusing on modern developments in the Muslim world. In his article *Der Islam als Problem* (Islam as a Problem) in the first issue of the journal, Becker presented his approach to Islamic studies. The

---

46. In his lecture *Ist der Islam eine Gefahr für unsere Kolonien* Becker emphasized, for instance, that all German colonial administrators working in East and West Africa should have thorough knowledge of Islam in the way in which the Colonial Institute in Hamburg conveys it. Similar to Snouck Hurgronje, Becker perceived this knowledge as a clear precondition of colonial Islam politics and for the ability to integrate Muslims into colonial state-building projects (Becker 1909, 186).

article was interpreted as "an attempt to bid resolute farewell" to some of the almost axiomatic assumptions that had dominated oriental studies so far (Batunsky 1981, 288). Becker defined Islam as representing both a multiplicity of historical faces and a cultural unity, a civilization that was once built on religion. However, this religion did not shape Islamic civilization. The religious element only flourished on the fertile soil which was prepared by other forces. The central problem for Islamic studies he saw thus in the question of how this cultural unity of Islam came into existence and in which ways religion did play a role in this historical process (Becker 1910, 4). Becker identified the unifying factor of Islamic civilization in its absorbing of Hellenism (1910, 15). Like the Christian civilization, according to Becker's thesis, the Muslim civilization was built on the heritage of classical Hellenism, making Islam a part of European history and the crucial link between Europe and Asia (Becker 1922b, 20–21). This model of the historical unity of Christian and Islamic culture served three purposes in Becker's foundation of Islamic studies. Firstly, he was able to integrate Islamic history into the framework of universal history with which Becker was familiar from the intellectual milieu in Heidelberg. Secondly, in perceiving Islam as a distinct part of universal history, he justified the relative independence of Islamic studies as a unique field of scholarship. Finally, Becker could integrate research on the contemporary Muslim world in the paradigm of Islamic civilization (Haridi 2005, 66).

Based on this model, Becker suggested looking upon Islam with benevolent neutrality if not even with a certain appreciation (1912, 600). In basing the Muslim world on the heritage of oriental antiquity, classical Hellenism and Christianity in its dogmatic and mystical forms (1922b, 23), he emphasized the shared cultural elements of Christianity and Islam by virtue of which the Muslim world would also be able to join in modern development (1916/17, 49). For Becker, the Islamic reform movement showed this adaptability to modernity. Consequently, he did not identify Islam as a religion as the major obstacle to the eventually inevitable modernization of the Muslim world, but the medieval world view of contemporary Muslims (1916/17, 51–52). What distinguished Europe from Islam was the historical fact that Europe had liberated itself from the bonds of medieval Christian Hellenism through the Reformation and the Renaissance, whereas the Orient remained confined in the cultural traditionalism of the Middle Ages (1907, 428). According to Becker, the medieval cultures of the Occident and of Islam were identical, only disguised by different religions and a multiplicity of languages and people (1907, 388): "Everywhere, we are confronted with the Christian world view as it was developed in the Orient of the seventh and eight centuries" (1907, 416). However, in the Occident, antiquity did not just live on, but Greek humanism was reborn and created modern men (1922b, 29). By contrast, the passing problems that had been faced in Christian antiquity became constant questions in Islam, a historical development reflected in the evolution of Islamic law (1907, 417). The stifling ideals of the Muslim world were, in his view, represented by Islamic law (1904, 238); and it was the "all-encompassing nature of this legal doctrine of duties" which prevented the modern development of Islam (cf. 1916/17, 44).

There is no doubt that Becker refuted a number of the orientalist stereotypes which were so well described by Edward Said. In Becker's conception, Islam was not a stagnating religiously determined entity, but a civilization with many historical facets and open to change. He rejected the dominant narrative of Islamic conversion by the sword, calling for a factual and temporal separation between the historical paths of political expansion and religious conversion in Islamic history (1910, 6).[47] Moreover, Becker transformed the notion of a Christian-Muslim dichotomy, the assumption of an essential difference between Occident and Orient, into the concept that they shared a cultural origin, although their historical trajectories diverged. Consequently, in his image of Islam there was no incompatibility in principle between modernity and Muslim culture. Becker consequently continued the historicization of oriental studies in line with Ignaz Goldziher and Snouck Hurgronje, on whose findings Becker's synthetic studies largely relied. That his work nevertheless contributed to consolidating some essentialist assumptions is closely linked to the way in which he singled out Islamic law as the core feature of Islam. Taking Snouck Hurgronje's point, i.e. the sharp contrast between the normative ideal and social practices, Becker also presented this ideal system of religious and legal duties as the essence of Islam.[48] His historicist concept of Christian-Muslim cultural unity did not prevent him from perceiving Islamic tradition as a holistic world view based on the ideal conceptions of Islamic law (cf. Haridi 2005, 33). For Becker, although it developed historically, Islamic law represented Islam in substantial terms, characterizing its concept of the world in which the ideal is in constant protest against reality (Waardenburg 1962, 249). Based on the implicit dichotomy between tradition and modernity, Becker re-introduced the essentialist motive of difference into his own model, in which an oriental world remains dormant in its traditions, only to be modernized through the helping hands of European powers.

In his essays on colonial politics, Becker therefore stresses the justification for and necessity of the European civilizing mission. Civilizing the colonized is the historical and moral task of Europe, demanding an elaborated policy toward Islam which must rely on solid knowledge of the local conditions in the colonies (1912, 176 and 186). From an evolutionary perspective, Becker perceived the course of civilization as the transformation of primitive societies permeated by religion into modern societies in which religion no longer represents a systematic world view but only an element of individual human experience (Waardenburg 1962, 276). Although he himself did not live through such a religious experience, Becker played off religious subjectivity against institutionalized and orthodox forms of religion (van Ess 1980, 44), reflecting the anti-clerical and anti-orthodox attitudes of the intellectual secular European mainstream. Yet this evolution

---

47. In this context, Becker refers to Thomas Arnold's book and the rather peaceful spread of Islam via commerce and trade. This position is in sharp contrast to Weber's concept of the warrior religion and might thus contradict further Bryan Turner's assertion already discussed in footnote 45.

48. In a letter to Martin Hartmann, Becker expressed his awareness of being a follower of Hurgronje in this strong emphasis on the role of Islamic law (Hanisch 1992, 51).

from primitive to modern societies needed religion as a transitional force, and it is this role which Islam could play in German colonial policies in Africa by contributing to the moral civilization of an inferior people in close collaboration with the colonial powers. For Becker, Islam made headway in Africa because of the simplicity and practicality of its message. In opening the continent for trade and commerce, colonial policies facilitated the spread of Islam, the continuation of which he perceived as unavoidable. Consequently, in his view German policy-makers should not support the efforts of Christian missionaries but perceive Islam as their natural ally in colonial politics in Africa (cf. Becker 1910).

The implicit theoretical assumptions behind Becker's colonial policy advice, which closely reminds us of the Islam politics of Snouck Hurgronje, bring us back to the scholarly environment in which he developed his model of Islamic studies. Becker's approach to Islam was guided by the modern concept of religion as developed through liberal Protestant theologians and the early sociologists of religion. He constructed universal history according to an evolutionary idea of human civilization in which the progressive rationalization of religious ideas played a central role. C.H. Becker's studies on Islam were framed by the Protestant academic milieu of Heidelberg in which he lived the formative years of his scholarly life (1895–1908). He applied some core concepts of Germany's Cultural Protestants in general and of the Eranos in Heidelberg in particular. Prime amongst these elements of Cultural Protestantism was Becker's belief in the civilizing role of education, his concept of the autonomous individual and his humanism which he juxtaposed with the orthodoxy of Islamic law.[49] In some parts of his work, Becker makes direct and indirect references to Weber's sociology of religion (1916a, 54; 1916b, 366; 1922b, 28 and 33),[50] and his essay *Der Islam im Rahmen einer allgemeinen Kulturgeschichte* (Islam in the Framework of Universal Cultural History) was directly inspired by the theologian Ernst Troeltsch. In contrast to Troeltsch, however, who was a Christian apologist and excluded Islam from his world history of Europe, Becker insisted on the inclusion of Islam into European cultural history, distinguishing between religion and civilization (cf. Becker 1922b; Schaeder 1923, van Ess 1980; Schäbler 2008). Given this intellectual background, Becker is an excellent example of the social and cultural milieu out of which the academic discipline of Islamic studies evolved and which molded its theoretical perspectives and core analytical concepts.

---

49. While the implicitly applied framework of his academic work shows this impact of the Cultural Protestant milieu, Becker's world view was also influenced by intellectual currents such as "life philosophy" (*Lebensphilosophie*) and the youth movement, which often faced explicit and strong critique from modernist "mandarins" like Max Weber (cf. Essner and Winkelhane 1988, 160–163).

50. In a letter to Erich Wede, Becker described Weber's sociology of religion as fantastic reading (Müller 1991, 345).

Conclusions: Colonialism, Islamic Studies and the Modern "*Doxa*" on Islam

Beginning with Ignaz Goldziher, this chapter dealt with four scholars who played important roles in the formation of Islamic studies as a distinct field of modern scholarship. Perceived from the level of individuals, Goldziher and Snouck Hurgronje were crucial in giving the new academic discipline its contours. Their work was essential to the eventual emancipation of Islamic studies from the classical realm of orientalism. Even more important, in putting Islamic law at the center of research, they emphasized the image of Islam as a "legal religion" and founded a major line of research for the new discipline. In addition, Goldziher and Snouck Hurgronje mark — in very different ways — nodal points of a network connecting European scholars with colonial politics and the Islamic reform movement. Apart from these important individuals, structural developments in the evolution of modern science as a function system also played a role in the formation of Islamic studies and the rise of a new generation of scholars focusing on Islam. At the macro level, the progressive evolution of modern society as global society and the concomitant internal differentiation of the systems of modern science and education provided the structural framework in which the new discipline emerged. The academic activities of the four scholars in this chapter closely reflected these processes of internal differentiation: they engaged in the organization of academic conferences, the formation of national and international associations, the foundation of scientific journals and the elaboration of university curricula for Islamic studies.

While macro-sociological changes strongly framed the birth of Islamic studies, historical conditions largely decided the success and the social relevance of the new discipline. In this process, the formation of the global political system as a "society of national states," as well as its historical face, the asymmetric power-relations and the imperial competition among these states, had a significant impact on the establishment of Islamic studies. The "German Jihad" episode and Snouck Hurgronje's colonial policies show in which ways national and international political agendas enhanced the relevance of Islamic studies. The "ghost of Panislamism" played a significant role in the justification of the new discipline in the eyes of the political elite (cf. Landau 1990). In particular European colonial powers began to perceive Islam as a threat in military and moral terms (Hourani 1991a, 301). With the insurrections in Dutch East India, the antagonism between Mughal rule and British colonialism in India and the Ottoman Empire as a part in Europe's imperial power struggle, anti-Imperialism attained a profoundly Muslim character. In this way, the rise of Islamic studies and of Islamic modernism took place in an ideological context of Islam against the West. To a certain extent, this role of Islam in international politics contributed to the successful separation of Islamic studies from oriental studies. In the second part of the nineteenth century, having specific knowledge of Islam appeared to be a crucial resource in international politics. Yet it was a resource for quite different ways of implementing Islam policies in the international system. In the Netherlands, for instance, the interest in Islamic studies as an "applied science" was close-ly linked to colonial domination. In Germany, by contrast, Islamic studies as a resource was intended to inform the political strategy behind the German-Ottoman alliance.[51] In both cases, studies on contemporary Islam were able to attract pub-lic resources for the academic institutionalization of the discipline and for field studies by individual scholars who began to leave the ivory tower of textual desk studies. From this historical perspective, the colonial situation did indeed play a very significant role regarding the rise and public attractiveness of Islamic stud-ies. Edward Said's thesis of a straight-forward legitimization of colonial domina-tion by orientalist scholarship is, however, by far too reductive. It neglects the societal complexities of both the historical structures of international politics and the systemic logic of the autonomization of modern sciences.

Said's thesis is even more questionable when it comes to the micro level. The colonial habitus, the conviction of the superiority of European culture and civili-zation, was a firm feature of the general social imaginary that characterized the world views of our four founding fathers of Islamic studies. Regardless of their dif-ferent nationalist, religious and political positions, for all of them the standards of modern civilization were without doubt given by the European experience.[52] They were confident "that the West had made a leap forward, morally and intel-lectually" (Marchand 2009, 497). Advocating the civilizing mission of Europe was less a legitimizing strategy than an inherent and thus unquestioned feature of the moral beliefs prevalent among European intellectuals. This becomes appar-ent when looking at the striking differences that drove our scholars with respect to their personal motivations. While Snouck Hurgronje's study on Aceh might be described as a piece of "counter-insurgency research," there is mutual agreement among the biographers of Ignaz Goldziher that his devotion to the study of Islam was of religious origin. Although often a critic of The Hague's colonial policies, Hurgronje was captivated by the nationalist idea of making Indonesia an inte-gral part of a greater Netherlands. The Hungarian "marginal man" Goldziher, by contrast, was driven by a universalist agenda of religious reform. What is impor-tant here, despite the strikingly different personal backgrounds of Hurgronje and Goldziher, is that their works clearly converged into a particular image of Islam.

This convergence must be explained in theoretical terms. It is a result of the background knowledge behind the studies of Goldziher, Hurgronje, Becker and Hartmann. Filtered through this implicitly shared theoretical framework, their rather different individual approaches to Islamic studies converged into a particular modern image of Islam. In their studies we can clearly discern the conceptual debates about religion and modernity which were the topic of chap-

---

51. It has to be noted, as already mentioned in chapter three, that at that point of time Germany did not identify with the West.

52. In his oriental diary, the young Goldziher gave a rather ambiguous picture, sometimes expressing this superiority of Europe, sometimes criticizing Muslim attempts to fol-low the European example. In his later correspondence and autobiographical notes, however, the colonial habitus is also clearly detectable in Goldziher's world view.

ter four of this book. The four scholars interpreted their observations through conceptual lenses whose origins we found in the interlacing rationalizations of Protestant theology, sociology and comparative religion. They all began their academic careers by studying theology, more specifically with the interpretations of Christianity by liberal Protestant theologians who represented the Tübingen and Leiden schools. Yet they applied this conceptual apparatus in a rather undeliberated manner. The theoretical frameworks of our four scholars constitute taken-for-granted cognitive platforms, epistemological predispositions, for the erection of Islamic studies, a kind of analytically applied background knowledge which was decisive in shaping the modern image of Islam. In comparing the studies of the four scholars, I identify at least four core elements which in conceptual terms characterized the intellectual milieu in general out of which Islamic studies emerged: an evolutionary approach to history, the paradigmatic dichotomy between tradition and modernity, a modern concept of religion, and the civilizing role of secular education.

Firstly, there is a shared understanding of history as a process of sociocultural evolution. In interpreting Islamic history, Goldziher was interested in the unfolding of Islam's internal principles, while Becker constructed it as part and parcel of a universal history of human kind. Hurgronje and Hartmann emphasized rather the continuing adaptation of Islam to its historically changing environments. From a position of historical criticism, all four refuted in principle the classical orientalist assertion that the Orient was an unchanging entity and pointed out various processes of historical change in the Muslim world. The normative standard applied to their interpretations of Islamic history, however, was the history of European civilization and its more or less hidden assumptions regarding the evolution of Christianity.

Secondly, they introduced the sociological dichotomy between tradition and modernity into Islamic studies, albeit in a specific way. The identification of orthodox religion with traditional society by sociologists appears among these pioneers of modern Islamic studies in the distinction between traditional Islamic orthodoxy and modern culture. They juxtaposed the teachings of classical *fiqh* with the then contemporary ideas of religious reform. More specifically, they made the dogmatization and orthodoxification of Islamic law and the societal role of the *ulama* responsible for the patterns of stagnation and decline which they claimed to observe in Islamic history; a point of view that was further enhanced by their critical stance toward Europe's clerical establishment and the papacy in Rome.

Thirdly, the four founding fathers of Islamic studies perceived religion according to the modern concept into which sociologists had transformed the liberal Protestant interpretations of the Christian faith. From the sincere believer Goldziher to the socialist-agnostic Hartmann, regardless of their individual religious attitudes, all four scholars conceived religion in terms of "religious privacy." They defined religion as being a subjective collection of spiritual experiences and an ethical system of belief that provide a rational path toward individual salvation. Based on this theoretical background knowledge, they no longer saw a fundamental incompatibility between Islam and modern culture. Instead, they narrated the theme of Islam and the West in the semantics of a sharp distinction between medieval and modern world views. Consequently, Muslims only had to transform their faith in accordance with the model of a modern religion. They had to follow the "necessary" steps of sociocultural evolution and get rid of their "medieval traditions."

The means of achieving this transformation, and this is the fourth cognitive core element, they saw as being modern secular education. Consequently, the observed "inferiority" of the Muslim world was not intrinsically due to Islamic culture but to the lack of modern knowledge that could be transmitted through a secular system of education. Like Durkheim in his concern about national cohesion, Snouck Hurgronje perceived modern education as a major means for Dutch colonial nation-building. For Hartmann and Becker, educational policies were a major part in Germany's international "cultural" politics. Spreading modern forms of education was therefore an integral part of the measures which the four scholars suggested in order to raise Muslim societies to the level of "contemporary civilization."

In combining these key concepts on a common interpretative ground, early Islamic studies produced a rather ambivalent image of Islam. In the scholarly productions of Goldziher, Hurgronje, Becker and Hartmann we can find both the historical deconstruction and the scholarly confirmation of an essentialist ontology of Islam. On the one hand, a closer examination of their works clearly shows that they did not share some of the attitudes which were prevalent among many of their orientalist predecessors. In comparison to the pejorative value judgments of Ernest Renan and William Robertson Smith, for instance, they perceived Islam in a much more neutral if not even benevolent way.[53] This might be due to the fact that they were no longer driven by apologetic interests, trying to prove the solemn authenticity and modern compatibility of the Christian revelation. For them, Islamic studies represented a genuine field of research in itself and not an auxiliary discipline to prove the eternal truth of the Christian faith. Furthermore, they shared a firm belief in the autonomous principles of academic reasoning without following the deification of science in a positivist way. Even the religiously motivated Goldziher rigorously applied the rules of modern scientific communication in his academic work. These founding fathers of Islamic studies were neither searching for a religion of humanity, nor did they explicitly declare modernity as a form of advanced Christianity. They derived the central values of their academic ethos from the historicist norms which were so crucial to the formation of the social sciences and the humanities, and their world views reflected a kind of "natural" acceptance of the relatively autonomous logics of the functionally differentiated realms of modern society.

On the other hand, and in sharp contrast to these academic credentials, we can nevertheless detect a number of positions in their works that helped to corroborate the essentialist image of Islam. In making Islam the common denominator

---

53. Except for the young Goldziher, the absence of a romantic longing for the past characterized these founding fathers of Islamic studies. Instead, Islamic studies were pursued in a more "scientific" and professional way.

for the scientific study of the Muslim world, the very foundation of the discipline looks like a confirmation of the orientalist stereotype of religious determinism so heavily criticized by Edward Said. Under the impact of holistic and organicist theories, they tried to address Islam as a cultural whole, and they identified the origin of this all-encompassing unity in religion. Consequently, the founding fathers even strengthened the tradition of writing and understanding the history of Muslim peoples as a concise history of Islam.[54] Writing this kind of Islamic history implies that "everything that took place in the countries inhabited by Muslims had some essentially 'Islamic' component" (Owen 1973, 295). At least on the surface, Islamic studies made Islam, and thus religion itself, the central and independent variable in studying the complex history of Muslims. Besides the inherent religious determinism of Islamic studies as an academic discipline, we can discern three recurrent themes in the works of Goldziher, Hurgronje, Becker and Hartmann which are closely associated with the essentialist image of Islam: the "dormant" orient; the conception of Islamic history as a political history; and the dogmatic and legalistic image of "true Islam."

Like Heinrich Leberecht Fleischer, our four scholars perceived the Muslim world as being in a kind of stagnation which called for an awakening. To be sure, all four rejected the orientalist attitude of neglecting contemporary Islam as an object of study. For them, Islamic studies meant much more than the analysis of classical texts alone, and they established the new discipline by stripping it of its merely philological bonds. Yet they addressed contemporary questions of Islam within the narrative of Islamic history as a history of decline. This decline, according to the narrative, resulted in a social stagnation which called for a complete revision of Islamic history. Martin Hartmann expected this revision to come from the secular national awakening of the Arabs and the Turks, whereas Goldziher supported the ideas of Islamic reform. Snouck Hurgronje and C.H. Becker demanded the relegation of Islam to the private religious sphere. They set their hopes on a process of secularization in which the European experience should serve as both example and guidance. In sum, all four conveyed the rather bleak picture of a Muslim world whose historical course made it unfit for the challenges of modern times.

In line with many Islamic modernists, the four scholars identified in the political and religious institutions of Islam the cause for this historical decline. In doing so, the founding fathers of the discipline largely adopted Wellhausen's assertion according to which the real importance of Islam in human history is not of a religious, but of a political nature. To be sure, they wanted to understand the Muslim world from its religious core, but they perceived this core as being compromised in Medina. Consequently, already in early Islam true religion gave way to religious politics. The nineteenth-century tradition of political history writing has

---

54. From my point of view, Ursula Wokoeck underestimates the role of this theoretical and conceptual dimension in explaining the origin of Islamic studies in Germany. Even if the discipline came into being by default and Islamic studies might represent a misnomer, the very fact of its coming into existence and survival under this "misnomer" Islamic studies must be explained (Wokoeck 2009, 164–184).

strongly impacted on the discipline. In his review of the *Cambridge History of Islam* (Holt, Lambton, and Lewis 1970), Albert Hourani, the late Professor of Islamic and Middle Eastern History at St. Anthony's College, Oxford University, criticized the volume for being almost completely taken up with the genre of political narratives (Hourani 1972, 349). For Hourani the *Cambridge History* is a perfect example of this tradition of political history writing in Islamic studies. The volumes are paradigmatic of the way in which Western studies of Muslim countries and Muslim lives in general have focused on issues such as politics, law, and unity, at the expense of investigations into the varieties of religious belief, mystical paths, and the actual diversity of a multiplicity of Islamic social practices.

The mainstream of Islamic studies has interpreted Islamic history as a political history that transformed its religious core into the petrified system of Islamic law. As a historical religion, Islam is therefore represented by the Sunni orthodoxy, and it has fallen hostage to the doctrines of the *ulama*. In the work of Goldziher, Hurgronje, Becker and Hartmann, "true Islam" represents a compromised form of religion whose original message has been submerged by historical developments. In line with Rabbinical Judaism and Catholicism, they perceived Islam as being socially represented by the *ulama* as a form of medieval world view, a traditional form of religion that had suppressed its original spirituality. While this original spirituality shared the monotheistic core messages of Judaism and Christianity, still free of rituals and dogmas, its historically established form was based on the normative ideal of a holistic system of duties represented by Islamic law. The central problem of the Muslim world is therefore this historical deviation of Islam from its originally religious core.

To a certain extent, this representation of Islam seems to be compatible with the set of centuries-old narratives that characterized the image of the Muslim religion in Europe. According to Norman Daniel, the medieval canon of knowledge about Islam was entirely based on Christian concepts. Although the scholastics often took Islam as the "sum of all heresy," Muhammad's "heretical teachings" were interpreted as a "corroboration of the Gospel" and a "witness to the truth of the Christian faith" (Daniel 1960, 272). Rejecting Muhammad's prophetic character, Christian apologists saw him as a "deliberate deceiver" who invented Islam by borrowing randomly from existing religions. In Christian opinion, the Prophet was not distinguished by receiving a divine revelation, but by his "sexual license" and "violent nature." Consequently, Islam was perceived as a "practical religion," i.e. preoccupied with worldly affairs, with determinist ethics and established by force (Daniel 1960, 272–275). In Daniel's assessment, this medieval concept of Islam proved to be extremely durable and still visible in post-Reformation times, whether in presenting Muhammad and Islam as the head and body of the Antichrist, the use of the Muslim faith as a suitable mask by the Rationalists of the Enlightenment to attack Christianity itself, or in the approach of the Romantics who turned the pejorative image of Islam up-side-down. From the Western perspective it was Christianity that formed the central point of reference in dealing with Islam (Daniel 1960, 274–294).

Although far from following Christian apologetic aims, our four founding fathers not only continued the narrative of Islam as a practical (read: political) religion, but also made in the modern concept of religion a revised interpretation of Christianity the conceptual fundament of their studies on Islam. There is no doubt that they did not question the religious sincerity of Muhammad. In their eyes, the Prophet was not a heretic, and they did not perceive Islam as a heretical wing of Christianity. Rather, they interpreted Muhammad as receiving the same universal message of monotheism which he subsequently transformed according to specific historical and social conditions. Based on a new cognitive foundation, however, they continued questioning the original character of his revelation and narrating Islamic history as a history of worldly affairs. Moreover, they identified true Islam with a determinist system of binding ethics in worldly and otherworldly affairs. The sophistication of their historicist understanding of Islamic history disappeared in the dissemination of their results. While it was able to inform the future methodological development of Islamic studies as an academic discipline, it did not resonate in the public at large. The general readers most probably glossed over the parts of academic erudition and found at home in the standard narratives about the East which were the context for the transmission of new scholarly knowledge. Martin Hartmann's works provide a good example of the ways in which the public dissemination of modern knowledge of Islam became compatible with historically entrenched public narratives. In his journalistic articles and popular books, Hartmann translated the scholarly findings of Islamic studies into the vernacular of the public discourse. In doing so, he not only employed many of the stereotypes of the orientalist tradition, but also consciously trivialized the findings of his discipline in order to find the acceptance of the general German readership.[55]

It is through the choice of themes and the popularization of its findings that Islamic studies itself contributed to the dominance of the essentialist image of Islam in its particularly modern form. Prime in this selective process is the elevation of Islamic law to become the epitome of the Muslim religion. From the perspective of modern religion, Islamic studies conveyed to us that historically true Islam is a law religion claiming to provide an all-encompassing social order. Even more important, as a field of modern scholarship it gave this image academic authority. The strength and resilience of this modern knowledge about Islam is reminiscent of the "plain truth" that Clifford Geertz once discerned in the structures of "common sense." As in Geertz' *Common Sense as a Cultural System*, the essentialist image of Islam is historically constructed and rests on the conviction

---

55. In his popular book on Islam, Hartmann presents Muhammad as an honest, however, mentally sick character. Hartmann largely trivialized Goldziher's description of the Prophet using the voice of popularly known stereotypes and molded by his personal world view. Religion and prophecy, thus, appear as naïve, simple and sick interpretations of the world, based on a primitive search for truth. Yet in moral terms, Muhammad's naivety in Mecca was preferable to his subsequent turn to politics in Medina. The primitive search for knowledge became substituted by a non-compromising search for power (Hartmann 1909, xx).

held by those in whose possession this knowledge is that it is valuable and valid (Geertz 1975, 8). In the wording of the French sociologist Pierre Bourdieu, viewing Islam as a holistic and all-encompassing system has become a part of a *doxa* of global public discourse, an experience of the social world—here of Islam—in which specific relations of social and cognitive orders shape an object accepted as self-evident (Bourdieu 1986a, 471). Orientalist and Islamist narratives have become a simple, natural, and authoritative story about Islam. In common modern knowledge, the essentialist image represents Islam simply "as it is"—as a holistic order intrinsically different from the West.

6

Orientalist Constructions, Islamic Reform and Islamist Revolution

...this religion is essentially a unity, worship and work, political and economic theory, legal demands and spiritual exhortations, faith and conduct, this world and the world to come...

(Sayyid Qutb)

In *Social Justice in Islam* Sayyid Qutb, probably Egypt's most influential Islamist intellectual of the twentieth century, constructs Islam as an ideal and all-encompassing socio-religious system.[1] Qutb, who is often seen as the intellectual mastermind behind the ideologies of contemporary Islamist militancy, provides an image of Islam that reminds us closely of some of the Western constructions which we have discussed in the previous chapters of this book. In line with Ignaz Goldziher, for instance, Qutb based his interpretation of Islamic history on the assumption that the real religious spirit of Islam had been lost with the establishment of the Umayyad dynasty (Algar 2000, 14). Like Ernest Renan, he narrates Jewish history as the way into "a system of rigid and lifeless ritual" against which Jesus Christ stood up in preaching spiritual purity (Qutb 2000, 20–21). Of course not mentioning him by name, Sayyid Qutb seemingly agreed with Theodor Nöldeke that true Muslim philosophy cannot be found in the work of Ibn Rushd or other Islamic philosophers who were inspired by the Greek philosophical heritage (2000, 38).[2] Moreover, he apparently shared the opinion of

---

1. The English translation to which I refer here is a revised version of John B. Hardie's translation from the Arabic by Hamid Algar. Hardie's translation was based on the first edition of *Social Justice in Islam* from 1948. Between 1948 and 1964, the book appeared in six editions. William Shepard showed in which way the revisions in these subsequent volumes indicate the radicalization of Sayyid Qutb's ideological outlook. Shepard discerned three tendencies: an increasing theocentrism; an increase in emphasis "on Islam as a distinct, stable and inwardly consistent religious-social order"; and a partly revised picture of Islamic history, replacing the notion of progress by "a series of abrupt rises and gradual declines" (Shepard 1996, xxiv, iiv).

2. For support of his argumentation, however, Qutb refers directly to orientalist scholars

Julius Wellhausen that Islam's world historical importance lies in its nature as a "political religion" of "practical work" (2000, 29).

At the same time, Sayyid Qutb's religiopolitical ideology contains a number of the central elements of nineteenth-century Islamic modernism.[3] In his books, he refers to modernist authors such as Afghani, Abduh and Muhammad Iqbal and advocates the "Salafi method" (Moussalli 1992, 43). In *Social Justice in Islam*, for instance, he defines the Koran and the traditions of the early community as the sole authorities in finding the true Islamic way of life. In order to develop his "Islamic concept," Qutb returns to the pristine community of the prophet and his companions (2000, 38). Sayyid Qutb rejects the mode of traditional imitation (*taqlid*), holds a critical position with respect to Islamic jurisprudence (*fiqh*), advocates independent reasoning (*ijtihad*), stresses the theological concept of divine unity (*tawhid*) as a means of Muslim solidarity, and indiscriminately associates his Islamic system with the establishment of a social order based on the *sharia*. Undoubtedly, Qutb's writings highlight some of the core ideas of the modern Islamic reform movement in which the Egyptian Muhammad Abduh was one of the key figures. Like Abduh, Sayyid Qutb grounded his world view in the conviction that Islam's transnational and trans-historical mission was that of a universal religion (cf. Ahmad 1963, 114). Moreover, he shared with the mainstream of Islamic reformers the belief in the inherently spiritual and moral qualities of Eastern culture, sharply distinguishing it from the alleged materialism of the West. In short, in the Islamist world view of Sayyid Qutb we find many traces of both the reinterpretation of Islamic traditions by the modernist Salafiyya and the orientalist constructions of their Western contemporaries who reshaped the modern image of Islam while defining it as a field of academic scholarship. Sayyid Qutb is thus one of the important voices in the global negotiations about the modern image of Islam.

Apart from its constant explicit and implicit references to the different semantics of Western orientalism and Islamic reform, Sayyid Qutb's Islamist reconstruction of Islamic traditions is also firmly rooted in the conceptual apparatus of the modern *epistemé*. For instance, his philosophy of history is based on the model of a sequence of religious evolutions according to which Judaism was replaced by Christianity, and the history of humanity will be completed by the eventual institution of true Islam as the universal and comprehensive religion of the human kind (Qutb 2000, 23, 37, 41).[4] Reminding us to Ernest Renan's theory of reli-

---

who were his contemporaries such as, for instance, Hamilton Gibb (Qutb 2000, 267).

3. This relationship to Islamic modernism is less visible in his later works and the later editions of *Social Justice in Islam* in which Qutb apparently tried to distance himself from this world of modernist thoughts (cf. Shepard 1996).

4. Apparently, Qutb also changed his view on Christianity throughout the subsequent editions of *Social Justice in Islam*. With respect to the last edition, Shepard writes: "On this view the essential difference between original Christianity and Islam seems, by implication, to be minimized. Christianity thus becomes not a stage in the historical development of religion culminating in Islam, but one more example of the pattern of high point followed by decline" (Shepard 1996, liii).

gious evolution, Qutb adds here another narrative of human history as a history of religious evolution in combining the Islamic tradition about Muhammad as the seal of prophecy with the general evolutionary trope that has informed the global debate about religion and modernity from its outset. Later on in this chapter, we will see that this evolutionary perspective on Islam was already a fundamental part of the thought of Muhammad Abduh, who perceived pre-Islamic religions as necessary steps toward the final revelation of Islam (Hildebrandt 2002, 238).

A second example is Qutb's theory of the Islamic system. In constructing Islam as a comprehensive way of life, Qutb fused the holistic concepts of culture and civilization with the core category of Islamic theology *tawhid,* the absolute unity of God.[5] The writings of Sayyid Qutb draw on the same cognitive foundations on which the ideas of Islamic reform and Western studies on religion and Islam rested. Based on this very same conceptual structure, however, he elaborated a rather different kind of semantic. In the Islamist narrative of Qutb, true Islam is sharply dissociated from the orientalist view of the alleged backwardness of Sunni Orthodoxy and the petrified system of Islamic law. Instead he draws a picture in which true Islam appears not as a rigid normative force devoid of spirituality, but as an in essence flexible and dynamic one that provides mankind with a firm framework for encompassing solutions to the societal problems of all times.

In sharp contrast to Islamic modernists, Qutb did not expect to find some of these solutions for the Muslim world in Europe. He strongly opposed the modernist idea of an Islamization of European models. Instead, he further radicalized the modern search for Islamic authenticity. In this search, Sayyid Qutb deviated from the rationalist approach of the modernist Salafiyya of proving the intrinsic rationality of Islam. Contrary to Afghani, Abduh and Rida, Qutb's world view is deeply molded by the romanticist stream of modern thinking. He interpreted Islamic traditions from a strongly existentialist perspective and questioned the pretensions of modern reason from an romanticist Islamic point of view. To a certain extent, Sayyid Qutb's Islamist semantics combine the interpretative elements of the nineteenth-century reform movement with the fierce anti-Western attitude of nationalist movements and the conservative *ulama,* who were fighting against the intellectual movement of Islamic modernism. Qutb forcefully refutes Western culture in an traditionalist attitude while reconstructing true Islam with the help of modern conceptual tools.

Sayyid Qutb is an excellent example of Sadik al-Azm's critique of Edward Said's blindness toward the discursive unity which has actually characterized

---

5. This application of the modern system concept to Islamic traditions is, for instance, apparent in Qutb's commentary on Islamic criminal law. In references to Surah 5, 28–40 he writes: "The Islamic order is an integrated whole. You cannot properly understand the reason for particular legislation within it unless you look at the nature of the system, its basic principles and its safeguards. Likewise, this particular legislation can only be validly applied when the whole system is in effect. It is of no use to separate out one law or one principle and apply it within a system that is not fully Islamic" (quoted in Carré 2003, 287).

the modern imaging of Islam by Western and Muslim intellectuals. Firmly anchored in the modern discursive formation, his writings add to the various semantics which have cross-cut in negotiating the modern image of Islam in the global public sphere. In dealing with the fields of politics, economics, law and education, *Social Justice in Islam* implicitly understands society within the general modern framework of functional differentiation. In his attempt to find an authentic Islamic answer to the fragmented nature of the modern social condition, Qutb developed his ideas in constant dispute with Christianity and Western political ideologies such as socialism and liberalism, which themselves are an attempt to make sense of the imperatives of functional differentiation.[6] He eventually tried to dissolve modern fragmentation in the ideal of an all-encompassing Islamic unity. From the perspective of modern systems theory, in Qutb's ideology religion represents society as a whole, and religious communication penetrates the other functionally differentiated fields of social action. While Islam served many orientalists as the ideal representation of a pre-modern form of religious holism which obstructed the modern reality of functional differentiation, in Sayyid Qutb's thinking Islamic holism emanates from the unity of God (*tawhid*) and provides the essential means for a romantic resolution of the deep sense of contingency that human kind has experienced in its confrontation with the modern transformation.

This brings me back to the central concern of this book, namely, to reconstruct the origin and spread of the essentialist image of Islam that has dominated the contemporary debate about Islam and the West. The previous chapters presented both a theoretical framework and steps in a genealogical analysis for this purpose. The main focus of these chapters was on the ways in which European intellectuals, sociologists and Western scholars of Islam, contributed to the making of this modern image of Islam. From my theoretical vantage point of world society, I have embedded the rise of this image within the larger social and discursive context of the global expansion of patterns of modern society. Chapter four discussed the cognitive foundations, problematic themes and specific semantics through which nineteenth-century Europeans comprehended the role of religion in modern society. Chapter five, then, put its focus on the evolution of Islamic studies and the way in which Western scholars of Islam contributed to shaping the contemporary image of the Muslim religion. Together, these two chapters give an insight into the multi-faceted and extended intellectual networks in which modern knowledge of Islam has emerged. They give an analytically guided account on the discursive practices and social relations that have connected Western scholars of different nations and various academic disciplines. We have examined the themes and semantics through which the modern images of religion and, more specifically, of Islam have been constructed in an

---

6. In her study on Sayyid Qutb as a "political theorist," Roxanne Euben mentions this "preoccupation" of Qutb with modern political theories and concludes that he unintentionally incorporated "many of the terms and concerns of those discourses while insisting on philosophical 'purity'" (Euben 1999, 84).

emerging global public sphere. The aim of this concluding chapter is now to add an "Islamic" perspective to this investigation. So far, I have only hinted at the fact that Muslim intellectuals were an inherent part of this process. On the following pages I shall demonstrate how different generations of Muslim thinkers have been engaged in this increasingly global process of shaping and disseminating a particularly modern image of Islam.

In doing so, this chapter aims at giving further proof of the analytical utility and historical reality of my concept of an emerging global public sphere. I shall demonstrate the ways in which the different semantics of Islamic modernism and Islamist ideologies relate to the very same cognitive deep structures of the modern *episteme*, adding to Islamic traditions new meanings. Furthermore, I want to show that the negotiations of Muslim thinkers among each other and with the West reflect the more general themes that have accompanied the evolution of a global modernity. Just as European intellectuals were concerned about the relationship between Christianity and modernity, Islamic reformers were occupied with the nature of Islam as a modern religion, with the definition of Islam in light of other religions, with the historical evolution of these religions, and with the reconciliation between modern scientific and revealed knowledge. In discussing these general themes Muslim intellectuals also employ concepts of religion, law, education, science and politics that they derive from the modern social structure of a functionally differentiated society. However, they have articulated these core themes of modernity in different semantics which are historically and culturally conditioned; and it is this conditionality together with the asymmetric power relations of the international system that we observe as both conflict and difference between Islam and the West.

To make it clear from the beginning, this chapter remains a sketch. I will not be able to present the reader of this book an equally detailed analysis of the life and work of my Muslim sample as is the case with the European intellectuals in chapters four and five. In a more comprehensive fashion, this analysis ought to be based on a similar scrutiny of primary and secondary sources; consequently, it demands another book. Given this imbalance between the previous two chapters and chapter six, I nevertheless hope the following pages will be sufficient to convince the reader of the validity of my thesis that the modern essentialist image of Islam has to be understood within the analytical framework of an emerging global modernity. With regard to this purpose, this chapter primarily has its focus on the close discursive and social connections with Europe in which modern Muslim intellectuals have developed their thoughts. In addition, this chapter will indicate the historical path that these thoughts about an Islamic reformation have taken from the nineteenth-century period of Islamic reform to the contemporary aspirations of a transnational Islamist revolution. In this way, I shall answer my question about the historical origin of the similarities between the shared essentialist images of Islam by Western orientalists and contemporary Islamists. Furthermore, I will contribute to the understanding of the linkage between the global rise and dissemination of this image and the assumption of a confrontation between Islam and the West.

In the coming section, I first look at the discursive and social interconnect-edness among Muslim reformers from India, the Ottoman Empire and Egypt, as well as with their Western intellectual counterparts. In emphasizing the over-lapping nature of various Muslim and European intellectual milieus, I try to give evidence for my thesis that the construction of modern images of Islam was an undoubtedly collaborative process among Islamic and European thinkers. Then we will move to a closer analysis of some of the core revisions of Islam undertak-en by the modernist Salafiyya, which is connected to the life and work of Jamal al-Din al-Afghani, Muhammad Abduh, and Rashid Rida. I have chosen these three individuals with regard to their central roles in reshaping Islam throughout the Muslim world. I will analyze core ideas of the modernist Salafiyya movement in the light of both the conceptual foundations of the modern *epistemé* and the above mentioned typical themes which became intercultural templates of nego-tiating the modern social condition. This sociological analysis adds the broader historical context of imperialist power relations and the strong impact which the formation of national states in general made on the modern reconstruction of Is-lam in the late nineteenth and throughout the twentieth century. Then, I sketch the transformative path on which the ideas of the modernist Salafiyya have travelled in becoming core elements of Islamist thinking during the twentieth century. Starting with the "conservative" re-interpretation of Abduh's thoughts by Rashid Rida,[7] this sketch looks at changing concepts and patterns of orga-nization, leading via the founders of the Egyptian Muslim Brotherhood, Hasan al-Banna, and the Pakistani Jamaat-i Islami, Abu al-Ala Mawdudi, to the ideology of Sayyid Qutb, whose conceptual revisions to a large extent have informed the ideologues of a transnational Islamist revolution such as Abdallah Azzam or Osa-ma bin Laden. These two sections further point at the ways in which intellectual concepts become stereotypical patterns of common global knowledge through popularization, dissemination and trivialization by social movements, organiza-tions and the media.[8]

---

7. Because of his increasingly more rigid and purist interpretations of the reform ideas which originated in Muhammad Abduh's thought, Rashid Rida is often described as a "neo-fundamentalist" or "conservative" thinker. In spite of this particular label, it is important to differentiate this turn toward conservativism from the traditionalist attitude of the *ulama*. Rida fully remains within the modernist paradigm whose con-servative leanings are based on conscious political reflection.

8. Given the limits of both time and space, this chapter is largely based on secondary sources, referring to primary sources in a more sporadic way. A real study of the con-ceptual transformations that Islamic reformers and Islamist thinkers have made in their modern reconstructions of Islamic traditions must be based on the same array of original sources as I have used in chapters four and five.

Muslim and European Public Spheres:
The Overlapping Nature of Modern Intellectual Deliberations

Islamic Modernism in India:
Sayyid Ahmad Khan, Muhammad Iqbal and the Aligarh Movement

In a letter from September 1910, Martin Hartmann asked his Hungarian colleague Ignaz Goldziher whether he knew an Indian Muslim by the name of Muhammad Iqbal. The German orientalist had just received a letter from Iqbal in which he asked Hartmann to send him his article on Germany and Islam (*Deutschland und der Islam*) (Hanisch 2000, 365). The tone with which Martin Hartmann tells this episode slightly ridicules Iqbal's request and Hartmann remains silent about whether he eventually sent the article or not.[9] Apparently, he did not know that Iqbal had studied in Germany and was in contact with a number of Western orientalists. Today, Muhammad Iqbal is remembered for his important role in providing the ideological foundation for the Pakistani state, and his poetry and philosophical writings have found worldwide recognition. While Martin Hartmann is only known to a few specialists in the field of Islamic studies, Muhammad Iqbal represents one of the leading Muslim intellectuals of South Asia in the twentieth century. Not only are there a mausoleum and an Iqbal academy in Lahore, but the university city of Heidelberg in Germany also named a riverside road after him. Close to Heidelberg University, the road is named in honor of the time Iqbal spent studying in Heidelberg and, more generally, in Europe.

In 1905, Iqbal left India for Europe, where he lived in England and Germany. He studied law in London and at Cambridge and submitted his PhD thesis on Persian metaphysics to the faculty of philosophy at Ludwig Maximilian University in Munich. From June to November 1907, Muhammad Iqbal studied German in Heidelberg, in an intellectual milieu that was strongly characterized by the ideas of Germany's Cultural Protestants. His stay in Heidelberg coincided with the activities of the Eranos around Ernst Troeltsch and Max Weber, as well as with C.H. Becker's starting his innovative series of lectures on modern Islam. Of course, I cannot provide any evidence that Iqbal was directly in touch with the intellectual circles around Weber and Becker. Iqbal's writings, however, revolve around similar themes to those discussed in Germany's Protestant intellectual milieu. In particular the question of a reconciliation of religious experience with modern scientific culture was a central concern in Iqbal's work (cf. Vahid 1953). In addition, the German cultural debate might have resonated in his emphasis on the importance of culture in human life and his definition of culture in organicist language as a

---

9. The article was published together with C.H. Becker's *Der Islam als Problem* in the first issue of the newly established journal *Der Islam*. Hartmann describes the Muslim world as not yet prepared to follow its own interest in developing forms of modern statehood and capitalist economy due to the religious mindset of its population. In this situation, according to Hartmann, it must be the aim of German foreign policy to raise the economic and cultural level of Muslim countries in their own and in the German national interest (Hartmann 1910).

comprehensive expression of human activity (Abdul Rahim 1998, 31–33).

With respect to South Asian Islam, Muhammad Iqbal is an excellent example of the discursive and social integration of the Muslim reform movement into the global public sphere. In his modern revitalization of Islam, Iqbal was not only "deeply influenced" by the work of Nietzsche (Schimmel 1954, 153). In his lectures and essays the Indian thinker refers to the ideas of such different Western authors as Bergson, Comte, Fichte, Hegel, Kant, Rousseau, Schleiermacher, Schopenhauer, Spencer and Spinoza, and he read the works of orientalists such as the Dutchmen Snouck Hurgronje and Reinhardt Dozy or the Austrian von Kremer, whose cultural history of Islam so profoundly inspired the work of Ignaz Goldziher (Iqbal 2006). Iqbal was especially versed in German philosophy, which he perceived to be central to modern learning (Robotka 1996, 350). Fascinated by Goethe and Rumi, Iqbal presents in his poetry a perfect fusion of European and Muslim horizons. In social and intellectual terms, he was very close to his teacher Thomas Walker Arnold, whom he met at the Government College in Lahore. Arnold himself was a scholar of modern Islam and received his education in oriental studies under William Robertson Smith at Cambridge (Watt 2002, 7–8). From 1888–1898, Arnold taught at the Muhammadan Anglo-Oriental College in Aligarh, which was founded by the famous Indian Muslim reformer Sayyid Ahmad Khan (1817–1898) in 1875.[10]

In 1869–1870, Ahmad Khan travelled Great Britain, where his son resided after having received a scholarship. Inspired by the example of Cambridge and impressed by the accomplishments of British education, Khan decided to build up a modern Muslim university in India. For Ahmad Khan, the education system was the foundation of British strength, and building a similar system of education in India would therefore lead to the desired empowerment of Indian Muslims. Since the "Indian Mutiny" in 1857/58, Ahmad Khan had "tried to counteract the British belief" that this revolt had been a specifically Muslim uprising (Lelyveld 1996, 74). Working closely with the British authorities, he was advocating a revival and reform of Muslim culture for which he perceived the reconciliation of religion and modern science as vital. In interpreting the Koran from a naturalistic perspective, Ahmad Khan reformulated Islamic theology "in order to prove the consistency of God's revelation with nineteenth-century European rationalism" (1996, 110). He propagated the importance of religion for social cohesion and moral progress. Partly informed by methods of biblical criticism, he underpinned his apologetic mission with modernist reinterpretations of Islamic traditions. For instance, he transformed the military concept of *jihad* ("holy war") into a civic

---

10. Sayyid Ahmad Khan was born on October 17, 1817 in Delhi. He came from a noble Muslim family, which for generations had served the higher bureaucracy of the Moghul court. He received a basic education in Islamic sciences and studied Islamic philosophy and modern sciences. At the age of twenty, he joined the administrative service of the British East India Company. Before founding the college in Aligarh, Ahmad Khan worked at the court in Agra and later became a judge in the Islamic legal system of the country (Peters 1989, 112).

religious obligation for the active advancement of learning. Ahmad Khan was striving for a religiously inspired reform of Indian education and the College in Aligarh as a self-consciously planned institution became the central means for his project of an Islamic reformation (1996, 146).

Sharing the vision of Ahmad Khan, Thomas Walker Arnold was fully engaged in this educational project at Aligarh. His thinking about and attitude toward Islam became "most profoundly affected by his experiences at Aligarh's Muhammadan Anglo-Oriental College" (Watt 2002, 9). With his sympathy for Islam and his promotion of the educational and cultural ideals of Ahmad Khan's movement, Thomas Arnold won "considerable respect" among Muslim reformers (2002, 70). For Muhammad Iqbal, Arnold was an important personal linkage between India's Islamic modernism and the world of Western scholarship. In the Preface to *Preaching of Islam,* Arnold expressed his gratitude for the "valuable suggestions" William Robertson Smith made to his book (Arnold 1896, xi). At Cambridge, Robertson Smith taught Arnold the methods of biblical criticism which he himself once had learnt while studying with the leading Protestant theologians at the Universities of Bonn and Göttingen in Germany. Arnold later applied this historical-critical approach to his studies on Islam and spread them while teaching in India. Moreover, Robertson Smith influenced Arnold with the very same anthropological ideas that later impacted so strongly on the development of Durkheim's sociology of religion (Watt 2002, 8).

Studying philosophy, English literature and Arabic at the Government College in Lahore, Iqbal was encouraged by Arnold to come to Europe and to engage more with Western literature and philosophy. The British scholar and his Indian disciple were bound by a lasting friendship and intellectual affinities. It was Arnold who convinced Iqbal not to give up the medium of poetry, and it was his advice and recommendation that enabled Iqbal to receive his doctoral degree from the University of Munich (Watt 2002, 68). There, he defended his thesis under the formal supervision of Fritz Hommel (1854–1936), a Professor of Semitic languages who himself once was a student of Heinrich Leberecht Fleischer in Leipzig. Apparently, Hommel based his evaluation of the thesis on Arnold's assessment and examined Iqbal only in Arabic (Robotka 1996, 355). There is no doubt that Thomas Arnold exerted a significant influence on the Muslim Indian educational movement and on leading figures among India's Islamic reformers such as Iqbal (cf. Watt 2002, 71).[11]

Islamic Modernism in the Ottoman Empire: From the Young Ottomans to the Young Turk Revolution

Whereas the life and work of Muhammad Iqbal was closely connected to the intellectual milieus of Great Britain and Germany, the Islamic modernists of the Ottoman Empire and Egypt were equally closely knit with discursive structures and

---

11. In terms of Islamic reform, Muhammad Iqbal was also strongly influenced by Afghani and Abduh, whose ideas about Muslim unity, the relation between science and religion, and the vices of European nationalism he shared (cf. Abdul Rahim 1998).

social networks which had their gravity center in France. A well-known example of this connection is Ernest Renan's lecture *L'Islam et la science*. His speech at the Sorbonne in 1883 triggered immediate responses by Jamal al-Din al-Afghani and the Ottoman writer Namik Kemal. Both defended Islam against Renan's accusations, however, in very different ways. In talking to a European audience, Afghani conceded the incompatibility between traditional religion and modern science, a position which earned him public recognition by Ernest Renan himself and might have been the reason why Afghani's response was not published in Arabic. However, he rejected Renan's assertions regarding the never-changing nature of Islam and the intellectual inferiority of the Arabs.[12] Namik Kemal, by contrast, refuted Renan's denigrating picture of Islam vehemently from an apologetic perspective (Kemal 1962). Born in 1848, Namik Kemal was a leading figure among the "Young Ottomans," a group of reform-minded bureaucrats, journalists, writers and younger *ulama* that in 1865 began to spread their ideas about Islamic modernization and constitutional reform (Mardin 1988, 31). In their attempt to reconcile modern science with religion they were aiming at a synthesis of Islamic values with the ideas of the Enlightenment. In political terms, they advocated the introduction of representative institutions based on Islamic principles. The Young Ottomans propagated a form of "Ottoman nationalism" in which the traditional loyalties to the *millet*, the religiously defined communities of the empire, should be replaced by the fatherland (*vatan*), which they perceived as above religious, ethnic or regional divisions (Karpat 1972, 262–265).

The Young Ottomans represented a group of modernizers who were nationally minded and liberal in their institutional concepts and who reverted to the symbolic power of Islamic traditions. In this sense they were the prime representatives of Islamic modernism at the political center of the Ottoman Empire. With their critique of the "over-Westernized" bureaucratic elite of the empire, this lower stratum of the educated bourgeoisie pursued their own aspirations to participate in the power resources of the modern sectors of Ottoman society. They were pioneers of a modern discourse of constitutionalism, religious reform and Ottoman-Turkish nationalism, a discourse which grew out of both the societal changes of the Tanzimat reform period (1839–1878) and the legalist spirit of its reform edicts.[13] In December 1876, the opposition around the Young Ottomans

---

12. Afghani defends Arab civilization as a carrier of science and knowledge which has fallen into darkness; a form of stagnation for which he does, indeed, make the "Muslim religion" responsible. In Arab history, however, Islam only played a similar role to that of Christianity in Europe. There is a constant struggle between religion and philosophy, between free thinking and religious dogmas. Reforming Islam, therefore, is the right way to overcome the stagnation of Arab civilization (cf. Afghani 1883). The argumentative logic of Afghani's response to Renan very much resembles the way in which Renan himself defended his Christian ideals against both Catholicism and modern disbelief.

13. The major administrative changes under the Tanzimat comprised: the introduction of a monetized and rationalized system to levy taxes; the part secularization and formaliza-

achieved the promulgation of an Ottoman constitution and the establishment of a representative assembly. In the context of continuous military defeats, financial crises and separatist insurgencies, the predominantly Muslim constitutional movement tried to curb the authoritarian powers of the sultan and the higher bureaucrats. Yet this first constitutional period was only a short interlude in the authoritarian state tradition of Ottoman-Turkish modernization.

In December 1878, Sultan Abdülhamid II dissolved parliament and suspended the Ottoman constitution. For a couple of years, the Young Ottomans moved the centers of their intellectual and political activities to Europe. In 1867, Namik Kemal first arrived in Paris and then went to London before returning via Vienna to Istanbul in 1871. During his exile, Namik Kemal continued his journalistic and literary work, as well as the translation of French literature into Turkish.[14] Through his life-long contact with European literature and the years of exile, Europe became for him a model for the modernization of the Muslim world; however, "a model to be copied with discrimination and not slavishly" (Menemencioglu 1967, 32). Until the so-called Young Turk Revolution in July 1908, Abdülhamid II ruled the country for more than 30 years in a repressive and absolutist manner. As an ideology of unity, the ideas of Young Ottoman constitutionalism had failed and Sultan Abdülhamid embarked on an Islamization of state and society in order to face the legitimacy crisis the policies of centralization had brought about. In international politics, the foreign policies of the Ottoman Sultan were from now on increasingly perceived as expressions of Panislamism (Deringil 1998).

In their attempts to modernize state and society in the Ottoman Empire both the higher bureaucrats of the Tanzimat and the Young Ottomans were primarily oriented toward French institutional models and philosophical streams. Similar to European intellectuals, Ottoman modernists articulated their ideas in different semantics ranging from apologetic argumentations, of which Namik Kemal's work is a good example, to a full embrace of French positivist thought. In particular among leading bureaucrats, positivist attitudes were enormously attractive and traditional Islam was perceived as "a major obstacle to social progress" (Hanioglu 2005, 28). Similar to the world view of Renan, that of these Ottoman intellectuals was strongly based on the idealization of modern science. They expressed strong anti-clerical tendencies and aimed at a separation of political and religious institutions. Abdullah Cevdet (1869-1932), for instance, a graduate from the Ottoman Royal Medical Academy and leading intellectual behind the Young Turk Movement, even translated an essay by Reinhard Dozy (1820-1883) in which the Dutch orientalist suggested the Islamic revelation derived from Muhammad allegedly having a mental disease (Hanioglu 2005, 50). Yet this radi-

---

tion of education and of the administration of justice; the differentiation of branches of government; the differentiation of the state's monopoly of physical force into military and police forces; the introduction of a new system of provincial administration, as well as representative institutions and formal civic rights (Jung 2001a, 40).

14. Namik Kemal translated authors such as Rousseau, Montesquieu, Bacon, Volney and Condillac into Turkish (al-Azmeh 1996, 107).

cal stance against traditional religion did not necessarily lead to a total rejection of Islam. Another Young Turk leader, Ahmet Riza (1859–1930), for instance, combined his fierce anti-clericalism with an idea of "pure Islam" which would be compatible with the modern scientific world view and could serve as a moral means of cohesion in modern social life (Zürcher 2005, 17).[15] Embracing a positivist world view did not necessarily exclude the adoption of Islam as an ideology of social cohesion and anti-imperialist unity.

The societal negotiations between authoritarian Panislamist state ideologues, traditionalist *ulama*, liberal-minded Muslim apologists and a variety of positivist intellectuals made the period of Hamidian absolutist rule (1878–1908) into the most formative phase of Turkish nationalism. In this period, Turkish nationalism evolved as an ideology and as a social movement in close interplay between domestic opposition groups and exiled communities in Europe. Furthermore, the development of Turkish nationalism reflected the historical reality of a territorially shrinking empire. In ideological terms, the concept of territorial political loyalty to the fatherland (*vatan*), first adopted by the Young Ottomans, acquired a more pronounced Muslim and later Turkish connotation, eventually revolving around Anatolia as its territorial core. Against the background of Armenian and Greek nationalist separatism, intellectual circles developed an idealized history of the Turks, promoted the idea of a Turkish civilizing mission and attempted to purify and standardize the Turkish language (Kushner 1977, 29–80). In social terms, the modern educational institutions of the empire, in particular the training centers for the military and the state bureaucracy, developed into the main breeding grounds for Turkish nationalists. Their most influential organization, the Committee of Union and Progress (CUP),[16] eventually instigated the Young Turk Revolution against Abdülhamid II in 1908.

The CUP, basically the predecessor of the Turkish national movement that later founded the Turkish republic, began as a secret circle of students in 1889. Initially advocating the Ottomanist ideology of unity by promoting constitutionalism and parliamentarian representation, the CUP soon adopted a more nationalist stance, now integrating ideological elements of Islam and Turkishness. In their ethnic composition, however, the CUP still reflected the ethnic mosaic of the Muslim *millet*. The Young Turks were Turks, Kurds, Arabs, Albanians and Circassians who shared the social patterns of an urban, educated middle class with close ties to both the military and the state administration (Zürcher 2002). In this sense they epitomized the fact that Turkishness was not an "awakening," as the German orientalist Martin Hartmann put it, but the creation of a particular

---

15. This resurrection of Islam by Ottoman positivists is very much reminiscent of the French resurrection of the essence of Christianity in their search for a religion of humanity as previously discussed in the works of Renan and Durkheim.

16. The strong influence of positivism on the Young Turk movement is underlined by the fact that the CUP derived its name from Auguste Comte's "Order and Progress," which its leaders transformed in the Ottoman historical context into "Unity and Progress" (Parla 1985, 21).

ethno-national identity within certain historical conditions.[17]

In this process of the modern construction of Turkishness, Ziya Gökalp assumed a crucial role. He was a key figure in fusing various streams of European thought with Islamic modernism into the intellectual foundations of Turkish nationalism. In Gökalp's thought, we can identify the fusion of Ottoman intellectual traditions with the scientific approach to sociology by Emile Durkheim. Born in 1876 in the Southeastern Anatolian town Diyarbakir, Gökalp became the central intellectual figure within the Turkish nationalist movement. For more than ten years he was a member of the Central Committee of the CUP (1908–1920), and the founder of the Turkish republic, Mustafa Kemal Atatürk, called him the "intellectual father of the new republic" (Özelli 1974, 81). In *The Principles of Turkism* Ziya Gökalp responded to the political and cultural threats of European imperialism as follows:

> There is only one way to escape these dangers, which is to emulate the progress
> of Europeans in science, industry and military and legal organization, in other
> words to equal them in civilization. And the only way to do this is to enter Euro-
> pean civilization completely. (Gökalp 1968, 45–46)

This political vision of Ziya Gökalp marks the end result of an intellectual jour-ney which he began from the Young Ottoman world of thoughts, aiming at a synthesis of modern science, the national state and Islam. Gökalp saw himself torn between the rationalism of European philosophy and the religious mysti-cism in which he was brought up by his Sufi-oriented family. It was Abdullah Cevdet who introduced him to French positivism and the organicist sociology of Herbert Spencer. While residing in Salonika (1910–1918), Gökalp became ac-quainted with the sociology of Emile Durkheim, which became the new basis of his more systematic thinking. He combined the ideas of "nationalist cultural Turkism" with "ethical Islamism" and "Durkheimian solidarism." The distillate of these three ideological elements provided the essence for the social corporat-ism which has characterized the Kemalist state ideology of the Turkish republic. Deeply influenced by Durkheim's sociology of religion, Gökalp stripped Islam of its theological functions and perceived it first and foremost as a moral source of social cohesion (Parla 1985, 21–38). In the Ottoman-Turkish context, the seman-tics of positivism and the secularizing stream among Islamic modernists became dominant and developed into core elements of the Kemalist state doctrine of republican Turkey.

Islamic Modernism in Egypt: State-Centered Reforms, British Occupation and the Modernist Salafiyya Movement

In Egypt, Muhammad Ali (1769–1849) embarked on a massive reform program even before his Ottoman overlords initiated the Tanzimat. After the massacre of the Mamluks in 1811, the Egyptian ruler, who was formally subordinate to

---

17. While in Europe the terms Turk, Turkish and Turkey were already used in relation to the Ottoman Empire, until the end of the nineteenth century the term Turk was alien to the Ottoman elite, implying the notion of an "uneducated peasant" (Poulton 1997, 51).

the Ottoman Sultan, embarked on a conscious program to transform the economic and political structures of the country according to European standards.[18] He launched a long-lasting reform project under which French literature on science, law and the military was translated into Arabic, and he sent several study groups to Paris (Arafat 2001, 382).[19] From 1826 to 1831, Rifaat Tahtawi, a representative of the *ulama*, stayed in Paris as the Imam of such a group of Egyptians.[20] There he immersed himself in French thought and met with orientalists such as Silvester de Sacy and his German student Heinrich Leberecht Fleischer (Hourani 1962, 69–70). Tahtawi was attracted by the European ideas of social progress, modern sciences, freedom of thought and representative institutions of government. In his eyes the state had to facilitate the rationalization of society and the *ulama* should spearhead this process of social modernization while giving it an Islamic face. Tahtawi did not advocate blind imitation of Europe. Firmly rooted in Egyptian Muslim culture, he suggested the self-conscious reformation of public institutions, in particular in the field of education, in selectively borrowing from European models (Livingston 1995, 219).

The writings of Tahtawi set the stage for a number of themes which occupied Muslim thinkers in Egypt and beyond throughout the nineteenth century (Hourani 1962, 82). These themes, however, were not yet associated with Europe as a cultural and political threat. Only with the subsequent political domination of the Arab world by France and Great Britain did the relationship of Muslim intellectuals with Europe enter a severe dilemma: under the impact of imperialist politics Europe could not be embraced, but because of its advances in science and its political and intellectual liberties it could not easily be rejected (Johansen 1967, 12).[21] This ambivalence toward Europe decisively characterized the lives and thoughts of the Egyptian Islamic reform movement which became known

---

18. There is no doubt that these reforms to a large part were experienced as repressive acts of the state and did not have beneficial effects on all parts of society. Mervat Hatem, for instance, argued that the educational and health reforms impacted women in a way which "domesticated femininity" and denied them autonomy (Hatem 1997, 67).

19. As already mentioned in previous chapters, for many intellectuals from Europe and the rest of the world, Paris became the intellectual gravity center. At the same time as Egyptian study groups frequented the French capital, German writers such as Heinrich Heine or Ludwig Börne, for instance, found their way to Paris. There, they could not only mingle with the leading intellectuals of their time but also enjoy the comparatively high level of freedom of expression.

20. Rifaat Tahtawi gave a comprehensive account of his experiences in Paris in his book *An Imam in Paris* (2004).

21. Muslim intellectuals were not only critical of Europe because of the colonial condition. Muhammad Iqbal, for instance, developed a distinct dislike of the nationalist and racist leanings he could observe while in Europe (Vahid 1953, 6). Later, Muslims took the cruelties of the First World War and the rise of Fascist and Stalinist rule as proof of the moral degeneration of European culture and the failure of its secular liberal pretentions (cf. Gershoni 1999; Johansen 1967, 125–158).

under the label of the modernist Salafiyya, closely associated with the names of Jamal al-Din al-Afghani, Muhammad Abduh and Rashid Rida.

In March 1871, Jamal al-Din al-Afghani arrived in Cairo from Istanbul. He had to leave the Ottoman capital after the Sheikh al-Islam, the highest religious authority of the empire, declared a public lecture held by Afghani as being heretical and derogatory to the dignity of Islam (Adams 1933, 6). Afghani was one of the most exceptional figures among Islamic reformers to arrive in Egypt. Eloquent in various languages and versed in both Islamic and European philosophy, Afghani was labeled a religious philosopher, a political manipulator, a revolutionary conspirator, and a radical proponent of Islamic reform (Hourani 1962, 112; Livingston 1995, 221; Euben 1999, 97). His restless life in itself is an expression of the interconnected nature of Muslim and European public spheres. Afghani lived and travelled in India, Afghanistan, Iran and different provinces of the Ottoman Empire, and his political ambitions brought him to London, Paris and St. Petersburg. In Cairo, he assembled around him a group of students who discussed works of Sufism, logics, philosophy and theology (Hildebrandt 2002, 215). In this circle participated not only important Egyptians such as Muhammad Abduh, Saad Zaghlul or Ali Yussuf,[22] but also the young Ignaz Goldziher while on his study tour in Egypt (1873–1874). In his diary, Goldziher described Afghani as one of the most original characters among his friends.[23] He met him and his group of students in a coffee shop in Abedin, where he regularly joined their circle which discussed subjects which Goldziher described as being of a "free-thinking and heretical" nature. Ten years later, in 1883, Goldziher and Afghani met again in Paris. There, according to the Hungarian orientalist's notes, Goldziher's wife Laura supposedly discussed with Afghani matters of philosophy and even "lectured him on European culture" (Goldziher 1978, 68).[24]

Taking up the essential themes of previous reformers, Afghani's central concern was the call for Muslim unity in order to fight European, in particular British, imperialism. In 1876, the European powers began to seriously interfere with Egypt's administration. At the appeal of the Khedive Ismail, European controllers

---

22. Saad Zaghlul (1859–1927) joined Afghani's circle as an Azhar student. He later became the leader of the liberal-nationalist Wafd Party and served a short period as Egyptian prime minister in 1924. Ali Yussuf became a well-known journalist and published the anti-British and reformist journal *al-muayyad*. In contrast to Abduh, however, he was a staunch supporter of Khedive Abbas II (1874–1944), who formally ruled Egypt from 1892–1914 (Lutfi al-Sayyid 1968, 96–97).

23. In his diary, Ignaz Goldziher refers to Afghani as the "exiled, anti-British agitator, journalist and polemicist against Renan Abd-al-Dschakal the Afghan" (*der Afghane Abd-al-Dschakal*) who invited him to join his group of students in Abedin (Goldziher 1978, 68).

24. The picture of Goldziher's wife lecturing the Muslim intellectual and anti-imperialist Afghani about European culture seems rather odd and this note in Goldziher's diary stands in striking contradiction to Nikki Keddie's assertion that "an expressed hostility toward relations with women" was one of the peculiar qualities of Afghani's personal character (Keddie 1983, 33).

headed the "Caisse de la Dette Publique," supervising the strained public finances of Egypt. The establishment of this foreign control over Egypt's state finances
was only a prelude to the eventual occupation of the country by Great Britain in
1882 (cf. Lutfi al-Sayyid 1968, 1–37). These developments sharply distinguish the
historical context of Afghani's times from the earlier period of reform in which
Tahtawi formulated his ideas. Directly threatened by imperial politics, Afghani
used Islam as a symbolic means of political distinction to the West and subordinated the strife for social and religious reform to his anti-imperialist policies.
Afghani, thus, synthesized Islamic reform with fierce anti-colonial agitation.

In contrast to Afghani's "paramount concern with Imperialism" and Muslim
unity (Euben 1999, 99), his disciple Muhammad Abduh's life ambition was the
internal revitalization of Egyptian society through religious and educational
reform as a means of achieving political independence (Livingston 1995, 216).
Initially fascinated by Afghani and supporting his revolutionary ideas, Abduh
was later willing to cooperate with the British administration in pursuing his
reform ambitions. He even established a friendly relationship with Lord Cromer
(1841–1917), the head of the British colonial administration in Egypt.[25] The kaleidoscopic nature of Muhammad Abduh's intellectual universe makes him a real
crossroads of Islamic and Western thoughts (cf. Hildebrandt 2002, 210). In his
intellectual history of the nineteenth-century Middle East, Albert Hourani tells
us, for instance, about Abduh's strong interest and personal contact to European
intellectuals and that the library of the Azhar Sheikh and later Mufti of Egypt
comprised several books by Ernest Renan as well as a copy of David Friedrich
Strauss' *Life of Jesus* (Hourani 1962, 135), the most radical outcome of the Protestant revision of Christianity by the Tübingen School.[26]

At the age of 44, Abduh learnt French and he read, among others, the works
of Comte, Descartes, Guizot, Taine, and Max Nordau (Arafat 2001, 377). He frequently travelled to Europe, lived in Paris, London and Beirut, studied in the
libraries of Oxford and Cambridge, corresponded with Tolstoy and visited the
British evolutionist Herbert Spencer (Livingston 1995, 233–234). In the year 1900,
he entered into an exchange of newspaper articles with Gabriel Hanotaux (1853–
1944), a French historian, foreign minister and later representative of France in
the League of Nations. Hanotaux criticized Islam in contrast to Christianity for

---

25. For a critical portrait of Lord Cromer, see the book by Roger Owen (2004).

26. For a Muslim theologian the books of the Protestant Strauss and the Catholic Renan,
    basically confirming the human nature of Jesus Christ, might have been proof of the
    unity of God which plays such a central role in Islamic theology and in the theories
    of both Islamic reformers and Islamist ideologues. In his introduction to the French
    translation of Abduh's *Risalat al Tawhid* (The Theology of Unity), Mustafa Abd al-Raziq
    emphasizes how close Abduh's definition of religion came to the individualistic Protes-
    tant concepts represented in the works of Adolf von Harnack and William James (Abd
    al-Raziq 1925, xlix). Adams mentions Abduh's view of Christianity as appealing to emo-
    tions and ascetic spirituality, also reminiscent of the discussions around the Protestant
    reformulations of Christianity during the nineteenth century (Adams 1933, 174–176).

insinuating fatalism and the helplessness of human beings *vis-à-vis* an utterly transcendent God (Adams 1933, 87). Similar to Namik Kemal in his refutation of Ernest Renan's *L'Islam et la science,* Abduh defended the civilizing potential of Islam in a fiery essay. Abduh's powerful reply triggered a response by Hanotaux, again followed by a rejoinder by Abduh published in three subsequent articles (Adams 1933, 89; Haj 2009, 91–92). As a teacher in Beirut and Cairo, Abduh introduced his students to the ideas of François Guizot (1787–1874), the French historian and conservative statesman whose *Cours d'histoire moderne* also impacted the thought of European thinkers such as Alexis Tocqueville, John Stuart Mill and Karl Marx (Sedgwick 2010, 17). Muhammad Abduh's attempt to amalgamate Western models of modernity and scientific reason with the Islamic tradition made him a true apologist of Islam. Combining his erudition in Islamic classics with his knowledge of European thought he propagated the unity of Islam with modern science and education. He was convinced that a rational interpretation of Islamic traditions would open the way for a self-conscious and authentic integration of the economic, political and scientific achievements of Europe into the modern Muslim context.

For Abduh, science and faith were not opposite but mutually reinforcing forces. The reformist ideas of Abduh were spread throughout the entire Muslim world. He visited Tunis twice and established a vibrant exchange of thought between the Maghreb and Cairo which also involved a network of Egyptian, Levantine and Turkish friends who lived, among other places, in Cairo, Italy and Paris (Tunger-Zanetti 1996, 163 and 202). In 1903, Muhammad Abduh issued the "Transvaal fatwa" at the request of the small Muslim minority of this province in South Africa. The previous Boer republic had just been conquered by Great Britain and the Muslim community asked for legal advice pertaining to disputes between the Shaafi and Hanafi schools of law and the slaughtering of animals (Sedgwick 2010, 97–99). In South-East Asia, Abduh's ideas were predominantly transmitted by the journal *al-manar,* which was edited by his disciple Rashid Rida. In Indonesia, *al-manar* became an "important vehicle for the transmission of reform ideas from Cairo" (Burhanudin 2005, 26). The thoughts of Abduh, especially in its interpretation by Rida, were central for the engagement of Indonesian Muslims in the Islamic reform movement (2005, 10). The importance of Rashid Rida and *al-manar* in the dissemination and re-interpretation of Abduh's reform agenda can hardly be underestimated. Not only was Rida the biographer of Abduh, but he also continued to write and publish Abduh's Koran commentary and became the leading "mouthpiece of Abduh's ideas" (Hourani 1962, 226).[27] However, as the next section in this chapter will show, under Rida's interpretation the rather "liberal

27. The Koran commentary of Muhammad Abduh is called *tafsir al-manar* when it was subsequently published in the journal between 1901 and 1935. In distancing himself from the classical form of Koranic exegesis with its almost inaccessible technicalities, terminologies and disciplinary knowledge, Abduh wanted to write a *tafisr* that explains the Koran in a practical manner readable for a broader public (Jansen 1980, 19). Most of the commentary actually was written after Abduh's death in 1905 by Rashid Rida.

thoughts" of Abduh suffered visible and decisive changes.[28] From Rashid Rida's interpretations, the ideas of the modernist Salafiyya evolved into an intellectual resource for the essentialist reconstructions of the Muslim religion by Islamist ideologues in the twentieth century.

In sharp contrast to Rashid Rida, who reformulated Islamic modernism in a form often labeled as "fundamentalist," a number of Abduh's students left the path of religious apology and developed the Imam's modernist ideas further into a more secular reform agenda. Prime amongst them were Egyptian intellectuals such as Lutfi al-Sayyid (1872–1963), Mustafa Abd al-Raziq (1882–1947) or Taha Husain (1889–1973). Similar to Ziya Gökalp in Turkey, they advocated a complete integration of Egypt into European civilization (cf. Johansen 1967, 8). In clearly deviating from Abduh's position, they were no longer apologists of Islam but became "apologists of European culture" (Tahar 1976, 22). For this more secular-oriented stream of Egyptian modernists, Comte, Durkheim, Mill, and Spencer seemingly represented an important intellectual canon (Arafat 2001, 400). Taha Husain and Mustafa Abd al-Raziq, for instance, began their studies under Abduh at the Azhar. Later they continued to study at the Egyptian University, which was considered the secular alternative to the Azhar. Founded in 1908, Western orientalists played a vital role among its teachers during the first two decades of its existence. Both Ignaz Goldziher and Snouck Hurgronje were invited to teach at the Egyptian University but turned the offers down. In its seminars, young Egyptians were introduced to the methods of historicist and critical European scholarship, leading to a fierce public dispute about the applicability of these methods to the sacred scriptures of Islam (Reid 1987).[29] From the Egyptian University, Abd al-Raziq and Taha Husain went to Paris, where their studies included sociology under Emile Durkheim.[30] In 1919 Taha Husain returned from Paris deeply influenced by Durkheim and his sociological conceptualization of religion

---

28. I completely support Samira Haj's opinion that it is wrong to label Abduh as a liberal thinker in the sense of twentieth century liberalism (Haj 2009). He certainly did not promote a liberal imaginary of the self, but still had an elitist and status-oriented perception of society, as Haj shows with regard to Abduh's program to reform Egyptian education. While Abduh promoted free education for all Egyptians, the system in his mind was not only gendered but also structured according to social status groups. What made him in the context of nineteenth-century Egypt a liberal was his advocacy of constitutional governance and more general political, social and religious reforms.

29. A part of this public debate is linked to the scandal around Taha Husain's book on pre-Islamic poetry. In this book, first published in 1926, Taha Husain questions the Ibrahim legend in the Koran from a historically critical position. This critique was a well-known topic in the discussions of Western orientalists, first mentioned by Alois Sprenger (1813–1893) and further elaborated by Snouck Hurgronje (cf. Ryad 2002, 99–100).

30. Already familiar with French thought through his studies at the Egyptian University, Taha Husain spent the years from November 1914 to October 1919 in France, furnished with a scholarship which he received for his Egyptian doctoral degree (Mahmoudi 1998, 116). Until his death in November 1917, Emile Durkheim was, together with the orientalist Paul Casanova, the supervisor of Taha Husain's doctoral dissertation on Ibn Khaldun.

(Tahar 1976, 78). In Egypt, he remained for more than three decades at the "very center of literary and academic life" (Hourani 1962, 326). His fellow student at the Sorbonne, Mustafa Abd al-Raziq, became first a professor of philosophy at the Egyptian University before he served from 1945 until his death in 1947 as rector of the Azhar (Hourani 1962, 163). Together with his brother, Ali Abd al-Raziq (1888–1966),[31] Mustafa represented a form of unity of thought, combining Islamic modernism with the conceptual background of the rising social sciences in Europe. Understanding himself and his brother as very close students of Abduh, whose father was a personal friend of the Imam (Adams 1933, 252), Mustafa Abd al-Raziq later rationalized Islam with the help of concepts which he derived from the writings on religion by Max Müller and Emile Durkheim (Arafat 2001, 413).

With Mustafa Abd al-Raziq's modern reconstruction of Islam through the theoretical lenses of Max Müller's comparative religious studies, we can find our way back to the dinner party in Leipzig with which we started in chapter four. The host of this meeting between Friedrich Nietzsche and Richard Wagner, the orientalist Hermann Brockhaus, was the Sanskrit teacher of Max Müller. It was in Leipzig where Müller got his education, which eventually brought him to Oxford. Through his readings of Max Müller, we can put Mustafa Abd al-Raziq, for a short period rector of the center of Sunni Islamic learning, the Azhar in Cairo, indirectly into contact with the German orientalist and founder of the *Deutsche Morgenländische Gesellschaft*, Hermann Brockhaus. In discursive and indirect social terms, this connection between Brockhaus and Mustafa Abd al-Raziq closes the circle that combines the empirical investigations of this book.

It was one purpose of this book to elaborate on and to employ the analytical concept of a global public sphere in order to demonstrate the dense interconnection of a broad variety of culturally, nationally and disciplinarily distinct intellectual milieus. In social and discursive terms, the above histories on the life and work of a number of important Muslim thinkers form another example for the applicability of this concept of a global public sphere. They show in which ways the intellectual milieus of Europe and the Muslim world overlapped in the production of modern knowledge. Thinkers such as Muhammad Iqbal, Namik Kemal, Ziya Gökalp and Muhammad Abduh developed their ideas on Islamic reform by fusing the various horizons of their indigenous cultures, Islamic traditions, European philosophy and the conceptual world of the emergent social sciences. In discussing the relationship between divine revelation and modern

---

31. Ali Abd al-Raziq first studied at the Azhar and later went to Oxford. In 1925, he published a book about the fundaments of government in Islam (*Islam wa usul al-hukm*) in which he dealt with the Islamic Caliphate, which had been abolished only a year before by Mustafa Kemal Atatürk. In this contribution to the debate about the Caliphate, Abd al-Raziq came to the conclusion that an Islamic system of government does not exist. In his analysis, the Islamic unity of the *umma* does not represent a state and Muhammad was nothing more than a Prophet who received a divine revelation. The book raised a storm of protest and Rashid Rida declared it "an attempt of the enemies of Islam to weaken and divide it from within" (Hourani 1962, 189).

scientific knowledge, as well as in their concern for the establishment of modern systems of political authority and education, these Muslim intellectuals shared some of the central thematic themes of their European contemporaries. Moreover, in reflecting the global rise of a social structure predominantly based on functional differentiation, modern thinkers with Muslim and European cultural backgrounds referred to a common cognitive basis that facilitated their discursive exchanges in a global public sphere. On the surface, the various semantics of this public sphere produced a cacophony of voices. An apparent diversity, however, which rested on an increasingly unified modern *epistemé*.

To be sure, the intellectual gravity centers of the nineteenth century—Paris and London—were simultaneously the centers of power in the imperial world order. The evolution of modern knowledge on religion and Islam took place within the coordinates of this center-periphery relationship and they were deeply embedded in the structure of the discursive formation from which the cognitive dimension of the global public sphere emerged. Consequently, the participation of the periphery in the choir of global voices demanded its adjustment to the underlying grammar of the center. In discussing religious matters with the West, Muslim intellectuals had to employ as a point of reference the concept of religion as was developed in nineteenth-century Europe. Likewise, the call for political independence and self-determination in the Muslim world had to refer to the blueprint of political organization that emerged in Europe, the national state. Yet to rationalize these processes of coercive and creative borrowing using the simplistic dichotomy between East and West misses the point. On the one hand, these new modern cultural features and institutional templates also met with strong resistance in Europe. As we have seen, long into the twentieth century both Catholic establishments and German intellectuals strongly rejected what they interpreted as the imposition of an alien Western culture. For many Europeans, the development of "Western modernity" was not a matter of choice either. On the other hand, many non-traditionalist Muslim intellectuals of the nineteenth century shared with their European contemporaries the conviction that some of the modern scientific, institutional and organizational patterns that first developed in Europe were superior, and in their search for societal models and intellectual inspiration it was in particular France with its capital Paris which almost magically attracted nineteenth-century intellectuals from within and outside Europe. Instead of reducing non-European modernization to the colonial dichotomy of international power politics, we should rather conceptualize it from the theoretical angle of the emerging structure of a global modernity. This emergence involved actors of various religious, cultural and social backgrounds, however, historically certainly not on equal footing. With regard to the Muslim world, the modernist Salafiyya represents one of the leading intellectual movements in this emergent process. The following section will look at the ways in which some of its key figures negotiated the inherited Islamic traditions in light of the principal and historical challenges of modernity.

The Modernist Salafiyya:
Imperial Politics, Religious Reform and the Islamic State

In 1966, Malcolm Kerr published a book on the political and legal thought of Muhammad Abduh and Rashid Rida. In this book, *Islamic Reform*, Kerr concluded that their attempts to reform the Muslim world by returning to the pristine teachings of the early "Golden Age" of Islam had failed in political and intellectual terms (Kerr 1966). Measured according to the standards of their own goals, the nineteenth-century Salafiyya around Muhammad Abduh had apparently failed.[32] During their lifetimes, Abduh and Rida did not succeed in shaping a dynamic social reform movement that was able to achieve both a fundamental reformation of Muslim societies and put an end to the political, economic and cultural domination of the Middle East by Europe. Yet their somewhat elitist re-interpretation of Islamic traditions provided one of the core intellectual reservoirs of ideas for the development of Muslim religious and political thought in the twentieth century. Abduh and his associates bequeathed to later generations of Muslim intellectuals a completely revised platform of Islamic concepts. They reinvented Islamic traditions and imbued a number of traditional religious concepts with entirely new meanings. They did so based on new cognitive foundations which they shared with their European contemporaries, making the different cultural semantics of modernity mutually intelligible. Perceived from this angle, the nineteenth-century Salafis contributed successfully to establishing an Islamic public sphere which in itself was an integral part of the larger global public sphere. The contemporary essentialist image of Islam rests on a number of trivialized and popularized concepts of this intellectual movement which so closely associated the themes of internal reform with the colonial encounter between Islam and the West.

The Modernist Salafiyya: Shaping an Islamic Modernity

According to the standard literature on the modern history of Islam, the modernist Salafiyya is directly connected to the lives and works of Jamal al-Din al-Afghani, Muhammad Abduh and Rashid Rida. Representing a chain of teachers and disciples, the three reformers have contributed to the modern image of Islam in different ways. Afghani, still venerated for his fierce anti-colonialist stance by Islamists and Arab nationalists, was one of the main figures in the subsequent politicization of Islam. In emphasizing the political distinction between Islam and the West, his heritage is still a part of the confrontational scenario that characterizes the political world view of contemporary Islamists. Although Islamist thinkers owe a lot to Abduh's reinterpretation of Islamic traditions, they appreciated

---

32. I fully agree with Samira Haj's opinion that this failure cannot be explained by a principle incompatibility of the Islamic tradition with modernity. The failure of Abduh and Rida must be understood within the social and historical context in which their reform efforts took place (cf. Haj 2009, 198).

his role in Islamic history much less than Afghani's.[33] Abduh's legacy is primarily visible in the meanwhile rampant independent interpretation of the religious sources. Although himself a leading representative of the *ulama*, Abduh's struggle against imitation (*taqlid*) and for independent reasoning (*ijtihad*) contributed substantially to undermining the clerics' monopoly of religious knowledge in the Muslim world. Rashid Rida played an important role in initiating the continuing legalization of Islam. The idea of an Islamic state based on the *sharia*, as well as the increasing convergence between Salafi thinking and Hanbali interpretations of Islam such as Saudi Wahhabism, is linked to his later work.

In spite of their very different personal characters and their intellectual legacies, the profiles of these three reformers point to three telling similarities. These similarities comprise both their individual religious and intellectual developments and the political diagnosis of their times. Firstly, they all received a classical education in Islamic sciences and they acquired substantial knowledge on modern science. These Salafi thinkers were still connected to the *madrasa*, the traditional institution of Islamic learning. At the same time, however, they were familiar with modern knowledge and shared the universalist and rationalist outlook of the new group of Westernized Muslim intellectuals (Skovgaard-Petersen 2001a, 95). In this way, the Salafiyya acted between the two opposite poles of the Muslim educated classes in the nineteenth century: the *ulama* as defenders of traditional fields of religious knowledge, on the one hand, and the proponents of secular Western modern education on the other. While challenging the monopoly of knowledge of the traditional Islamic learned, the Salafi reformers also opposed the uncritical acceptance of European cultural innovations by the Westernizing elite.

The second common denominator regards their personal religious experiences. Afghani, Abduh and Rida share an intense encounter with Islamic mysticism before later becoming staunch defenders of Islamic rationalism. Despite this, they never condemned Sufism entirely (Hourani 1981, 91). On the contrary, in different ways they framed their reformist agendas with reference to ideas of the philosophical tradition in Sufi Islam.[34] Yet they fought against the various forms of popular mysticism which were particularly widespread in Egypt. Religious practices linked to local saints, for instance, they perceived as backward superstitious attitudes of the ignorant masses. In turning vehemently against widespread forms of magic, witchcraft and sorcery, Abduh and Rida put a fresh emphasis on the Koran as the central religious and spiritual source of guidance (Jansen 1980, 24). Targeting traditionalist *ulama* and popular forms of Islamic mys-

---

33. Rather than viewing Abduh as an intellectual predecessor of their thought, Islamist intellectuals perceive and disdain him as a "Westernizer."

34. For Muhammad Abduh's future, for instance, the spiritual and philosophic approach to Islam which he learnt from his uncle Sheikh Darwish Khidr was very decisive (Haj 2009, 21). Darwish was an adherent of the Madaniyya, an internationally oriented revivalist Sufi Movement that spread from Libya. Critical of forms of popular Islam, the Madaniyya was a scholarly and intellectual order which stressed the proper practice of Islam together with the role of spiritual experience in faith (Sedgwick 2010, 4).

ticism at the same time, they promoted a rationalist and textual interpretation of Islamic traditions as "true Islam." Clearly, their attempts to rationalize Islam had parallels with the reinterpretations of Protestantism in the nineteenth century as analyzed in chapter four. Finally, witnessing the imperial domination of the Middle East by the European powers, all three identified the political weakness of the Muslim world in a historical deviation from true Islam by incompetent intellectual and political Muslim leaders. Consequently, they equated the defense of Muslim countries against external enemies with the necessity for internal reform. Between the outer poles of traditionalism and positivism, Afghani, Abduh and Rida represent three individual variations of apologetic Muslim thinkers.[35] In this respect, they resemble the various types of Christian apologists with whom we have dealt in the previous chapters. What distinguishes them from European apologists, however, is the experience of Muslim political inferiority and the feeling of cultural decline in the light of European hegemony. In turning orientalist pretentions upside-down, however, they declared Islam to be not the cause of the predicament but the only reliable source of change.

From an apologetic perspective, Abduh and Rida were convinced that Islam as a religion was in principle ideally prepared to meet the challenges caused by modernization. Dealing with the fields of Sufism, Islamic jurisprudence, modern science and anti-colonial nationalism (Eich 2003, 80), the nineteenth-century Salafiyya perceived the rational interpretation of pristine Islamic principles as the primary condition for an authentic appropriation of the scientific, political and economic achievements of Europe (Brown 2000, 139). Representing a method of thinking rather than a specific school of thought, the Salafiyya located the ultimate religious authority in the holy scriptures themselves (Dallal 2000, 347). Their political and intellectual encounter with Europe marks the watershed between them and the generation of eighteenth century Islamic reformers. While for the latter the Islamic past was an unchallenged and ever-present reality, the nineteenth-century reformers had to rediscover and reconstruct Islamic history in the light of Europe's encompassing hegemony (Dallal 2000, 334), and they undertook this reconstruction on fundamentally different cognitive grounds in comparison to their revivalist predecessors. Confronted with the "imperative intellectual authority of the West," they adopted the inevitable tropes of modernity without sacrificing the credibility of the Koran and other foundational texts of Islam (al-Azmeh 1996, 106, 101). In combining modern science with the symbolic authority of Islam, they demanded a reform of the traditional system of education in which they identified the core obstacle that caused the alleged stagnation of Muslim societies. Even more important, they combined reform with new forms of political and social activism. Afghani appealed to his follow-

---

35. Amongst these three reformers, Rashid Rida probably was the most obvious religious apologist. With reference to Abduh's rationalism, some authors suspected him of being a closet agnostic. In the case of Afghani, the mainstream literature strongly questions his religious convictions and perceives his apology of Islam often as a mere political strategy.

ers to present and disseminate their views in public and to contribute to the development of a conscious and educated public opinion. Abduh underpinned this call for activism theologically. In his elaborations on free will, for instance, he defended the idea of an "Islamic responsibility of men." For Abduh, Islam encouraged hard work and personal sacrifice in daily life, which is far removed from generating forms of "Muslim fatalism" (Ibrahim 1999, 71).[36] According to Afghani and Abduh, Islam was synonymous with activity, and only ignorance had led the Muslims toward stagnation (Lutfi al-Sayyid 1968, 88).

Afghani and Abduh: Muslim Unity and Islamic Civilization

Their promotion of general public engagement and various forms of social activism, however, almost naturally brought the reformers into confrontation with both their indigenous and colonial rulers. In particular the life of Jamal al-Din al-Afghani was deeply molded by the shifting phases of cooperation and conflict which he experienced with the various political establishments of his times. Due to his revolutionary zeal, Afghani was constantly on the move. His profound anti-colonial stance and specific hatred of the British can most probably be traced back to the years of his early stay in India, which coincided with the "mutiny" of 1857/58.[37] The years between 1866 and 1869 Afghani spent in Afghanistan, where he became deeply involved in national and international politics. A shift in political leadership eventually led him to leave the country in dismay. After short stays in Mecca and Cairo, Afghani arrived in Istanbul in late 1869. In the Ottoman capital, Afghani soon frequented high educational circles and may have become acquainted with the reformist thoughts of the Young Ottomans (Keddie 1972, 60). After being attacked by the religious establishment of the empire, however, he was forced to leave Istanbul for Egypt only a year later. Establishing himself in Cairo, he first had the sympathy of the government. Yet his continuous call for Islamic reformation, active interest in Egyptian politics and persistent anti-colonial agitation increasingly aroused the opposition of such powerful forces as the *ulama*, Egypt's indigenous ruling elite and Great Britain. Soon after coming to power, the Khedive Tawfiq expelled Afghani from Egypt in September 1879. Afghani went back to India, where he lived in Hyderabad and Calcutta before travelling via London to Paris.

In Paris, he was joined by his disciple Muhammad Abduh in 1884. Due to his involvement in the nationalist uprising of the officer group around Ahmad Urabi,

---

36. In a similar way, the Indian reformers Ahmad Khan and Muhammad Iqbal advocated the ideal of the active and responsible Muslim who should engage practically in ordinary life (Robinson 2000, 111–116).

37. There is not much information about Afghani's early life. He most probably was born in October or November 1838 in Iran. Outside Iran he pretended to be of Afghan origin, a claim which he apparently fabricated after he was expelled from Afghanistan in 1869. In claiming to be of Afghan origin, he most likely tried to avoid being associated with the Shia minority branch of Islam, as this might have undermined his agitation for Muslim unity (Keddie 1972, 10–11).

Abduh also had to leave Egypt for some years. In December 1882, he went to Damascus before spending a year in Beirut. There, he mingled with other Egyptian exiles, among whom were also some members of the Afghani group from Cairo. From Beirut, Abduh moved to Paris, where he and Afghani published an Arabic weekly called *al-urwa al- wuthqa* (The Indissoluble/Firmest Bond). Its title referring to the Koran, eighteen issues of the paper were published and freely distributed between March and October 1884, when it most probably was discontinued because of a lack of funding (Keddie 1972, 214). In this fiercely anti-British journal, Afghani and Abduh expressed their ideas about the necessary fusion of Islamic reform and anti-colonial resistance. They strongly criticized the corruption of Islam by ignorance and accused the "greedy" and "selfish" Muslim rulers of surrendering their countries to foreign domination. Turning the theological concept of *tawhid* into an ideology of political unity, the journal used religious rhetoric to call for the national self-determination of Muslim people, challenging European imperialism in line with the Panislamist quest of the Ottoman Sultan (Lutfi al-Sayyid 1968, 88).[38]

After having invented "what would now be called radical Islamist journalism in Arabic" (Sedgwick 2010, 56), the ways of Jamal ad-Din al-Afghani and Muhammad Abduh diverged. Abduh left Paris for Tunis and soon severed his ties with Afghani. In the literature, this split is often explained by the increasingly diverging strategies of the two reformers. While Afghani enhanced his stress on the dichotomy between Islam and the West, transforming Islam from a religious faith into a politico-religious ideology to fight colonialism, Abduh was much more interested in the combination of religious and social reform. In his focus on internal reform, he chose a more conciliatory approach to the West, in particular to the British colonial administration in Egypt. From Tunis, Muhammad Abduh went to Damascus and later back to Egypt, pursuing his struggle for political independence and Islamic reform in a different way. With British support he eventually even became the Mufti of Egypt. Afghani instead continued his restless political efforts and left Europe in 1885 for Iran. However, as a result of his propagating ideas of reform and meddling in internal affairs, the shah urged him to leave the country in 1887. From Iran, Afghani went to Russia, where he was engaged in anti-British activities in Moscow and St. Petersburg. From Russia, Afghani returned to Iran, after he was apparently invited back by the "Iranian Chief Minister" Amin al-Sultan on the occasion of a meeting in Munich in August 1889 (Keddie 1972, 307). Yet again his stay in Iran developed into a conflict over the despotic nature of Shah Nasir al-Din's rule and his—in Afghani's eyes—rather accommodating foreign policies. In 1891, Afghani was deported from Iran. He first went to Basra and Baghdad, from where he supported the Iranian opposition movement against the tobacco concessions given to a British company. Then he returned to London for another year (Keddie 2005, 21). In summer 1892, the Ottoman Sultan

---

38. The journal was financed by a group of sympathizers. Amongst these sympathizers was Wilfrid Blunt, an essayist and adventurer who supported the Urabi rebellion and opposed British imperialism (Sedgwick 2010, Chapter 4).

Abdülhamid II invited him to Istanbul. In the beginning, Afghani was close to the sultan and enjoyed his sympathy. Yet Abdülhamid II resented his constant public criticism of the shah of neighboring Iran. After Afghani's alleged involvement in the assassination of the Iranian shah in May 1896, the Ottoman ruler put him under house arrest. Living the last months of his life under close surveillance of the Ottoman authorities, Afghani died in March 1897.

There is no doubt that the reform agendas of Jamal al-Din al-Afghani and Muhammad Abduh were firmly anchored in Islamic traditions. Yet in the re-interpretation of these traditions they draw equally on themes and concepts which they derived from their reading of modern science and their engagement with European philosophical and political thought. The ideas of these key figures of Islamic reform developed on the cognitive foundations of the modern *episteme*. It is precisely this merger of modern knowledge with Islamic traditions that makes Islamic modernists into an integral part of the emergence of modern society as multiple modernities. A good example of the fusion of different cultural horizons based on common cognitive structures and mutually faced problems is the reception of Guizot's *History of Civilization in Europe* by Afghani and Abduh.

In his search for a coherent interpretation of the evolution of the West, Guizot combined such diverse ingredients as his personal commitment to Calvinism, French social thought, German idealism and ideas of the romantic movement in a theory of history which enabled him to present European civilization as an ordered totality. Interested in civilization as a total way of life, he narrated European history as a continuous process of social progress (Weintraub 1966, 14). For Guizot, the evolution of European civilization could not be reduced to the development of a single nation, although he saw France at the centre of the civilizing process in Europe (Guizot 1828, Chapter 1, 4–6). In European civilization he found an intrinsic aim for humanity as a whole, the realization of a divine plan (1828, Chapter 2, 12). While ancient civilizations such as in Greece, India or Egypt rested on a "single idea," according to Guizot, this simplistic nature does not apply to modern European civilization. On the contrary, European unity is not based on a single principle but emanates from its diversity. For the first time, a civilization was not stagnant but dynamic and resembled the diversity of the world as a whole (1828, Chapter 2, 1–15). Belonging to France's Protestant minority, Guizot played an important role in the apologetic fight against French positivism together with the Bishop of Orleans, who once facilitated Renan's theological studies with a scholarship (Robertson 1924, 5). During the 1860s, Guizot also published apologetic works in which he condemned French positivism as an ideology that with its radically inner-worldly epistemology would in the end lead to fatalism (Plé 1996, 100–108).

In the course of the nineteenth century, Guizot's lectures on European civilization appeared in 20 editions in France alone, and Afghani and Abduh first read it in an Arabic translation (Weintraub 1966, 83). Obviously Guizot's lectures not only fascinated a Western audience, but also made a deep impression on Muslim intellectuals (Arafat 2001, 376). How is a complex and diverse cultural entity to be presented as a unified whole (cf. Weintraub 1966, 17)? The answer to this central question posed by Europe's historians of civilization was of particular interest for Afghani in his search for Muslim unity. In Guizot's holistic conceptualization of European diversity, Afghani found a way to construct the desired unity of a Muslim world that was in reality politically fragmented. Although rooted in a very different tradition, Afghani and Abduh were confronted with a similar set of problems to those of Guizot and other European intellectuals: unity in diversity, providence and human progress, divine order and historical change.

In his critique of Ahmad Khan's Indian reform movement, Afghani takes up Guizot's interpretation of the Christian Reformation and refers to the rise of Protestantism as the decisive turning point for the progressive development of European civilization.[39] According to Afghani, however, Martin Luther was only following the example of the righteous early Muslims when in order to free European Christianity from the stifling influence of the clerics he directed them to search for proof of the fundamentals of their belief. By portraying Islam as "the only religion that censures belief without proof," Afghani applied a theory of religious rationalization similar to that of Christian apologists, in which he only substituted the role of Protestantism by the world historical role of Islam (Afghani 1880–1881, 171–172).[40] Also for the modernist ideas of Ziya Gökalp, Protestantism was a central reference to show the in principle "modern" content of Islam and therewith its historical superiority to the Christian faith. In his essay on Islam and modern civilization, for instance, Gökalp declared Protestantism as entirely being in contradistinction to the traditional principles of Christianity and he poses the question: "Are we not justified if we look at this religion as a more or less Islamicized form of Christianity?" (Gökalp 1959, 222).

In Afghani's theoretical edifice, Guizot's thoughts could underpin his call for the abolition of blind imitation (*taqlid*) and provided a framework for challenging the widespread equation of modern rationalism with the West (cf. Euben 1999, 97). This attempt to put the Western (read: Protestant) view on modern rationalism up-side-down and bestow Islam with the predicate of an intrinsically rational and modern religion also permeated the thought of other Muslim modernists such as Ziya Gökalp. Moreover, in borrowing from Guizot, Afghani was able to fuse the Islamic theological concept of the unity of God (*tawhid*) with the concept of civilization as a totality. Consequently, it was possible for Afghani to

---

39. In substance, the reform ideas of Ahmad Khan were not so far from Afghani's thinking. Afghani's attack, therefore, has to be understood in the context of his anti-British stance. This becomes particularly visible in the short essay *The Materialists in India*, in which he accuses Ahmad Khan of "hovering around the English in order to obtain some advantage from them" (Afghani 1884, 176). In this essay, Afghani paints the picture of a Muslim unity in India, subverted by Ahmad Khan and the British.

40. This is also apparent in his answer to Renan, in which he points to the civilizing role of religion in general. Although Afghani admits the intolerant attitudes of all religions, he emphasizes the role of Islam and Christianity in leading humanity from barbarism toward "more advanced civilization" (Afghani 1883, 183).

construct Islam as a strict form of rationalized monotheism corresponding to an all-encompassing cultural whole, to a comprehensive and systematically closed Islamic way of life which he utilized in both his fight against imperialism and his attempt to modernize the Muslim world.

Muhammad Abduh: Independent Reasoning and the Modern Muslim Subject

Given Guizot's apologetic mission and his belief in the civilizing function of education, it is not surprising that the *History of Civilization in Europe* made an even stronger impact on Muhammad Abduh's thought. Abduh and Guizot were brothers in thought. It was through Guizot that Abduh first became acquainted with a number of French ideas which influenced his approach to reforming the Azhar and Egyptian education in general (Arafat 2001, 377). Dealing with issues such as liberty, independent reasoning, self-help and the evolution of religions, this reinterpretation of Islamic history based on modern ideas becomes especially visible in Abduh's lectures published in *risalat al-tawhid* (The Theology of Unity) (cf. Sedgwick 2010, 63–70). In these theological lectures to his students at the Sultaniyya in Beirut he applied an evolutionary view to religious history and presented the Koran as the first holy book in which "revelation and reason merge through the voice of the messenger of God" (Abduh 1965, 8). Moreover, Guizot's emphasis on the civilizing role of Christian morality was easily convertible for Abduh's apologetic purposes. Supported by the conceptual fundaments of Guizot's history of civilization, Abduh was able to give his program a coherent form in which the reform of Islamic jurisprudence and education was synthesized with the central role which the ethics of Islam should play for modern civilization (cf. Hildebrandt 2002, 235).

Contrary to the European model of a history of progress, the Muslim reformers constructed Islamic history as a history of decay. This inverse narrative of history was, on the one hand, a result of the experience of Western cultural hegemony and political domination. The nineteenth-century Muslim intellectuals agreed with Western orientalists on the miserable and feeble condition of the Muslim world. On the other hand, this narrative of decay was compatible with a traditional template of interpreting Islamic history. Given the exemplary and revered era of the Prophet, Islamic history was traditionally narrated as a "progressive retreat" from the ideal community. This retreat demanded a continuum of renewal (*tajdid*), revival (*ihya*) and reform (*islah*). In conceptualizing Islamic history anew, Afghani and Abduh inscribed a new meaning into the traditional idea of historical degeneration (Haj 2009, 8 and 72). They applied the modern historicist concept of civilization within the context of this traditional view on Islamic history, identifying the totality of Islam as a civilization in the ideal of a Golden Age in early Islam. Unlike contemporary Salafists, however, Abduh did not reduce this ideal of the *umma*, the community of all Muslims, to the first generation of Muslims. His concept of the Salaf included the first centuries during which Islamic philosophy and jurisprudence developed (Hourani 1962, 149).

For both Afghani and Abduh, true Islam was synonymous with inner-worldly engagement. In keeping with the modern idea of human progress and related to the above-mentioned reform tradition, they perceived the active and educated individual as a necessary precondition for shaping a better future. Therefore, Afghani's and Abduh's recourse to the Golden Age had nothing to do with the uncritical acceptance of traditions or mere nostalgic leanings. On the contrary, they called upon Muslims to reinterpret the ideal Islamic community and its traditions in light of contemporary challenges. They perceived both blind following of traditions and uncritically imitating Europe as forms of *taqlid* which prevented Muslims from living authentic lives. In principle, every educated Muslim should be able to undertake this reinterpretation of the traditions. Yet Abduh was aware of the dangers of using this right of interpretation indiscriminately and he saw it as restricted to the religious dimensions of the *sharia* (Eich 2003, 83). Nevertheless, in order to develop an Islamic modernity, the modernist Salafiyya demanded that the right to individual interpretation of the traditions, the *ijtihad*, must be freed from the confines of the religious and legal orthodoxy of the *ulama*.

According to the standard narrative, this right to individually interpret the religious sources in order to tackle new societal problems was not in question during the formative centuries of Islam. At the beginning of the ninth century, however, the general opinion gradually took shape according to which all essential questions of Islamic jurisprudence were successfully settled. Consequently, individual scholars were no longer authorized to conduct *ijtihad*.[41] The Salafi reformers turned against this assumed "closure of the gate of *ijtihad*." They rejected the principle of *taqlid* as propagated by the traditionalist *ulama* and demanded the individual right to interpret the *sharia* in light of new problems. Moreover they opposed the strict application of the interpretations and methods of a particular school of law (*madhab*) and advocated the principle of *talfiq*, the possibility of drawing in the process of legislation eclectically from different schools of law (*madhahib*). This fight against *taqlid* and the segregated domains of schools of law was directed against the traditionalist *ulama* and their authority to define Islamic orthodoxy. In order to shape an authentic Muslim modernity, the Islamic reform movement struggled with the traditionalists about the authoritative interpretation of the traditions and factually undermined the interpretative monopoly that for centuries was under control of the *ulama*.

In line with so many Christian apologists, Muhammad Abduh strove for a reconciliation of revealed knowledge with the modern sciences. Yet he did not fully share the belief in the concept of natural law and the separation between legal and moral realms held by European scholars. For Abduh, faith and reason were not separate domains. In principle, he continued to perceive questions of faith, morality and law as inseparably interconnected. This is apparent in his concept of the modern Muslim subject and the societal role of the *sharia*. According to Samira Haj, Abduh was searching for a civil Muslim subject, able to make rational

---

41. See: *Encyclopaedia of Islam*, CD-ROM Version (2002), keyword *Ijtihad*. This interpretation of the legal history of Islam, however, has largely lost its authoritative character. As a matter of fact, the application of *ijtihad* in later centuries also seems to correspond more with the historical reality (cf. Johansen 1999).

political and social decisions. In being self-regulatory, self-disciplining, orderly, productive, rational, and fundamentally moral with a concern for the public good and healthy in body and mind, Abduh's modern Muslim subject reflects most of the standard features of an ideal type of the modern individual. What distinguished his concept from the independent liberal individual that has dominated the European social imaginary was that his Muslim subject was grounded in Islamic ethics and the essential role which the religious community should play in realizing his imaginary of the modern Muslim (Haj 2009, 118). Despite the reality of increasing functionally differentiated spheres of communication and social action, Islam remained pivotal for Abduh in informing and regulating social practices under modern conditions. The reform of Islamic education and of Islamic law was the institutional means for creating a Muslim society conducive to the evolution of the modern Muslim individual.

Muhammad Abduh perceived the application of the *sharia* not as antithetical to the modern idea of the rule of law. On the contrary, in line with the relative distance to political authority in which the evolution of Islamic law took place (Johansen 1999, 268), Abduh's reform of the *sharia* was intended to reduce the state's role to administrative and managerial functions in legal processes. In light of the heterogeneity of the Egyptian legal system of his times, the *sharia* served Abduh as a means of national politics and legal unification toward preventing the further Europeanization of Egyptian law (Haj 2009, 137–143). At the same time, he understood the *sharia* as a set of general principles, open to legislative processes according to historically changing needs. Abduh attempted an authentic formal rationalization of the legal system in which religion would continue to play an authoritative role in moral and legal terms. The application of the general principles of the *sharia* would guarantee the legal system would be founded in religious authority. While this legal theory could be interpreted as an Islamic version of the foundational role of natural law in the European context, it nevertheless contained a tendency to perceive the *sharia* in terms of a code book to be implemented by the state (Kerr 1966, 103–109). In the legal thought of Abduh's disciple Rashid Rida, this tendency to reconstruct the meaning of the *sharia* within the new conceptual frameworks of the modern legal system and the national state became more prominent. To be sure, Rida still emphasized the flexibility and the adaptability of Islamic law to changing historical circumstances. Yet to advocate putting the ideal of the *sharia*—to represent a comprehensive legal system based on divine authority—into practice, he laid the foundation for the positivist interpretation of the *sharia* as a law code which was to increasingly characterize the legal theories of Islamist movements in the twentieth century.[42] In his theory about the Caliphate, Rida envisioned a strong Islamic state which was able to enforce the *sharia* without foreign interference (Haddad 1997, 256; Rida 1938).

---

42. Posing the question as to why the introduction of European law in Egypt during the nineteenth century did not result in open rebellion, Nathan Brown shows in which ways the *sharia* has been transformed from a rather heterogenous amalgamation of institutions, discourses and social practices into a normative set of rules (Brown 1997).

Rashid Rida: Religious Arab Nationalism and the Islamic State

Rashid Rida's role as a switchman linking Muhammad Abduh with the Islamist thinkers of the twentieth century is due to the shift in his intellectual development (cf. Dallal 2000, 342). Fascinated by the essays of Afghani and Abduh which he read in *al-urwah al-wuthqa* Rida left his Syrian home in 1897 to join the Islamic reform movement in Cairo (Ryad 2008, 3). In Egypt, Rida established the journal *al-manar* with which he wanted to perpetuate the tradition of *al-urwah al-wuthqa* (Adams 1933, 181). In the beginning, he was, like his mentor Abduh, very open to the indigenization of Western institutions and ideas. In his struggle for an Islamic renaissance, Rida aimed at combining modern science, technology, rationalism and constitutionalism with the moral and ethical values of Islam. In his later years, however, he shifted to a more rigid and "traditionalist" attitude toward Islamic reform, merging modernist Salafi thinking with the puritan school of Hanbalism. He deviated from Abduh's broad understanding of the Golden Age of Islam, increasingly restricting the notion of the Salafi to the life of the Prophet and the first generation of pious Muslims (Hourani 1962, 230). Moreover, he abolished the approach of gradual reform and selective collaboration with Britain, an approach which once led Abduh to separate from the more radical Afghani. Returning to Afghani's confrontational and revolutionary stance, Rida now became one of the intellectuals behind the idea of a principle antagonism between Islam and the West (Tauber 1989, 124-27).

In order to clarify Rida's intellectual shift, a brief glance at his political activities seems necessary. We can also identify major changes in his political views during his lifetime. First embracing Panislamist ideas and defending the Ottoman Caliphate, Rida later promoted various Arab nationalist agendas, eventually advocating the establishment of an Arab Caliphate (Haddad 1997, 254). His shifting political loyalties are closely linked to the frustrations which he faced in his political endeavors. In 1909, for instance, he went to Istanbul to lobby for the establishment of an institute to teach "true Islam." Inspired by the example of Christian missionaries, Rida founded a society of "mission and guidance" (*dawa wa al-irshad*), which he wanted to transform into an educational institute. Given his critical attitude toward the traditionalist class of the *ulama* and the fact that he perceived an Arab cultural and political awakening as the prerequisite for an Islamic revival, the response of the Ottoman government caused in him a major disappointment with the empire. The Supreme Porte demanded from Rida, a religious Arab nationalist, that Turkish be the language of instruction at the institute and that the institute should be under the fiscal and theological supervision of the Ottoman Sheikh al-Islam. Rida went back to Egypt and finally established his institute there in March 1912 on Rawda Island in Cairo (Ryad 2002, 88; Tauber 1989, 104–106).

Another example is Rida's political activities during the First World War, when he lobbied intensively for the establishment of an Arab state comprising the Arab Peninsula and geographical Syria. At the same time as the Ottoman Empire was proclaiming its "*Jihad* made in Germany," Rida was undermining this war strategy by submitting a memorandum to the British that requested support for his plan for an independent Arab state. In July 1915, he had a conversation with Mark Sykes (1879–1919), the advisor to the British Cabinet in Middle Eastern affairs, and he met a year later with Sharif Husain in Mecca. In a letter to US President Wilson in 1918, Rida demanded the self-determination of the Arabs. In the same year he also met the French diplomat François Georges-Picot (1870–1951), who secretly negotiated the Anglo-French agreement about the partition of the Ottoman territories in 1916 with Mark Sykes. Finally, Rida dispatched another memorandum on the establishment of an Arab state to the British Prime Minister Lloyd George (1863–1945) in 1919. These encounters with the Western powers and the Hashemites, however, all ended with no results (Tauber 1989, 1995a, 1995b). Apparently, the representatives of the West did not take him seriously, and the Arab leaders were willing to sacrifice Arab nationalist ambitions for the sake of their own dynastic interests. In light of this series of political frustrations, Rashid Rida's eventual affiliation with Ibn Saud and his religious approach to Wahhabism certainly was not the result of intellectual affinities alone (Commins 2006, 138).

In the context of Middle Eastern state formation and the introduction of Western systems of law, Muhammad Abduh and Rashid Rida initiated a public debate on forms of sovereignty and the legislative authority of political institutions. Based on the modern concepts of state and law, they perceived an authentic Islamic system of law with its foundations in a thorough reinterpretation of the *sharia* as a crucial bulwark against the political and cultural encroachments from the West. Rida developed these thoughts further and became in the course of the crisis of the caliphate one of the founding fathers of the modern idea of an Islamic state. For the constitutional foundation of this Islamic state he sought inspiration from the general religious principles of the Koran and the Sunna. According to Rida, Muslims should utilize the immanent potential of the *sharia* for developing an authentic Islamic social order. The theological, juridical and political ideas of the modernist Salafiyya provided the intellectual platform from which both the secular and Islamist streams of reform in the twentieth century evolved (Brown 2000, 90). The Salafiyya created a conceptual amalgamation of Islamic traditions with modern political ideas and initiated a fundamental transformation of the orders of knowledge in the Muslim world. In this sense, the Islamic public sphere and intellectuals such as Afghani, Abduh and Rida were from the very beginning inherent parts of the emerging global public sphere.

The basic concepts and the clusters of thematic problems of the modernist Salafiyya clearly reflect the "deep structure" of the modern discursive formation of the nineteenth century. The various semantics of Islamic reform and Western interpretations of Islam emerged with close reference to these discursive structures, articulated in different cultural programs. The focus on Islam as the central variable in shaping a modern Muslim world and the Salafiyya's textual hermeneutics with regard to the primary sources of Islam find their parallels in the methods and interpretation of Western oriental studies. In liberating traditional Islamic concepts from their particular context, Muslim reformers created a religious-symbolic "tool-kit" applicable to any issue of political and social reform (cf. al-Azmeh 1996, 106–110). They initiated a fundamental change in meaning with regard to the most significant elements of Islamic traditions. This applies in particular to the societal role and understanding of the *sharia*. Originally representing a metaphor for "a mode of behavior that leads to salvation" (Kelsay 2007, 44), the *sharia* developed into a "total intellectual discourse," representing a religious, scholarly, and holistic field of social reflection and deliberation (Messick 1993, 3). Under the impact of nineteenth-century Islamic reform and modern state formation, however, the meaning of the *sharia* was transformed into a rather fixed set of rules. This transformation took place with reference to the modern functional relationship between positive law and the state; a relationship that implied the idea of the enforcement of legal rules by the coercive means of the state.

The close and complex linkages among Muslim and European intellectual milieus, however, should not be misinterpreted by conceptualizing Islamic modernities only as derivates of European modernities. The theoretical perspective applied here explains diversity through unity, the emergence of multiple modernities due to a global process of social transformation which I try to grasp by the over-arching category of world society. From this perspective, the content of the modernist Salafi world view cannot be reduced to a confrontation of Muslim reformers with colonial modernization. On the contrary, Islamic modernities built on strong indigenous components. In developing their thoughts through concepts such as *ijtihad, jihad, sharia, tawhid,* and *umma,* as well as with their reference to the Golden Age of Islam, Afghani, Abduh and Rida articulated their visions of an Islamic modernity in correspondence with their own traditions. It is significant, however, that they did so by emphasizing a specific and influential stream of thought to which John Voll once referred as the "fundamentalist" and Marshall Hodgson as the "*sharia*-minded" line of Islamic tradition (Voll 1979).[43] While Voll looked at revivalist movements when employing the label of fundamentalism, Hodgson put his focus on the *ulama*. According to him, the *sharia*-minded tradition has mainly been represented by the *ulama* who worked out a program under which the life of society and individuals should be "directly under the guidance of God's laws" (Hodgson 1974, 238). Even more important, in their focus on this particular dimension of the Islamic tradition they were in line with Western orientalists, who perceived the same stream of thought as the most genuine expression of Islam.[44] In political terms, the revivalist version of this stream of thought was especially important when the Muslim community was threatened from outside, for

---

43. For a thorough critique of this selective perception on Islamic traditions by both Western and Muslim scholars of Islam, see, for instance, Lumbard (2004).

44. In a letter to Ignaz Goldziher from December 1912, Martin Hartmann describes Rashid Rida as the prime thinker among Muslim intellectuals. Apparently Hartmann largely endorsed Rida's points of view and intended to visit his missionary institute in Cairo (Hanish 2000, 419).

instance, the life and work of the Hanbali scholar Ibn Taymiyya (1263–1328). His example and teachings play a central role in the complex of nineteenth-century Salafi and later Islamist thinking and must be understood in the context of the Mongol invasion. Ibn Taimiyya was a strict proponent of *tawhid*, advocated a literal interpretation of the holy scripture and stressed the exemplary role of the early Muslims. His interpretation of the Hanbali school of law then played a central role in the revivalist thoughts of pre-modern reformers such as Muhammad ibn Abd al-Wahhab (1703–1792), whose puritan theology was integrated into the state doctrine of Saudi Arabia. In his conservative turn, Rashid Rida took up this fundamentalist line of Islamic traditions and combined it with his interpretation of Abduh's reform ideas.

From National Islamic Reform to Transnational Islamist Revolution

Pre-modern religious reform movements, the modernist Salafiyya and contemporary Islamist organizations share this feature of combining religious revivalism with the resistance against external threats. This combination seems almost to be a constant in Islamic history. Against the background of the erosion of Islamic empires, we can observe the rise of various revivalist movements throughout the eighteenth century. Oriented toward the ideal of the early Muslim community, the central concern of these religiopolitical movements was the revitalization of the Muslim *umma*, which they perceived as internally degenerated. This concern almost automatically brought them into confrontation with the colonizing European powers, combining the struggle for religious and moral reform with anti-colonial resistance. From the perspective of the European public this Islamic revivalism was perceived as a confusion of religion and politics, a perception which essentially contributed to the assumption that Islam represents a violent form of religion antagonistic to Western rationalism (Lapidus 1983, 11–13). Yet these pre-modern forms of Islamic revivalism were radically different from the modernist Salafiyya with regard to their social and historical contexts, as well as the particular meanings which they ascribed to the Islamic tradition. The reform movement around Afghani, Abduh and Rida provided an entirely new discursive foundation for Islamic revivalism, reinventing Islamic traditions in a modern conceptual environment. Significantly, they did so in constant reference to Europe and not from the position of the self-sufficient embeddedness in traditional culture as their revivalist predecessors. Thus, the modernist Salafiyya marks the most significant break with the past. It is this new context of meaning provided by the nineteenth-century Salafiyya from which Islamist movements have evolved during the twentieth century. Despite semantic parallels with pre-modern revivalists, these Islamist thinkers and their religiopolitical ideologies are firmly anchored in the global discourse of modernity.

When referring to religious concepts such as *tawhid*, the *umma* or the *sharia*, Islamists do so on the basis of entirely modern concepts such as holistically closed systems, the authority structure of national states or the codified nature of positive law. The world views and actions of Islamist movements have been shaped through contested negotiation within the confines of an emerging global public sphere, and they adopted the globally dominant narrative of difference between the East and the West. In their search for Islamic authenticity, Islamist ideologues present us with a mirror image of the essentialist cultural dichotomies that characterized the work of nineteenth-century orientalists. The essentialist assumptions of Western civilization are echoed in the concepts of an Islamic system and state. Moreover, twentieth-century Islamist movements subsequently translated religious reform into inner-worldly activism and applied modern forms of organization in their striving for political and social change. The history of the Egyptian Muslim Brotherhood and the biography of its founder Hasan al-Banna (1906–1948) are paradigmatic for this development of Islamist ideas and organizations in the twentieth century.

Hasan al-Banna: From Intellectual Movement to Mass Organization

The primary-school teacher Hasan al-Banna grew up in Mahmudiyya, a provincial town in the Nile delta. In his youth, he joined the Hasafiyya Sufi order, a strongly *sharia*-minded group with a strict observance of scripture in their rituals and ceremonies. As secretary of the order's charitable society, al-Banna propagated Islamic morals and fought against the influence of Christian missionaries. In 1923 he moved to Cairo, where he studied at the Dar al-Ulum, the modern teacher training college of Egypt (Commins 2005, 129). In Cairo, al-Banna was apparently appalled by the Europeanizing features of social life and the "defection of the 'educated youth' from the 'Islamic way of life'" (Mitchell 1969, 5). While he perceived the Azhar as stuck in traditions not able to defend Islam, he observed the recently founded Egyptian University as a force that fostered secularist and libertarian ideas. Al-Banna frequented the circles around Rashid Rida and became influenced by the reform ideas of Afghani and Abduh in Rida's interpretation. In July 1939, al-Banna even continued the publication of *al-manar*, which was interrupted after the death of Rida in August 1935 (cf. al-Banna 2004, 14; Hourani 1962, 360; Ryad 2008, 5). From Rashid Rida, Hasan al-Banna took the concept of the Islamic state and the dominant function of the *sharia* in shaping an authentic Islamic order. Al-Banna emphasized the Salafi idea that it is necessary to return to the exemplary order of the Golden Age of Islam in order to overcome the political subordination and social crisis of the Muslim world. For al-Banna, the Prophet and the first four caliphs truly represented Islam as a faith and a just social order (Mitchell 1969, 210). To bring about a national and religious revival in Egypt, according to al-Banna, Muslims have to direct themselves toward the "true Islam" as lived by the early Muslim community. While vigorously promoting this Salafi approach, al-Banna downplayed the other central feature of nineteenth-century modernism, the conscious but critical appropriation of European ideas and institutions into an Islamic context. This incorporation of European models was meanwhile the central and almost exclusive claim of the rather secularist stream of Muslim modernists such as Taha Husain in Egypt or the new republican elite in

Turkey. This group of secular Muslim intellectuals al-Banna identified, however, with the threat of cultural Westernization and the spread of immorality and atheism in society; and it was these Muslim Westernizers, as well as the presence of colonial powers, against which the Muslim Brotherhood was struggling for an Islamization of Egyptian society.

In increasing the stress on authenticity, this rather one-sided continuation of the thought of the Salafiyya developed into the corner stone of a modern world view, which William Shepard called "Islamic totalism." According to Shepard, in this world view Islam represents a hermetically closed system of political, economic, cultural and social forms of life (Shepard 1987, 308), precisely the essentialist image of Islam that is central to the investigation of this book. Abduh and his associates reconstructed Islam with the help of the holistic concepts of culture and civilization which were also key categories in the historical self-reflection of societies in the course of European modernization (Reckwitz 2000, 67–78). Islamist theories in the twentieth century adopted this holistic view and developed it further into the ideal of a comprehensive Islamic system. Apparently, the Islamist rejection of so-called Western models is in itself predicated on the application of organicist theories and on conceptual tools which informed the formation of the social sciences in Europe. The new semantics of Islamist revival, thus, rest on a modern discursive formation which Muslim and European intellectuals established in the second part of the nineteenth century. In addition, this Islamic totalism builds on a utopia of progress in which Islamist ideologies implicitly follow modern models of human development and progress (Shepard 1987, 315). In their philosophies of history, Islamists fuse the modern idea of progress with the traditional Islamic conceptions of deviation from ideal origins and the necessity of revivalism.

This conceptual fundament and the utopian turn with respect to the ideal community clearly separates contemporary Islamist thinkers from the pre-modern world of ideas which characterized the teachings of revivalist thinkers such as Ibn Taymiyya or Muhammad ibn Abd al-Wahhab. Modern revivalist movements clearly reflect the essential question of modern culture: How to actively form individuals and collectives in light of their contingent forms? They combined this sense for modern contingency with the conscious shaping of social practices and a new consciousness of time (cf. Reckwitz 2006, 77). In theory and practice, the Islamist movements of the twentieth century radicalized and politicized Afghani's and Abduh's call for activism further. Islamists left the world of intellectual circles and popularized the ideas of Islamic reform as a means of mass mobilization advocating social change. Most of the Islamist thinkers of the twentieth century did not enjoy an education in traditional Islamic sciences, and like Hasan al-Banna they took the "defense of Islam" directly to the people (Mitchell 1969, 211). The Egyptian Muslim Brotherhood also played a paradigmatic role in this transformation of Islamic reform from an elitist intellectual movement into a mass organization. Starting from the point of religious awakening, it quickly grew into a social movement and then into a comprehensive organization with activities in societal fields such as health care, sports, education and social welfare.

The Brotherhood included pressing political and economic questions in its reform program and gradually extended its Islamic discourse into functional domains separate from the religious realm. The modernist Salafiyya once provided the intellectual basis for this expansion. In giving secular European institutions a form of Islamic legitimacy, the nineteenth-century reformers generated a pervasive and all-encompassing intellectual Islamic discourse (Dallal 2000, 337). Hasan al-Banna popularized this elitist discourse of the Salafiyya and, with the Muslim Brotherhood, gave the Islamic reform movement an organizational form. Combining features of bureaucratic institutions with structures reminiscent of Sufi leadership, Hassan al-Banna built the Muslim Brotherhood as an efficient organization with an enormously broad societal reach. Most important, he applied to the Brotherhood the organizational templates and the patterns of public mobilization that characterized the popular political mass movements in the first part of the twentieth century in general. In the rapid social transformation of the 1930s, the Brotherhood was able to provide public services for which the state or private enterprises were not yet prepared. In an atmosphere of the failure of liberal politics in both Egypt and Europe, it additionally could present itself as a viable and indigenous political alternative.[45] The Muslim Brotherhood was thus able to establish itself in society at large and developed during the twentieth century into an organization with more than a million members. Today, it represents the most important socio-political force in Egypt, whose membership is not limited by specific social, educational or regional boundaries (Krämer 1999, 173).[46]

In content, the Islamist ideologies of the twentieth century clearly reflect the modern thoughts of "social engineering," the idea of a conscious reconstruction of society, which also was an essential feature in the formation of the modern national state in Europe. The increasingly political character of Islamist movements is highlighted by the central role of the Islamic state in the disciplining and structuration of society. In developing his idea of the comprehensive Islamic order further, Hasan al-Banna expanded the regulative role of the Islamic government from the fields of education and economic and fiscal organization to the disciplinary state control over the arts and the correct observance of religious practices (Commins 2005, 140). His Islamic state had the duty to implement the ideal order revealed in the *sharia* in the name of social and moral progress. This concept of Islamic governance has developed historically within the context of the formation of the postcolonial state in the Muslim world. Yet at the same time it has continued the political efforts of indigenous rulers and colonial administrations of the late nineteenth century that made the supervision of people's

---

45. In the inter-war period, Egypt experienced an Islamic revival of various sorts. The Muslim Brotherhood was one of its major representatives; however, there also were strong liberal voices increasingly referring to Islamic traditions in order to defend an open society in light of authoritarian and fascist ideologies (Gershoni 1999).

46. For more detailed descriptions of the ideology, organizational structure and the historical development of the Egyptian Muslim Brotherhood, see the works of Lia (1998), Mitchell (1969) and Zollner (2009).

health, the policing of urban neighborhoods, the reorganization of streets, and, above all, the schooling of the people the central responsibility of government (Mitchell 1988, 103). From this perspective, the ideology of the Muslim Brotherhood replaced "Colonizing Egypt" with Islamizing it, however, according to the very same modern ideas of politics as a state-dominated form of social practice (cf. Mitchell 1988). The political theories of Islamist movements therefore are not only inscribed into the imperialist power asymmetries of the international order, but they reflect equally strongly the repressive and authoritarian experiences of indigenous processes of state and nation building. In addition, Islamist thinkers developed their thoughts in close reference to European ideologies such as liberalism, socialism and fascism. Consequently, the often authoritarian political concepts of contemporary Islamists are also an expression of the political culture of the environments in which they emerged. Moreover, oriented toward the religious ideal of unity, the Muslim *umma*, Islamist activists have developed their political world views in constant tension between the supra-territorial nature of their religious ideals and the political reality of the territorial national state.[47]

Abu al-Ala Mawdudi: Islamist Party Organization and the Islamic State

This conflict between the normative ideal and the historical political realities was a constant theme in the life and work of Abu al-Ala Mawdudi (1903–1979), the founder of the Jamaat-i Islami in Pakistan. Born in 1903 in the South-Indian principality of Hyderabad, Mawdudi came from a notable North Indian family which left Delhi after it had lost its social status in the final fall of the Moghul Empire during the mutiny of 1857/58. He was brought up in a strongly religious environment where he received a traditional Islamic education. Later Mawdudi became a politically engaged journalist and together with his brother moved to Delhi. There he came in close contact with the Muslim intellectual environment and supported the Khilafat movement which was formed in support of the Ottoman Empire and collapsed after the abolition of the Islamic Caliphate by Mustafa Kemal Atatürk in 1924. In Delhi, Mawdudi learnt English, read Western literature and studied Islamic sciences with Deoband *ulama*.[48] Before moving back to

---

47. This tension between national and trans-national aspirations has characterized the Muslim Brotherhood as a politically minded religious movement. Originating in Egypt, the movement has spread beyond Egypt's borders into the Muslim world. However, it has done so by establishing national organizational branches with very different degrees of institutionalization and political strategies. The Jordanian example clearly shows the differences with regard to the political strategies with which the various national branches of the Muslim Brotherhood have pursued their agendas of Islamist reform. In sharp contrast to Egypt, in Jordan the monarchy co-opted the Brotherhood right from the beginning and made it together with other Salafi-oriented organizations part of the country's political establishment. Only in the aftermath of the Jordanian-Israeli peace agreement (1994) and in particular since September 11, 2001, this collaboration between the Islamist movement and the Jordanian state has seemed to deteriorate (see Wiktorowicz 2001).

48. The reform college of Deoband was established in 1867. The curriculum of the col-

Hyderabad, he published his first major book on *jihad* in Islam (*al-jihad fil-islam*). Presenting a systematic discussion of the Muslim positions on *jihad*, Mawdudi defended the concept against being simply equated with aggression and warfare. Comparing the early Muslims with "freedom fighters," Mawdudi conceptualized *jihad* as an encompassing struggle for justice and to worship God alone. The book marks the starting point for his career as one of the leading Islamist revivalist thinkers of the twentieth century (Cook 2005, 100–101; Nasr 2005, 99–102).

The political and theological writings of Mawdudi play a foundational role for the radical Islamist ideologies which developed within Sunni Islam in the course of the twentieth century. In addition they comprise the most comprehensive thoughts about the Islamic state among Sunni Islamists (Enayat 1982, 102).[49] In Mawdudi's eyes, political authority was an integral part of the religious field. His concept of the Islamic state is first and foremost an "ideological state," deriving its legitimacy from the sovereignty of God. In his political theory, divine sovereignty implies absolute suzerainty derived from the theological principle of *tawhid* (Moten 2003, 27). Consequently, he combines the modern understanding of political authority with a religious core element of Muslim belief. It is therefore the central task of Islamic governance to establish God's will on earth according to the revealed knowledge in the Koran and the Sunna. Apart from the idea of classical consultancy (*shura*), the Islamic state—in theory—does not need specific mechanisms and institutions for political decision-making.[50] Due to the essentially homogeneous nature of the *umma*, any pluralistic conflict of interests is absent. Mawdudi's concept of Islamic governance therefore does not need an elaborated institutional theory. The ideal ruler of the Islamic state is a competent and pious person who does not strive for power and position (Brown 2000, 152–153).

In 1938, Mawdudi moved from Hyderabad to Punjab at the invitation of Muhammad Iqbal. The Indian poet and philosopher wanted to establish an "Institute for Advanced Research" with purely educational purposes. Its aim was to combine classical Islamic studies with contemporary social sciences in order to analyze current political and economic questions from an Islamic point of view.

---

lege combined classical Islamic with modern sciences and aimed at a reform and standardization of Islamic belief and practices. In disseminating its message of the "true practices of Islam" the school of Deoband spread over the whole of South Asia and cultivated widespread middle-class support (Lapidus 2002, 626).

49. In comparison to Khomeini's theory of the *velayat-e faqih* (the rule of the religious jurisprudents), which heavily draws on the doctrine of the Imamat in Shia tradition, the political theories of Sunni Islamists are generally weak in institutional terms. Khomeini's theory, however, did not lead to a similar development of an institutionally more elaborated political theory in Sunni Islam.

50. The application of the traditional concept of *shura* by Islamists can easily be traced back to the modernist Salafiyya. Muhammad Abduh already identified in *shura* a form of Islamic governance which he, however, strongly associated with the European idea of parliamentary democracy. Also for Rida, *shura* represented a legislative and decision-making procedure that was binding to rulers (Hourani 1962, 144, 234).

Mawdudi became the founding director of the institute in Pathankot under the name Daru'l Islam only a month before Muhammad Iqbal's death. In deviating from the mere educational purposes which Iqbal had in mind, however, Mawdudi soon clashed with the sponsors, who accused him of violating his own agreements with Iqbal. In January 1939, Mawdudi therefore resigned from his position and moved to Lahore, where he founded the Jamaat-i Islami in 1941 (Malik and Malik 1971, 33; Nasr 1996, 38–39). With the foundation of the Jamaat, Mawdudi reacted to the nationalist aspirations of India's Muslim elite to form an independent Muslim state, Pakistan. In propagating Islamic reform first and foremost as a means of combating internal decay rather than external threats, Mawdudi did not directly support the aim of the Indian Muslim League to establish a territorial state based on religious arguments. However, as a convinced communalist he also strongly opposed Indian secular nationalism as propagated by the Congress Party, as this would have meant "Hindu rule" (Nasr 1994, 109). In 1938, he proposed an Indian federation of nations in which each nation enjoys cultural autonomy, and state sovereignty was to be divided between the center and the various national units (Khalidi 2003, 418–419).[51]

After India's partition in 1947, Mawdudi accepted the *fait accompli* and made the Islamization of the Pakistani state to his program. The Jamaat decided to play an active part in Pakistani politics and gradually changed its initial call for religious awakening into a strategy to capture political power by constitutional means (Moten 2003, 60). This political program was in line with Mawdudi's general principle according to which the realization of the Islamic state should not result from a violent revolution. Rather he believed in incremental change, in the moral and spiritual transformation of the individual and therewith of Muslim society. On this premise, the Islamic state was not at the beginning but at the very end of this process (Enayat 1982, 104). Regarding the organizational structure of the Jamaat-i Islami, Mawdudi was, despite his strong anti-Western sentiment, guided by the example of the European vanguard parties of the 1920s and 1930s. He quickly reshaped the Jamaat from being a revivalist movement into being a political pressure group and later an Islamist cadre party (cf. Moten 2003, 137).

This elitist self-perception was one reason why the Jamaat has never developed into a mass party such as the Muslim Brotherhood in Egypt. While both have been integral parts of the broader Islamist movement, they evolved very different organizational formats. Whereas the Muslim Brotherhood became a political, religious and social mass organization, the Jamaat-i Islami established itself as an Islamist cadre party. Consequently, the Jamaat's political influence in Pakistan was not a result of large-scale support among the population, but

---

51. Mawdudi did not oppose the establishment of Pakistan, but it was not the number one solution on his list of priorities. The Muslim League's territorial form of Muslim nationalism, according to Mawdudi, excluded Islam from India proper and surrendered the domains of the Moghul Empire to the Hindus (Nasr 1994, 6). Moreover, he was antagonistic to the largely secular leadership of the Muslim League, which wanted to found a territorial national state for India's Muslims but not an Islamic state.

more due to a specific constellation of social forces. In Pakistan's internal power configuration, the military and the state elite gained the support of Islamist intellectuals and related religious circles of the upper middle class in exchange for a gradual Islamization of society (Kepel 2002, 99). Since the establishment of the Pakistani state, the country's political forces oscillated between religious nationalism and transnational Islamist aspirations (cf. Roy 2004, 65).Within these domestic power structures, Mawdudi and his movement had to face repressive measures from the state authorities in the foundational period of Pakistan and in particular under the military rule of Ayub Khan (1958–1969). Later, however, the Jamaat made its way toward becoming an influential political party. Rallying the opposition against the rule of first President and then Prime Minister Zulfikar Bhutto (1971–1977), Mawdudi and his party gained significant influence in Pakistani politics. In its opposition to Bhutto, the Jamaat coalesced Islam and democracy, a coalescence that increasingly became problematic after the military coup of Zia ul-Haq in July 1977, whose regime co-opted the Islamic forces in the country (Nasr 1994, 188). Yet both opposition to Bhutto and aligning with Zia ul-Haq's regime offered Mawdudi the possibility of pursuing his political vision within the framework of the national state.

Sayyid Qutb: Modern Barbary and Islamist Revolution

In comparison with Mawdudi, Sayyid Qutb took a very different path in life. Born in Upper Egypt in 1906, Qutb grew up in a rural environment and began his career as a writer and intellectual in the Cairo of the 1920s. There, like Hasan al-Banna he studied at the Dar al-Ulum, from which he graduated in 1933. From 1940 to 1948 he served as a school inspector for the ministry of education, which, in 1948, sent him for two years to the United States, where he took an MA in education from the University of Colorado (Bergesen 2008, 3). Sayyid Qutb first published literary criticisms and novels which reflected the nationalist and secularist atmosphere of Egypt's liberal intellectual circles of this time. During this period, Taha Husain was one of his intellectual mentors. In the international and domestic contexts of decolonization and Egyptian state formation, however, Qutb made his way from being a nationalist "man of letters" to becoming a radical Islamist and prime enemy of the Nasserist regime (cf. Musallam 2005). In 1951, after coming back from the United States, Qutb became a member of the Egyptian Muslim Brotherhood.[52] Initially supporting the military coup of the "Free Officers" in 1952, he soon became an antagonist of Nasser's regime. During the state campaign against the Muslim Brotherhood in 1954, Sayyid Qutb was arrested for the first time and sentenced to 25 years of forced labor in 1955. Released in 1964, the regime arrested him again only a year later, accused him of conspiring against Nasser, and publicly executed him in August 1966.

---

52. There are many speculations about the role of this stay in Qutb's life and his increasing radicalization. A number of articles he wrote for Egyptian magazines between 1949 and 1950, as well as letters to his friends, expressed a very negative reaction to American culture. In his opinion, Americans did not lack all virtues, but they were poor with regard to leadership and morality (Musallam 2005, 118–119).

The major part of his Islamist thought Qutb wrote down during his time in prison. Behind bars, he revised and completed the 30 volumes of his commentary on the Koran, *fi zilal al-quran* (In the Shade of the Koran). This commentary has found an enormously wide distribution throughout the world and is a work of religiopolitical literature rather than belonging to the exegetic Islamic *tafsir* tradition (Carré 2003, vii–ix). With his socio-political reflections and reinterpretations of both Islamic traditions and the modernist Salafiyya, Sayyid Qutb created an ideological environment from which revolutionary and militant Islamist ideologies have emerged. This applies in particular to Qutb's efforts to develop a consciously modern and authentically Islamic vocabulary (Shepard 1996, xivii). At the center of these efforts, Qutb elaborated on three concepts which semantically are deeply rooted in the Islamic tradition, but to which he added completely new meanings.

Firstly, Qutb gave the social dimension of Islam a new meaning. In his effort, to conceptualize Islam as a comprehensive ideology, as a sort of "third way" to capitalism and communism, Qutb extended the traditional religious concept of justice (*adala*) into a concept of social justice (*al-adala al-ijtimaiyya*) that could inform revolutionary political action. This new meaning of justice appeared relatively suddenly during the 1940s in Muslim political writing and reflects European debates about the fair re-distribution of societal resources (Akhavi 1997, 380–386). In addition, the newly introduced concept of social justice refers to global politics regarding the decolonization of the Third World. Secondly, in his concept of divine authority (*hakimiyya*) he fused the Koranic concept of *hukm* (to rule or to judge) with the modern notion of political sovereignty as was formulated with regard to modern statehood. From the theological perspective of the absolute unity of God, the concept of *tawhid*, Qutb subordinates the sovereignty of the state to the authority of God. Politics, therefore, must represent divine authority on earth, and the sovereignty of the Islamic state is derived from the sovereignty of God. The organization of society according to the *sharia* is the means of establishing divine sovereignty on earth. In light of this political theory, Qutb declared any other form of governance as illegitimate (Khatab 2006, 7–46).

In combining the sovereignty of the modern state with the religious core concept of *tawhid*, Sayyid Qutb followed to a large extent Mawdudi's theory of the Islamic state. Although hardly mentioning Mawdudi directly, in his later years Sayyid Qutb drew heavily from the ideas and concepts of the Indian Islamist (Osman 2003, 480).[53] This applies even more so to his third conceptual revision, the Koranic notion of *jahiliyya*. Together with his theory of divine sovereignty, Qutb's concept of the modern *jahiliyya* became not only a corner stone in radical Islamist ideologies (Musallam 2005, 155), but also played an important role in justifying the militarization of Islamist movements.[54] Often translated as the "epoch

---

53. Sayyid Qutb refers to Mawdudi in footnotes but seemed in his later work to be profoundly influenced by him with respect to terminology and the stress on the systematic nature of Islam (Shepard 1996, lv).

54. In terms of institutions, the Egyptian Muslim Brotherhood already had a military

of ignorance," *jahiliyya* refers to the times before the revelation of the Koran. Deeply anchored in the world view of ordinary Muslims, this classical concept reflects in temporal terms the boundary between belief and un-belief. Mawdudi imbued *jahiliyya* with the new meaning of "modern barbarism," referring to the abandonment of divine guidance in modern society.[55]

In addition to being influenced by Mawdudi's writings, Qutb's theories of divine sovereignty and modern barbarism were strongly influenced by the thoughts of Alexis Carrel. In 1959/60, Qutb read an Arabic translation of Carrel's *L'homme, cet inconnu* (Man, the Unknown) in which the French medical doctor equates modern civilization with a new form of barbarism (Choueiri 1997, 150).[56] In order to re-establish the unity of men and to overcome modern fragmentation, Carrel proposed a holistic theory of science and faith in which he fused elements of Christian fundamentalism, life philosophy and eugenic theories. Without following Carrel in his racist and eugenic leanings, Qutb "extensively quotes" from Carrel's book in his attempt to prove the incompatibility of modern civilization with the needs of a just order of humanity (Choueiri 1997, 149–157; Musallam 2005, 158–159; Walther 2003).

In his last and most prominent book *maalim fi al-tariq* (Signposts on the Road), Sayyid Qutb further radicalized his concept of the modern *jahiliyya* and gave it a distinct political meaning. Though written in prison, the Egyptian regime allowed its publication in five subsequent editions before it became the major source of evidence in the conspiracy trial against Qutb, eventually leading to his execution (Tripp 2005, 160). In *maalim fi al-tariq*, Qutb extended the meaning of *jahiliyya* to all kinds of worldly rule which supposedly have replaced the sovereignty of God. Consequently, he branded all existing forms of state authority as

---

wing before Sayyid Qutb's radicalization. The secret apparatus was developed in the context of the Brotherhood's concern for Palestine during the 1930s. In the 1940s, it was the movement's defense against the security forces of the Egyptian government (Mitchell 1969, 31–32). After Nasser's campaign against the Brotherhood in the 1950s, however, the Muslim Brothers under Hasan al-Hudaybi, the successor of Hasan al-Banna, pursued a reformist agenda. In sharp contrast to Sayyid Qutb, al-Hudaybi followed a policy of moderation with regard to the regime and the desired religious transformation of Egyptian society (cf. Zollner 2009).

55. Mawdudi's writings were first translated into Arabic in the early 1950s by a small publishing group in Cairo, where his systematic thought found an interested audience among the Egyptian Muslim Brotherhood. In the years from 1956 to 1974, Mawdudi travelled the Arab world giving lectures in cities such as Amman, Cairo, Damascus, Jeddah, Kuwait, Mecca, Medina and Rabat (Osman 2003, 466–467).

56. First published in 1935, Carrel's book was translated into 19 languages. Born in 1873, Carrel was a surgeon and medical doctor who received the Nobel Prize in medicine in 1912. Partly in protest against the secularist policies of the Third Republic, the strongly Catholic Carrel left France for the United States in 1905. There he worked at the University of Chicago and the Rockefeller Institute. He went back at the beginning of the Second World War and worked for the Vichy regime under Marshall Pétain, expressing affinity with the eugenic policies of Nazi Germany (Walther 2003).

pagan and equated them with the time of ignorance of pre-Islamic Arabia. While primarily justifying resistance to Nasser's rule in Egypt, with his politicized concept of *jahiliyya* Qutb delivered an encompassing construct for revolution. Based on this concept, Islamist action against incumbent rulers resembles the example of the Prophet who struggled for the acknowledgment of the Islamic revelation in Arabia's pagan society. Consequently, the political action of militant Islamists against incumbent governments found religious legitimacy (cf. Qutb 1991, 66, 98). Sayyid Qutb radicalized the rather reformist agenda of Mawdudi and declared *jihad* against all non-believers. In excommunicating Muslims who he perceived as non-believers (*takfir*), Sayyid Qutb expanded the range of legitimate targets for *jihad* indiscriminately. In making fellow Muslims, especially Muslim rulers, into legitimate targets for *jihad*, Sayyid Qutb clearly positioned himself at the extreme fringe of all previous interpretations of *jihad* in the Islamic tradition.

Transnational Islamism: The Afghan Jihad and Global Revolution

In pursuing the aims of anti-colonial resistance and internal reform, the nineteenth-century Salafiyya made use of the semantic breadth of the term *jihad*, which reaches from individual moral conduct through social engagement to military campaigns. Consequently, the call for Muslim unity against European imperialism, for national self-determination and for political independence, as well as the fight for religious, educational and social change, could be associated with *jihad*. In sharp contrast to the pre-modern reform movements, the followers of Muhammad Abduh downplayed the violent and offensive notions of *jihad*, re-interpreting the traditional military concept in a defensive and predominantly non-violent way. From their apologetic perspective, they distinguished between two types of *jihad*: the "lesser *jihad*" in defense of Muslim territory and the "greater *jihad*," which refers to an internal and spiritual strife with all one's capacities (cf. Cook 2005, 32–48). While the concept of "greater *jihad*" traditionally was linked to Sufi asceticism, Abduh and Rida re-invented it—similar to Ahmad Khan in India—as a religious call to inner-worldly activism. For them, *jihad* was in the contemporary world first and foremost the Islamic equivalent to the kind of societal dynamism that they had observed in Europe (Hourani 1962, 129). The Muslim Brotherhood, then, used the concept of *jihad* in their fight against colonial domination, as well as in their struggle for the social and moral transformation of Egyptian society. At the same time, Hasan al-Banna still maintained the semantic breadth of the concept. Yet he clearly indicated that *jihad* inevitably implies physical fighting, leading—if necessary—to death and martyrdom (Mitchell 1969, 207). In combining *jihad* with the notion of striving for justice, Mawdudi gave the concept a revolutionary twist, however, still pursuing the apologetic purpose of downplaying its military connotations.

Following the late Sayyid Qutb, radical Islamists have employed *jihad* again in a much more narrow sense, strongly emphasizing the meaning of military combat. In sharp contradistinction to the classical *jihad* of the traditions, they do so in reference to but without being methodologically embedded in the scholarly debate of Islamic jurisprudence about just war. Unfolding among the *ulama* between the eighth and fourteenth centuries, this debate revolved around issues such as the just cause and the righteous intention of war. Even more important, the resort to war required "an order from a legitimate authority" (Kelsay 2007, 101). Contemporary Islamists have liberated the call for *jihad* from any religious or political authority. Once the sole prerogative of Caliphs and the Sheikh al-Islam, they take the right to declare *jihad* as their own. Inspired by the writings of Islamist ideologists such as Sayyid Qutb, contemporary *mujahidin* search for existential experiences in the name of Islam and declare indiscriminate warfare as a matter of policy (Kelay 2007, 196; Schulze 2003). The radical Islamist thus becomes a self-designated Jihadist, and it was the anti-Soviet war of resistance in Afghanistan that for these contemporary "warriors of Islam" achieved a paradigmatic appeal with a global reach (Franke 2002; Peters 1989).

In the course of the war in Afghanistan, militant Islamist groups increasingly became visible on the international political scene. Against the backdrop of the Cold War, their struggle attracted the interest of a global audience. In Peshawar, Pakistan, radical activists met, and under the supervision of the Pakistani secret service (ISI) they were recruited for the *jihad* against the Soviet troops in Afghanistan. The activities of these new "warriors of Islam" were financed by Saudi Arabia, and they went to Afghanistan equipped with weapons from the United States. There in Afghanistan, Mawdudi's Jamaat played an important role in the distribution of the financial resources, which were mainly channeled to their ideological allies and groups which promoted the Wahhabi version of Islam of the Saudi financiers.

One of the recruitment centers in Peshawar was founded and directed by Abdallah Azzam, a former Muslim Brother from Jordan with Palestinian background who was central in the spread of the Jihadist ideology. After being removed from his professorship in Islamic law at the University of Jordan, Azzam went to Saudi Arabia where he taught at the Abd al-Aziz University in Jiddah. There, Osama bin-Laden also attended some of his lectures. In 1984, Azzam opened his recruiting office in Peshawar and started the journal *al-jihad*, which published news from the Afghan resistance and ideological essays. Between 1985 and 1989, he traveled the United States several times in order to raise funds and to establish support centers that also spread his jihadist ideology (McGregor 2003, 105). Abdallah Azzam particularly attracted young militants and legitimized their inclination to violence with the concept of *jihad* as *fard ain*, as the personal religious obligation of every Muslim (Kepel 2002, 144–150). From a traditional point of view, *jihad* was normally perceived as a collective duty (*fard kifaya*) from which individual Muslims could receive dispensation. Abdallah Azzam turned against both apologetic interpretations of *jihad* and its character of being a collective duty. He refuted the assumption that the "greater *jihad*," the non-military struggle for moral and social progress, is at the heart of the Koranic doctrine. In Azzam's eyes, *jihad* is first and foremost military combat, and he declared the traditions to which the apologists refer in their theories about the "greater *jihad*" to be a mere fabrication. For Azzam, as long as there was Islamic territory under occupation, *jihad* remained a lifelong obligation, a constant and individual duty, which could not be delegated or relieved, for example, through money donations (McGregor 2003, 104; Roy 2004, 41–43).

The political practices of resistance in Afghanistan reduced the religious call to social activism to a militant struggle for Islam's mere existence. In the Jihadist ideologies the major ideas of the Salafiyya degenerated into slogans for the propagation of a transnational *jihad*. In his *Letter to the Pakistani Muslims*, for instance, Osama bin Laden took up the clash of civilization motive to present the world as divided between two camps, "one under the banner of the cross, … and one under the banner of Islam" (bin Laden 2001). In radical ideologies of the al-Qaida type, Islam is under siege, and the historical legacy of Islamic reform and anti-colonial resistance is re-interpreted as a total war against Islam. In underpinning their world view with rather randomly chosen and often decontextualized quotes from the Koran, the chief ideologues of a "global *jihad* for the defense of Islam" conduct *ijtihad* in the most simplistic way (cf. *Global Jihad* 2006). Besides quoting the Holy Scripture, Osama bin Laden and Ayman al-Zawahiri stress their religious mission through the application of rhetorical elements familiar to Islamic religious discourses. Furthermore in their attire they intend to resemble the appearance of the *salafiyyun*, the early Muslims and rightly guided companions of the Prophet. While their ideological constructs provide a religiously justified platform for rallying followers behind their militant cause, their propagation of the establishment of a just Islamic society profoundly lacks any kind of elaborate ideas about the institutional setting on which this Islamic order should rest. Therefore, their calls for the implementation of the *sharia* and the erection of an Islamic Caliphate epitomize only the crudest stereotypes that have traveled from orientalist perceptions and Islamist ideologies into the discursive universe of global public debates.[57] Their presentation of "Islamic totalism" has become the embodiment of a militant Islam easily connectible with the knowledge on Islam as a "warrior religion" that once was spread by scholars such as Julius Wellhausen and Max Weber.

The global receptiveness to this stereotypical representation of Islam can be explained on two different levels of analysis. Firstly, the global debate has been facilitated by the fact that the motive of difference which underlies both orientalist and Islamist narratives have become familiar to Muslim and non-Muslim audiences alike. Throughout the twentieth century the relationship between Islam and the West has publicly been discussed in various semantics, creating a mutually intelligible pool of expressive, normative and conceptual meanings. Secondly, this background of intelligibility has been supported by a cognitive deep structure on which the concepts of Islamist ideologies and the perceptive patterns of Western and other observers rest. Although connecting the semantics of difference with different traditions and historical narratives, as well as normative and evaluable

---

57. For a compilation of Osama bin Laden's messages between 1994 and 2004 in English, see Lawrence (2006).

patterns of meaning, the global debate about Islam and the West has conceptual foundations that make its various voices compatible. It was one of the central purposes of this book to validate this relationship between commonly shared cognitive foundations and different semantics in theoretical and empirical terms.

Yet this cognitive deep structure and the global familiarity with different semantics on religion and Islam have emerged within specific political contexts: first under the asymmetric power relations of imperialism and second within the coordinates of post-colonial state building. The multiple faces of a global modernity are therefore not only the result of different cultural programs, the way in which the modern *episteme* is connected to traditions, but are equally conditioned by the power relations under which this modern reinterpretation of traditions took place. Moreover, the way from orientalist constructions and Islamic reform to contemporary ideologies about Islamist revolution has been conditioned by technological and organizational innovations regarding our social site of a global public sphere.

In political terms, the formation of the Muslim public sphere has taken place in the context of authoritarian forms of domination. The intellectual deliberations of the early Islamic modernists still reflect the ideal of a relatively limited circle of an educated and cultivated bourgeoisie whose scope of public action, however, was decisively limited by both indigenous and colonial political authorities. Due to the repressive nature of indigenous rule the Muslim public sphere partly evolved in European places of exile from which Islamic reformers articulated their critique of domestic rulers and the colonial condition. The lives of Afghani, Abduh and Namik Kemal and Muhammad Iqbal give good examples of this spatial interconnection between Europe and the Muslim world in the formation of a global public sphere. In the twentieth century the experience of political domination and repression shifted more toward the internal consolidation of statehood in the post-colonial state. The lives of Hasan al-Banna, Mawdudi and Sayyid Qutb clearly show the growing impact which domestic forms of authoritarian rule exerted on the world views of Islamist thinkers. In most Muslim states, public spaces have been rigidly controlled by authoritarian regimes, and this experience has left its mark on theories of the Islamic state.

Under the impact of imperial asymmetries and domestic repression, Muslim intellectuals have increasingly turned orientalist stereotypes upside-down. This applies in particular to the idea of the moral superiority of Islam which has characterized modern Islamic revivalism from its outset. To a certain extent, Islamic reformers associated the experience with modern predicaments such as contingency, fragmentation and decentralization, as well as their fear of the loss of social cohesion, with the perceived moral deficiencies of a "materialist" Western culture. This conviction that the West is morally inferior is also an integral part of the thinking of contemporary Jihadists such as Abdallah Azzam and Osama bin Laden, whose political strategies refer precisely to the assumption that their enemies might be powerful in technology but are inferior in morality and individual strength (cf. Scheffler 2002, 35). On the way from reform to revolution, it is not the belief in the superiority of Islamic guidance that has changed, but the ways in which this conviction has been employed in the formulation of strategic action. While Afghani, Abduh and Rida perceived Islam as a moral source for the appropriation of European modern achievements without the vices of the West, Islamist thinkers have put their emphasis on uncompromised authenticity. They have replaced the reconciliation of religious traditions with modern reason through *ijtihad* with a form of "modern traditionalism" that has submerged the hermeneutical awareness of Islamic modernists in a literal understanding of the authoritative reading of the divine scripture. Consequently, they reject methods of interpretation and present their modern reformulations of Islamic traditions as the discovery of their authentic meaning.

The second development has been the transformation of the social composition and the infrastructure of the public sphere. With the foundation of the Egyptian Muslim Brotherhood, the Islamic public attained a very new social quality. The articulations of Islamic reform left the confines of a relatively small scholarly minded elite and became an integral part of mass politics in Muslim societies (cf. Lia 1998). The rising middle classes took over the banner of Islamic revivalism and combined the religious call to inner-worldly activism with their specific economic and political concerns. This broadening of the social basis of the Islamic reform movement went along with a trivialization and popularization of modern Salafist concepts and with a further erosion of the interpretative monopoly of the *ulama*. This is explicitly visible in the prolific writing of populist Koran commentaries (*tafsir*) by al-Banna, Mawdudi and Qutb. Sayyid Qutb even wrote one of the complete or *musalsal* commentaries, covering the whole of the Koran word by word (Jansen 1980, 13). In their return to the Golden Age, Islamists established a reading of the holy texts free of the methodological and scholarly constraints of the traditional science of Koranic exegesis. In comparison with the classical genre of exegetic commentaries, for instance, Sayyid Qutb's *In the Shade of the Koran* has the character of "an enormous collection of sermons," which has become an "icon-text" of contemporary Islamists (Jansen 1980, 79, fn 15; Carré 2003, 13). In the preface to the English version of his commentary, the translators praise Qutb's independent religiopolitical interpretations as a major contribution to a clearer understanding of the Koran (Salahi and Shamis 1992, vii).

The trivialization, popularization and global dissemination of Islamist revisions of Islamic traditions and of modernist reform ideas have been facilitated by the technological and institutional revolution that have radically transformed the infrastructure of the global public sphere. While Abduh's and Afghani's *al-urwa al wuthqa* was published in some hundred copies only,[58] the works of al-Banna, Mawdudi and Qutb have been translated into various languages and continue

---

58. About 551 copies were sent to Egypt, of which many were sent to the immediate entourage of the Khedive. The rest was distributed to Baghdad (5), Beirut (114), Damascus (23), Istanbul (88), Mecca and Medina (4), to North African destinations (11) and Tripoli (7). In addition, a number of copies went to other places in the wider Muslim world (Keddie 1972, 215).

to appear in numerous editions. In locating ultimate authority in the scripture itself and expanding the domains of religion into areas traditionally not covered (Dallal 2000, 347), modernist thinkers like Abduh "liberated the meanings of Islam from every context" (al-Azmeh 1996, 106). In this way, they provided a fertile ground for the holistic world views of Islamist ideologues. In the context of postcolonial state-formation, this pool of revised Islamic concepts has been a crucial resource for the political ideologies of both authoritarian Islamist regimes, such as in Iran, Sudan or Pakistan, and for the leaders of revolutionary movements against secular forms of authoritarianism in the Muslim world. In drawing from these resources, they were able to employ new means of communication technologies which facilitated not only the global spread but also the individual appropriation of various elements of Islamic totalism by individual Muslims and Western observers. The ways in which contemporary Jihadists disseminate their ideologies, for instance, further prove the deep integration of the Islamic public in the global public sphere. In the Lebanese Palestinian camp of Ain al-Helweh, for instance, young Palestinians entertain themselves by watching the war adventures of "Commander Khattab" in Afghanistan and Chechnya, who is fighting a technologically dominant enemy with the moral power of his Islamic faith (Rougier 2004).[59] In this way, young Muslims consume the products of a politically interested "cultural industry" which contributes further to disseminating an essentialist and militant image of Islam within the framework of an ongoing conflict between Islam and the West.

Conclusions: The Essentialist Image and the Multiple Voices of Islam

This chapter puts its focus on what I called in the introduction the "Muslim narrative." With this focus, I attempted to substantiate my claim that Western and Muslim public spheres were, from the beginning, inseparable parts of a rising global modernity, constructing modern knowledge on Islam within the coordinates of a wider global public sphere. As in the previous chapters, I apply the different levels of my analytical device of the public sphere. Beginning with the biographical accounts on the micro-sociological level of observation, I show in which ways Arab, Indian and Ottoman intellectual milieus factually interlaced with each other and with circles of European thinkers. They were all engaged in producing modern knowledge on Islam by interpreting Islamic traditions through modern concepts such as religion, culture, nation and civilization. Since the nineteenth century, Muslim intellectuals have been shaping a modern

---

59. Commander Khattab is the "warrior name" of Abdallah al-Suwailem, who was born in 1969 in Saudi Arabia. In 1987, Suwailem decided to join the *mujahidin* in Afghanistan to fight against the Soviets. According to a hagiographic presentation on the internet, Suwailem took on the name Khattab in reference to the deep impression which the second Caliph Omar ibn al-Khattab, a representative figure of the Salafiyyun, made upon him. From Afghanistan, Suwailem moved on to fight in Chechnya, where he was murdered by a poisoned letter in March 2002 (http://johnw.host.sk/articles/war_jihad_history/khattab.htm).

Islamic discourse which is inseparably linked to European deliberations about the modern condition and to European scholarship on religion and Islam. They have done so as part of a global discursive formation, of a particularly modern *epistemé*, whose social foundations can be comprehended through the category of world society, in this book predominantly conceptualized as the increasing functional differentiation of social life on a global scale.

Both this shared cognitive foundation and the confrontation with a historically specific form of social differentiation is reflected in a number of general problematic themes first discussed among various intellectual circles and later among the public at large. In the Muslim world of the nineteenth century, these circles were mainly represented by the modernist Salafiyya, the Aligarh movement and the Young Ottomans. These Islamic reform movements sharply distinguished themselves from previous forms of Islamic revival not only in their attempt to comprehend the apparent dissolution of traditional orders, but also in their aim to solve the problems of modern contingency by consciously building an alternative and authentic modern Islamic society. In this attempt they tackled the inherent ambiguities and tensions of modernity with close reference to Islamic traditions. Like the European orientalists, sociologists and theologians in chapters four and five, they posed the intertwined questions about the nature of modern religion, the interrelation among different religions, the relationship between the modern sciences (read: rationalism) and revealed knowledge, and the historical evolution of religions. They did so by deliberating on these questions in light of new forms of social activism, political authority and educational institutions. The core concerns of these Islamic reform movements display the very same themes which occupied European thinkers such as Renan, Robertson Smith, Weber, Durkheim and the founding fathers of Islamic studies.

Beginning with chapter four, I have "explained" this convergence as being the formative power of a common discursive formation, its rules, regulations and systematic order of concepts and themes. With core concepts such as evolutionary history, the dichotomy of tradition and modernity (translated by Muslim intellectuals into the jurisprudential language of *fiqh* as *taqlid* versus *ijtihad*), the autonomous functional definition of modern religion (in juxtaposing Islam's difference against the individualized Christian spirituality as a holistic "way of life") or the civilizing force of formal education, we have met in the Islam interpretations of both Islamic reformers and Islamist ideologues the same elements of the discursive formation that conditioned the works of our founding fathers of Islamic studies in chapter five. From this theoretical perspective, the works of all these very different personalities ranging from Muhammad Abduh to Sayyid Qutb and Ernest Renan to Marin Hartmann were embedded in a general modern discourse on religion and Islam.

To be sure, for the generation of modern knowledge on Islam, the personal relationships among these individuals were rather of an accidental nature. The remarkable unanimity between orientalist and Islamist interpretations of Islam are not the outcome of such personal and intellectual contacts as between C.H.

Becker and Muhammad Abduh, Ignaz Goldziher and Jamal al-Din al-Afghani, Thomas W. Arnold and Muhammad Iqbal, or Christiaan Snouck Hurgronje's interaction with Sheikh Dahlan in Mecca. To a large extent the commonly shared essentialist image of Islam has been a result of discursive practices alone. The personal and intellectual encounters that I have demonstrated here, however, illustrate on a different level of analysis the historical reality of the global public sphere not only as an invisible discursive structure, but also as a directly observable history of social interaction. The European and Muslim protagonists in this book show, on the one hand, in which ways discursive formations enable cross-cultural communication, while on the other hand, the social interactions of orientalists and Muslim reformers are also an example of the enactment of discursive structures by social actors. In this way, this book has argued from two different analytical perspectives against the essentialist assumption of two hermetically distinct cultural worlds of Islam and the West.

Employing the first two levels of observation of my analytical concept of the public sphere, the levels of the *episteme* and of general themes, we can detect a large degree of unity among Muslim and non-Muslim thinkers. It is on these levels where we can discern the origin of the striking unanimity between the orientalist and Islamist imaging of Islam. In cognitive terms, their worlds of thought are deeply rooted in the modern *episteme* and they comprehend the modern condition through similar categories. Diversity, then, appears with a shift in analytical perspective. Analyzing Islamic modernism and Islamist ideologies on the third level of observation, the concrete semantics through which the general themes attain socially relevant meaning, we can discern multiple cultural voices of modernity. At this level, not only do European and Muslim voices diverge, but the formation of European and Islamic modernities also appear as internally highly contested fields of discursive practices. It is at this level that the formative struggles about identity, knowledge and world view take place and to which our public debates refer. Similar to the development in Europe, a large variety of semantics between the outer poles of positivism and traditionalism in the Muslim world can be observed. Islamic modernism has evolved into such different ideological projects of societal reconstruction as represented by Mawdudi's and Qutb's ideal of the Islamic state, Khomeini's political theory of the *velayat-e faqih* or the secularist state doctrine of Turkish Kemalism. Again, in between these extreme poles of Islamist and secularist modern thought, we must locate a broad variety of Muslim apologetic attitudes, which represent Islamic reform ideologies in the more narrow sense, aiming at a reconfiguration of religious traditions with general features of modernity. This becomes apparent in the different ways in which Muslim intellectuals have attached new meanings to classical Islamic concepts such as *ijtihad, jihad, sharia, taqlid, tawhid* and *umma*. Based on the modern *episteme*, these traditional concepts have been revised under the impact of changing historical conditions. I briefly investigated this historical contingency in the construction of these various semantics and new patterns of meaning by examining the paths leading from the Young Ottomans to the Kemalists, from Aligarh to the Pakistani Jamaat-i

Islami, and from the modernist Salafiyya to the Jihadist world view of contemporary radical and transnationally oriented Islamists. In so doing, I stressed the impact of international politics and domestic state-building processes on these different trajectories in which nineteenth-century Islamic modernism evolved. Here the history of ideas meets with the institutional history of modern state formation; and it is within this context that the essentialist image of Islam not only has achieved its hegemonic position in public debates, but also has been embedded in the narrative of a confrontation between Islam and the West.

According to my analysis, beginning with the joint reform efforts of Jamal al-Din al-Afghani and Muhammad Abduh, we can reconstruct the rise and spread of the essentialist image of Islam along six paths:

First, there is the gradual transformation of the religious concept of divine unity, *tawhid,* into the all-encompassing idea of an Islamic system. Employing *tawhid* first as a means of achieving Muslim political unity, Afghani and Abduh further transformed its meanings based on the modern holistic concepts of culture and civilization. Like European orientalists, Muslim intellectuals began to represent Islam as the unity of a comprehensive Islamic civilization. The Islamists of the twentieth century, then, made this holistic image of Islamic civilization the core of their political ideologies. Constructing it as a hermetically closed system, they perceived Islam as a distinct alternative to Western culture and its liberalist and socialist world views. In the context of a global rise of political mass movements in the 1920s and 1930s, Islamists trivialized major ideas of Islamic modernism and turned them into core elements of their populist religio-political ideologies. Even more important, they fused this image with the institutional patterns of modern statehood, turning their holistic pretensions into an aim of political action.

Second, in turning Islamic unity into an anti-imperialist ideology, Afghani took part in firmly establishing the theme of Islam against the West as one of the leading fault-lines in international politics. During the period of high imperialism, both Muslims and non-Muslims articulated this theme in reference to the idea of Panislamism. In this tradition, the political world view of contemporary Islamists still resembles the colonial antagonisms of international politics which were perpetuated throughout the twentieth century.[60] At the end of the twentieth century, transnational Islamist militancy resurrected the ghost of Panislamism, however, in new transnational attire.

Third, this dichotomy between Islam and the West was additionally stressed by the attempt of the modernist Salafiyya to justify the borrowing of secular modern European institutions by assigning them Islamic symbols. Consequently, any claim to authenticity was based on Islamic traditions. This Islamization of modern Muslim culture was further emphasized by the rigorous quest for authenticity of Islamist movements in the twentieth century. In their eyes, every-

---

60. There is a host of historical events associated with the Arab-Israeli conflict, US support of the shah in Iran, or the recent military interventions in Afghanistan and Iraq that both Arab nationalists and Islamist have interpreted through this prism of colonial power relations.

thing authentic had to be Islamic, which is reminiscent of the role which Islam has played as the independent explicative variable in orientalist scholarship. It is contemporary Islamists who fully live up to Edward Said's orientalist stereotype to make Islam the representative of "all at once a society, a religion, a prototype, and an actuality" (Said 1978, 299).

Fourth, in employing the concept of *sharia* as a means of conscious reform of Muslim society, the modernist Salafiyya initiated a form of the juridification of Islam that has taken place in close reference to the evolution of the modern legal system. Islamist political action continued to narrow the meaning of *sharia* in close reference to the essentially modern idea of positive law, on the one hand, and to expand its utility as a political instrument for the implementation of their ideal vision of an encompassing Islamic order on the other.[61] The *sharia* attained the character of a body of law that should be implemented by the coercive power of the modern national state. The preoccupation of Islamic studies with the Islamic legal tradition thus found empirical confirmation in the juridification of the *sharia* by Muslim thinkers. Throughout the twentieth century orientalists and Islamists mutually contributed to further emphasizing the image of Islam as a "law religion."

Fifth, in translating *jihad* into a synonym for social activism, the nineteenth-century reformers opened an avenue for the appropriation and instrumentalization of an important religious concept by modern political movements. Under the historical experience of colonial domination and domestic state repression, twentieth-century Islamists have transformed this call to political action into a means of popular resistance. Relating it back to the Golden Age of Islam and the armed campaigns of the Prophet, they resurrected the traditional military character of *jihad* and provided religious legitimacy for the use of force by national and transnational groups of Islamist terrorists. In this way, the re-emergence of *jihad* has revitalized the orientalist narrative of Islam as a "violent" or "warrior religion" which the founding fathers of Islamic studies already saw on the death bed of modern history.

---

61. It is important to note that—in theory—many Islamist intellectuals have maintained elements of the interpretation of Abduh and Rida, which views the *sharia* as a historically flexible basis of general divine principles for legislation according to changing needs and historical circumstances. Sayyid Qutb, for instance, perceived religious law not in the sense of concrete regulations and procedures, but in the sense of general principles binding rulers and ruled. The finding of historically appropriate regulations is therefore a legitimate form of legislation under the rule of the *sharia* (cf. Moussalli 1992, 154–155). In terms of practicality, however, a problem arises with the definition and interpretation of these general principles. Here the historical account does not match at all the ideals of the modernist Salafiyya or the more ambiguous theoretical elaborations of Islamist intellectuals. The concrete application of Islamic law by Islamist regimes or its propagation by Islamist movements was subject to factual state authority or to the individual interpretations of the vanguards of Islamist revolution. Without an elaborated and acknowledged set of legal institutions, the application of general principles and legislation based on them becomes a hostage of political power and interests, religious law turns into the *de facto* legislation of state authorities.

Sixth, in their struggle against the religious establishment and their preroga-tive of *taqlid*, the representatives of the modernist Salafiyya opened the "gates of *ijtihad*" wider than they most probably intended. The Islamic reformers under-mined the traditional authority structures of Islamic knowledge without being able to establish an authoritative modern structure of religious learning. They sparked the dissolution of the monopoly of knowledge which the class of the *ulama* had held for centuries. Yet they did not succeed in providing the Muslim masses with a new hermeneutical access to the religious traditions. Instead, the Holy Scriptures became subject to trivial and populist interpretations. Together with the translation of the Koran and the revolution in media technology, the popularization of *ijtihad* in the twentieth century provided Islamist movements with an opportunity to draw on Islamic traditions almost randomly.

In the ideologies of contemporary radical Islamists, these six paths have con-verged into an image of Islam as an all-encompassing world view, based on a rigid and transhistorical system of normative principles. In a reinforcing process among Islamist ideologies and orientalist narratives and stereotypes, this repre-sentation of Islam has gained primacy in global debates. While Islamists present this Islamic system as morally superior to Western culture, spread it through political movements and make its implementation the personal religious duty of every Muslim, Western observers comprehend Islamist agitation as a continu-ation of the orientalist narrative about Islam as a backward, anti-modern and essentially violent religion. Clearly, the once enlightened, rationalist revisions of nineteenth-century Muslim reformers have travelled a long way, on which they have—unwillingly—corroborated the orientalist image of Islam as produced by their scholarly contemporaries in Europe. Facilitated by the technologically advancing communicative means of the global public sphere, orientalist and Is-lamist semantics reinforced each other throughout the twentieth century, estab-lishing the hegemony of an essentialist global public knowledge on Islam.

These findings of my empirical investigation bring me to the field of the sociology of knowledge. In which ways does this book contribute to theoretical discussions about knowledge? First and foremost, this contribution has been the development and application of my analytical device of the global public sphere. In chapters four to six I analyzed certain genealogical steps in European and Mus-lim intellectual history in order to underpin my hypothesis about the origin and spread of the modern essentialist image of Islam. I did so by employing the four levels of observation of the public sphere. The argumentation, presentation and selection of data in these chapters were guided by this analytical device. Through-out the book I have tried to demonstrate the ways in which my approach of a global public sphere, combining structuralism with hermeneutics, can facilitate research in cultural sociology. In addition to demonstrating the paramount role of the global public sphere, I have made a number of observations during this study that might be relevant for discussion in the field of the sociology of knowledge. These rather sketchy observations pertain to the relation between academic and ordinary knowledge, the dissemination of scholarly concepts and ideas among larger audiences, and the universalization of particular forms of knowledge.

Like Edward Said, I have located the origin of popular and stereotypical knowledge in scholarly debates. I have traced back the essentialist image of Islam to rather elitist discourses on religion, Islam and modernity by Western scholars and—in contradistinction to Said—by Islamic modernists. Ordinary knowledge draws on these sophisticated debates in a reductive way. In the process of dissemination, scholarly concepts and ideas become de-contextualized and enter the body of generally accepted knowledge as "public truths" or *doxas*. The narrative of secularization, the spiritual and individual character of Christianity, the association of "true Islam" with Sunni orthodoxy, the character of Islam as a "law religion," or the holistic image of Islam in general are cases in point. With respect to the Muslim intellectual environment, this chapter has shown how Islamist thinkers of the twentieth century were active in the trivialization and popularization of knowledge that they selectively drew from the more sophisticated debates of Islamic modernism. Divorced from their intellectual contexts, they made some of the core concepts of the modernist revision of Islamic traditions into building-blocks of their Islamist ideologies and attached to them new meanings. Even more important, in founding social movements based on these ideological platforms Islamist ideologues such as Hasan al-Banna and Abu al-Ala Mawdudi spread this trivialized and popularized knowledge on Islam in society at large.

Looking at Western scholarship, the work of Ernest Renan is a good example of these forms of reductive transfer of knowledge to larger audiences. The scarce, passing and therefore also extremely stereotypical references to Islam in his *Life of Jesus* were disseminated to an international readership who did not even intend to read about Islam. It was not so much Ernest Renan the orientalist, but the celebrated author of a bestseller on Jesus Christ who spread and reinforced stereotypical images of Islam in the European public. Further, the founding fathers of Islamic studies in chapter five did not only establish a new field of scholarly research which was methodologically more versed and by far less stereotypical in its findings than the works of previous generations of orientalist scholarship. In their public lectures and popular writings they also contributed to the trivialization of academic knowledge on Islam. Prime among our four protagonists in chapter five is Martin Hartmann. In writing for the broader German public he deliberately embedded his scholarly knowledge in common sense narratives about Islam. Consequently he deprived his books and journalist articles, which were directed to the general German reader, of the factually detailed erudition he had on Islam. Moreover, he bestowed these popular narratives with a kind of academic authority which they did not deserve.

Generally speaking, it is difficult to set clear borders that separate academic from ordinary knowledge. Rather we can observe a complex cross-fertilization of both. This even becomes apparent in Max Weber's work. In his Islam interpretation we gained the impression that he relied on a very narrow and selective source basis. Some of the popular nineteenth-century narratives such as the association of Islam with violence and war-prone politics of expansion he seemingly took for granted. Consequently, in his studies on Islam he combined sophisticated thinking on the socio-historical evolution of religions with then contemporary truisms about Islam. In analyzing the scholarly interactions among orientalists and the early sociologists of religion, the generation of knowledge in both fields reminds us more of a circular than an accumulative process. The particular findings of one discipline were utilized in building up the general conceptual apparatus of another discipline and vice-versa. Also in the field of academic scholarship, the production of knowledge was characterized by a trivialization of the concepts and models which were imported from other disciplines. In Snouck Hurgronje's "applied research" in Islam politics in Dutch East India, for example, we could discern a very crude application of some basic assumptions of the secularization theory. The so-called sociological method of Martin Hartmann was based on a number of modernist clichés which he took from the social sciences in a random and unsystematic way. Rather than accumulating knowledge on a specific subject, scholars have gradually revised and re-invented their interpretations and concepts in a spiraling process that has cross-cut disciplinary boundaries.

In these complex processes of the production of knowledge, we can discern a version of Roland Robertson's model of the universalization of the particular and the particularization of the universal. Through chapters four to six, for instance, runs the implicit story of the universalization of some very particular Protestant reform ideas which appeared first at the Universities of Tübingen and Leiden. From these local centers of liberal Protestant theology they entered broader discussions about modern religion in the social sciences, philosophy and the humanities. In this way, these interpretations of the Christian faith not only developed into generally acknowledged representations of Christianity, but also served as central points of reference for the formulation of universally applicable concepts of religion in modern times. Increasingly stripped of their context of origin in liberal Protestant thought, these concepts of religion and Christianity entered Muslim deliberations about Islam as a modern religion. In their efforts to define the particularities of Islam, Muslim reformers and Islamist thinkers took the universalized model of liberal Protestantism as a major conceptual reference. They juxtaposed Islam against this subjective, spiritual and strongly transcendental construction of modern religion; a process of religious reconstruction in which the idea that Islam is "more than a religion," that it, in contradistinction to the Christian faith, represents an all-encompassing way of life, gained hegemony. The elaborations of Sayyid Qutb about the differences between Islam and Christianity as documented in *Social Justice in Islam* are an excellent example of this re-invention of Islam against the foil of a universalized concept of liberal Protestant Christianity.

It is important to keep in mind, however, that despite its global dissemination this essentialist image is only one out of a multiplicity of modern representations of Islam. This chapter has indicated the multiple directions in which Islamic modernism has developed and that, although rather marginalized at the moment, its secular stream still continues to exist.[62] The question is thus how this specific image of Islam has achieved its global dominance. Here, I agree with *Orientalism*. We can only answer this question by taking into account the impact of power on the generation and dissemination of knowledge. The lives and works of our central protagonists clearly show that the production of knowledge takes place within historically specific frames of social power. In this process we observed the exertion of power as both a structural force, such as in the modern discursive formation, and a social relationship, that is to say the interdependent social ties that mediated the respective positions of our individual protagonists in their different fields of social interaction.

In his partisan approach, Edward Said simplified these complexities of the relationship between power and knowledge, reducing them to a rather one-dimensional colonial situation. The evolution of the essentialist image of Islam, therefore, wrongly appears in *Orientalism* as a mere tool for imperialist policies. However, the fact that Islam turned into the general oriental signifier in representing Muslim life in oriental scholarship cannot be explained by the power asymmetries of colonialism alone. In the orientalist obsession with religion, the political, economic and cultural hegemony of Europe rather played a contextual role. The lives and works of the European scholars we have examined here all indicate how deeply their production of knowledge was entrenched in the intellectual and socio-political conflicts of Europe and their respective national and religious environments. In the social transformation of Europe itself, the role of religion in society was one of the most significant issues of the nineteenth century; and the founding fathers of Islamic studies shared this obsession with religion and a pronounced antagonism toward traditional religion and orthodox institutions, regardless of being a convinced secularist (Hurgronje), a sincere believer (Goldziher), a Cultural Protestant (Becker), or an agnostic who left the church (Hartmann).The construction of the essentialist image of Islam by Western scholars therefore reflects such different power struggles as between national governments and the papacy in Rome, secular and religious forms of education, religious lay reformers and the clergy, or the mandarins of modern science and the traditionally learned of Christianity and Judaism. Moreover, each of our protagonists was working within highly contested new fields of scholarship in which social power was functional in shaping the future contours of their respective disciplines. From the perspective of this book, power and knowledge interlace at different levels of analysis in a much more complex way than Said's thesis suggested. While the macro-structures of international politics and the modern discursive formation formed the coordinates in which European and Muslim intellectuals worked and lived, their individual strategies and motivations were subject to a web of social power which we should not reduce to the international structural context.

---

62. A good example of this secular position among Arab intellectuals is the book *Myth and Reality in the Contemporary Islamist Movement* by Fuad Zakariyya (2005).

In light of the "successful" promotion of the essentialist image of Islam by orientalists and Islamists, it is nevertheless important to stress the broad variety of thoughts that the current intellectual streams in the Muslim world expose. The radical ideas of a transnational *jihad* held by Sayyid Qutb and his militant successors represent nothing but a small minority within these streams. As an organization, the Muslim Brotherhood, for instance, has never endorsed Qutb's radical theory, and many contemporary Islamist thinkers have gradually incorporated elements of the global discourse on human rights and democracy into their world views (Dagi 2004; Zollner 2009). Even the idea of Islam as a comprehensive system seems slowly to be giving way to different forms of interpretation which include elements of a secular world view. As in Western scholarship on Islam, the hegemony of the essentialist image is highly contested among Muslim thinkers and activists. This contestation of the alleged holistic nature of Islam applies in particular to the institutional level of the secularization theory, the separation of state and religion. Having its roots in Turkey's Islamist political wing, the Turkish Justice and Development Party (AKP), for instance, has transformed itself into a conservative party with religious leanings, in principle accepting the secular constitution of the Turkish state (Önish 2006). Iranian intellectuals and religious scholars such as Mohsin Kadivar, Abdolkarim Soroush and the late Ayatollah Montazeri have publicly voiced their critique of the *velayat-e faqih* in Iran. Today, they advocate the legitimization of the state on popular instead of divine sovereignty. They promote an independent judiciary, freedom of expression and the restriction of the religious establishment to matters of religious and moral guidance (Abdo 2001; Hunter 2009b, Soroush 2000). From a theological perspective, the critical hermeneutics of the Ankara school show the compatibility of Islamic theology with historical criticism. With reference to the reformist thought of the Pakistani scholar Fazlur Rahman (1919–1988), the theologians at Ankara University engage in Koran interpretations that replace simplistic textual approaches with historically critical methods (Körner 2006). Without any doubt there are many and very different "liberal Islamic voices" audible in the Muslim world (Kurzmann 1998). Although it still remains at the center of the global public debate, the essentialist image does not represent "true Islam" in any exclusive way.

It was precisely this resilience of the essentialist image of Islam in public knowledge which provided the incentive to write this book. It understands the continuing but contested dominance of this image as being rooted in the global discursive structures of popular knowledge. Constructed since the end of the nineteenth century, popular knowledge of Islam has been predicated on a number of stereotypical truths about the Muslim religion. These *doxas* of public knowledge still continue to inform global public debates, despite empirical counter-evidence and the multi-faceted approach that most scholars in Islamic studies apply to the Muslim world today. Although this historical process has taken place within the coordinates of international power relations, the globalization of the essentialist image of Islam has not been just a mere function of them. In light of Edward Said's omission, disregarding the phenomenon of "orientalism in reverse," the purpose of this final chapter has been to show the various ways in which Muslim intellectuals took an active part in the creation of these stereotypical truths which have emerged in the cognitive context of a globally shared modern discursive formation.

References

Abaza, Mona and Georg Stauth. 1988. Occidental Reason, Orientalism, Islamic Fundamentalism: A Critique. *International Sociology* 3(4): 343–364.

Abd al-Raziq, Mustafa. 1925. Introduction, La vie du Cheickh Mohammed Abdou. In *Rissalat al Tawhid — Expose de la religion Musulman,* traduit de l'Arabe par B. Michel et le Cheikh Moustapha Abdel Razik. Paris: Librairie Orientaliste Paul Geuthner.

Abdo, Geneive. 2001. Re-Thinking the Islamic Republic: A 'Conversation' with Ayatollah Hossein Ali Montazeri. *Middle East Journal* 55(1): 9–24.

Abduh, Muhammad. 1965. *Risalat al-tawhid,* Cairo.

Abdul Rahim, Adibah Binti. 1998. *A Critical Assessment of Muhammad Iqbal's Concepts of the Spirit of Muslim Culture and the Principle of Movement in the Structure of Islam,* MA thesis, International Islamic University of Malaysia.

Abu-Lughod, Lila. 1989. Zones of Theory in the Anthropology of the Arab World, *Annual Review of Anthropology* 18: 267–306.

Abu-Rabi, Ibrahim. 2002. Sayyid Qutb and His Influence. Interview with Professor Ibrahim Abu-Rabi, *Religioscope,* www.religioscope.com. 26.01.2002.

Adams, Charles C. 1933. *Islam and Modernism in Egypt: A Study of the modern Reform Movement Inaugurated by Muhammad Abduh.* London: Oxford University Press.

Adorno, Theodor W. Gesellschaft. 1975. In *Evangelisches Staatslexikon,* 2. Auflage. Stuttgart und Berlin: Kreuz Verlag.

———. 2000. *Introduction to Sociology.* Edited by Christoph Gödde and translated by Edmund Jephcott. Cambridge: Polity Press.

Adorno, Theodor W. and Max Horkheimer. 1989. *Dialectic of Enlightenment.* London: Verso.

al-Afghani, Jamal al-Din. 1880–81. The Truth about the Neicheri Sect and an Explanation of the Neicheris. In *An Islamic Response to Imperialism,* edited by Nikki R. Keddie, 130–174. Berkeley: University of California Press, 1983.

———. 1883. Answer of Jamal ad-Din to Renan. In *An Islamic Response to Imperialism,* edited by Nikki R. Keddie, 181–187. Berkeley: University of California Press, 1983.

———. 1884. The Materialists in India. In *An Islamic Response to Imperialism,* edited by Nikki R. Keddie, 175–180. Berkeley: University of California Press, 1983.

Ahmad, Abdelhamid Muhammad. 1963. *Die Auseinandersetzung zwischen Al-Azhar und der modernistischen Bewegung in Ägypten von Muhammad Abduh bis zur Gegenwart.* Hamburg: Philososphische Fakultät der Universität Hamburg.

Ahmad, Aijaz. 1991. Between Orientalism and Historicism. Reprinted in *Orientalism. A Reader,* edited by A.L. Macfie, 285–297. Edinburgh: Edinburgh University Press, 2000.

Ahmed, Akbar S. and Hastins Donnan, eds. 1994. *Islam, Globalization and Postmodernity*, London: Routledge.

Ahmed, Akbar S. 2002 (1988). *Discovering Islam. Making Sense of Muslim History and Society.* Revised edition. London: Routledge.

Akhavi, Shahrough. 1997. The Dialectics of Contemporary Egyptian Social Thought: The Traditionalist and Modernist Discourses of Sayyid Qutb and Hassan Hanafi. *International Journal of Middle East Studies* 29: 377–401.

Albert, Mathias and Lothar Brock. 2000. Debordering the World of States: New Spaces in International Relations. In *Civilizing World Politics. Society and Community Beyond the State,* edited by Mathias Albert, Lothar Brock and Klaus Dieter Wolf, 19–44. Boston, MA: Rowman and Littlefield.

Alejandro, Roberto. 1993. *Hermeneutics, Citizenship, and the Public Sphere.* New York: State University of New York Press.

Alexander, Jeffrey C. 1998. After Neofunctionalism: Action, Culture, and Civil Society. In *Neofunctionalism and After,* by Jeffrey C. Alexander, 210–233. Oxford: Blackwell Publishers.

———. 2003. *The Meanings of Social Life. A Cultural Sociology.* Oxford: Oxford University Press.

———. 2005. The Dark Side of Modernity: Tension Relief, Splitting, and Grace. In *Comparing Modernitites. Pluralism versus Homogenity. Essays in Homage to Shmuel N. Eisenstadt,* edited by Ben-Rafael Eliezer and Yitzhak Sternberg, 171–182. Leiden: Brill.

Algar, Hamid. 1969. *Religion and State in Iran 1785-1906. The Role of the Ulama in the Qajar Period.* Berkeley: University of California Press.

———. 2000. Introduction. In *Social Justice in Islam,* by Sayyid Qutb. Translated from the Arabic by John B. Hardie, translation revised and introduction by Hamid Algar. Kuala Lumpur: Islamic Book Trust.

Almog, Shmuel. 1988. The Racial Motif in Renan's Attitude to Jews and Judaism. In *Antisemitism Through the Ages,* edited by Shmuel Almog, 241–278. Oxford: Pergamon Press.

Allardt, Erik. 2005. Europe's Multiple Modernities. In *Comparing Modernitites. Pluralism versus Homogenity. Essays in Homage to Shmuel N. Eisenstadt,* edited by Ben-Rafael Eliezer and Yitzhak Sternberg, 413–442. Leiden: Brill.

Anderson, Jon W. 1999. The Internet and Islam's New Interpreters. In *New Media in the Muslim World: The Emerging Public Sphere,* edited by Dale. F. Eickelman and Jon W. Anderson, 41–56. Second ed. Bloomington: Indiana University Press.

Anjum, Ovamir. 2007. Islam as a Discursive Tradition: Talal Asad and His Interlocutors. *Comparative Studies of South Asia, Africa and the Middle East* 27(3): 656–672.

Ansari, Ali M. 2007. *Iran under Ahmadinejad. The Politics of Confrontation.* Adelphi Paper 393. London: IISS.

Arabi, Oussama. 2001. The Dawning of the Third Millennium on Shari´a: Egypt's Law No. 1 of 2000, or Women May divorce at Will. *Arab Law Quarterly* 161. 2–21.

Arafat, Ala ad-Din. 2001. Al-alaqat al-masriyyah al-faransiyyah min at-taaun ila at-tawatu 1906–1923 (The Egyptian-French Relations from Cooperation to Agreement 1906–1923). Cairo: Al-Arabi.

Archer, Margaret S. *Culture and Agency.* 1988. *The Place of Culture in Social Theory.* Cambridge: Cambridge University Press.

Arenhövel, Mark. 2005. "Die Erfindung der Pancasila. Zur Konstruktion einer staatsreligiösen Einheitsvision in Indonesien." In *Unfriedliche Religionen? Das politische Gewalt- und Konfliktpotenzial von Religionen,* edited by Matthias Hildebrandt and Manfred Brocker, 139–152. Wiesbaden: VS Verlag.

Arnold, Thomas W. 1896. *Preaching of Islam. A History of the Propagation of the Muslim Faith.* Westminster: Archibald Constable.

Asad, Talal. 1993. *Genealogies of Religion. Discipline and Reasons of Power in Christianity and Islam.* Baltimore, MD: Johns Hopkins University Press.

———. 2003. *Formations of the Secular: Christianity, Islam, Modernity.* Stanford, CA: Stanford University Press.

Ashcroft, B., G. Griffiths and H. Tiffin, eds. 1995. *The Post-Colonial Studies Reader.* London: Routledge.

al-Azm, Sadik Jalal. 1981. Orientalism and Orientalism in Reverse. *Khamsin* 8: 5–26. Reprinted in *Orientalism. A Reader,* edited by A.L. Macfie, 217–238. Edinburgh: Edinburgh University Press.

al-Azmeh, Aziz. 1996. *Islams and Modernitites.* Second Edition. London: Verso.

Azzam, Abdallah. 1990. *Hamas: al-judur at-tarikhiya wa al-mithaq* (Hamas: The Historical Roots and the Manifesto). Amman: n.p.

Badie, Bertrand. 1997. *La fin des territoires—Essay sur le désordre international et sur l'utilité social du respect.* Paris: Fayard.

al-Banna, Ahmad Saif al-Islam, Hasan, ed. 2004. *Maqasid al-Quran li al-Imam Hasan al-Banna.* Kuwait: Dar al-Wathiqa li al-Nashr wa al-Tawzia.

Baird, William. 1992. *History of New Testament Research, Volume One: From Deism to Tübingen.* Minneapolis, MN: Fortress Press.

Batunsky, Mark. 1981. Carl Heinrich Becker: From Old to Modern Islamology. Commemorating the 70th Anniversary of "Der Islam als Problem." *International Journal of Middle East Studies* 13: 287–310.

Bayart, Jean-François. 2004. *Le gouvernement du monde.* Paris: Fayard.

Beck, Ulrich. 1986. *Risikogesellschaft. Auf dem Weg in eine andere Moderne.* Frankfurt a.M.: Suhrkamp.

———. 1992. *Risk Society: Towards a New Modernity.* London: Sage.

———. 1993. *Die Erfindung des Politischen.* Frankfurt a.M.: Suhrkamp.

———. 1997. *The Reinvention of Politics: Rethinking Modernity in the Global Social Order.* Cambridge: Polity.

Beck, Ulrich and Nathan Sznaider. 2006. Unpacking Cosmopolitanism for the Social Sciences: A Research Agenda. *British Journal of Sociology* 57(1): 1–23.

Beck, Ulrich, Wolfgang Bonss and Christoph Lau. 2003. The Theory of Reflexive Modernization: Problematic, Hypotheses and Research Programme. *Theory, Culture & Society* 20(2): 1–33.

Beckford, James. 2003. *Social Theory and Religion.* Cambridge: Cambridge University Press.

Becker, Carl Heinrich. 1904. Panislamismus. In *Islamstudien: Vom Werden und Wesen der islamischen Welt.* Vol. 2. Hildesheim: Georg Olms Verlagsbuchhandlung.

———. 1907. Christentum und Islam. In *Islamstudien. Vom Werden und Wesen der islamischen Welt,* Vol. 1. Hildesheim: Georg Olms Verlagsbuchhandlung.

———. 1909. Ist der Islam eine Gefahr für unsere Kolonien? In *Islamstudien. Vom Werden und Wesen der islamischen Welt.* Vol. 2. Hildesheim: Georg Olms Verlagsbuchhandlung.

———. 1910. Der Islam als Problem. *Der Islam* 11: 1–21.

———. 1912. Islam. *Archiv für Religionswissenschaft.* 15: 530–602.

———. 1915. Die Kriegsdiskussion über den Heiligen Krieg (A. Deutschland und der Heilige Krieg). In *Islamstudien: Vom Werden und Wesen der islamischen Welt.* Vol. 2. Hildesheim: Georg Olms Verlagsbuchhandlung.

———. 1916a. Islam und Wirtschaft. In *Islamstudien: Vom Werden und Wesen der islamischen Welt,* Vol. 2. Hildesheim: Georg Olms Verlagsbuchhandlung.

278 • *Orientalists, Islamists and the Global Public Sphere*

————. 1916b. Das türkische Bildungsproblem. In *Islamstudien: Vom Werden und Wesen der islamischen Welt*. Vol. 2. Hildesheim: Georg Olms Verlagsbuchhandlung.

————. 1916/17. Der Islam als Weltanschauung in Vergangenheit und Gegenwart. In *Islamstudien: Vom Werden und Wesen der islamischen Welt*. Vol. 1. Hildesheim: Georg Olms Verlagsbuchhandlung.

————. 1920. Martin Hartmann. In *Islamstudien: Vom Werden und Wesen der islamischen Welt*. Vol. 2. Hildesheim: Georg Olms Verlagsbuchhandlung.

————. 1922a (1967). "Ignaz Goldziher." In *Islamstudien. Vom Werden und Wesen der islamischen Welt*. Vol. 2. by C.H. Becker. Hildesheim: Georg Olms Verlagsbuchhandlung.

————. 1922b. Der Islam im Rahmen einer allgemeinen Kulturgeschichte. *Zeitschrift der Deutschen Morgenländischen Gesellschaft* 761: 18–35.

————. 1932 (1967). "Ernst Nöldeke." In *Islamstudien. Vom Werden und Wesen der islamischen Welt*, Band II, by C.H. Becker: Hildesheim: Georg Olms.

Beidelman, Thomas. 1974. *W. Robertson Smith and the Sociological Study of Religion*. Chicago, IL: University of Chicago Press.

Benda, Harry J. 1972. *Continuity and Change in Southeast Asia. Collected Journal Articles of Harry J. Benda*. New Haven, CT: Yale University Press.

Bender, Thomas. 1997. Politics, Intellect, and the American University. *Dædalus* 126(1): 1–38.

Berger, Peter and Thomas Luckmann. 1967. *The Social Construction of Reality: A Treaties in the Sociology of Knowledge*. London: Penguin Press.

Bergesen, Albert J. 2008. The Sayyid Qutb Reader. Selected writings on politics, religion, and society. Edited by Albert J. Bergesen. London: Routledge.

Bermbach, Udo. 1997. *Wo Macht ganz auf Verbrechen ruht. Politik und Gesellschaft in der Oper*, Hamburg: Europäische Verlagsanstalt.

Berkes, Niyazi 1964. *The Development of Secularism in Turkey*, Montreal: McGill University Press.

Beyer, Peter L. 1994. *Religion and Globalization*. London: Sage.

————. 1998. The Modern Emergence of Religions and a Global Social System for Religion. *International Sociology* 132: 151–172

————. 2003. Social Forms of Religion and Religions in Contemporary Global Society. In *Handbook of the Sociology of Religion*, edited by Michele Dillon, 45–60. Cambridge: Cambridge University Press.

————. 2006. *Religion and Global Society*. London: Routledge.

Bhaba, Homi. 1997 (1983). The Other Question. In *Contemporary Postcolonial Theory: A Reader*, edited by Padmini Mongia, 37–54. London and New York: Arnold.

bin Laden, Osama. 2001. *Letter to the Pakistani Muslims*, accessed on September, 13, 2006, under: http://news.bbc.co.uk/2/hi/world/monitoring/media_reports/1633204.stm.

Bickel, Cornelius. 1988. Ferdinand Tönnies' Weg in die Soziologie. In *Simmel und die frühen Soziologen: Nähe und Distanz zu Durkheim, Tönnies und Max Weber*, edited by Ottheim Rammsted, 86–163. Frankfurt: Suhrkamp.

Black, John Sutherland and George Chrystal. 1912. *The Life of William Robertson Smith*. London: Adam and Charles Black.

Blinkenberg, Andreas. 1923. *Ernest Renan. Bidrag til belysning af hans filosofisk-religiøse ungdomskrise*. Copenhagen: Engelsen and Schrøder.

Bloch, Charles. 1972. *Die Dritte Französische Republik. Entwicklung und Kampf einer parlamentarischen Demokratie (1870-1940)*. Stuttgart: K.F. Koehler Verlag.

Boli, John and George M. Thomas. 1999. INGO's and the Organization of World Culture, in: Boli, John and George M. Thomas, eds. *Constructing World Culture. International Non-governmental Organizations since 1875.* Stanford: Stanford University Press.

Bossy, John. 1982. Some Elementary Forms of Durkheim. *Past & Present,* 94–97: 3–18.

Bourdieu, Pierre, 1986a. *Distinction. A Social Critique of the Judgement of Taste.* London and New York: Routledge.

———. 1986b. The Forms of Capital, in: John G. Richardson, ed. *Handbook of Theory and Research for the Sociology of Education.* Westport: Greenwood Press.

———. 1992. *Die verborgenen Mechanismen der Macht.* Hamburg: VSA Verlag.

———. 1996. *The State Nobility. Elite Schools in the Field of Power.* Oxford: Polity Press.

———. 2000. *Pascalian Meditations.* Oxford: Polity Press.

Bousquet, G.-H. 1957. Christiaan Snouck Hurgronje (1857–1936). In *Selected Works of C. Snouck Hurgronje,* edited by G.-H. Bousquet and Joseph Schacht, xi-xxi. Leiden: Brill.

Breckenridge, Carol A. 1989. The Aesthetics and Politics of Colonial Collecting: India at World Fairs. *Comparative Studies in Society and History* 31(2): 195–216.

Breuer Stefan. 2006. *Max Webers tragische Soziologie. Aspekte und Perspektiven.* Tübingen: Mohr Siebeck.

Brockelmann, Carl. 1922. Die morgenländischen Studien in Deutschland. *Zeitschrift der Deutschen Morgenländischen Gesellschaft* 76(1): 1–17.

Brown, Carl. 2000. *Religion and State: The Muslim Approach to Politics,* New York: Columbia University Press.

Brown, Nathan J. 1997. Sharia and State in the Modern Middle East. *International Journal of Middle East Studies* 29 (3): 359–376

Bruch, Rüdiger vom, Friedrich Wilhelm Graf and Gangolf Hübinger, eds. 1989. *Kultur und Kulturwissenschaften um 1900. Krise der Moderne und Glaube an die Wissenschaft.* Stuttgart: Frank Steiner Verlag.

Buchta, Wilfried 1997. *Die iranische Schia und die islamische Einheit 1976–1996.* Hamburg: Deutsches Orient-Institut.

Burhanudin, Jajat. 2005. Aspiring for Islamic Reform: Southeast Asian requests for *Fatwas* in *Al-Manar. Islamic Law and Society* 12(1): 9–26.

Buruma, Ian and Avishai Margalit. 2004. Occidentalism. London: Atlantic Books.

Buss, Martin. 1999. *Biblical Form Criticism in ist Context.* Sheffield: Sheffield Academic Press.

Bürgel, Johann Christoph. 1991. *Allmacht und Mächtigkeit. Religion und Welt des Islam.* Munich: C.H.Beck.

Buzan, Barry. 2004. *From International to World Society? English School Theory and the Structure of Globalisation.* Cambridge: Cambridge University Press.

Calhoun, Craig, ed. 1997. *Habermas and the Public Sphere.* Cambridge, MA: MIT Press.

Carré, Olivier. 2003. Mysticism and Politics. A Critical Reading of Fi Zilal al-Qur'an by Sayyid Qutb (1906–1966). Leiden: Brill.

Carrier, James G. ed. 1995. *Occidentalism. Images of the West.* Oxford: Clarendon Press.

Casanova, José. 1994. *Public Religions in the Modern World.* Chicago, IL: University of Chicago Press.

———. 2001. Civil Society and Religion: Retrospective Reflections on Catholicism and Prospective Reflections on Islam. *Social Research* 68(4): 1041–1080.

Cashdollar, Charles D. 1989. *The Transformation of Theology, 1830–1890. Positivism and Protestant Tought in Britain and America.* Princeton, NJ: Princeton University Press.

Celik, Zeynep. 1992. *Displaying the Orient. Architecture of Islam at Nineteenth-Century World's Fairs.* Berkeley: University of California Press.

Chabbi, Jacqueline. 1996. Histoire et tradition sacrée: la biographie impossible de Mahomet. *Arabica* 43(1): 189–205.

Chakrabarty, Dipesh. 1992. Postcoloniality and the Artifice of History: Who Speaks for "Indian" Pasts? *Representations* 37 (1992): 1–26.

Charlton, D.G. 1963. *Secular Religions in France, 1815-1870.* London: Oxford University Press.

Chaudhuri, Sibidas. 1982. *Index to the Transactions of the International Congress of Orientalists 1873-1973,* index asia series in humanities. Calcutta: Centre for Asian Dokumentation.

Chen, Xiaomei. 1995. *Occidentalism: A Theory of Counter-Discourse in Post-Mao China.* Oxford: Oxford University Press.

Cheyne, Alec C. 1995. Bible and Confession in Scotland: The Background to the Robertson Smith Case. In *William Robertson Smith: Essays in Reassessment,* edited by William Johnstone, 24–40. Sheffield: Sheffield Academic Press.

Choueiri, Youssef M. 1997. *Islamic Fundamentalism.* Revised edition. London: Pinter.

CIO 1876 (1998). *Congrès International Des Orientalists,* vol. 3, Bristol: Ganesha Publishing.

Commins, David. 2005. Hasan al-Banna (1906-1949). In *Pioneers of Islamic Revival,* edited by Ali Rahnema, 125–153. New edition. London: Zed books.

———. 2006. The Wahhabi Mission and Saudi Arabia. London: I.B. Tauris.

Conrad, Lawrence I. 1990. The Near East Study Tour Diary of Ignaz Goldziher. *Journal of the Royal Asiatic Society* 1990: 105–126.

———. 1993. The Pilgrim from Pest: Goldziher's Study Tour to the Near East (1873-1874). In *Golden Roads. Migration, Pilgrimage and Travel in Mediaeval and Modern Islam.* edited by Ian Richard Netton, 110–148. Richmond: Curzon Press.

———. 1999. Ignaz Goldziher on Ernest Renan: From Orientalist Philology to the Study of Islam. In *The Jewish Discovery of Islam: Studies in Honor of Bernard Lewis,* edited by Martin Kramer, 137–180. Tel Aviv: Moshe Dayan Center and Tel Aviv University.

Cook, David. 2005. *Understanding Jihad.* Berkeley: University of California Press.

Cooke, Miriam and Bruce B. Lawrence, eds. 2005. *Muslim Networks: From Hajj to Hip Hop.* Chapell Hill: University of North Carolina Press.

Coulson, N.J. 1957. The State and the Individual in Islamic Law. *The International and Comparative Law Quarterly* 6(1): 49–60.

Crossley, Nick and John Michael Roberts, eds. 2004. *After Habermas: New Perspectives on the Public Sphere.* Oxford: Blackwell Publishing.

Dagi, Ihsan D. 2004. Rethinking Human Rights, Democracy, and the West: Post-Islamist Intellectuals in Turkey. *Critique: Critical Middle Eastern Studies* 13(2): 135–151.

Dahlgren, Peter. 1991. Introduction. *Communication and Citizenship: Journalism and the Public Sphere in the New Media Age,* edited by Peter Dahlgren and Colin Sparks, 1–24. London: Routledge.

Dahrendorf, Ralf. 2006 (1987). Max Weber and Modern Social Science. In *Max Weber and His Contemporaries,* edited by Wolfgang J. Mommsen and Jürgen Osterhammel, 574–580. London: Routledge.

Dallal, Ahmad. 2000. Appropriating the Past: Twentieth-Century Reconstruction of Pre-Modern Islamic Thought. *Islamic Law and Society* 7(1): 325–358.

Daniel, Norman. 1960. *Islam and the West. The Making of an Image.* Edinburgh: Edinburgh University Press.

Debesse, Maurice. 1973. Preface, in *Émile Durkheim: éducation et sociologie.* Paris: Presses Universitaires de France.

Demerath, N.J. III. 2001. *Crossing the Gods: World Religions and Worldly Politics.* New Brunswick, NJ: Rutgers University Press.

Deringil, Selim. 1998. *The Well-Protected Domains. Ideology and the Legitimation of Power in the Ottoman Enmpire, 1876-1909.* London: I.B. Tauris.

Desomogyi, Joseph. 1961. My Reminiscences of Ignace Goldziher. *The Muslim World* (LI): 5–17.

———. (ed.) 1968-1972. Ignaz Goldziher, Gesammelte Schriften in sechs Bänden. Hildesheim: G. Olms.

Dobbelaere, Karel. 2002. *Secularization: An Analysis at Three Levels,* Brussels: P.I.E.-Peter Lang Verlag.

Dörfler-Dierken, Angelika. 2001. *Luthertum und Demokratie. Deutsche und amerikanische Theologen des 19. Jahrhunderts zu Staat, Gesellschaft und Kirche.* Göttingen: Vandenhoeck and Ruprecht.

Douglas, Robert K. ed. 1876. *Transactions of the Second Session of the International Congress of Orientalists.* London: Trübner and Co.

Duri, A.A. 1987. *The Historical Formation of the Arab Nation: A Study in Identity and Consciousness.* Translated by Lawrence I. Conrad. London: Croom Helm.

Durkheim, Emil. 1898. L'individualisme et les intellectuals, translated by Steven Lukes. In Durkheim's 'Individualism and the Intellectuals,' 166–183. (Originally in French, *Revue Bleue* 4(10), (1898): 7–13.

———. 1964. *The Division of Labor.* New York: The Free Press.

———. 1995. *The Elementary Forms of Religious Life.* New York: The Free Press.

———. 2002. *Suicide: A Study in Sociology.* London: Routledge.

Dussaud, René. 1951. *L'Oeuvre scientifique d'Ernest Renan.* Paris: Librairie Orientaliste Paul Geuthner.

Ebach, Jürgen. 1982. Ewald, Georg Heinrich August (1803–1875). *Theologische Realenzyklopädie* Vol. 10. Berlin: de Gruyter.

Eich, Thomas. 2003. The Forgotten Salafi - Abu L-Huda as-Sayyadi. *Die Welt des Islams* 43(1): 61–87.

Eickelman, Dale F. and Jon W. Anderson, eds. 2003. *New Media in the Muslim World. The Emerging Public Sphere.* Second edition. Bloomington: Indiana University Press.

Eisenstadt, Samuel N. 1991. A Reappraisal of Theories of Social Change and Modernization. In *Social Change and Modernity,* edited by Hans Haferkamp and Neil J. Smelser, 412–431. Berkeley: University of California Press.

———. 2000. Multiple Modernities *Daedalus* 129(1): 1–29.

Elias, Norbert. 1986. *Was ist Soziologie?* Weinheim: Juventa.

———. 1987. The Retreat of Sociologists into the Present. *Theory, Culture & Society* 4: 223–47.

———. 1991. *The Society of Individuals.* Oxford: Blackwell.

———. 1994. *The Civilizing Process. The History of Manners and State Formation and Civilization.* Oxford: Basil Blackwell.

Enayat, Hamid. 1982. *Modern Islamic Political Thought: The Response of the Shi'i and Sunni Muslims to the Twentieth Century.* London: Macmillan Press.

Ende, Werner. 1989. Der schiitische Islam. In *Der Islam in der Gegenwart,* edited by Werner Ende and Udo Steinbach, 70–90. Munich: C.H. Beck.

Endress, Gerhard. 1982. *Einführung in die islamische Geschichte.* Munich: Beck.

Escovitz, Joseph H. 1986. "He was the Muhammad Abduh of Syria." A Study of Tahir Al-Jazairi and His Influence. *International Journal of Middle Eastern Studies* 18: 293–310.

Esposito, John L. and Dalia Mogahed. 2008. *Who Speaks for Islam? What a Billion Muslims Really Think.* New York: Gallup Press.

Esposito, John L. and John O. Voll. 1996. *Islam and Democracy.* Oxford: Oxford University Press.

Ess, Josef van. 1980. From Wellhausen to Becker. The Emergence of *Kulturgeschichte* in Islamic Studies. In *Islamic Studies: A Tradition and Its Problems,* edited by Malcom Kerr, 27–51. Malibu: Undena Publications.

————. 2003. Review Article. *Die Welt des Islams.* 43(1): 104–110.

Essner, Cornelia and Gerd Winkelhane. 1988. Carl Heinrich Becker (1876–1933), Orientalist und Kulturpolitiker. *Die Welt des Islams* 28: 154–177.

Euben, Roxanne L. 1999. Enemy in the Mirror. Islamic Fundamentalism and the Limits of Modern Rationalism. Princeton: Princeton University Press.

Euchner, Walter. 1996. Nation und Nationalismus. Eine Erinnerung an Ernest Renans Rede "Was ist eine Nation?" In Ernest Renan: *Was ist eine Nation? Rede am 11. März 1882 an der Sorbonne.* Stuttgart: Europäische Verlagsanstalt.

Euting, Joseph. 1896. *Tagebuch einer Reise in Inner-Arabien, Erster Theil.* Leiden: E.J.Brill.

————. 1914. *Tagebuch einer Reise in Inner-Arabien, Zweiter Theil,* herausgegeben von Enno Littman. Leiden: E.J.Brill.

Evans, Peter. 1995. *Embedded Autonomy: States and Industrial Transformation.* Princeton, NJ: Princeton University Press.

Fähndrich, Hartmut. 1988. Orientalismus und Orientalismus: Überlegungen zu Edward Said, Michel Foucault und westlichen "Islamstudien." *Die Welt des Islams* 28: 178–186.

Fairchild, Hoxie N. 1941. Romanticism and the Religious Revival in England. *Journal of the History of Ideas* 2(3): 30–38.

Fairclough, Norman. 2003. *Analyzing Discourse: Textual Analysis for Social Research.* London: Routledge.

Featherstone, Mike and Scott Lash. 1995. Globalization, Modernity and the Spatialization of Social Theory: an Introduction. In *Global Modernities,* edited by Mike Featherstone, Scott Lash and Roland Robertson, 1–24. London: Sage.

Feiner, Shmuel. 2004. *The Jewish Enlightenment.* Philadelphia: University of Philadelphia Press.

Findley, Carter Vaughn. 1998. An Ottoman Occidentalist in Europe: Ahmed Midhat Meets Madam Gülnar, 1889. *The American Historical Review* 103(1): 15–49.

Flint, Robert. 1893. *Historical Philosophy in France and French Belgium and Switzerland.* London: William Balckwood and Sons.

Fontane, Theodor. 1895 (1995). *Effi Briest.* Translated by Hugh Rorrison and Helen Chambers. London: Angel Books.

Foucault, Michel. 1980. *Power/Knowledge. Selected Interviews and Other Writings 1972-1977.* Edited by Colin Gordon. Brighton: Harvester Press.

————. 1989. *Archaeology of Knowledge.* London: Routledge. First published in French 1969.

————. 1994. *The Order of Things.* London: Routledge. First published in French 1966.

Franke, Patrick. 2002. Rückkehr des Heiligen Krieges? Dschihad-Theorien im modernen Islam. In *Religion und Gewalt: Der Islam nach dem 11. September,* edited by Andre Stanisavljevic and Ralf Zwengel, 46–68. Potsdam: Mostar Friedensprojekt.

Freitag, Ulrike. 2003. Der Orientalist und der Mufti: Kulturkontakt im Mekka des 19. Jahrhunderts. *Die Welt des Islams* 43(1): 37–60.

Frisby, David and Derek Sayer. 1986. *Society.* Chichester: Ellis Horwood.

Frye, R.N. ed. 1956. *Islam and the West.* S-Gravenhage: Mouton.

Fuchs, Eckhardt. 2002. Zwischen Wissenschaft und Politik. Die internationalen Historiker- und Orientalistenkongresse vor dem Ersten Weltkrieg. In *Wissenschaftsgeschichte und Geschichtswissenschaft: Aspekte einer problematischen Beziehung Wolfgang Küttler zum 65. Geburtstag,* edited by Stefan Jordan und Peter Th. Walther, 352–373. Waltrop: Harmut Spenner Verlag.

Fück, Johann 1955. *Die arabischen Studien in Europa. Bis in den Anfang des 20. Jahrhunderts,* Leipzig: Otto Harrassowitz.

Gadamer, Hans-Georg. 1993. *Truth and Method.* London: Sheed and Ward.

Geertz, Clifford. 1973. *The Interpretation of Cultures. Selected Essays.* New York: Basic Books.

———. 1975. Common Sense as a Cultural System. *The Antioch Review* 33: 5–26.

———. 2003a. Which Way to Mecca? (part I). *New York Review of Books,* 12 June 2003.

———. 2003b. Which Way to Mecca? (part II). *New York Review of Books,* 3 July 2003.

Geiger, Abraham. 1902. *Was hat Mohammed aus dem Judenthume aufgenommen?* Second edition. Leipzig: M.W. Kaufmann.

Geiger, Ludwig. 1910. *Abraham Geiger. Leben und Lebenswerk.* Berlin: Druck und Verlag von Georg Reimer.

Gershoni, Israel. 1999. Egyptian Liberalism in an Age of "Crisis of Orientation": Al-Risala's Reaction to Fascism and Nazism, 1933-39. *International Journal of Middle East Studies* 31: 551–576.

Ghazoul Ferial J. 1998. Review of: "Anatomy of a Dynamic Mind," by Abdelrashid Mahmoudi, Al-Ahram Weekly 5-11 Nov. No. 402.

Giddens, Anthony. 1972. Introduction. In *Selected Writings,* by Emile Durkheim. Cambridge: Cambridge University Press.

———. 1990. *The Consequences of Modernity.* Cambridge: Polity Press.

Global Jihad. 2006. In the words of Osama Bin Laden, Ayman Al Zawahiri, Musab Al Zarqawi. Philadelphia: Pavillon Press.

Glover, Willis B. 1954. *Evangelical Nonconformists and Higher Criticism in the Nineteenth Century.* London: Independent Press LTD.

Göbel, Karl-Heinrich. 1984. *Moderne schiitische Politik und Staatsidee.* Opladen: Leske and Budrich.

Gökalp, Ziya. 1959. *Turkish Nationalism and Western Civilization. Selected Essays of Ziya Gökalp.* Translated and edited by Niyazi Berkes. London: George Allen and Unwin.

———. 1968. *The Principles of Turkism.* Translated from the Turkish and annotated by Robert Devereux. Leiden: Brill.

Goddard, Hugh. 2000. *A History of Christian-Muslim Relations.* Edinburgh: Edinburgh University Press.

Goldstein, Warren S. 2009. Secularization Patterns in the Old Paradigm, *Sociology of Religion* 70(2): 157–178.

Goldziher, Ignaz. 1876. *Der Mythos bei den Hebräern und seine geschichtliche Entwicklung,* Leipzig: Brockhaus.

———. 1884. *Die Zairiten. Ihr Lehrsystem und ihre Geschichte. Ein Beitrag zur Geschichte der muhammedanischen Theologie,* mit einem Vorwort von Joseph Desomogyi. Hildesheim: Georg Olms Verlagsbuchhandlung, reprint 1967.

———. 1886 (1967-1973). Muhammedanisches Recht in Theorie und Wirklichkeit. In Gesammelte Schriften, Vol 2, (1878–1892), edited by Joseph Desomogyi. Hildesheim: G. Olms.

———. 1889. *Muhammedanische Studien, Erster Theil.* Halle: Max Niemeyer.

———. 1890. *Muhammedanische Studien, Zweiter Theil.* Halle Max Niemeyer.

———. 1897 (1967-1973). Real-Encyklopädie des Islam. In Gesammelte Schriften, Vol 4, (1896–1905), edited by Joseph Desomogyi, Hildesheim: G. Olms.

———. 1904 (1967-1973). Heinrich Leberecht Fleischer. In Gesammelte Schriften, Vol. 6, (1874–1907), edited by Joseph Desomogyi, . Hildesheim: G. Olms.

———. 1906. The Progress of Islamic Science in the Last Three Decades. In *Arts and Science. Universal Exposition, St. Louis, 1904, Vol. II: History of Politics and Economics, History of Law, History of Religion,* edited by Howard J. Rogers, 497–517. Boston, MA: Houghton, Mifflin and Company.

————. 1910a (1925). *Vorlesungen über den Islam,* zweite umgearbeitete Auflage. Heidelberg: Carl Winter's Universitätsbuchhandlung.

————. 1910b (1870-1877). Kämpfe um die Stellung des Hadith im Islam. In *Gesammelte Schriften,* Vol 5. edited by Joseph Desomogyi, 86-98. Hildesheim: G. Olms.

————. 1914. Katholische Tendenz und Partikularismus im Islam. In Gesammelte Schriften, Vol. 5, edited by Joseph Desomogyi, 285-312. Hildesheim: G. Olms.

————. 1916. *Streitschrift des Gazali gegen die Batinijja-Sekte.* Leiden: E.J. Brill.

————. 1920 (1952). *Die Richtungen der Islamischen Koranauslegung. An der Universität Upsala gehaltene Olaus-Petri-Vorlesungen,* unveränderter Neudruck. Leiden: E.J. Brill.

————. 1978. *Tagebuch.* Edited by Alexander Schreiber. Leiden: E.J.Brill.

————. 1994. *On the History of Grammar among the Arabs.* Amsterdam and Philadelphia: John Benjamins Publishing Company.

Goody, Jack. 2004. *Islam in Europe.* Cambridge: Polity Press.

Gore, Keith. 1970. *L'idée de progrès dans la pensée de Renan.* Paris: Editions A.-G. Nizet.

Gorski, Philip S. 2000. Historicizing the Secularization Debate: Church, State, and Society in Late Medieval and Early Modern Europe, ca. 1300 to 1700. *American Sociological Review* 65(1): 138-167.

Graf, Friedrich W. 1982. *Kritik und Pseudo-Spekulation. David Friedrich Strauss als Dogmatiker im Kontext der positionellen Theologie seiner Zeit.* Munich: CHR. Kaiser Verlag.

————. 1987. Max Weber und die protestantische Theologie seiner Zeit. *Zeitschrift für Religions- und Geistesgeschichte* 39: 122-147.

————. 2004. *Die Wiederkehr der Götter. Religion in der Modernen Kultur.* Munich: C.H.Beck.

————. 2006 (1987). Friendship between Experts: Notes on Weber and Troeltsch. In *Max Weber and His Contemporaries,* edited by Wolfgang J. Mommsen and Jürgen Osterhammel, 215-233. London: Routledge.

Greenhalgh, Paul. 1988. *Ephemeral Vistas. The Expositions Universelles, Great Exibitions and World's Fairs, 1851-1939.* Manchester: Manchester University Press.

Greil, Arthur L. and David G. Bromley, eds. 2003. *Defining Religion: Investigation the Boundaries between the Sacred and the Secular.* Oxford: Elsevier Science Ltd.

Gründer, Horst. 1985. *Geschichte der deutschen Kolonien.* Tübingen: UTB Schöningh.

Greyerz, Kaspar von. 2000. *Religion und Kultur: Europa 1500-1800.* Darmstadt: Wissenschaftliche Buchgesellschaft.

Guillén, Mauro. 2001. Is Globalization Civilizing, Destructive or Feeble? A Critique of Five Key Debates in the Social-Science Literature. *Annual Review of Sociology* 27: 235-260.

Guizot, François. 1828. *Cours d'histoire moderne—Histoire général de la civilization en Europe.* Paris: Pichon et Didier.

Haarmann, Ulrich. 1974. Die islamische Moderne bei den deutschen Orientalisten. In *Araber und Deutsche. Begegnungen in einem Jahrtausend,* edited by Friedrich H. Kochwasser and Hans R. Roemer, 56-91. Tübingen und Basel: Horst Erdmann Verlag.

————. 1975. Die Pflichten des Muslim – Dogma und geschichtliche Wirklichkeit. *Saeculum* 26: 95-110.

Haber, Peter. 2004. Bruchstellen einer ungarisch-jüdischen Symbiose: Ignaz Goldziher. In *Herausforderung Osteuropa. Die Offenlegung stereotyper Bilder,* edited by Thede Kahl, Elisabeth Vyslonzil and Alois Wondan, 69-80. Vienna: Verlag für Geschichte und Politik.

————. 2006a. *Zwischen jüdischer Tradition und Wissenschaft. Der ungarische Orientalist Ignác Goldziher 1850-1921).* Cologne: Böhlau Verlag.

————. 2006b. Verschiebungen: Jüdische Assimilation in Ungarn – Eine Skizze. *aufbau* 7/8: 29-31

————. 2006c. Sprache, Rasse, Nation. Der ungarische Turkologe Ármin Vámbery. In

Jüdische Identität und Nation, Fallbeispiele aus Mitteleuropa, edited by Peter Haber, Erik Petry and Daniel Wildmann, 19–49. Cologne, Vienna: Böhlau Verlag.

Habermas, Jürgen. 1962. *Strukturwandel der Öffentlichkeit,* Neuauflage 1990. Frankfurt a.M.: Suhrkamp.

———. 1986. *The Theory of Communicative Action: Lifeworld and System: A Critique of Functionalist Reason.* London: Polity Press.

———. 1987. *The Philosophical Discourse of Modernity.* Cambridge: Polity Press.

———. 1990 (1962). Vorwort zur Neuauflage 1990. In Jürgen Habermas, *Strukturwandel der Öffentlichkeit* Frankfurt a.M.: Suhrkamp.

———. 2005. *Zwischen Naturalismus und Religion. Philosophische Aufsätze.* Frankfurt a.M.: Suhrkamp.

Haddad, Mahmoud. 1997. Arab Religious Nationalism in the Colonial Era: Rereading Rashid Rida's Ideas on the Caliphate, *Journal of the American Oriental Society.* 117(2): 253–266.

Haddad, Yvonne. 2005. Muhammad Abduh: Pioneer of Islamic Reform. In *Pioneers of Islamic Revival,* edited by Ali Rahnema, 30–63. New edition. London: Zed books.

Hagen, Gottfried. 2004. German Heralds of Holy War: Orientalists and Applied Oriental Studies. *Comparative Studies of South Asia, Africa and the Middle East* 24(2): 145–162.

Haj, Samira. 2009. *Reconfiguring Islamic Tradition: Reform, Rationality, and Modernity.* Stanford, CA: Stanford University Press.

Halliday, Fred. 1993. Orientalism and Its Critics. *British Journal of Middle Eastern Studies* 20(2): 145–163.

———. 1995. *Islam and the Myth of Confrontation: Religion and Politics in the Middle East.* London: I.B. Tauris.

Haltern, Utz. 1971. *Die Londoner Weltausstellung von 1851. Ein Beitrag zur Geschichte der bürgerlich-industriellen Gesellschaft im 19. Jahrhundert.* Münster: Verlag Aschendorff.

Hamilton, Malcolm. 2002. *The Sociology of Religion. Theoretical and Comparative Perspectives.* Second edition, London and New York: Routledge.

Hanioglu Shükrü. 2005. Blueprints for a Future Society: Late Ottoman Materialists on Science, Religion, and Art. In *Late Ottoman Society: The Intellectual Legacy,* edited by Elisabeth Özdalga, 28–116. London: Routledge.

Hanisch, Ludmila, ed. 1992. *Islamkunde und Islamwissenschaft im Kaiserreich. Der Briefwechsel zwischen Carl Heinrich Becker und Martin Hartmann 1900-1918.* Leiden: Rijksuniversiteit Leiden.

———. ed. 2000. *Machen Sie doch unseren Islam nicht gar zu schlecht. Der Briefwechsel der Islamwissenschaftler Ignaz Goldziher und Martin Hartmann 1894-1914.* Wiesbaden: Harrassowitz Verlag.

———. 2003. *Die Nachfolger der Exegeten. Deutschsprachige Erforschung des Vorderen Orients in der ersten Hälfte des 20. Jahrhunderts.* Wiesbaden: Harrassowitz.

Hardin, Russell. 2009. *How Do You Know? The Economics of Ordinary Knowledge.* Princeton, NJ: Princeton University Press.

Haridi, Alexander. 2005. *Das Paradigma der 'islamischen Zivilisation' - oder die Begründung der deutschen Islamwissenschaft durch Carl Heinrich Becker (1876-1933). Eine wissenschaftliche Untersuchung.* Würzburg: Ergon Verlag.

Harms, John B. 1981. Reason and Social Change in Durkheim's Thought: The Changing Relationship Between Individuals and Society. In *Emile Durkheim: Critical Assessments.* Volume IV, edited by Peter Hamilton, 393–407. London and New York: Routledge (reprint 1990).

Hartmann, Martin. 1899a. *Islam und Arabisch* In *Der islamische Orient: Berichte und Forschun-*

gen, Vol. 1. Berlin: Wolf Peiser Verlag.

———. 1899b. *The Arabic Press of Egypt.* London: Luzac.

———. 1900a. China und der Islam. In *Der islamische Orient: Berichte und Forschungen,* Vol. 1. Berlin: Wolf Peiser Verlag.

———. 1900b. Strassen durch Asien. In *Der islamische Orient: Berichte und Forschungen,* Vol. 1. Berlin: Wolf Peiser Verlag.

———. 1907. Islam und moderne Kultur. *Internationale Wochenschrift für Wissenschaft, Kunst und Technik,* Vol. 1. 858–866.

———. 1908. *Die Mekka-Bahn.* Abdruck aus der Orientalischen Literatur-Zeitung. Berlin: Wolf Preiser Verlag.

———. 1909a. *Der Islam: Geschichte - Glaube - Recht. Ein Handbuch.* Leipzig: Verlag von Rudolf Haupt.

———. 1909b. Die Arabische Frage mit einem Versuche der Archäologie Jemens. In *Der Islamische Orient, Berichte und Forschungen,* Vol. 2. Leipzig: Rudolf Haupt Verlag.

———. 1910. Deutschland und der Islam. *Der Islam* 1(81): 72–92.

———. 1911. Die Islamische Verfassung und Verwaltung. In *Die Kultur der Gegenwart, Teil II: Allgemeine Verfassungs- und Verwaltungsgeschichte.* Leipzig and Berlin: B.G. Teubner.

———. 1912. Das Seminar für Orientalische Sprachen in Berlin. Zum 25jährigen Bestehen, *Internationale Wochenschrift für Wissenschaft, Kunst und Technik.* Vol 6: 611–618.

———. 1916. Kriegsurkunden: Die fünf heiligen Fetwas (Rechtsgutachten). *Die Welt des Islams* 3(1): 1–23.

Hartmann, Richard. 1922. Ignaz Goldziher. *Zeitschrift der Deutschen Morgenländischen Gesellschaft* 76: 285–290.

Hatem, Mervat F. 1997. The Professionalization of Health and the Control of Women's Bodies as Modern Governmentalitites in Nineteenth-Century Egypt. In *Women in the Ottoman Empire. Middle Eastern Women in the Early Modern Era,* edited by Madeline C. Zilfi, 66–80. Leiden: Brill.

Haynes, Jeffrey. 1998. *Religion in Global Politics.* Harlow: Longman.

———. 2006. Religion and International Relations in the 21st Century: Conflict or Cooperation? *Third World Quarterly* 27(3): 535–541.

Hayward, J.E.S. 1960. Solidarist Syndicalism: Durkheim and Duguit. In *Emile Durkheim: Critical Assessments.* Volume IV, edited by Peter Hamilton, 128–144. London and New York: Routledge (reprint 1990).

———. 1963. "Solidarity" and the Reformist Sociology of Alfred Fouillée, I. *The American Journal of Economics and Sociology* 22(1): 205–222.

Held, David *et al.* 1999. *Global Transformations, Politics, Economics and Culture.* Cambridge: Polity Press.

Held, David and Anthony McGrew, eds. 2003. *The Global Transformation Reader. An Introduction to the Globalization Debate.* Cambridge: Polity Press.

Hennis, Wilhelm. 1988. *Max Weber: Essays in Reconstruction.* London: Allen Unwin.

Hildebrandt, Thomas. 2002. Waren Jamal Al-Din al-Afghani und Muhammad Abduh Neo-Mu'taziliten? *Die Welt des Islams* 42(2): 207–262.

Hitti, Philip K. ed. 1962. *Islam and the West: A Historical Cultural Survey.* Princeton, NJ: Princeton University Press.

Hirst, Paul and Graham Thompsen. 1995. Globalization and the Future of the Nation State. *Economy and Society* 24(3): 408–442.

Hodgson, Marshall. 1974. *The Venture of Islam: Conscience and History in a World Civilization,* vol. one. Chicago, IL: University of Chicago Press.

Hoffman, Dieter M. 1988. *Renan und das Judentum. Die Bedeutung des Volkes Israel im Werk des "Historien philosophe."* Würzburg: Julius-Maximilians-Universität.

Holt, P.M., Ann K.S. Lambton, and Bernard Lewis. eds. *The Cambridge History of Islam,* two volumes. Cambridge: Cambridge University Press.

Honigsheim, Paul. 2000. *The Unknown Max Weber.* New Brunswick: Transaction.

Hourani, Albert. 1962. *Arabic Thought in the Liberal Age 1798-1939,* reissued with a new preface 1983. Cambridge: Cambridge University Press.

———. 1972. Review of the Cambridge History of Islam. *The English Historical Review* 87(343): 348–357.

———. 1981. The Emergence of the Modern Middle East. Berkeley: University of California Press.

———. 1991a. *A History of the Arab Peoples.* London: Faber and Faber.

———. 1991b. *Islam in European Thought.* Cambridge: Cambridge University Press.

Hübinger, Gangolf. 1994. *Kulturprotestantismus und Politik: Zum Verhältnis von Liberalismus und Protestantismus im wilhelminischen Deutschland.* Tübingen: Mohr.

Huff, Toby E. and Wolfgang Schluchter, eds. 1999. *Max Weber and Islam.* New Brunswick: Transaction.

Humphreys, Stephen R. 1995. *Islamic History. A Framework for Inquiry.* Revised edition. London: I.B. Tauris.

Hung, Ho-Fung. 2003. Orientalist Knowledge and Social Theory: China and the European Conceptions of East-West Differences from 1600 to 1900. *Sociological Theory* 21(3): 254–280.

Hunter, Shireen T. 2009a. Introduction. In *Reformist Voices of Islam. Mediating Islam and Modernity,* edited by Shireen T. Hunter, 3–32. Armonk and London: M.E.Sharpe.

———. 2009b. Islamic Reformist Discourse in Iran: Proponents and Prospects. In *Reformist Voices of Islam. Mediating Islam and Modernity,* edited by Shireen T. Hunter, 33–97. Armonk and London: M.E.Sharpe.

Hurgronje, Christiaan Snouck. 1885 (1923). Aus Arabien. In *Verspreide Geschriften van C. Snouck Hurgronje, Deel III.* Bonn and Leipzig: Kurt Schroeder.

———. 1887 (1923). Über eine Reise nach Mekka. In *Verspreide Geschriften van C. Snouck Hurgronje, Deel III.* Bonn and Leipzig: Kurt Schroeder.

———. 1888. *Mekka. Die Stadt und ihre Herren,* Haag: Martinus Nijhoff.

———. 1889. *Mekka. Aus dem heutigen Leben.* Haag: Martinus Nijhoff.

———. 1899. Besprechung von Eduard Sachaus: Muhammedanisches Recht nach schafiitischer Lehre. *Zeitschrift der Deutschen Morgenländischen Gesellschaft* 53: 125–167.

———. 1903. *Het Gajoland en zijne bevoners: Met en overzichtskaart van de Gajo- en Alaslanden.* Batavia: Landsdrukkerij.

———. 1906a. *The Achehnese.* Vol. I. Translated by A.W.S. O'Sullivan. Leiden: Brill.

———. 1906b. *The Achehnese.* Vol. II. Translated by A.W.S. O'Sullivan. Leiden: Brill.

———. 1907 (1924). L'Arabie et les indes néerlandeaises. In *Verspreide Geschriften van C. Snouck Hurgronje, Deel IV.* Bonn und Leipzig: Kurt Schroeder.

———. 1909. Jong-Turkije, Herinneringen uit Stambol, 25. Juli bis 23 September 1908, *De Gids* 1.

———. 1911 (1924). Politique musulmane de la hollande. In *Verspreide Geschriften van C. Snouck Hurgronje, Deel IV.* Bonn und Leipzig: Kurt Schroeder.

———. 1915a (1923). The Holy War "Made in Germany." In *Verspreide Geschriften van C. Snouck Hurgronje, Deel III.* Bonn and Leipzig: Kurt Schroeder.

———. 1915b (1923). Deutschland und der heilige Krieg. In *Verspreide Geschriften van C. Snouck Hurgronje, Deel III.* Bonn and Leipzig: Kurt Schroeder.

————. 1916a (1923). The Revolt in Arabia. In *Verspreide Geschriften van C. Snouck Hurgronje, Deel III*. Bonn and Leipzig: Kurt Schroeder.

————. 1916b (1989). *Islam: Origin, Religious and Political Growth and Its Present State*. Reprint of Mohammedanism, Lectures on Its Origin, Its Religious and Political Growth and Its Present State. New Delhi: Mittal Publications.

————. 1924. Der Islam. In *Lehrbuch der Religionsgeschichte*, 4. vollständig neu bearbeitete Ausgabe. Tübingen: J.C.B. Mohr.

————. 1931. Theodor Nöldeke. *Zeitschrift der Deutschen Morgenländischen Gesellschaft* 10: 239–281.

Huq, Mozammel and Michael Tribe. 2004. Economic Development in a Changing Globlized Economy. *Journal of International Development* 16(7): 911–923.

Ibrahim, Haslina. 1999. Free Will and Predestination: A Comparative Study of the Views of Abu Al-Hassan Al-Ash'ri and Muhammad 'Abduh, unpublished MA thesis, Kulliya of Islamic Revealed Knowledge and Human Sciences, International Islamic University Malaysia.

Irwin, Robert. 2006. *For Lust of Knowing. The Orientalists and their Enemies*. London: Penguin Books.

Iqbal, Muhammad. 2006. *Speeches, Writings and Statements of Iqbal*. Edited by Latif Ahmad Sherwani. New Delhi: Adam Publishers.

Jackson, Robert H. 1990. *Quasi-States: Sovereignty, International Relations, and the Third World*. Cambridge: Cambridge University Press.

Jäschke, Gotthart. 1941. Islamforschung der Gegenwart: Martin Harmann zum Gedächtnis. *Die Welt des Islams* 23 (1941): 111–121.

Jansen, J.J.G. 1980. *The Interpretation of the Koran in Modern Egypt*. Leiden: Brill.

Joas, Hans. 1993. Durkheim und der Pragmatismus. Bewusstseinspsychologie und die soziale Konstitution der fundamentalen Kategorien. In Emile Durkheim, *Schriften zur Soziologie der Erkenntnis*. Frankfurt a. M.: Suhrkamp.

Johansen, Baber. 1967. *Muhammad Husain Haikal. Europa und der Orient im Weltbild eines ägyptischen Liberalen*. Beirut: Orient-Institut der Deutschen Morgenländischen Gesellschaft

————. 1999. *Contingency in a Sacred Law: Legal and Ethical Norms in the Muslim Fiqh*. Leiden: Brill.

Jones, Robert Alun. 1999. *The Development of Durkheim's Social Realism*. Cambridge: Cambridge University Press.

Juergensmeyer, Mark. 2003. *Terror in the Mind of God. The Global Rise of Religious Violence*. Berkeley: University of California Press.

Jung, Martin H. 2000. *Der Protestantismus ind Deutschland von 1815 bis 1870*. Leipzig: Evangelische Verlagsanstalt.

Jung, Dietrich 2001a. *Turkey at the Crossroads: Ottoman Legacies and a Greater Middle East*, with Wolfango Piccoli. London: ZED.

————. 2001b. The Political Sociology of World Society. *European Journal of International Relations* 7(4): 443–474.

————. 2004a. World Society, Systems Theory and the Classical Sociology of Modernity. In *Observing International Relations: Niklas Luhmann and World Politics*, edited by Mathias Albert and Lena Hilkermeier, 103–118. London: Routledge.

————. Jung, Dietrich. 2004b. Global Conditions and Global Constraints: The International Paternity of the Palestine Conflict. In *The Middle East and Palestine. Global Politics and Regional Conflict*, edited by Dietrich Jung, 3–36. New York: Palgrave McMillan.

Jung, Dietrich, Klaus Schlichte and Jens Siegelberg. 2003. *Kriege in der Weltgesellschaft. Strukturgeschichtliche Erklärung kriegerischer Gewalt (1945-2002)*. Wiesbaden: Westdeutscher Verlag.

Käsler, Dirk 1988. *Max Weber: An Introduction to His Life and Work,* translated by Philippa Hurd. Cambridge: Polity Press.

Kamali, Mohammad H. 2000. Law and Society. The Interplay of Revelation and Reason in the Sharia. In *The Oxford History of Islam,* edited by John L. Esposito, 107–153. Oxford: Oxford University Press.

Karachouli, Regina 1994. Vermutungen über das Orientbild des Leipziger Arabisten. Heinrich Leberecht Fleischer (1801–1888). In *Gedenkschrift Wolfgang Reuschel,* edited by Dieter Bellmann, 175–184. Stuttgart: Franz Steiner.

Karpat, Kemal H. 1972. The Transformation of the Ottoman State, 1779-1908. *International Journal of Middle East Studies* 3: 243–281.

Keddie, Nikki R. 1972. Sayyid Jamal al-Din al-Afghani: A Political Biography. Berkeley: University of California Press.

———. 1983. *An Islamic Response to Imperialism. Political and Religious Writings of Sayyid Jamal ad-Din "al-Afghani."* Berkeley: University of California Press.

———. 2005. Sayyid Jamal al-Din 'al-Afghani'. In *Pioneers of Islamic Revival,* edited by Ali Rahnema, 11–29. New edition. London: Zed books

Kelsay, John 2007. *Arguing the Just War in Islam.* Cambridge, MA: Harvard University Press.

Kemal, Namik. 1962. *Renan Müdafaanamesi (Islamiyet ve Maarif).* Ankara: Milli Kültür Yayinlari.

Kepel, Gilles. 2002. *Jihad. The Trail of Political Islam.* Cambridge, MA: The Belknap Press of Harvard University Press.

Kerr, Malcom. 1960a. Rashid Rida and Islamic Legal Reform: An Ideological Analysis – Part I. *The Muslim World* 50(2): 99–108.

———. 1960b. Rashid Rida and Islamic Legal Reform: An Ideological Analysis – Part II, *The Muslim World* 50(2): 170–181.

———. 1966. *Islamic Reform. The Political and Legal Theories of Muhammad Abduh and Rashid Rida.* Berkeley: University of California Press.

———. 1980. Orientalism – Book Review. *International Journal of Middle East Studies* 12: 544–547.

Kessler, Clive S. 2000. Globalization: Another False Universalism? *Third World Quarterly* 21(6): 931–942.

Khalidi, Omar. 2003. Mawlana Mawdudi and the Future Political Order in British India. *The Muslim World* 93(3/4): 415–427.

Khatab, Sayed. 2006. *The Power of Sovereignty. The Political and Ideological Philosophy of Sayyid Qutb.* London: Routledge.

Khatami, S. Mohammad. 1998. "Text of Speech Delivered by H.E. Seyyed Mohammad Khatami President of the Islamic Republic of Iran at the UN General Assembly." *Iranian Journal of International Affairs* 10(1/2): 127–136.

Khomeini, A.R. 1981. *Islam and Revolution. Writings and Declarations of Imam Khomeini.* Translated by Hamid Algar. Berkeley, CA: Mizan Press.

Kinzer, Stephen. 2001. *Crescent and Star: Turkey Between Two Worlds.* New York: Farrar, Straus and Giroux.

Kippenberg, Hans G. 1993. Max Weber im Kreise von Religionswissenschaftlern. *Zeitschrift für Religions- und Gesellschaftsgeschichte* 45(1): 348–366.

Kopf, David. 1980. Hermeneutics versus History. *Journal of Asian Studies* 39(3): 495–506.

Köpf, Ulrich. 2002. Tübinger Schulen. In *Theologische Realenzyklopädie.* Berlin: Walter de Gruyter.

Körner, Felix. 2006. *Alter Text - neuer Kontext. Koranhermeneutik in der Türkei heute,* eingeleitet, übersetzt und kommentiert von Felix Körner SJ. Herder: Freiburg, Basel und Wien.

Koningsveld, P. Sj. van. ed. 1985. *Orientalism and Islam, the Letters of C. Snouck Hurgronje to Th. Nöldeke from the Tübingen University Library.* Leiden: Brill.

Koselleck, Reinhart. 1979. *Kritik und Krise.* Neuauflage, Frankfurt a.M.: Suhrkamp.

Kramer, Martin. 1989. Arabistik and Arabism: The Passions of Martin Hartmann. *Middle Eastern Studies* 25(3): 283–300.

Krämer, Gudrun. 1999. *Gottes Staat als Republik. Reflexionen zeitgenössischer Muslime zu Islam, Menschenrechten und Demokratie.* Baden-Baden: Nomos.

Kratz, Reinhard G. 2003. Wellhausen, Julius (1844–1918). In *Theologische Realenzyklopädie,* vol. 35. Berlin: Walter de Gruyter.

Krech, Volkhard. 2002. *Wissenschaft und Religion. Studien zur Geschichte der Religionsforschung in Deutschland 1871–1933.* Tübingen: Mohr Siebeck.

Krüger, Hilmar. 2000/2001. The Study of Islamic Law in Germany: A Review of Recent Books on Islamic Law. *Journal of Law and Religion* 15(1/2): 303–330.

Küenzlen, Gottfried. 1980. *Die Religionssoziologie Max Webers.* Berlin: Duncker and Humblot.

———. 1978. Unbekannte Quellen der Religionssoziologie Max Webers. *Zeitschrift für Soziologie* 7: 215–227.

Kushner, David. 1977. *The Rise of Turkish Nationalism.* London: Frank Cass.

Kurzmann, Charles. 1998. ed. *Liberal Islam - A Sourcebook.* Oxford: Oxford University Press.

Laffan, Michael F. 2002. *Islamic Nationhood and Colonial Indonesia: The Umma Below the Winds.* London: Routledge/Curzon.

Laldin, Mohamad Akram. 2006. *Introduction to Shariah and Islamic Jurisprudence.* Kuala Lumpur: CERT Publications.

Landau, Jacob M. 1990. *The Politics of Pan-Islam.* Oxford: Clarendon Press.

Lapidus, Ira M. 1975. The Separation of State and Religion in the Development of Early Islamic Society. *International Journal of Middle Eastern Studies* 6: 363–385.

———. 1983. *Contemporary Islamic Movements in Historical Perspective, Policy Papers in International Affairs,* Number 18. Berkeley: University of California.

———. 2002. *A History of Islamic Societies.* Second edition. Cambridge: Cambridge University Press.

Lassner, Jacob. 1999. Abraham Geiger: A Nineteenth-Century Jewish Reformer on the Origins of Islam. In *The Jewish Discovery of Islam: Studies in Honor of Bernard Lewis,* edited by Martin Kramer, 103–135. Tel Aviv: Moshe Dayan Center and Tel Aviv University.

Lawrence, Bruce, ed. 2006. *Messages to the World. The Statements of Osama Bin Laden.* London: Verso.

Lee, David C.J. 1996. *Ernest Renan: In the Shadow of Faith.* London: Duckworth.

LeGouis, Catherine. 1997. *Positivism and Imagination: Scientism and Its Limits in Emile Hennequin, Wilhelm Scherer, and Dimitri Pisarev.* Cranbury and London: Associated University Press.

Lelyveld, David. 1996. *Aligarh's First Generation. Muslim Solidarity in British India.* New Delhi: Oxford University Press.

Lepsius, Rainer M. 1990. *Interessen, Ideen und Institutionen.* Opladen: Westdeutscher Verlag.

Lessing, Eckhard. 2000. *Geschichte der deutschsprachigen evangelischen Theologie von Albrecht Ritschl bis zur Gegenwart, Band 1: 1870–1918.* Göttingen: Vandenhoeck and Ruprecht.

Lewis, Bernard. 1988. *The Political Language of Islam.* Chicago, IL: The University of Chicago Press.

———. 1990. The Roots of Muslim Rage. *The Atlantic Monthly* 266(3): 47–60.

———. 1993. The Question of Orientalism, chapter 6 of his *Islam and the West,* reprinted in *Orientalism. A Reader,* edited by A.L. Macfie, 249–272. 2000. Edinburgh: Edinburgh University Press.

Lewis, Geoffrey. 1975. The Ottoman Proclamation of Jihad in 1914. *The Islamic Quarterly* 19 (3/4): 157–163.

Lia, Brynjar 1998. *The Society of the Muslim Brothers in Egypt: The Rise of an Islamic Mass Movement 1928-1942*. Reading: Garnet.

Lichtblau, Klaus. 1999. Differentiations of Modernity. *Theory, Culture and Society* 16(3): 1–30.

Littman, Enno. 1936. Christiaan Snouck Hurgronje. *Zeitschrift der Deutschen Morgenländischen Gesellschaft* 90: 445–458.

Livingston, John W. 1995. Muhammad 'Abduh on Science. *The Muslim World* 85(3/4): 215–234.

Lockman, Zachary. 2004. *Contending Visions of the Middle East: The History and Politics of Orientalism*. Cambridge: Cambridge University Press.

Lombard, Maurice. 1971. *L'Islam dans sa première grandeur*. Paris: Flammarion.

Lozachmeur, Hélène. 2007. Le Cabinet du Corpus Inscriptionum Semiticarum. http://www.aibl.fr (accessed in July 2007).

Luckmann, Thomas. 1963. *Das Problem der Religion in der modernen Gesellschaft*. Freiburg: Rombach.

Luhmann, Niklas. 1970. Öffentliche Meinung. *Politische Vierteljahresschrift* 11(1): 2–28.

———. 1981. Geschichte als Prozess und die Theorie sozio-kultureller Evolution. In Niklas Luhmann, *Soziologische Aufklärung*, Band 3. Opladen: Westdeutscher Verlag.

———. 1985. Society, Meaning, Religion—Based on Self-Reference. *Sociological Analysis*, 64(1): 5–20.

———. 1986. *Ökologische Kommunikation: Kann sich die moderne Gesellschaft auf ökologische Gefährdungen einstellen?* Opladen: Westdeutscher Verlag.

———. 1990. The World Society as a Social System. In Niclas Luhmann, *Essays on Self-Reference*. New York: Columbia University Press.

———. 1991. *Soziale Systeme: Grundriss einer allgemeinen Theorie*. Frankfurt a.M.: Suhrkamp.

Lukauskas, Arvid. 1999. Managing Mobile Capital: Recent Scholarship on the Political Economy of International Finance. *Review of International Political Economy* 6(2): 262–287.

Lukes, Steven. 1969. Durkeim's 'Individualism and the Intellectuals.' In *Emile Durkheim: Critical Assessments*. Volume IV, edited by Peter Hamilton, 166–183. London and New York: Routledge (reprint 1990).

———. 1985. *Emile Durkhiem: His Life and Work, A Historical and Critical Study:* Stanford, CA: Stanford University Press.

Lumbard, Joseph E.B. ed. 2004. *Islam, Fundamentalism, and the Betrayal of Tradition: Essays by Western Muslim Scholars*. Bloomington, IN: World Wisdom.

Lutfi al-Sayyid, Afaf. 1968. Egypt and Cromer: A Study in Anglo-Egyptian Relations. London: John Murray.

Lynch, Marc. 2006. *Voices of the New Arab Public: Iraq, al-Jazeera, and Middle East Politics Today*. New York: Columbia University Press.

MacEoin, Denis and Ahmed Al-Shahi, eds. 1983. *Islam in the Modern World*. New York: St. Martin's Press.

Macfie A.L. ed. 2000. Introduction. In *Orientalism: A Reader*, edited by A.L. Macfie. Edinburgh: Edinburgh University Press.

Mahmoudi, Abdelrashid. 1998. *Taha Husain's Education: From the Azhar to the Sorbonne*. London: Curzon.

Makdisi, Ussama. 2002. After 1860: Debating Religion, Reform, and Nationalism in the Ottoman Empire. *International Journal of Middle East Studies* 34(4): 601–617.

Malik, Hafeez and Lynda P. Malik. 1971. The Life of the Poet-Philosopher *Iqbal: Poet-Philosopher of Pakistan,* edited by Hafeez Malik, 3–20. New York: Columbia University Press.

Mangold, Sabine. 2004. *Eine "weltbürgerliche Wissenschaft"—Die deutsche Orientalistik im 19. Jahrhundert.* Stuttgart: Frank Steiner Verlag.

Mani, Lata and Ruth Frankenberg. 1985. The Challenge of Orientalism. *Economy and Society* 14(2): 174–192.

Mann, Golo. 1992. *Deutsche Geschichte des 19. und 20. Jahrhunderts.* Frankfurt a.M.: Fischer.

Mann, Thomas. 1918 (2002). *Betrachtungen eines Unpolitischen.* Frankfurt a.M.: Fischer.

Manuel, Frank E. 1962. *The Prophets of Paris.* Cambridge, MA: Harvard University Press.

Marchand, Suzanne L. 2009. *German Orientalism in the Age of Empire. Religion, Race, and Scholarship.* Cambridge: Cambridge University Press.

Marden, Peter. 2003. *The Decline of Politics: Governance, Globalization and the Public Sphere.* Aldershot: Ashgate.

Mardin, Serif. 1988. Freedom in an Ottoman Perspective. In *State, Democracy and the Military: Turkey in the 1980s,* edited by in: Ahmet Evin and Metin Heper, 23–35. Berlin: Campus.

Marti, Urs. 1988. *Michel Foucault.* Munich: C.H Beck.

Marty E. Martin and R. Scott Appleby. 1994. *Introduction.* In *Accounting for Fundamentalisms: The Dynamic Character of Movements,* edited by Martin E. Marty and R. Scott Appleby, 1–12. Chicago, IL: The University of Chicago Press.

Marx, Karl and Frederick Engels. 1848 (1976). Manifesto of the Communist Party. In *Collected Works, Volume 6.* London: Lawrence and Wishart.

Matthes, Joachim. 1967. *Religion und Gesellschaft, Einführung in die Religionssoziologie I.* Reinbek: Rowohlt.

———. 1993. Was ist anders an anderen Religionen? Anmerkungen zur zentristischen Organisation des religionssoziologischen Denkens. In *Religion und Kultur,* edited by Jörg Bergmann, Alois Hahn and Thomas Luckmann, 16–30. Opladen: Westdeutscher Verlag.

McGregor, Andrew. 2003. "Jihad and the Rifle Alone": Abdullah Azzam and the Islamist Revolution. *The Journal of Conflict Studies* 22(2): 92–113.

McGuigan, Jim. 1996. *Culture and the Public Sphere.* London: Routledge.

McGuire, Meredith B. 2003. Contested Meanings and Definitional Boundaries: Historicizing the Sociology of Religion. *Defining Religion: Investigation the Boundaries between the Sacred and the Secular,* edited by Arthur L. Greil and David G. Bromley, 127–138. Oxford: Elsevier Science.

McLeod, Hugh 1996. *Piety and Poverty: Working-Class Religion in Berlin, London and New York, 1870-1914.* New York: Homes and Meier.

———. 2003. Introduction. In *The Decline of Christendom in Western Europe, 1750-2000,* edited by Hugh McLeod, 1–28. Cambridge: Cambridge University Press.

Menemencioglu, Nermin. 1967. Namik Kemal Abroad: A Centenary. *Middle Eastern Studies* 4(1): 29–49.

Ménoret, Pascal. 2005. *The Saudi Enigma: A History.* London: ZED books.

Menzel, Ulrich. 1991. Das Ende der "Dritten Welt" und das Scheitern der grossen Theorie. Zur Soziologie einer Disziplin in auch selbstkritischer Absicht. *Politische Vierteljahresschrift* 32(1): 4–33.

Messick, Brinkley. 1993. *The Calligraphic State: Textual Domination and History in a Muslim Society.* Berkeley: University of California Press.

Meyer, John W., John Boli, George Thomas and Francisco Ramirez. 1997. World Society and the Nation State. *American Journal of Sociology* 103(1): 144–181.

Meyer, Michael. 1988. *Response to Modernity: A History of the Reform Movement in Judaism.* Oxford: Oxford University Press.

Michaelis, Paul. 1913. *Philosophie und Dichtung bei Ernest Renan.* Berlin: Verlag von Emil Ebering.

Minear, Richard H. 1980. Orientalism and the Study of Japan. *The Journal of Asian Studies,* 39(3): 507–517.

Mitchell, Marion M. 1931. Emile Durkheim and the Philosophy of Nationalism. *Political Science Quarterly* 46(1): 87–106. Reprinted in *Emile Durkheim: Critical Assessments,* vol. 4, edited by Peter Hamilton, 113–127. 1990. London: Routledge.

Mitchell, Richard P. 1969. *The Society of the Muslim Brothers.* London: Oxford University Press.

Mitchell, Timothy. 1988. *Colonising Egypt.* Cambridge: Cambridge University Press.

———. 1989. The World as Exhibition. *Comparative Studies in Society and History* 31(2): 217–36.

Mittelman, James H. 2000. Globalization: Captors and Captive. *Third World Quarterly* 21(6): 917–929.

Mommsen, Wolfgang J. 2006 (1987). Introduction. In *Max Weber and His Contemporaries,* edited by Wolfgang J. Mommsen and Jürgen Osterhammel, 1–22. London: Routledge.

Mongia, Padimini, ed. 1996. *Contemporary Postcolonial Theory, A Reader.* London: Arnold.

Moten, Abdul Rashid. 2003. *Revolution to Revolution: Jamaat-e-Islami in the Politics of Pakistan.* Karachi: Royal Book Company.

Motzki, Harald, ed. 2000. *The Biography of Muhammad: The Issue of the Sources.* Leiden: Brill.

Moussalli, Ahmad S. 1992. *Radical Islamic Fundamentalism: The Ideological and Political Discourse of Sayyid Qutb.* Beirut: American University of Beirut.

Muir, Edward. 1997. *Ritual in Early Modern Europe.* Cambridge: Cambridge University Press.

Müller, Guido. 1991. *Weltpolitische Bildung und akademische Reform. Carl Heinrich Beckers Wissenschafts- und Hochschulpolitik 1908-1930.* Cologne/Weimar and Vienna: Böhlau Verlag.

Müller, Hans-Peter. 1999. Emile Durkheim (1858–1917). In *Klassiker der Soziologie, Band 1: Von Auguste Comte bis Norbert Elias,* edited by Dirk Käsler, 150–170. Munich: C.H. Beck.

Münch, Richard. 1998. *Globale Dynamik, lokale Lebenswelten: Der schwierige Weg in die Weltgesellschaft.* Frankfurt: Suhrkamp.

———. 2001. *Offene Räume, soziale Integration diesseits und jenseits des Nationalstaats.* Frankfurt: Suhrkamp.

Musallam, Adnan A. 2005. From Secularism to Jihad. Sayyid Qutb and the Foundations of Radical Islam. Praeger: Westport and London.

Nagel, Tilman. 1981. Gab es in der islamischen Geschichte Ansätze einer Säkularisierung? In *Studien zur Geschichte und Kultur des Vorderen Orients,* edited by Hans Roemer and Albrecht Noth, 275–289. Leiden: Brill.

Nakash, Yitzhak. 2003. *The Shi'is of Iraq.* Second edition. Princeton, NJ: Princeton University Press.

Nasr, Seyyed Vali Reza. 1994. *The Vanguard of the Islamic Revolution: The Jama'at-i Islami of Pakistan.* London: I.B. Tauris.

———. 1996. *Mawdudi and the Making of Islamic Revivalism.* Oxford: Oxford University Press.

———. 2005. Mawdudi and the Jama'at-i Islami: The Origins, Theory and Practice of Islamic Revivalism. In *Pioneers of Islamic Revival,* edited by Ali Rahnema, 98–124. New edition. London: Zed books.

Nicholson, Ernest. 1998. *The Pentateuch in the Twentieth Century. The Legacy of Julius Wellhausen,* Oxford: Clarendon Press.

Nietzsche, Friedrich 1902. *Friedrich Nietzsches gesammelte Briefe, zweiter Band.* Edited by Elisabeth Förster-Nietzsche und Fritz Schöll. Berlin and Leipzig: Schuster and Löffler.

Nipperdey, Thomas. 1988. *Religion im Umbruch: Deutschland 1870-1918.* Munich: C.H. Beck.

Noer, Deliar. 1973. *The Modernist Muslim Movement in Indonesia 1900-1942.* Singapor and Kuala Lumpur: Oxford University Press.

Nöldeke, Theodor. 1884. Brief an J. Singer. In J. Singer, *Sollen Juden Christen werden? Ein offenes Wort an Freund und Feind.* Vienna: Verlag von Oskar Frank.

Nordbruch, Goetz. 2006. Defending the French Revolution during World War II: Raif Khoury and the Intellectual Challenge of Nazism in the Levant. *Mediterranean Historical Review* 21(2): 219–238.

Noth, Albrecht. 1980. Die Scharia, das religiöse Gesetz des Islam- Wandlungsmöglichkeiten, Anwendung und Wirkung. In *Entstehung und Wandel rechtlicher Traditionen* , edited by W. Fikentscher, W. Franke, and H. Köhler, 415–437. Freiburg and Munich: Alber.

———. 1987. Früher Islam. *Geschichte der arabischen Welt*, edited by Ulrich Haarmann, 11–100. Munich: C.H. Beck.

Al-Nowaihi, Mohamed. 1980. Towards the Reappraisal of Classical Arabic Literature and History: Some Aspects of Taha Husayn's Use of Modern Western Criteria. *International Journal of Middle East Studies* 11(2): 189–207.

Nowak, Kurt. 1998. Symbolisierung des Unendlichen. Ernest Renan und sein Verhältnis zum Protestantismus. *Zeitschrift für Kirchengeschichte* 109(1): 59–79.

Önish, Ziya. 2006. The Political Economy of Islam and Democracy in Turkey: From the Welfare Party to the AKP. In *Democratization and Development: New Political Strategies for the Middle East,* edited by Dietrich Jung, 103–128. New York: Palgrave MacMillan.

Önish, Ziya and Ahmet F. Aysan. 2000. Neoliberal Globalisation, the Nation-State and Financial Crises in the Semi-Periphery: A Comparative Analysis. *Third World Quarterly* 21(1): 119–139.

Olender, Maurice. 1992. *The Languages of Paradise. Race, Religion, and Philology in the Nineteenth Century.* Cambridge, MA: Harvard University Press.

Osman, Fathi. 2003. Mawdudi's Contribution to the Development of Modern Islamic Thinking in the Arabic-Speaking World. *The Muslim World* 93(3/4): 465–485.

Osterhammel, Jürgen. 1997. Edward W. Said und die "Orientalismus"-Debatte. Ein Rückblick. *asien afrika lateinamerika* 25 (1997): 597–607.

Owen, Roger. 1973. Studying Islamic History. *Journal of Interdisciplinary History* 4(2): 287–298.

———. 2004. Lord Cromer. Victorian Imperialist, Edwardian Proconsul. Oxford: Oxford University Press.

Özelli, M.T. 1974. The Evolution of the Formal Educational System and its Relation to Economic Growth Policies in the First Turkish Republic. *International Journal of Middle East Studies* 5: 77–92.

Pals, Daniel L. 1996. *Seven Theories of Religion.* Oxford: Oxford University Press.

Paret, Rudi 1930. *Die Legendäre Maghazi-Literatur.* Tübingen: J.C.B. Mohr.

Paris, Roland 2002. International Peacebuilding and the "Mission Civilisatrice." *Review of International Studies* 28: 637–656.

Paret, Rudi. 1968. *The Study of Arabic and Islam at German Universities: German Orientalists since Theodor Nöldeke.* Wiesbaden: Franz Steiner.

Parla, Taha. 1985. The Social and Political Thought of Ziya Gökalp 1876–1924. Leiden: Brill.

Patai, Raphael. 1987. *Ignaz Goldziher and His Oriental Diary: A Translation and Psychological Protrait.* Detroit, MI: Wayne State University Press.

Paul, Jürgen. 2003. Max Weber und die "Islamische Stadt." In *Max Webers Religionssoziologie in interkultureller Perspektive,* edited by Hartmut Lehmann and Jean Martin

Ouédraogo, 109–137. Göttingen: Vandenhoeck and Ruprecht.

Peters, Bernhard. 1994a. Der Sinn von Öffentlichkeit. In *Öffentlichkeit, öffentliche Meinung, soziale Bewegungen,* edited by Friedhelm Neidhardt, 42–76. Opladen: Westdeutscher Verlag.

Peters, F.E. 1991. The Quest of the Historical Muhammad. *International Journal of Middle East Studies* 23 (1991): 291–315.

Peters, Rudolph. 1989. Erneuerungsbewegungen im Islam vom 18. Bis zum 20. Jahrhundert und die Rolle des Islam in der neueren Geschichte: Antikolonialismus und Nationalismus. In *Der Islam in der Gegenwart,* edited by Werner Ende and Udo Steinbach, 91–131. Munich: C.H.Beck.

———. 1994b. The Islamization of Criminal Law: A Comparative Analysis. *Die Welt des Islams* 34: 246–273.

Peyre, Henri. 1969. *Renan.* Paris: Presses Universitaires de France.

———. 2007. *Émile Durkheim.* In Encyclopedia Britannica, www.britannica.com (accessed: August 2007).

Pickering, W.S.F. 1975. *Durkheim on Religion: A Selection of Readings with Bibliographies.* London: Rutledge and Kegan Paul.

———. 1984. *Durkheim's Sociology of Religion: Themes and Theories.* London: Routledge and Kegan Paul.

Pieterse, Jan Nederveen. 1995. Globalization as Hybridization. In *Global Modernities,* edited by Mike Featherstone, Scott Lash and Roland Robertson, 45–68. London: Sage.

Pietsch, Walter. 1999. *Zwischen Reform und Orthodoxie. Der Eintritt des ungarischen Judentums in die moderne Welt.* Berlin: Philo Verlagsanstalt.

Piscatori, James P. 1986. *Islam in a World of Nation-States.* Cambridge: Cambridge University Press.

Pitt, Alan. 2000. The Cultural Impact of Science in France: Ernest Renan and the *Vie de Jésus. The Historical Journal* 43: 79–101.

Plé, Bernhard. 1996. *Die "Welt" aus den Wissenschaften. Der Positivismus in Frankreich, England und Italien von 1848 bis ins zweite Jahrzehnt des 20. Jahrhunderts, eine wissenssoziologische Studie.* Stuttgart: Klett-Cotta.

Poggi, Gianfranco. 2001. *Forms of Power.* Cambridge: Cambridge University Press.

Pouchepadass, Jacques. 2004. Que reste-t-il des Subaltern Studies? *Critique internationale* 24 (July): 67–79.

Poulton, Hugh. 1997. *Top Hat, Grey Wolf and Crescent - Turkish Nationalism and the Turkish Republic.* London: Hurst.

Preissler, Holger. 1990. Friedrich Rückert und Heinrich Leberecht Fleischer. Beziehungen zwischen zwei Orientalisten. In *Friedrich Rückert. Dichter und Sprachgelehrter in Erlangen,* edited by Wolfdietrich Fischer and Rainer Gömmel, 23–34. Neustadt and der Aisch: Verlag Degener.

Qaradawi, al-, Yusuf. 2001. *The Lawful and the Prohibited in Islam.* Translated by Kamal El-Helbawy, M. Moinuddin Siddiqui and Syed Shurky. Kuala Lumpur: Islamic Book Trust.

Qutb, Sayyid. 1991. *Maalim fi al-tariq* (Singposts on the Road). Fourteenth edition. Cairo and Beirut: n.p.

———. 2000. *Social Justice in Islam.* Translated from the Arabic by John B. Hardie, translation revised and introduction by Hamid Algar. Kuala Lumpur: Islamic Book Trust.

Rammstedt, Otthein. 1988. Die Attitüden der Klassiker als unsere soziologischen Selbstverständlichkeiten. Durkheim, Simmel, Weber und die Konstitution der modernen Soziologie. In *Simmel und die frühen Soziologen. Nähe und Distanz zu Durkheim, Tönnies und Max Weber,* edited by Otthein Rammstedt, 275–307. Frankfurt a. M.: Suhrkamp.

Reckwitz, Andreas. 2000. *Die Transformation der Kulturtheorien: Zur Entwicklung eines Theorie-programms.* Weilerswist: Velbrück Wissenschaft.

———. 2006. *Das hybride Subjekt: Eine Theorie der Subjektkulturen von der bürgerlichen Moderne zur Postmoderne.* Weilerswist: Velbrück Wissenschaft.

Reid, Donald Malcolm. 1987. Cairo University and the Orientalists. *International Journal of Middle East Studies* 19: 51–76.

———. 1990. *Cairo University and the Making of Modern Egypt.* Cambridge: Cambridge University Press.

Reinkowski, Maurus 2005. Gewohnheitsrecht im multinationalen Staat: Die Osmanen und der albanische Kanun. In *Rechtspluralismus in der Islamischen Welt: Gewohnheitsrecht zwischen Staat und Gesellschaft,* edited by Michael Kemper and Maurus Reinkowski, 121–142. Berlin: Walter de Gruyter.

Renan, Ernest. 1863 (1991). *The Life of Jesus.* New York: Prometheus Books.

———. 1866. *Averroès et L'Averroïsme. Essai Historique.* Paris: Michel Lévy.

———. 1870. Renan an Strauss (letter of Ernest Renan to David-Friedrich Strauss). In Strauss, David Friedrich 1870. *Krieg und Friede. Zwei Briefe an Ernst Renan nebst dessen Antwort auf den ersten,* Leipzig: Verlag von S. Hirzel.

———. 1882 (1992). Qu'est-ce qu'une nation? Conférence faite en Sorbonne, le 11 mars 1882. In Ernest Renan, *Qu'est-ce qu'une nation? Et autres essais politiques.* Paris: Presses Pocket.

———. 1883a (1992). Le Judaïsme comme race et comme religion, in: Ernest Renan: *Qu'est-ce qu'une nation? Et autres essais politiques.* Paris: Presses Pocket.

———. 1883b. Islamism and Science. In *Poetry of the Celtic Races and other Essays by Ernest Renan.* London: Walter Scott Publishing (no date).

———. 1890. *L'Avenir de la science - Pensées de 1848 -.* Paris: Ancienne Maison Michel Lévy Frères.

———. 1936. *Souvenirs d'enfance et de jeunesse.* Paris: Nelson and Calmann-Lévy.

Repp, Richard C. 1988. Qanun and Shari'a in the Ottoman Context. In *Islamic law. Social and Historical Contexts,* edited by Aziz al-Azmeh, 124–145. London: Routledge.

Rida, Rashid. 1938. *Le califat. Dans la doctrine de Rashid Rida.* Translated by Henri Laoust. Beirut: Mémoires de l'instutut francais de damas.

Richardson, Michael. 1990. Enough Said. Reflections on Orientalism. *Anthropology Today* 6(4): 16–19.

Ringer, Fritz. 1969. *The Decline of the German Mandarins. The German Academic Community, 1890-1933.* Cambridge, MA: Harvard University Press.

———. 1992. *Fields of Knowledge: French Academic Culture in Comparative Perspective 1890-1920.* Cambridge: Cambridge University Press.

———. 2000. *Toward a Social History of Knowledge: Collected Essays.* New York: Berghahn Books.

Ritschl, Otto. 1892. *Albrecht Ritschls Leben, Erster Band, 1822-1864.* Freiburg: Mohr.

———. 1896. *Albrecht Ritschls Leben, Zweiter Band, 1864-1889.* Freiburg: Mohr.

Rittelmeyer, Friedrich. 1920. *Friedrich Nietzsche und die Religion.* Munich: Christian Kaiser Verlag.

Ritter, Heinrich. 1865. *Ernest Renan über die Naturwissenschaften und die Geschichte mit den Randbemerkungen eines deutschen Philosophen.* Gotha: Friedrich Andreas Perthes Verlag.

Ritter, Hellmut. 1922. Book Review: Die Richtungen der islamischen Koranauslegung *Der Islam* 12: 114–122.

———. 1937. Carl Heinrich Becker als Orientalist. *Der Islam* 24: 175–185.

Ritzer, Georg. 2003. Globalization: Glocalization/Grobalization and Something/Nothing. *Sociological Theory* 21(3): 193–209.

Robertson, J.M. 1924. *Ernest Renan.* London: Watts and Co.

Robertson, Roland. 1992a. *Globalization, Social Theory and Global Culture.* London: SAGE publications.

———. 1992b. Globality, Global Culture, and Images of World Order. In *Social Change and Modernity,* edited by Hans Haferkamp and Neil J. Smelser, 395–411. Berkeley: University of California Press.

———. 1993. Community, Society, Globality, and the Category of Religion. In *Secularization, Rationalism and Sectarianism, Essays in Honour of Bryan R. Wilson,* edited by Eileen Barker, James A. Beckford, and Karel Dobbelaere, 1–17. Oxford: Clarendon Press.

———. 1994. Religion and the Global Field. *Social Compass* 41(1): 121–135.

Robinson, Francis. 2000. *Islam and Muslim History in South Asia.* New Delhi: Oxford University Press.

Robotka, Bettina. 1996. Iqbal und Deutschland. In *Fremde Erfahrungen. Asiaten und Afrikaner in Deutschland, Österreich und in der Schweiz bis 1945,* edited by Gerhard Höpp, 347–358. Berlin: Das Arabische Buch.

Rodinson, Maxime. 1966. *Islam et capitalisme.* Paris: Ed. du Seuil.

———. 1974. The Western Image and Western Studies of Islam. In *The Legacy of Islam,* edited by Joseph Schacht and C.E. Bosworth, 9–62. Oxford: Clarendon Press.

———. 1988. *Europe and the Mystique of Islam.* Translated by Roger Veinus. (Published in French 1980). London: I.B. Tauris.

Rogers, Howard J., ed. 1906. *Arts and Science. Universal Exposition, St. Louis 1904,* two volumes. Boston and New York: Houghton, Mifflin and Company.

Rogerson, J.W. 1995. *The Bible and Criticism in Victorian Britain: Profiles of F.D. Maurice and William Robertson Smith.* Sheffield: Sheffield Academic Press.

Rohls, Jan. 1997a. *Protestantische Theologie der Neuzeit I.* Tübingen: J.C.B. Mohr.

———. 1997b. *Protestantische Theologie der Neuzeit II.* Tübingen: J.C.B. Mohr.

Roman, Joël. 1992. Introduction. In Ernest Renan, *Qu'est-ce qu'une nation? Et autres essais politiques.* Paris: Presses Pocket.

Rougier, Bernard. 2004. Religious Mobilization in Palestinian Refugee Camps in Lebanon: The Case of ain al-Helweh. In *The Middle East and Palestine: Global Politics and Regional Conflict,* edited by Dietrich Jung, 151–182. New York: Palgrave MacMillan.

Roy, Olivier. 1999. The Crisis of Religious Legitimacy in Iran. *Middle East Journal* 53(2): 201–216.

———. 2004. *Globalised Islam: The Search for a New Ummah.* London: Hurst and Company.

Rudolph, Kurt. 1983. Wellhausen as an Arabist. *Semeia* 25: 111–155.

Ruggie, John G. 1993. Territoriality and Beyond: Problematizing Modernity in International Relations. *International Organization* 47(1): 139–147.

Ryad, Umar. 2002. Rashid Rida and a Danish Missionary: Alfred Nielsen (d. 1963) and Three *Fatwas* from al-Manar. *IslamoChristiana* 28: 87–107.

———. 2008. *Islamic Reformism and Christianity: A Critical Reading of the Works of Muhammad Rashid Rida and his Associates (1898-1935).* Unpublished PhD thesis, Leiden University.

Sadowski, Yahya. 1993. The New Orientalism and the Democracy Debate. *Middle East Report* 183: 14–21.

Safranski, Rüdiger. 2005. *Nietzsche: Biographie seines Denkens.* Frankfurt a.M.: Fischer.

Said, Edward W. 1978. *Orientalism.* New York: Vintage.

———. 1981. *Covering Islam: How the Media and the Experts Determine How We See the Rest of the World.* London: Routledge & Kegan Paul.

———. 1994a. *Culture and Imperialism.* New York: Vintage.

————. 1994b. Afterword. In *Orientalism*, by Edward Said, 329–352. New York: Vintage.

————. 1996. A Devil Theory of Islam. *The Nation*, August, 12, 1996.

————. 1999. *Out of Place: A Memoir*. New York: Vintage.

————. 2000. Invention, Memory, and Place. *Critical Inquiry* 26 (winter): 175–192.

————. 2003. Preface to the 25th Anniversary Edition, In *Orientalism* by Edward Said, xv–xxx. New York: Vintage.

————. 2004. *Humanism and Democratic Criticism*. London: Palgrave MacMillan.

Salahi, Adil M. and Ashur A. Shamis. 1992. Introduction. In Sayyid Qutb, *In the Shade of the Quran*, vol. 30. New Delhi: Idara Ishaat e Diniyat.

Salvatore, Armando. 1997. *Islam and the Political Discourse of Modernity*. Reading: Ithaca Press.

Sawyer, Keith R. 2002. A Discourse on Discourse: An Archeological History of an Intellectual Concept. *Cultural Studies* 16(3): 433–456.

————. 2004. The Mechanisms of Emergence. *Philosophy of the Social Science* 34(2): 260–282.

————. 2005. *Social Emergence: Societies as Complex Systems*. Cambridge: Cambridge University Press.

Scaff, Lawrence A. 2000. Weber on the Cultural Situation of the Modern Age. In *The Cambridge Companion to Weber*, edited by Stephen Turner, 99–116. Cambridge: Cambridge University Press.

Schacht, Joseph. 1935. Zur soziologischen Betrachtung des islamischen Rechts. *Der Islam* 22: 207–238.

————. 1964. *Introduction into Islamic Law*. Oxford: Clarendon Press.

Schaeder, Hans Heinrich. 1926. Zum Entwurf einer orientalischen Kulturgeschichte In *Weltpolitische Bildungsarbeit an Preussischen Hochschulen*. Berlin: Verlag von Reimar Hobbing.

Schäbler, Birgit. 2008. Historismus versus Orientalismus? Oder: Zur Geschichte einer Wahlverwandtschaft. In *Das Unbehagen der Islamwissenschaft. Ein klassisches Fach im Scheinwerferlicht der Politik und der Medien*, edited by Abbas Poya and Maurus Reinkowski, 51–70. Bielefeld: transcript.

Schäfer, Rolf. 1998. Ritschl, Albrecht (1822-1889)/Ritschlsche Schule, in *Theologische Realenzyklopädie*, vol. 29. Berlin: Walter de Gruyter.

Schatz, Klaus 1990. Der päpstliche Primat. Seine Geschichte von den Ursprüngen bis zur Gegenwart. Würzburg: Echter.

————. 1992. *Vaticanum I, 1869-1870, Band I: Vor der Eröffnung*. Paderborn: Ferdinand Schönigh.

Schatzki, Theodore R. 2002. *The Site of the Social: A Philosophical Account of the Constitution of Social Life and Change*. University Park: Pennsylvania State University Press.

Scheffler, Thomas. 1995. Exotismus und Orientalismus, *kultuRRevolution* 32/33: 105–111.

————. 2002. Wenn hinten, weit, in der Türkei die Völker aufeinander schlagen ...": Zum Funktionswandel "orientalischer" Gewalt in europäischen Öffentlichkeiten des 19. und 20. Jahrhunderts. In *Europäische Öffentlichkeit. Transnationale Kommunikation seit dem 18. Jahrhundert*, edited by Jörg Requate and Martin Schulze Wessel, 205–230. Frankfurt: Campus.

Schimmel, Annemarie. 1954. Muhammad Iqbal 1873–1938. The Ascension of the Poet. *Die Welt des Islams* 3(2): 145–157.

Schluchter, Wolfgang, ed. 1987. *Max Webers Sicht des Islams, Interpretation und Kritik*. Frankfurt a.M.: Suhrkamp.

Schnädelbach, Herbert. 1984. *Philosophy in Germany 1831-1933*. Cambridge: Cambridge University Press.

Schöllgen, Gregor. 1981. "Dann müssen wir uns aber Mesopotamien sichern!" Motive deutscher Türkeipolitik zur Zeit Wilhelms II. in zeitgenössischen Darstellungen, *Saeculum* 32: 130–145.

Scholte, Jan Aart. 2000. *Globalization: A Critical Introduction.* London: Palgrave Macmillan.

Schröder, J.C.B. 1996. *Die kritische Identität des neuzeitlichen Christentums.* Tübingen: J.C:B: Mohr (Paul Siebeck).

Schulze, Reinhard. 2002. *A Modern History of the Islamic World.* New York: New York University Press.

———. 2003. Ein Leben für den Jihad, *taz,* December 2, 2003.

Schwab, Raymond. 1950. *La Renaissance Orientale.* Paris: Payot

———. 1984. *The Oriental Renaissance: Europe's Rediscovery of India and the East 1680-1880.* Translated by Gene Patterson-Black and Victor Reinking. Published in French 1950. New York: Columbia University Press.

Schwanitz, Wolfgang G. 2003. Djihad >Made in Germany<: Der Streit um den Heiligen Krieg 1914–1915. *Sozial.Geschichte* 18(2): 7–34.

Schweitzer, Albert. 1913. *Die Geschichte der Leben Jesu Forschung.* Tübingen: Mohr.

Sedgwick, Mark. 2010. *Muhammad Abduh,* Oxford: Oneworld Publications.

Serjeant, R.B. 1981. *Studies in Arabian History and Civilisation.* Reprint. London: Variorum.

Sfeir, George N. 1998. *Modernization of the Law in Arab States: An Investigation into Current Civil, Criminal and Constitutional Law in the Arab World.* San Francisco, CA: Austin and Winfield.

Shaberg, William H. 1995. *The Nietzsche Canon. A Publication History and Bibliography.* Chicago, IL: The University of Chicago Press.

Shahin, Emad Eldin. 1989. Muhammad Rashid Rida's Perspectives on the West as reflected in *Al-Manar.* The Muslim World 79(2): 113–132.

Sharabi, Hisham. 1970. *Arab Intellectuals and the West: The Formative Years, 1875-1914.* Baltimore, MD: Johns Hopkins University Press.

Sharot, Stephen. 2001. *A Comparative Sociology of World Religions: Virtuosos, Priests, and Popular Religion.* New York: New York University Press.

Shatzki, Theodore R. 2002. *The Site of the Social: A Philosophical Account of the Constitution of Social Life and Change.* University Park: Pennsylvania State University Press.

Shaw, Wendy M.K. 2003. *Possessors and Possessed. Museums, Archaeology and the Visualization of History in the Late Ottoman Empire.* Berkeley: University of California Press.

Sheikholeslami, Ali R. 1986. From Religious Accommodation to Religious Revolution: The Transformation of Shi'ism in Iran. In *The State, Religion, and Ethnic Politics: Afghanistan, Iran, and Pakistan,* edited by A. Banuazzizi and M. Weiner, 227–255. Syracuse, NY: Syracuse University Press.

Shepard, William E. 1987. Islam and Ideology: Towards a Typology, *International Journal of Middle East Studies.* 19: 307–336.

———. 1996. *Sayyid Qutb and Islamic Activism. A Translation and Critical Analysis of Social Justice in Islam.* Leiden: Brill.

Shiel, Judith B. 1995. William Robertson Smith in the Nineteenth Century in the Light of His Correspondence. *William Robertson Smith: Essays in Reassessment,* edited by William Johnstone, 78–85. Sheffield: Sheffield Academic Press.

Shilling Chris and Philip A. Mellor. 1998. Durkheim, Morality and Modernity: Collective Effervesence, homo duplex and the Sources of Moral Action. *British Journal of Sociology* 49(2): 193–209.

Simmel, Georg. 1992. *Soziologie. Untersuchungen über die Formen der Vergesellschaftung,* Frankfurt a.M.: Suhrkamp (first 1908).

————. 1995. *Philosophie der Mode, die Religion, Kant und Goethe, Schopenhauer und Nietzsche.* Gesamtausgabe Vol 10. Frankfurt a.M.: Suhrkamp.

Simon, Robert. 1986. *Ignác Goldziher. His Life and Scholarship as Reflected in His Works and Correspondence.* Leiden: Brill.

Sivan, Emmanuel. 1985. *Interpretations of Islam: Past and Present.* Princeton, NJ: The Darwin Press.

Sivaramakrishnan, K. 1995. Situating the Subaltern: History and Anthropology in the Subaltern Studies Project. *Journal of Historical Sociology* 8(4): 395–429.

Skovgaard-Petersen, Jakob. 2001a. Portrait of the Intellectual as a Young Man: Rashid Rida's *Muhawarat al-muslih wa-al-muqallid* (1906). *Islam and Christian-Muslim Relations* 12(1): 94–104.

————. 2001b. Den jødiske sheikh. *Udsyn* 16(1): 12–18.

————. 2006. Democratization and the New Arab Media. In *Democratization and Development: New Political Strategies for the Middle East,* edited by Dietrich Jung, 83–100. New York: Palgrave MacMillan.

Smend, Rudolf. 1995. William Robertson Smith and Julius Wellhausen. In *William Robertson Smith: Essays in Reassessment,* edited by William Johnstone, 226–242. Sheffield: Sheffield Academic Press.

Smelser, Neil J. 1976. *Comparative Methods in the Social Sciences,* London et al.: Prentice-Hall.

————. 1992. External and Internal Factors in Theories of Social Change. In *Social Change and Modernity,* edited by Hans Haferkamp and Neil J. Smelser, 369–394. Berkeley: University of California Press.

Smith, William Robertson. 1869 (1912). Christianity and the Supernatural. In *Lectures & Essays of William Robertson Smith,* edited by John Sutherland Black and George William Chrystal, 109–136. London: Adam and Charles Black.

————. 1871. The Fulfillment of Prophecy. In *Lectures and Essays of William Robertson Smith,* edited by John Sutherland Black and George William Chrystal, 253–284. London: Adam and Charles Black.

————. 1876. Two Lectures on Prophecy. In *Lectures and Essays of William Robertson Smith,* edited by John Sutherland Black and George William Chrystal, 341–366. London: Adam and Charles Black.

————. 1880–1881. A Journey in the Hejaz. In *Lectures and Essays of William Robertson Smith,* edited by John Sutherland Black and George William Chrystal, 484–600. London: Adam and Charles Black.

————. 1881. *The Old Testament in the Jewish Church. Twelve Lectures on Biblical Criticism,* Edinburgh: Adam and Charles Black.

————. 1882. *The Prophets of Israel and Their Place in History to the Close of the Eighth Century B.C. Eight Lectures.* Edinburgh: Adam and Charles Black.

————. 1887. Review of *Histoire du people d'Israël* by Ernest Renan. In *Lectures & Essays of William Robertson Smith,* edited by John Sutherland Black and George William Chrystal, 608–622. London: Adam and Charles Black.

————. 1894. *Lectures on the Religion of the Semites. First Series: The Fundamental Institutions.* New Edition. London: Adam and Charles Black.

————. 1903. *Kinship and Marriage in Early Arabia.* New Edition with additional notes by the author and by Professor Ignaz Goldziher, Budapest. London: Adam and Charles Black.

Soguk, Nevzat. 1993. Reflection on the "Orientalized Orientals." *Alternatives* 18: 361–384.

Soroush, Abdolkarim. 2000. *Reason, Freedom and Democracy in Islam: Essential Writings of Abdolkarim Soroush.* Oxford: Oxford University Press.

Southern, R.W. 1962. *Western Views of Islam in the Middle Ages.* Cambridge, MA: Harvard University Press.

Spickard, James V. 2003. *What is Happening to Religion? Six Sociological Narratives.* www.ku.dk/satsning/Religion

Spittler, Gerd. 1980. Abstraktes Wissen als Herrschaftsbasis. Zur Entstehungsgeschichte bürokratischer Herrschaft im Bauernstaat Preussen. *Kölner Zeitschrift für Soziologie und Sozialpsychologie* 32(1980): 574–604.

Spivak, Gayatri Chakravorty. 1985. Subaltern Studies: Deconstructing Historiography. In *Subaltern Studies IV: Writings on South Asian History and Society,* edited by Ranajit Guha and Gayatri Spivak, 330–363. Oxford: Oxford University Press.

Stark, Rodney. 1997. Bringing Theory Back In. In *Rational Choice Theory and Religion. Summary and Assessment,* edited by Lawrence A. Young, 3–23. London: Routledge.

———. 1999. Secularization, R.I.P. *Sociology of Religion* 60(3): 249–273.

Stauth, Georg. 1993. *Islam und westlicher Rationalismus: der Beitrag des Orientalismus zur Entstehung der Soziologie.* Frankfurt a.M.: Campus.

———. 2000. *Islamische Kultur und moderne Gesellschaft.* Bielefeld: transcript.

Steinberg, Guido. 2005. *Der nahe und der ferne Feind: Die Netzwerke des islamistischen Terrorismus.* Munich: C.H. Beck.

Steenbrink, Karel. 1993. *Dutch Colonialism and Indonesian Islam. Contacts and Conflicts 1596-1950.* Amsterdam: Editions Rodopi B.V.

Stepan, Alfred. 2000. Religion, Democracy and the "Twin Tolerations." *Journal of Democracy* 11(4): 37–57.

Steppat, Fritz. 1965. Der Muslim und die Obrigkeit. *Zeitschrift für Politik* 12(4): 319–332.

Stichweh, Rudolf 1984. *Zur Entstehung des modernen Systems wissenschaftlicher Disziplinen. Physik in Deutschland 1740-1890.* Frankfurt a.M.: Suhrkamp.

———. 1996. Science in the System of World Society. *Social Science Information* 35(2): 327–340.

Strange, Susan. 1996. *The Retreat of the State: The Diffusion of Power in the World Economy.* Cambridge: Cambridge University Press.

Strauss, David Friedrich. 1835/36. *Das Leben Jesu, kritisch bearbeitet.* Tübingen.

———. 1870. *Krieg und Friede. Zwei Briefe an Ernst Renan nebst dessen Antwort auf den ersten.* Leipzig: Verlag von S. Hirzel.

Swatos, William H. and Kevin J. Cristiano. 1999. Secularization Theory: the Course of a Concept. *Sociology of Religion* 60(3): 209–228.

Swatos, William H. and Peter Kivisto. 1991. Max Weber as "Christian Sociologist." *Journal for the Scientific Study of Religion* 30(84): 347–362.

Tagliacozzo, Eric. 2000. Kettle on a Slow Boil: Batavia's Threat Perceptions in the Indies' Outer Islands 1870-1910. *Journal of Southeast Asian Studies* 31(1): 70–100.

Tahar, Meftah. 1976. Taha Husayn sa critique littéraire et ses sources francaises. Paris: Maison Arabe du Livre.

Tahtawi, al-, Rifaat R. 2004. *An Imam in Paris. Al-Tahtawi's Visit to France 1826-1831).* Translated and introduced by Daniel L. Newman. London: Saqi.

Tauber, Eliezer. 1989. Rashid Rida as Pan-Arabist before World-War I. *The Muslim World* 79(2): 102–112.

———. 1995a. Rashid Rida's Political Attitudes During World War I. *The Muslim World* 85(1/2): 107–121.

———. 1995b. Rashid Rida and Faysal's Kingdom in Syria. *The Muslim World* 85(3/4): 235–245

Tavakoli Targhi Mohamad. 1996. Orientalism's Genesis Amnesia. *Comparative Studies of South Asia, Africa and the Middle East.* 16(1): 1–14.

Taylor, Charles. 1985. *Human Agency and Language: Philosophical Papers I.* Cambridge: Cambridge University Press.

———. 1989. *Sources of the Self: The Making of the Modern Identity.* Cambridge: Cambridge University Press.

———. 1991. *The Ethics of Authenticity.* Cambridge, MA: Harvard University Press.

———. 2002. Modern Social Imaginaries. *Public Culture* 14(1): 91–124.

———. 2007. *A Secular Age.* Cambridge, MA: The Belknap Press of Harvard University Press.

Tellenbach, Silvia. 1985. *Untersuchungen zur Verfassung der Islamischen Republik Iran vom 15. November 1979.* Berlin: Klaus Schwarz Verlag.

———. 1996. *Strafgesetze der Islamischen Republik Iran.* Berlin: Walter de Gruyter.

Tezcan, Levent. 2003. *Religiöse Strategien der >machbaren< Gesellschaft. Verwaltete Religion und islamistische Utopie in der Türkei.* Bielefeld: transcript.

Tibawi, A.L. 1963. English-Speaking Orientalists: A Critique of Their Approach to Islam and Arab Nationalism. *The Muslim World* 53(3): 185–204.

———. 1979. Second Critique of English-Speaking Orientalists and Their Approach to Islam and the Arabs. *The Islamic Quarterly* 23(1): 3–54.

Tilly, Charles. 1990. *Coercion, Capital, and European States, AD 990-1990.* Oxford: Basic Blackwell.

Tiryakian, Edward A. 1966. A Problem for the Sociology of Knowledge: The Mutual Unawareness of Emile Durkheim and Max Weber. *European Journal of Sociology* 7(2): 330–336.

Tocqueville, Alexis de. 1986. *De la démocratie en Amérique I.* Paris: Gallimard.

Tönnies, Ferdinand. 1887. *Gemeinschaft und Gesellschaft: Abhandlung des Communismus und des Socialismus als empirische Kulturformen.* Leipzig: Fues's Verlag.

Treiber, Hubert. 1999. Zur Genese des Askesekonzepts bei Max Weber. *Saeculum* 50(2): 247–297.

———. 2005. Der "Eranos"—Das Glanzstück im Heidelberger Mythenkranz? In *Asketischer Protestantismus und Geist des modernen Kapitalismus*, edited by Wolfgang Schluchter and Friedrich Wilhelm Graf, 75–153. Tübingen: Mohr Siebeck.

Tripp, Charles. 2005. Sayyid Qutb: The Political Vision. In *Pioneers of Islamic Revival,* edited by Ali Rahnema, 154–183. New edition. London: Zed books.

Trumpener, Ulrich. 1968: *Germany and the Ottoman Empire 1914-1918.* Princeton, NJ: Princeton University Press.

Tulloch, John. 1876–1877. Progress of Religious Thought in Scotland. *Contemporary Review* 29 (1876, Dec.–1877, May): 535–551.

Tunger-Zanetti, Andreas. 1996. *La communication entre Tunis et Istanbul 1860-1913: province et métropole.* Paris: L'Harmattan.

Turner, Bryan. 1974. *Weber and Islam: A Critical Study.* London: Routledge.

———. 1983. Accounting for the Orient. In *Islam in the Modern World,* edited by Denis MacEoin and Ahmed Al-Shahi, 9–26. New York: St. Martin's Press.

———. 1994. *Orientalism, Postmodernism and Globalism.* London: Routledge.

Tyrell, Hartmann von. 1990. Worum geht es in der Protestantischen Ethik? Ein Versuch zum besseren Verständnis Max Webers. *Saeculum* 41: 130–177.

Urry, John. 2003. *Global Complexity.* Cambridge: Polity Press.

———. 2005. The Complexities of the Global. *Theory, Culture & Society* 22(5): 235–254.

Vahid, S.A. 1953. *Introduction to Iqbal.* Karachi: Pakistan Publications.

Vásquez, Manuel A. and Marie Friedmann Marquardt. 2003. *Globalizing the Sacred: Religion Across the Americas.* New Brunswick, NJ: Rutgers University Press.

Vlekke Bernhard H.M. 1945. *The Story of the Dutch East Indies.* Cambridge, MA: Harvard University Press.

Vries Simon John de. 1968. *Bible and Theology in the Netherlands: Dutch Old Testament Criticism under Modern and Conservative Auspices, 1850 to World War I.* Wageningen: H. Veenman and Zonen.

Voll, John. 1979. The Sudanese Mahdi. Frontier Fundamentalist. *International Journal of Middle East Studies* 20: 145–166.

Waardenburg, Jacques. 1962. *L'islam dans le miroir de l'occident. Comment quelques orientalistes occidentaux se son penchés sur l'Islam et se sont formé une image de cette religion.* Paris: Mouton.

———. 1988. Muslim Enlightenment and Revitalization. *Die Welt des Islams* 28: 569–584.

Wagner, Falk. 1998. Rothe, Richard (1799-1867). In *Theologische Realenzyklopädie*, vol. 29. Berlin: de Gruyter.

Wagner, Peter. 1994. *A Sociology of Modernity: Liberty and Discipline.* London: Routledge.

Wallace, Ruth A. 1977. Emile Durkheim and the Civil Religion Concept. *Review of Religious Research* 18(3): 287–290. Reprinted in *Emile Durkheim: Critical Assessments*, vol. 4, edited by Peter Hamilton, 1990. London: Routledge.

Wallwork, Ernest. 1985. Durkheim's Early Sociology of Religion. *Sociological Analysis* 46(3): 201–218.

Walther, Rudolf. 2003. Die seltsamen Lehren des Doktor Carrel: Wie ein katholischer Arzt aus Frankreich zum Vordenker der radikalen Islamisten wurde. *Die Zeit*, 32-31: July, 31.

Warburg, Margit. 1989. William Robertson Smith and the Study of Religion. *Religion* 19: 41–61.

Wardman, H.W. 1964. *Ernest Renan. A Critical Biography.* London: The Athlone Press.

Watt, Katherine. 2002. Thomas Walker Arnold and the Re-Evaluation of Islam, 1864-1930. *Modern Asien Studies* 36(1): 1–98.

Watt, Montgomery W. 1956. *Muhammad at Medina.* Oxford: Clarendon Press.

———. 1972. *The Influence of Islam on Medieval Europe.* Edinburgh: Edinburgh University Press.

———. 1983. Islam and the West. In *Islam in the Modern World,* edited by Denis MacEoin and Ahmed Al-Shahi, 1-8. New York: St. Martin's Press.

Weber, Marianne 1975. *Max Weber: A Biography.* Translated and edited by Harry Zohn. New York: John Wiley and Sons.

Weber, Max. 1895. The Nation State and Economic Policy. In *Weber: Political Writings.* Cambridge: Cambridge University Press.

———. 1904. "Objectivity" in Social Science and Social Polity. In Max Weber, *The Methodology of the Social Sciences,* translated and edited by Edward A. Shils and Henry A. Finch, 1949. New York: The Free Press.

———. 1915a. The Social Psychology of the World Religions. In *From Max Weber: Essays in Sociology,* edited by H.H. Gerth and C. Wright Mills, 267–301. London: Routledge (New Edition, 1991).

———. 1915b. Religious Rejections of the World and Their Directions. In *From Max Weber: Essays in Sociology,* edited by H.H. Gerth and C. Wright Mills, 323–359. London: Routledge. New Edition, 1991.

———. 1917. Science as Vocation. In *From Max Weber: Essays in Sociology,* edited by H.H. Gerth and C. Wright Mills, 129–156. London: Routledge (New Edition, 1991).

———. 1930. *The Protestant Ethic and the Spirit of Capitalism.* Translated by Talcott Parsons. London: Routledge. Reprint 2004.

———. 1948. *From Max Weber: Essays in Sociology.* Edited by H.H. Gerth and C. Wright Mills. London: Routledge. (New edition, 1991).

———. 1968. *The Religion of China: Confucianism and Taoism.* New York: The Free Press.

————. 1978a. *Economy and Society,* vol. 1. Edited by Guenther Roth and Claus Wittich. Berkeley: University of California Press.

————. 1978b. *Economy and Society,* vol. 2. Edited by Guenther Roth and Claus Wittich. Berkeley: University of California Press.

————. 1994. *Political Writings.* Cambridge: Cambridge University Press.

Wedel, H. 1996. Binnenmigration und ethnische Identität—Kurdinnen in türkischen Metropolen. *Orient* 37(3): 437–452.

Wehler, Hans-Ulrich. 1975. *Modernisierungstheorie und Geschichte.* Göttingen: Vandenhoeck and Ruprecht.

Welsch, Wolfgang. 1987. *Unsere postmoderne Moderne.* Weinheim: VCH.

Weintraub, Karl J. 1966. Visions of Culture: Voltaire, Guizot, Burckhardt, Lamprecht, Huizinga, Ortega Y Gasset. Chicago, IL: University of Chicago Press.

Wellhausen, Julius. 1882. *Muhammed in Medina: Das ist Vakidi's Kitab al-Maghazi.* Berlin: G. Reimer Verlag.

————. 1883. Mohammedanism. *Encyclopaedia Britannica* 16(9): 545–565.

————. 1889. *Skizzen und Vorarbeiten: Viertes Heft, Muhammads Gemeindeordnung von Medina.* Berlin: G.Reimer Verlag (Reprint 1985).

————. 1898. *Reste Arabischen Heidentums,* 2. Ausgabe. Berlin: G. Reimer Verlag.

————. 1901 (1965). Heinrich Ewald. In *Julius Wellhausen. Grundrisse zum Alten Testament,* edited by Rudolf Smend, 120–138. Munich: Chr. Kaiser Verlag.

————. 1902. *Das Arabische Reich und sein Sturz,* Berlin: G. Reimer Verlag.

Wende, Erich. 1959. C.H. Becker: Mensch und Politiker. Stuttgart: Deutsche Verlags-Anstalt.

Wensinck, Arent Jan. 1975. *Muhammad and the Jews of Medina: With an Excursus on Muhammad's Constitution of Medina by Julius Wellhausen.* Freiburg: Schwarz.

Wertheim, W.F. 1972. Counter-insurgency Research at the Turn of the Century—Snouck Hurgronje and the Acheh War. *Sociologische gids* 19(5/6): 320–328.

Whitelam, Keith W. 1995. William Robertson Smith and the So-called New Histories of Palestine. In *William Robertson Smith: Essays in Reassessment,* edited by William Johnstone, 180–189. Sheffield: Sheffield Academic Press.

Wiener, Max 1962. *Abraham Geiger and Liberal Judaism: The Challenge of the Nineteenth Century.* Philadelphia: The Jewish Publication Society of America.

Wiktorowicz, Quintan. 2001. *The Management of Islamic Activism: Salafis, the Muslim Brotherhood and State Power in Jordan.* New York: State University of New York Press.

Winder Bayly. 1965. *Saudi Arabia in the Nineteenth Century.* London: Macmillan.

————. 1981. Orientalism—Review Article. *The Middle East Journal* 35(4): 615–619.

Wokoeck, Ursula. 2009. *German Orientalism: The Study of the Middle East and Islam from 1800 to 1945.* London: Routledge.

Worsely, P.M. 1956. Emile Durkheim's Theory of Knowledge. In *Emile Durkheim: Critical Assessments.* Volume IV, edited by Peter Hamilton, 12–25. London: Routledge (reprint 1990).

Young, Robert J.C. 2003. *Postcolonialism: A Very Short Introduction.* Oxford: Oxford University Press.

Zakariyya, Fuad. 2005. *Myth and Reality in the Contemporary Islamist Movement.* Translated and with and introduction and bibliography by Ibrahim M. Abu-Rabi. London: Pluto Press.

Zaman, Muhammad Qasim. 2002. *The Ulama in Contemporary Islam. Custodians of Change,* Princeton: Princeton University Press.

————. 2005. The Scope and Limits of Islamic Cosmopolitanism and the Discursive Language of the Ulama. In *Muslim Networks: From Hajj to Hip Hop,* edited by Miriam Cooke and Bruce B. Lawrence, 84-104. Chapel Hill: The University of Carolina Press.

Zeghal, Malika. 1999. Religion and Politics in Egypt: The Ulema of Al-Azhar, Radical Islam, and the State (1952–1994). *International Journal of Middle Eastern Studies* 31: 371–399.

Zeleny, Milan. 1993. Autopoiesis: A Paradigm Lost? In *Autopoiesis, Dissipative Structures, and Spontaneous Social Orders,* edited by Milan Zeleny, 3–43. Boulder: West View.

Zöckler, Otto. 1907. *Geschichte der Apologie des Christentums.* Gütersloh: C. Bertelsmann.

Zollner, Barbara H.E. 2009. *The Muslim Brotherhood: Hasan al-Hudaybi and Ideology.* London: Routledge.

Zubaida, Sami. 1997. Is Iran an Islamic State? In *Political Islam,* edited by J. Beinin and J. Stork, 103–119. London: I.B. Tauris.

Zürcher, Erik-Jan. 1993. *Turkey: A Modern History.* (Reprint 1998). London: I.B.Tauris.

————. 2002. *The Young Turks—Children of Borderlands?* Working Paper, Department of Turkish Studies, University of Leiden.

————. 2005. Ottoman Sources of Kemalist Thought In *Late Ottoman Society. The Intellectual Legacy,* edited by Elisabeth Özdalga, 14–27. London: Routledge.

Index